Murray Brothers

Quality Helm & Fighting Chairs

- *Fighting Chairs*

- *Fishing Chairs*

- *Helms Chairs*

- *Rocket Launchers*

- *Hi-Lo Tables*

- *Casual Furniture*

FACTORY
1306 53rd Street
West Palm Beach, Florida 33407
407-845-1366 • Fax 407-844-4355

1995
EDITION

McKnew & Parker's
BUYER'S GUIDE TO

SPORTFISHING BOATS

From the Editors of the POWERBOAT GUIDE

Ed McKnew and Mark Parker

International Marine
Camden, Maine

PUBLISHED BY
International Marine
A Division of McGraw-Hill, Inc.
Blue Ridge Summit, PA 17294
1-800-822-8158

COMPILED BY
American Marine Publishing, Inc.
P.O. Box 30577
Palm Beach Gardens, FL 33420
1-800-832-0038

FOR ADVERTISING INFORMATION
Contact Ben Wofford, Director of Advertising
407-627-3640 • Fax 407-627-6636

ISBN 0-07-045171-0
Printed and bound in the United States of America.

CONTENTS

This book is written to help buyers sort through the hundreds of different production sportfishing boats 24 feet to 83 feet in length currently available on the nation's new and used markets. Over 300 popular models are featured in these pages—center consoles and cuddies, express fishermen and convertibles, inboards and outboards, and even a couple of jackshaft designs—a wide cross section of sportfishing boats ranging in price from the affordable to the truly opulent. For each, we have included complete factory specifications together with floorplan options, real-world performance data, production history, engine choices, and production updates. Throughout, the authors' opinions are oftentimes freely expressed. Advertising hype notwithstanding, some boats are simply better than others, and those that stand out at either extreme are occasionally noted. No attempt has been made to maliciously abuse a particular model, however, and the comments represent nothing more or less than the opinions of the authors. Needless to say, the services of experienced marine professionals are strongly recommended in the sale or purchase of any boat.

The prices quoted in this book reflect the market conditions projected by our staff for 1995. Those wishing to establish a consistent pattern for depreciation will be disappointed: We know of no such schedule. Rather, we have evaluated each model on its own merits and assigned values based on our own research and experience. While we are aware of the prices other appraisal guides assign to various models, we often disagree with those values and believe that our estimates are more reflective of actual cash values. No matter what the various price guides (including ours) might say, the fact remains that the only *real* value of a boat is what someone is willing to pay for it on a given day.

McKnew & Parker's Buyer's Guide to Sportfishing Boats is one of three annual consumer publications written by Ed McKnew and Mark Parker. (The other two are *McKnew & Parker's Buyer's Guide to Motor Yachts & Trawlers* and *McKnew & Parker's Buyer's Guide to Family & Express Cruisers.*) The series is a spin-off of the hugely successful *PowerBoat Guide,* a now standard industry reference originally compiled for the exclusive use of marine professionals. As the *PowerBoat Guide* grew in content and cost over the years, it became evident that we needed to break the book down into three smaller publications, each aimed at a specific segment of the market. Future additions to the series will include guides for cruising sailboats, trailerable fishing boats, etc., and other under-25-foot pleasure boats.

ACKNOWLEDGMENTS

We wish to thank the following individuals for their support. Without their help we would never have come this far.

Floyd Appling, Jr.

Bill Burgstiner

Steve & Delores Brown

Top & Sandy Cornell

George & Helene Gereke

Edward & Betty Groth

Freddy & Patti Hamlin

For the most part, the contents of this book are straightforward and easily understood. There are a few conventions, however, that should be kept in mind. Failure to do so will result in a good deal of confusion and misunderstanding.

Factory Specifications

The specifications listed for each model are self-explanatory, although the following factors are noted:

1. Clearance refers to bridge clearance, or the height above the waterline to the highest point on the boat. Note that this is often a highly ambiguous piece of information since the manufacturer may or may not include such things as an arch, hardtop, or mast. Use this figure with caution.

2. Designer refers to the designer of the hull only.

3. NA means that the information is not available.

Performance Data

Whenever possible, performance figures have been obtained from the manufacturer or a reliable dealer or broker. When such information was unavailable (or—as in many cases—manufacturers refused to provide it) the authors have relied on their own research together with actual hands-on experience. The speeds are estimates and (in most cases) based on boats with average loads of fuel, water, options, and gear.

Speeds are reported in knots. Those in the Great Lakes or inland waterways may convert knots to miles per hour by multiplying a given figure by 1.14.

Cruising Speeds, Outboard Engines

On average, we calculate the cruising speed of an outboard engine at about 4,000 rpm, or 1,200–1,500 rpm off a motor's top rpm rating.

Cruising Speeds, Gas Engines

Unless otherwise noted, the cruising speed for gas-powered inboard boats is calculated at 3,000–3,200 rpm.

Cruising Speeds, Diesel Engines

The cruising speeds for diesel-powered boats are calculated as follows:

1. Detroit (two-stroke) Diesels: about 250–300 rpm off the top rpm rating.

2. Other (four-stroke) diesels: about 350–400 rpm off the manufacturer's maximum rpm rating.

Floorplans

When there are two or more floorplans, the most recent layout comes last.

Pricing Information

Used-boat prices have been compiled from 1975, the base year for our calculations. Boats whose production runs were previous to that year are noted in the Price Schedule with four asterisks (****).

In the Price Schedule, six asterisks (******) indicate that we have insufficient data to render a value for a particular year.

A single asterisk (*) next to outboard models indicates that the price is for the hull only.

While diesel engines always add significant value to any boat, there are some cases where the differences in the *type* or *horsepower* of diesel engines installed in a particular model will seriously affect the average resale value. Those cases in which we believe the diesel options do indeed affect the value of an individual boat have been noted in the Price Schedule.

The Retail High is the average selling price of a clean, well-equipped, and well-maintained boat with low-to-moderate engine hours. Boats with an exceptional equipment list or those with unusually low hours will often sell at a figure higher than the published Retail High.

The Retail Low is the average selling price of a boat with below-average maintenance, poor equipment, high-time engines, or excessive wear. High-time boats in poor condition may sell for less than the published Retail Low.

Used boats located in the following markets are generally valued at 10–15% higher than published prices:

1. Great Lakes

2. Pacific Northwest

3. Inland Rivers and Lakes

The prices presented in this book reflect our best estimates of new and used boat prices for the model year 1995. They are intended for general use only and are not meant to represent exact market values.

TWENTY FREQUENTLY ASKED QUESTIONS ABOUT SPORTFISHING BOATS

In an effort to clear away some of the confusion regarding the purchase of a new or used sportfishing boat, we have listed below some of the more common questions asked by potential buyers. The answers presented to these questions are our own and we welcome responses from others who hold differing views. For the most part, however, we believe the information presented here will address several important issues confronting buyers of boats listed in this publication.

1. I hear a lot of brokers talking about deep-V hulls. Should I be looking for this in my next boat?

The majority of manufacturers of over-30-foot designs build their boats on modified-V hulls because it provides owners with the best combination of performance, stability, and economy. Other builders specialize in fishing boats with deep-V hulls, most notably Bertram and Blackfin. It's true that deep-V designs offer superior rough-water performance, but at a cost. They tend to roll more at trolling speeds (especially in a beam sea) and they're more sensitive to the added weight of a tower. They also require more power to get up on plane, although there's no serious penalty in cruising economy once they're up and running.

Aside from their excellent headsea capabilities, deep-V hulls generally track much better than a modified-V design of similar length and displacement. A Bertram 46, for example, will require a lot less steering effort in a quartering or following sea than an Ocean 46 or Egg Harbor 54—boats with relatively flat bottoms. Although less stable at slow speeds, the deep-V is more stable at cruising speeds.

Note that while deep-V hulls involve some compromise in larger boats (over 30 feet) they are almost the standard in smaller designs.

2. I'm looking at a boat with prop pockets. What are the advantages and disadvantages?

Prop pockets are used to reduce shaft angles, which often results in improved fuel economy and engine efficiency at cruising speeds. Manufacturers like Sea Ray and Phoenix have used them for years. A secondary benefit to owning a hull with prop pockets is evident—the ability to operate with less fear of clipping a prop in shallow waters.

One criticism we've often heard of boats with prop pockets is that they don't back down on a fish as well since they lack the "bite" that a more exposed propeller can get. Most experienced captains agree that backing a boat with prop pockets into a slip takes a little more finesse than with a conventional hull. Also, because pockets reduce the lifting surface area back where it counts the most, at least some of the advantages of lower shaft angles are compromised.

3. Should my budget allow for diesel engines?

Yes. Range is always a factor in sportfishing boats and diesels can deliver up to 50% more range than a similar gas-powered boat. If diesels are not in the budget make sure that the speed and range capabilities of a prospective boat are sufficient for the type of running you will be doing.

In a family cruising boat the choice between gas and diesel isn't always so clear, but more and more builders are installing diesels in their models under 35 feet. Diesels are becoming more affordable, too, as new technology allows manufacturers to reduce both the size and weight of diesel engines while increasing their performance. At least with sportfishing boats, the resale value of a diesel-powered model will usually go a long way toward justifying the added up-front expense.

4. I know that engine hours are important, but what constitutes a lot of hours on a particular set of motors?

This is always a hard question to answer, so we'll just offer some general guidelines. When it comes to gas engines (inboards and I/Os), most brokers figure that motors with over 1,000 hours are probably tired. With turbocharged diesels 3,500 hours is a lot of running time, and with naturally aspirated diesels it's not uncommon to pile up 5,000 hours before an overhaul is required. The tragedy is that many of today's ultra-high-performance diesels never see 2,000 hours before an overhaul. Sometimes this is a manufacturer problem, but premature marine diesel death usually results from improper owner care and maintenance. Lack of use and poor exercise habits may be the number-one killer. Humidity (moisture) on cylinder components can be avoided with regular running and engine heaters. Diesel engines should be run under a load whenever possible. If your mechanical surveyor suggests new oil, fuel, or water hoses, do it. Trying to save money here can be expensive.

Having said that, it's important to note that there are far too many variables to make any buying decisions based upon engine hours alone. It's imperative to have the diesels in a used boat surveyed just as you have the boat itself professionally examined before reaching a final decision. It's not quite so critical with gas engines since they cost far less to rebuild than diesels; however it's always worth the small expense of having a compression test done on gas engines just to see what you're getting into.

Determining the actual hours on an engine (or a set of engines) can be difficult. There are generally hour meters installed in boats over 25 feet (that often aren't working) but they're not always found in smaller gas-powered boats and outboard models. Even if you have access to all the service records, we strongly suggest that you rely on an expert to evaluate the engines in any boat you have a serious interest in owning.

5. How can I spot a boat that's been fished hard?

Many owners of expensive sportfishermen employ full-time captains to maintain their vessel to new-boat standards. Generally, how a boat has been maintained will determine what kind of service to expect more than the number of hours she's been fished. It's obvious that a five-year-old Davis 47 with a tuna tower, outriggers, and a full electronics package sitting in Palm Beach with 1,500 hours on the meters has been fished—the question is whether she's been well maintained during her lifetime.

6. Can I rely on the boat tests that I read in the national magazines?

Yes, they're usually accurate as far as they go. For example, the performance figures—speeds at various rpm's, fuel burn data, etc.—are quite reliable although it's always wise to keep in mind that these are new boats with light loads and plenty of factory preparation. Don't look for a lot of hard-hitting criticism in these tests, however, because boating magazines depend on boat manufacturers for a major part of their advertising revenues.

We've read a lot of boat tests over the years. In our opinion, the best and most comprehensive are conducted by Boating magazine. Sea and Sport Fishing also have some excellent reviews.

8. Are freshwater boats really worth more?
Sure, no question about it. Salt water is hard on a boat, especially the gelcoat, electronics, paint,

metalwork, and engine room components. And while nearly all diesel-powered boats have closed cooling systems, the same is not always true of gas engines. In a saltwater environment it's wise to look for a boat with a closed cooling system since it usually lengthens engine life considerably.

Another reason why freshwater boats often bring a premium price has to do with the fact that they generally have fewer engine hours. The boating season in most freshwater regions is shorter than many of the largest saltwater boating areas. Furthermore, the majority of freshwater vessels spend their winters out of the water—many in a protected environment with reduced exposure to the corrosive effects of sun, wind, and rain.

As you might imagine, a well-maintained saltwater vessel is probably a better investment than a poorly maintained freshwater boat. One final factor that equalizes the values between the two is equipment. Especially with fishing boats, an East Coast saltwater boat is often outfitted with better equipment and more elaborate electronics.

9. Should I avoid a boat if the manufacturer has gone out of business or is currently undergoing hard times?

Emphatically, no. There are plenty of good used boats on the market from manufacturers who couldn't survive the poor economy of the past several years. The parts you will need from time to time are always available from catalog outlets or suppliers. Engine parts, of course, are easily secured from a number of sources. Generally speaking, there are no components used in a production model that cannot be replaced (or repaired) by a good yard.

Note that many of the most popular models on today's brokerage market were built by companies now out of business.

10. Why do I see so few Asian-built sportfishing boats?

While Asian builders have secured a significant share of today's motor yacht market (and near-domination of the market for trawlers), their products have enjoyed very limited success with the hard-core sportfishing market. Aside from Ronin, Mikelson and Pace, there are very few Taiwanese imports taken seriously among tournament-level anglers on either coast. There's probably a good deal of pro-American sentiment and pride at work here but it's a situation that's not likely to change anytime soon.

11. Outboard brackets are becoming more and more common. What are the pros and cons?

The benefits of an outboard bracket are increased cockpit space, reduced engine noise, and the ability to trim the boat even further, thus reducing wetted surface and increasing speed.

The drawbacks inherent in a boat with outboard brackets are reduced fishability (it's harder to get a rod tip out around the motors) and shifted weight distribution. The farther aft the weight load, the harder it is to keep the hull up on plane at slower speeds.

12. For resale, should I consider only a brand of boat with big-name market recognition?

There is no question that certain popular brands have consistently higher resale values. There are, however, many designs from small or regional builders that are highly sought after by knowledgeable boaters. Often, the market for these models is tighter and generally less saturated than the high production designs—a factor that often works to a seller's advantage.

13. Why is a 27-foot boat with twin 200-hp outboards faster than the same boat with 200-hp inboard engines?

Simple. You can trim outboard engines to gain maximum prop efficiency for speed and conditions. Inboards have fixed shaft angles regardless of speed or sea conditions. Trimming outboards also lifts the hull farther out of the water, reducing the wetted surface and drag considerably.

Also, two-stroke outboards are designed for cruising at a higher percentage of maximum rated rpm than the four-stroke gas inboard, and the outboard's horsepower-to-weight ratio is better. It should be said that in rough-water conditions inboard models are generally better designs since the centralized weight of the engines allows the boat to stay on plane at much lower speeds than outboard designs.

14. I'm considering the purchase of a 40-foot convertible. I've heard several times that I need a boat capable of 30 knots wide open. How important is that?

It's nice to have a fast boat—the less time it takes you to get there, the more time you have to fish. Speed is especially important in tournament-level boats where it's often necessary to travel long distances in order to drop a line.

In fact, however, the top speed isn't anywhere near as important as the ability to attain a fast cruising speed. (Running wide open for long periods shortens engine life considerably.) A 40-foot boat capable of cruising at 27 knots is considered fast by the standards of most knowledgeable skippers. For a smaller boat with outboards, 40 knots is a fast cruising speed. While a fast boat is nice (and often a measure of efficiency), sea conditions often equalize the speed of the fleet.

15. Should I reject a boat with bottom blisters?

Generally, no. Blisters can almost always be repaired, although the process can require a fair amount of time and expense. With that in mind, it is rare indeed to see a blistering problem so severe that it actually affects the integrity of the hull.

While some boats tend to re-blister again and again, most bottoms properly dried and protected should remain blister-free for five years or longer.

16. What are the differences between a West Coast fishing boat and an East Coast model?

The differences are relatively minor. West Coast anglers do a lot of their fishing off the bow, so it's common to see their boats with wider sidedecks and more elaborate pulpits. Too, since the weather is often cooler, many West Coast boats have the helm all the way forward on the bridge—just behind the windscreen—to enjoy some protection from the wind and to better see the foredeck fishing action. Traditional East Coast boats have the helm aft on the bridge so the captain can see the action in the cockpit and handle the boat accordingly.

17. How important is a lower helm?

That depends on your location. A lower helm is a great convenience (a luxury, actually) when you're getting an early start on a chilly morning. For visibility (and to avoid seasickness), however, most skippers prefer the bridge station for heavy-weather running.

On the other hand, aside from the added expense (which can be considerable), a lower helm takes up room in the salon which would otherwise be devoted to living space. Too, a lower helm requires a front windshield—something a lot of yacht designers and builders are trying to eliminate in their newer models.

Note that a lower helm in Florida (or along the Gulf Coast) is sometimes a hindrance to a boat's resale value since it's often viewed as a useless feature on a fishing boat in a warm climate.

18. Why do I want (or not want) a tower on my next boat?

Towers are designed for spotting bait, feeding or traveling gamefish, birds, rip and weed lines, and other changing surface conditions. They are also handy for working through reefs or other underwater obstructions. Many people buy boats with towers because they look good and are fun to ride in.

Consideration should also be given to the fact that towers require substantial maintenance. Proper care in a saltwater environment requires a weekly wash and chamois, and periodic waxing and repairs. Towers also add weight and windage and raise the boat's center of gravity—a design factor of more significance for a flybridge boat than for a low-profile express model.

19. How much does it cost to fish-rig a new boat or a cruise-equipped used model?

Obviously this depends on the size of the boat, but there are some general guidelines. A full tower for a mid-size flybridge convertible will run between $20,000 and $28,000 including options and accessories. A smaller tower for a 33-foot express model will run around $12,000 to $18,000. A half tower (or hardtop) on the aforementioned convertible will run between $10,000 and $15,000 and about $6,000 to $10,000 for the express.

A full-size tuna chair will cost from $4,500 to $6,500. A smaller (marlin) chair should run $3,500 to $5,500. Outriggers sell for $2,000 to $4,000 depending on length, brand, and number of spreaders.

Electronics are expensive. Theoretically, the only piece of electronics needed for serious fishing pursuits is a video depth recorder. It's common, however, for serious fishing boats to be fitted out with more and better electronics than comparably sized cruising boats.

20. If I decide to buy a used boat, should I use a broker?

If you have plenty of time on your hands you could locate a good boat at a fair price without a broker. Unless you find a boat for sale by the owner, you end up working with a broker anyway—the listing agent.

When choosing a broker consider that you are about to spend a large amount of money. Do your homework and end up with an agent that you feel has your long-term interests at heart. You're not paying for his time and expertise until you purchase a boat through him. Keeping many brokers in competition against one another often results in no one giving you the time and attention that you'll require.

USEFUL TERMS

Abaft—behind

Athwartships—at a right angle to the boat's length

Bulkhead—an upright partition separating compartments in a boat

Bulwark—a raised portion of the deck designed to serve as a barrier

Chine—the point at which the hullsides and the bottom of the boat come together

CID—referring to the cubic inch displacement of an engine, i.e., 454-cid gas engine

Coaming—vertical surface surrounding the cockpit

Cuddy—generally refers to the cabin of a small boat

Deadrise—the angle from the bottom of the hull (not the keel) to the chine

Deep-V Hull—a planing hull form with at least 18° of constant deadrise

Displacement Hull—a hull designed to go through the water and not capable of planing speed

Forefoot—the underwater shape of the hull at the bow

Freeboard—the height of the sides of the boat above the waterline

GPH—gallons per hour (of fuel consumption)

Gunwale—(also gunnel) the upper edge of the sheerline

Hull Speed—the maximum practical speed of a displacement hull. To calculate, take the square root of the load waterline length (LWL) and multiply by 1.34.

Knot—one nautical mile per hour. To convert knots to statute mph, multiply by 1.14.

Modified-V Hull—a planing hull form with less than 18° of transom deadrise

Nautical Mile—measurement used in salt water. A nautical mile is 6,076 feet.

Planing Speed—the point at which an accelerating hull rises onto the top of the water. To calculate a hull's planing speed, multiply the square root of the water-line length by 2.

Semi-Displacement Hull—a hull designed to operate economically at low speeds while still able to attain efficient planing speed performance

Sheerline—the fore-and-aft line along the top edge of the hull

Sole—a nautical term for floor

Statute Mile—measurement used in fresh water. A statute mile equals 5,280 feet.

Tender—refers to (*a*) a dinghy, or (*b*) lack of stability

WOT—wide open throttle

Directory of Yacht Brokers & Dealers

ALABAMA

A&M Yacht Sales/Mobile Hatteras
5004 Dauphin Island Pkwy.
Mobile, AL 36605
205-471-6949, Fax: 205-479-4625
Hatteras, Viking

Bay Yacht Sales
4960 Dauphin Island Pkwy.
Mobile, AL 36605
205-476-8306, Fax: 205-473-3802

KV Yacht Brokerage
27844 Canal Rd., Sportsman's Marina
Orange Beach, AL 36561
205-981-9600, Fax: 205-981-4304

The Marine Group
Sportsman's Marina, Box 650
Orange Beach, AL 36561
205-981-9200, Fax: 205-981-9137

CALIFORNIA

Ballena Bay Yacht Brokers
1150 Ballena Blvd., #121
Alameda, CA 94501
415-865-8601, Fax: 415-865-5560
Krogen

Bill Gorman Yachts
1070 Marina Village Pky., #100
Alameda, CA 94501
510-865-6151, Fax: 510-865-1220

Cruising World Pacific
2099 Grand St.
Alameda, CA 94501
415-521-1929, Fax: 415-522-6198

Don Trask Yachts
1070 Marina Village Pkwy., #108
Alameda, CA 94501
510-523-8500, Fax: 510-522-0641
Sabreline

Kensington Yacht Brokers
1535 Buena Vista Ave.
Alameda, CA 94501
510-865-1777, Fax: 510-865-8789

Nor-Cal Yachts
2415 Mariner Square Dr.
Alameda, CA 94501
510-523-8773, Fax: 510-865-4383
Ocean Alexander, Cruisers, Riviera, Luhrs

Richard Boland Yacht Sales
1070 Marina Village Pkwy., #107
Alameda, CA 94501
510-521-6213, Fax: 510-521-0118
Viking, Ocean

Newmarks Yacht & Ship Brokerage
3141 Victoria
Channel Islands, CA 93030
805-985-9898, Fax: 805-985-9982

Yachtline International
3150 South Harbor Blvd.
Channel Islands Harbor, CA 93035
805-985-8643, Fax: 805-985-3889
Ocean Alexander

Cays Boat Sales
509 Grand Caribe Isle
Coronado, CA 92118
619-424-4024, Fax: 619-575-7716

Lemest Yacht Sales
24703 Dana Drive
Dana Point, CA 92629
714-496-4933, Fax: 714-240-2398
Mason, Nordhavn

Huntington Harbour Yacht Exchange
16400 Pacific Coast Hwy., #107
Huntington Beach, CA 92649
714-840-2373, Fax: 310-592-9315

Wescal Yachts
16400 Pacific Coast Hwy., #106
Huntington Beach, CA 92649
310-592-4547, Fax: 310-592-2960

Marina Boat Sales
14900 West Highway 12
Lodi, CA 95242
209-367-0111
Carver, Tollycraft, Formula, Larson

Far West Marine
718 W. Anaheim St.
Long Beach, CA 90813
310-437-6461, Fax: 714-673-0733

Flying Cloud Yachts
6400 Marina Dr.
Long Beach, CA 90803
310-594-9716, Fax: 310-594-0710

Long Beach Yacht Sales
6400 E. Pacific Coast Hwy.
Long Beach, CA 90815
213-431-3393, Fax: 213-598-9483

Naples Yacht Sales
5925 Naples Plaza
Long Beach, CA 90803
310-434-7278, Fax: 310-434-0738

Stan Miller Yachts
245 Marina Dr.
Long Beach, CA 90803
310-598-9433, Fax: 310-598-5349
Catalina, Grand Banks, Blackfin

Bob Seldon Yacht Sales
14120 Tahiti Way
Marina del Rey, CA 90292
310-821-5883, Fax: 310-301-1020

Cruising World Pacific
14025 Panay Way
Marina del Rey, CA 90292
310-823-3838, Fax: 310-305-1941

Executive Yacht Management
646-A Venice Blvd.
Marina del Rey, CA 90291
310-306-2555

Purcell Yachts
14000 Palawan Way, #C
Marina del Rey, CA 90292
310-823-2040, Fax: 310-827-1877

Rick Ermshar Yachts
4601 Admiralty Way
Marina del Rey, CA 90292
213-822-4727, Fax: 310-822-6730

Tom Murdock Yachts
13915 Panay Dr.
Marina del Rey, CA 90292
310-822-8333, Fax: 310-822-9404

Yahama Marina Del Rey
13555 Fiji Way
Marina del Rey, CA 90292
310-823-8964, Fax: 310-821-0569
Tiara, Wellcraft

Thorsen Marine
6038 Shelter Bay Ave.
Mill Valley, CA 94941
415-461-5957, Fax: 415-461-6958

Ardell Yacht & Ship Brokers
2101 W. Coast Hwy.
Newport Beach, CA 92663
714-642-5735, Fax: 714-642-9884

Avion Yacht Sales, Ltd.
177 Riverside Ave., Suite F
Newport Beach, CA 92660
714-642-2827, Fax: 714-642-4127
Princess, Sunseeker

Bayliner Yacht Center
101 Shipyard Way, Cabin G
Newport Beach, CA 92663
714-723-0473, Fax: 714-723-0475
Bayliner

Chuck Hovey Yachts
717 Lido Park Dr. , Ste. A
Newport Beach, CA 92663
714-675-8092, Fax: 714-673-1037
Riva, Fleming, Island Gypsy, Azimuth

Craig Beckwith Yacht Sales
101 Shipyard Way, Suite J
Newport Beach, CA 92663
714-675-9352, Fax: 714-675-2519

Crow's Nest
2801 W. Coast Hwy., #260
Newport Beach, CA 92663
714-574-7600, Fax: 714-574-7610
Bertram, Davis, Hatteras, Tiara, Trojan

Emerald Yacht & Ship Brokers
3300 Irvine Avenue, Ste. 308
Newport Beach, CA 92660
714-553-0695, Fax: 714-752-0462

Falmouth Yachts
510 31st St., Suite D
Newport Beach, CA 92663
714-723-4225, Fax: 714-723-4093

Fraser Yachts
3471 Via Lido, #200
Newport Beach, CA 92263
714-673-5252, Fax: 714-673-8795
Chicago, IL 60614
312-993-7711, Fax: 312772-0891
Tiara

Fredericks Power & Sail
201 Shipyard Way, #A/3
Newport Beach, CA 92663
714-854-2696, Fax: 714-854-4598

H&S Yacht Sales
2001 W. Coast Highway
Newport Beach, CA 92663
714-642-4786, Fax: 714-642-1568
Mainship, Silverton, President

Lido Yacht Brokeage
3412 Via Oporto, #301
Newport Beach, CA 92663
714-675-0915, Fax: 714-675-0805
Rampage

Marine Center,
2200 W. Coast Hwy.
Newport Beach, CA 92663
714-645-3880
Bayliner

Newport Yacht Brokers
Box 5741, 400 S. Bayfront
Newport Beach, CA 92662
714-723-1200, Fax: 714-723-1201

Orange Coast Yachts
201 E. Coast Hwy.
Newport Beach, CA 92660
714-675-3844, Fax: 714-675-3980
Ocean Alexander

Seaward Yacht Sales
101 Shipyard Way, Suite K
Newport Beach, CA 92663
714-673-5950, Fax: 714-673-1058
Vitech, Nordic, Tayana

Venwest Yachts
2505 W. Coast Highway, #201
Newport Beach, CA 92663
714-642-1557, Fax: 714-548-0257
Viking

World Wide Custom Yachts
3412 Via Oporto, #301
Newport Beach, CA 92663
714-675-2179, Fax: 714-675-8210
Symbol

Yacht & Ship Brokers International
2507 W. Coast Hwy. #202
Newport Beach, CA 92663
714-722-7740, Fax: 714-722-8733

D'Anna Yacht Center
11 Embarcadero West, #100
Oakland, CA 94607
510-451-7000, Fax: 510-451-7026
Silverton, Wellcraft, Mainship

Integre Marine Ltd.
1155 Embarcadero
Oakland, CA 94606
415-465-6060, Fax: 415-465-6078

Admiralty Yacht Sales
3600 South Harbor Blvd.
Oxnard, CA 93035
805-985-1686
Wellcraft

Executive Yacht & Ship Brokers
3205 S. Victoria Ave.
Oxnard, CA 93035
805-984-1004, Fax: 805-985-4365

Wright Marine Sales,
3600 S. Harbor Blvd.
Oxnard, CA 93035
800-237-7174, Fax: 805-985-4586
Sea Ray

ACA Marine Yacht Sales
4262 Dauntless
Rancho Palos Verdes, CA 90274
213-541-6186, Fax: 213-541-6053

Pacific Coast Boats
2413 Cormorant Way
Sacramento, CA 95815
916-372-1500
Cruisers

Bower & Kling Yachts
955 Harbor Island Dr., #180
San Diego, CA 92101
619-299-7797, Fax: 619-299-3811

Cabrillo Yacht Sales
2638 Shelter Island Dr.
San Diego, CA 92106
619-523-1745, Fax: 619-523-1746

California Yacht Sales
2040 Harbor Island Dr., #111
San Diego, CA 92101
619-295-9669, Fax: 619-295-9909

Continental Yachts
333 West Harbor Dr.
San Diego, CA 92101
619-696-7400, Fax: 619-696-8029

CR Marine Yacht Sales
PO Box 82838
San Diego, CA 92138
619-295-0305, Fax: 619-298-5738

Crow's Nest
2515 Shelter Island Dr.
San Diego, CA 92106
619-222-1122, Fax: 619-222-3851
Bertram, Davis, Hatteras, Tiara, Trojan

Cruising World Pacific
2323 Shelter Island Dr.
San Diego, CA 92106
619-224-3277, Fax: 619-224-9225

Driscoll Yacht & Ship Brokerage
1050 Anchorage Lane
San Diego, CA 92106
619-222-0325, Fax: 619-222-0326

Fraser Yachts
2353 Shelter Island Dr.
San Diego, CA 92106
619-225-0588, Fax: 619-225-1325

H&S Yacht Sales
955 Harbor Island Dr., #110
San Diego, CA 92101
619-291-2600, Fax: 619-291-2613
Mainship, Silverton, President

Knight & Carver Yacht Sales
1500 Quivira Way
San Diego, CA 92109
619-224-4102, Fax: 619-222-6014

MacDonald Yacht Management
1450 Harbor Island Dr.
San Diego, CA 92101
619-294-4545, Fax: 619-294-8694

Mikelson Yachts
2330 Shelter Island Dr., #202
San Diego, CA 92106
619-222-5007, Fax: 619-223-1194
Mikelson

R.D. Snyder Yacht Sales
1231 Shafter St.
San Diego, CA 92106
619-224-2464, Fax: 619-224-7396

San Diego Yacht Sales
2525 Shelter Island Dr.
San Diego, CA 92106
800-221-8116, Fax: 619-221-0308
Hylas

Shelter Island Yacht Sales
2330 Shelter Island Dr., #200
San Diego, CA 92106
619-222-0515, Fax: 619-222-5283

Suncoast Yachts & Charters
955 Harbor Island Dr., #140
San Diego, CA 92101
619-297-1900, Fax: 619-297-1994
Grand Banks

Sunset Marine
2590 Ingraham St.
San Diego, CA 91209
619-224-3221
Sea Ray

Yachts West
333 West Harbor Dr.
San Diego, CA 92101
619-230-8989

Newmarks Yacht & Ship Brokerage
210 Whalers Walk
San Pedro, CA 90731
310-833-0887, Fax: 310-833-0979

ABC Yachts
One Gate 5 Road
Sausalito, CA 94964
415-332-7245, Fax: 415-332-4580

Fraser Yachts
320 Harbor Dr.
Sausalito, CA 94965
415-332-5311, Fax: 415-332-7036

Lager Yacht Brokerage Corp.
400 Harbor Dr. #C
Sausalito, CA 94965
415-332-9500, Fax: 415-332-9503

Nor-Cal Yachts
400 Harbor Dr., Suite C
Sausalito, CA 94965
415-332-0393
Ocean Alexander, Cruisers, Riviera, Luhrs

Oceanic Yacht Sales
308 Harbor Dr.
Sausalito, CA 94965
415-331-0533, Fax: 415-331-1642
Grand Banks, Midnight Lace

Sausalito Yacht Brokerage
100 Bay St.
Sausalito, CA 94965
415-331-6200, Fax: 415-331-6213

Western California Yacht Sales
6649 Embarcadero
Stockton, CA 95209
209-952-7672, Fax: 209-952-6443

Premier Yacht Sales
1801 Sonoma Blvd., #607
Vallejo, CA 94590
510-652-2109, Fax: 510-658-1635

Larry Dudley Yacht Sales
1559 Spinnaker Dr. #202
Ventura, CA 93001
805-644-9665, Fax: 805-644-9695

Ventura Yacht Sales
1101 Spinnaker Dr.
Ventura, CA 93003
805-644-1888
Grand Banks, Riviera

Newmarks Yacht & Ship Brokers
Berth 204
Wilmington, CA 90744
310-834-2830, Fax: 310-835-7206

CONNECTICUT

Randall Yacht Sales
145 S. Montowese St.
Branford, CT 06405
203-481-3866, Fax: 203-481-8699

Cedar Island Marina
PO Box 181, Riverside Dr.
Clinton, CT 06413
203-669-8681, Fax: 203-669-4157

Coastal Marine
143 River Rd., Box 228
Cos Cob, CT 06807
203-661-5765, Fax: 203-661-6040
Albin

Norwalk Cove Marina
Beach Road
East Norwalk, CT 06855
203-838-2326, Fax: 203-838-9258
Hatteras, Grand Banks, Tollycraft,
Cheoy Lee

Boatworks Yacht Sales
PO Box 668
Essex, CT 06426
203-767-3013, Fax: 203-767-7178
Sabreline, Grand Banks

Eastland Yachts
33 Pratt St.
Essex, CT 06426
203-767-8224, Fax: 203-767-9094

Essex Island Yachts
Foot of Ferry St.,
Essex Island Marina
Essex, CT 06426
203-767-8645, Fax: 203-767-0075

Hank Aldrich Yacht Sales,
37 Pratt St., Box 72
Essex, CT 06426
203-767-4988, Fax: 203-767-4998
Ocean

Photo-Boat
PO Box 504
Mystic, CT 06355
203-536-9333, Fax: 203-535-4801

Storm Haven Yachts
PO Box 85
Newtown, CT 06470
203-426-0806

Noank Shipyard
PO Box 9248
Noank, CT 06340
203-536-9651, Fax: 203-572-8140

Don Zak's Shoreline Yacht Sales
54 Ferry Rd.
Old Saybrook, CT 06475
203-395-0866, Fax: 203-395-0877

Northeast Blackfin,
PO Box 429
Portland, CT 06480
203-342-1988, Fax: 203-342-4132

Petzold's Yacht Sales
37 Indian Hill Ave.
Portland, CT 06480
203-342-1196, Fax: 203-342-0462
Silverton, Mainship, Egg Harbor, Stamas,
Cruisers

Portland Boat Works,
1 Grove St.
Portland, CT 06480
203-342-1085, Fax: 203-342-0544
Post, Tiara

Boatworks Yacht Sales
PO Box 265
Rowayton, CT 06853
203-866-0882, Fax: 203-853-4910
Sabreline, Grand Banks

Rex Marine Center
144 Water St.
South Norwalk, CT 06854
203-866-5555, Fax: 203-866-2518
Stamas, Formula, Island Packet

Chan Moser Yachts
6 Woodridge Drive
Stamford, CT 06905
203-322-6668, Fax: 203-322-8288

Brewer Yacht Sales
63 Pilots Point Dr.
Westbrook, CT 06498
203-399-6213, Fax: 203-399-4379

Louis Marine, Ltd.
438 Boston Post Rd.
Westbrook, CT 06498-1722
203-664-4230
Wellcraft, Chris Craft

Sail Westbrook
PO Box 1179
Westbrook, CT 06498
203-399-5515

FLORIDA

Aventura Yacht Sales
20801 Biscayne Blvd.
Adventura, FL 33180
305-933-8285, Fax: 305-933-8287

South Florida Marine Liquidators
4800 N. Federal Hwy., Suite 113B
Boca Raton, FL 33431
407-750-5155, Fax: 407-750-8533

O'Brien Yacht Sales
3010 SW 14th Place
Boynton Beach, FL 33426
407-738-6676, Fax: 407-738-1658

The Boatworks
6921 14th St. W. (U.S. 41)
Bradenton, FL 34207
813-756-1896, Fax: 813-753-9426
Bayliner, Wellcraft

Harbour Yacht Sales
25 Causeway Blvd.
Clearwater Beach, FL 34630
813-446-5617, Fax: 813-441-9173

Hatteras in Miami
2550 S. Bayshore Dr.
Coconut Grove, FL 33133
305-854-1100, Fax: 305-854-1186
Hatteras, Tiara

Reel Deal Yachts
2550 S. Bayshore Dr.
Coconut Grove, FL 33133
305-859-8200, Fax: 305-854-8044
Blackfin, Luhrs, Phoenix, Mainship, Mako

Cozy Cove Marina
300 N Federal Hwy.
Dania, FL 33004
305-921-8800, Fax: 305-922-0173
Blackfin

HMY Yacht Sales
850 NE 3rd. St.
Dania, FL 33004
305-926-0400, Fax: 305-921-2543
Post, Hines-Farley, Viking, Cabo

Intrepid Southeast
850 NE 3rd. St.
Dania, FL 33004
305-922-7544, Fax: 305-922-3858
Intrepid

Oviatt Marine
850 NE 3rd St., Suite 201
Dania, FL 33004
305-925-0065, Fax: 305-925-8822

Daytona Marina & Boatworks
645 S. Beach St.
Daytona Beach, FL 32114
904-253-6266, Fax: 904-253-8174

Eagle Yachts
721 Ballough Rd
Daytona Beach, FL 32114
904-258-7578, Fax: 904-257-5179

Yacht Brokerage USA
3948 S. Peninsula Dr.
Daytona Beach, FL 32127
904-760-9353

Universal Yachts,
1645 SE 3rd Ct., #214
Deerfield Beach, FL 33441
305-786-2911, Fax: 305-786-1937

Yacht Registry
343 Causeway Blvd.
Dunedin, FL 34698
813-733-0334, Fax: 813-733-6754

Alexander Yachts
2150 SE 17th St., Suite 201,
Ft. Lauderdale, FL 33316
305-763-7676, Fax: 305-763-7758

Allied Marine
401 SW First Ave., 2nd Fl.,
Ft. Lauderdale, FL 33301
305-462-7424, Fax: 305-462-0756

American Trading Industries
500 SE 17th St., #220,
Ft. Lauderdale, FL 33316
305-522-4254, Fax: 305-522-4435

Ameriship Corporation
3285 SW 11th Ave.,
Ft. Lauderdale, FL 33315
305-463-7957, Fax: 305-463-3342
Exporter

Ardell Yacht & Ship Brokers
1550 SE 17th Street,
Ft. Lauderdale, FL 33316
305-525-7637, Fax: 305-527-1292

Atlantic Pacific Sailing Yachts
2244 SE 17th St.,
Ft. Lauderdale, FL 33316
305-463-7651, Fax: 305-779-3316

Bollman Yachts
2046 SE 17th St.,
Ft. Lauderdale, FL 33316
305-761-1122, Fax: 305-463-9878

Bradford International
3151 State Road 84,
Ft. Lauderdale, FL 33312
305-791-2600, Fax: 305-791-2655

Broward Yacht Sales
1535 SE 17th St., Suite 202,
Ft. Lauderdale, FL 33316
305-763-8201, Fax: 305-763-9079

Bruce A. Bales Yacht Sales
1635 S. Miami Rd., #2,
Ft. Lauderdale, FL 33316
305-522-3760, Fax: 305-522-4364

Castlemain,
300 SW 2nd St., Suite 4,
Ft. Lauderdale, FL 33312
305-760-4730, Fax: 305-760-4737
Swiftships

Chas. P. Irwin Yacht Brokerage
801 Seabreeze Blvd.
(Bahia Mar Yachting Ctr.),
Ft. Lauderdale, FL 33316
305-463-6302, Fax: 305-523-0056

Colonial Yacht Sales
901 SE 17th St., #203,
Ft. Lauderdale, FL 33316
305-463-0555, Fax: 305-463-8621

Dave D'Onofrio Yacht Sales
1875 SE 17th St. (Marriott Marina),
Ft. Lauderdale, FL 33316
305-527-4848, Fax: 305-462-6817

Dave Pyles Yacht Sales
2596 SW 23rd Terrace,
Ft. Lauderdale, FL 33312
305-583-8104, Fax: 305-797-7669

Emerald Yacht & Ship Brokers
801 Seabreeze Blvd.,
Ft. Lauderdale, FL 33316
305-522-0556, Fax: 305-522-3194

Everglades Marina
2409 NE 26th Ave.,
Ft. Lauderdale, FL 33305
305-763-3030, Fax: 305-763-3167
Baja, Fountain

Florida Yacht & Ship Brokers
1700 E. Las Olas Blvd.,
Ft. Lauderdale, FL 33316
305-467-1122, Fax: 305-467-0011

Frank Gordon Yacht Sales
801 Seabreeze Blvd.
(Bahia Mar Yachting Center),
Ft. Lauderdale, FL 33316
305-525-8476, Fax: 305-525-6024

Fraser Yachts
2160 SE 17th St.,
Ft. Lauderdale, FL 33316
305-463-0600, Fax: 305-763-1053

Garcia Yacht Sales
1323 SE 17 St, #220,
Ft Lauderdale, FL 33316
305-763-6152, Fax: 305-763-6152

Hal Jones & Co.
1900 SE 15th St.,
Ft. Lauderdale, FL 33316
305-527-1778, Fax: 305-523-5153
Grand Banks

Hatteras of Lauderdale
401 SW 1st Ave.,
Ft. Lauderdale, FL 33301
305-462-5557, Fax: 305-462-0029
Hatteras, Tiara

Helms • Kelly • MacMahon International Yachting
1650 SE 17th St., Suite101,
Ft. Lauderdale, FL 33316
305-525-1441, Fax: 305-525-1110

High-Tech Marine
1535 SE 17th St. Quay,
Ft. Lauderdale, FL 33316
305-524-6911, Fax: 305-524-7107

J. Woods Marine Group
808 NE 20th Ave.,
Ft. Lauderdale, FL 33304
305-764-8770, Fax: 305-764-8771

Jackson Marine Sales
1915 SW 21st Ave.,
Ft. Lauderdale, FL 33312
305-792-4900, Fax: 305-587-8164

Jet Sea Yacht Brokerage
1650 SE 17th St., #204,
Ft. Lauderdale, FL 33316
305-766-2600, Fax: 305-766-2611
Tecnomarine

Luke Brown & Assoc.
1500 Cordova Rd., #200,
Ft. Lauderdale, FL 33316
305-525-6617, Fax: 305-525-6626

Mares Yacht Sales
1535 SE 17th St., #107,
Ft. Lauderdale, FL 33316
305-523-2287, Fax: 305-523-2236
Mares

Marina 84
2698 SW 23rd Ave.,
Ft. Lauderdale, FL 33312
305-581-3313, Fax: 305-797-8986

Merle Wood & Associates
1535 SE 17th St., #201B,
Ft. Lauderdale, FL 33316
305-525-5111, Fax: 305-525-5165

Merritt Yacht Brokers
2040 SE 17th St,
Ft. Lauderdale, FL 33316
305-761-1300, Fax: 305-463-8617

Northrop & Johnson
1901 SW 4th Avenue,
Ft. Lauderdale, FL 33316
305-522-3344, Fax: 305-522-9500

Peter Kehoe & Associates
2150 SE 17th St., #107,
Ft. Lauderdale, FL 33316
305-767-9880, Fax: 305-767-9884

Rex Yacht Sales
2152 SE 17th Street,
Ft. Lauderdale, FL 33316
305-463-8810, Fax: 305-462-3640
Ocean Alexander, Cheoy Lee

Richard Bertram & Co.
651 Seabreeze Blvd.,
Ft. Lauderdale, FL 33316
305-467-8405, Fax: 305-763-2675

Royce Yacht & Ship Brokers
1600 SE 17th St., #418,
Ft. Lauderdale, FL 33316
305-764-0100, Fax: 305-764-0192

Sea Yachts
837 NE 20th Ave.,
Ft. Lauderdale, FL 33304
305-522-0993, Fax: 305-768-9027

Tom Klein Yacht
5200 N. Federal Hwy., Suite 2,
Ft. Lauderdale, FL 33308
305-772-7070, Fax: 305-772-7086

Trans America Yacht Brokers
1535 SE 17th St., Ste. 109,
Ft. Lauderdale, FL 33316
305-462-1177, Fax: 305-462-7858

Trans-Coastal Yacht Brokerage
515 Seabreeze Blvd.,
Ft. Lauderdale, FL 33316
305-767-8830, Fax: 305-767-8942

Walsh Yachts
1900 S.E. 15th Street,
Ft. Lauderdale, FL 33316
305-525-7447, Fax: 305-525-7451

Woods & Oviatt
Pier 66 Marina, 2301 SE 17th St.,
Ft. Lauderdale, FL 33316
305-463-5606, Fax: 305-522-5156

Yacht Brokerage USA
1700 E. Los Olas Blvd., Suite 101,
Ft. Lauderdale, FL 33301
305-463-1255, Fax: 305-463-7733

Yacht Search—The Professional Brokerage
2150 SE 17th St.,
Ft. Lauderdale, FL 33315
305-524-1823, Fax: 305-525-3074

Yacht & Ship Brokers,
2501 S. Federal Hwy.,
Ft. Lauderdale, FL 33316
305-779-7447, Fax: 305-779-3735

Great American Marine
1310 Lee Street,
Ft. Myers, FL 33901
813-334-8622, Fax: 813-334-0207
Grand Banks, Hatteras

Yacht Brokerage USA
1700 Medical Lane,
Ft. Myers, FL 33907
813-936-5595, Fax: 813-936-0544

Yacht-Eng,
13601 McGregor Blvd., #16,
Ft. Myers, FL 33919
813-481-3511, Fax: 813-481-3064

East-West Yachts
10 Avenue A, Ft. Pierce Yacht Center,
Ft. Pierce, FL 34950
407-466-1240, Fax: 407-466-1242

Waterline Yacht Brokerage
2010 Harbortown Dr.,
Ft. Pierce, FL 34946
407-466-5747, Fax: 407-466-5966

Yacht Brokerage USA
PO Box 1552,
Ft. Walton Beach, FL 32549
904-664-1212, Fax: 904-244-1751

Grantour Yachts,
2422 NE 9th St.
Hallandale, FL 33009
305-936-0337, Fax: 305-936-0338
Riviera

Palm Beach Yacht Center
7848 S. Federal Hwy.
Hypoluxo, FL 33462
407-585-2003, Fax: 407-585-9933
Bayliner

Ortega River Boat Yard
4451 Herschel St.
Jacksonville, FL 32210
904-387-5538, Fax: 904-388-7476
Luhrs

Roger Hansen Yacht Sales
3344 Lake Shore Blvd.
Jacksonville, FL 32210
904-384-3113, Fax: 904-384-6550
Californian, Bertram

Jax Beach Yacht Brokerage
13846 Atlantic Blvd.
Jacksonville Beach, FL 32225
904-246-4975, Fax: 904-246-7573
Halvorsen

North Florida Yacht Sales
2305 Beach Blvd., #105
Jacksonville Beach, FL 32250
904-249-8444, Fax: 904-247-0050

Card Sound Yachts
9 Barracuda Lane
Key Largo, FL 33037
305-367-2727, Fax: 305-367-3962

Perdue Dean,
#2 Fishing Village Dr. ORC
Key Largo, FL 33037
305-367-2661, Fax: 305-367-2128

Marine Unlimited
232 Basin Dr.
Lauderdale-by-the-Sea, FL 33308
305-491-0430, Fax: 305-771-6122

Oceanus Institute,
4332 E. Tradewinds Ave.
Lauderdale-by-the-Sea, FL 33308
305-772-5773

SGK Yacht Sales
218 Commercial
Lauderdale-by-the-Sea, FL 33308
305-776-5525

Donhuser's Yacht Brokerage
3142 N. Federal Hwy.
Lighthouse Point, FL 33064
305-946-9484, Fax: 305-946-9487

Rhodes Yacht Brokers
2901 NE 28th Court
Lighthouse Point, FL 33064
305-941-2404, Fax: 305-941-2507

Waterline Yacht Brokerage
905 N. Harbor City Blvd.
Melbourne, FL 32935
407-254-0452, Fax: 407-254-0516

Cruising Yachts & Ships,
3051 Orange St.
Miami, FL 33133
305-448-3481, Fax: 305-567-9750

Custom Brokerage Yacht Sales
11422 SW 87th Terrace
Miami, FL 33173
305-598-9875, Fax: 305-598-2239

Frank Stanzel Yachts
7350 SW 96th St.
Miami, FL 33156
305-669-0962, Fax: 305-669-0961

Merrill-Stevens Yacht Sales
1270 NW 11th St.
Miami, FL 33125
305-858-5911, Fax: 305-858-5919

Richard Bertram & Co.
3660 NW 21st St.
Miami, FL 33152
305-633-9761, Fax: 305-634-9071

Florida Yacht Charters & Sales
1290 Fifth Street
Miami Beach, FL 33139
305-532-8600, Fax: 305-672-2039

Naples Yacht Brokerage
P.O. Box 882
Naples, FL 33939
813-434-8338, Fax: 813-434-6848

Walker's Yacht Sales
895 10th St. South
Naples, FL 33940
813-262-6500, Fax: 813-262-6693
Parker, Tiara, Formula, Albemarle

Blake Davis Yacht Brokerage
7601 E. Treasure Dr.
North Bay Village, FL 33141
305-866-8329

Gilman Yacht Sales
1212-A U.S. Hwy 1
North Palm Beach, FL 33408
407-626-1790, Fax: 407-626-5870

Camper & Nicholson
450 Royal Palm Way
Palm Beach, FL 33480
407-655-2121, Fax: 407-655-2202

Hatteras in Palm Beach
2410 PGA Blvd., #155
Palm Beach Gardens, FL 33410
407-775-3531, Fax: 407-775-8790
Hatteras, Tiara

Shear Yacht Sales
2385 PGA Blvd., Box 30308
Palm Beach Gardens, FL 33420
407-624-2112, Fax: 407-624-1877
Albin, Island Gypsy, Novatec, DeFever

Singer Island Yacht Sales
11440 U.S. Highway 1
Palm Beach Gardens, FL 33408
407-622-0355, Fax: 407-622-0339

Stella Marine
2385 PGA Blvd.
Palm Beach Gardens, FL 33410
407-624-9950, Fax: 407-624-9949

The Marine Group
2401 PGA Blvd., Suite 104
Palm Beach Gardens, FL 33410
407-627-9500, Fax: 407-627-9503

Coastal Yacht Sales
1496 Treetop Dr.
Palm Harbor, FL 34683
813-787-9300
Ocean

Carson Yacht Brokerage
1035 Riverside Dr.
Palmetto, FL 34221
813-723-1825, Fax: 813-729-8254

K&H Yachts
1055 N. Riverside Dr.
Palmetto, FL 34221
813-729-4449
Albin

Regatta Point Yacht Sales
985 Riverside Dr.
Palmetto, FL 34221
813-722-7755, Fax: 813-722-7757

Grand Lagoon Yacht Brokers
3706 Thomas Dr.
Panama City Beach, FL 32408
904-233-4747, Fax: 904-233-4741

Treasure Island Marina
3605 Thomas Dr.
Panama City Beach, FL 32408
904-234-6533, Fax: 904-235-1299
Sea Ray

Prestige Yachts
600 Barracks St., Suite 102
Pensacola, FL 32501
904-432-6838, Fax: 904-432-8999
Tiara, Silverton

Four Points Yacht & Ship Brokers
101 N. Riverside Dr., Suite 214
Pompano Beach, FL 33062
305-941-5500, Fax: 305-941-5521
Ocean, Jefferson

Ocean Harbor Marine
1500 N. Federal Hwy.
Pompano Beach, FL 33062
305-946-9900, Fax: 305-946-4040
Wellcraft

Cape Yacht Brokerage
800 Scallop Dr.
Port Canaveral, FL 32920
407-799-4724, Fax: 407-799-0096

Taber Yacht Sales
Pirates Cove Marine, Box 1687
Port Salerno, FL 34992
407-288-7466, Fax: 407-288-7476

Bain Yacht Sales
1200 W. Retta Esplanade
Punta Gorda, FL 33950
813-637-1335, Fax: 813-637-8057
Onset

Yacht Perfection
1601 W. Marion Ave #203 D
Punta Gorda, FL 33950
813-637-8111, Fax: 813-637-9918

Wayne Roman Yachts
207 E. Blue Heron Blvd.
Riviera Beach, FL 33404
407-844-5000, Fax: 407-848-5422

Yacht Brokerage USA
613 Rockledge Dr.
Rockledge, FL 32955
407-636-3600, Fax: 407-636-3606

Great American Marine
1889 N. Tamiami Trail
Sarasota, FL 33580
813-365-1770, Fax: 813-365-1787
Grand Banks, Hatteras

Modern Classic Yachtworks
1666 Main St.
Sarasota, FL 34236
813-955-7733, Fax: 813-957-3132

Sarasota Yacht & Ship Services
1306 Main St.
Sarasota, FL 34236
813-365-9095, Fax: 813-955-1727

First Coast Yacht Sales
103 Yacht Club Dr.
St. Augustine, FL 32095
904-824-7293, Fax: 904-829-6779

Offshore Yacht & Ship Brokers
256-B Riberia St.
St. Augustine, FL 32084
904-829-9224, Fax: 904-825-4292

St. Augustine Yacht Center
3040 Harbor Dr.
St. Augustine, FL 32095
904-829-2294, Fax: 904-829-2298

D.M. Savage Yacht
4326 Central Ave.
St. Petersburg, FL 33711
813-327-1288, Fax: 813-321-0491

Anchor Yachts International
1110 Pinellas Bayway Dr.
St. Petersburg, FL 33715
813-867-8027, Fax: 813-864-1359

Capt. Jack's Yacht Brokerage
101 16th Ave So.
St Petersburg, FL 33701
813-825-0757, Fax: 813-822-6415

Charles Morgan Associates
200 Second Ave. S.
St. Petersburg, FL 33701
813-894-7027, Fax: 813-894-8983

Great American Marine
6810 Gulfport Blvd.
St. Petersburg, FL 33707
813-384-3428, Fax: 813-381-1401
Grand Banks, Hatteras

Mariner Yacht Sales
12022 Gandy Blvd.
St. Petersburg, FL 33702
813-576-3307, Fax: 813-576-4767

Royal Yacht & Ship Brokers
3859 Central Ave.
St. Petersburg, FL 33713
813-327-0900, Fax: 813-327-7797

The Harborage Marina
1110 3rd St. South
St. Petersburg, FL 33701
813-894-7497, Fax: 813-898-2028
Carver, Sport Craft

West Florida Yachts
4880 37th St. South
St. Petersburg, FL 33711
813-864-0310, Fax: 813-867-6860

Yacht Brokerage USA
4401 Central Ave.
St. Petersburg, FL 33713
813-328-1255, Fax: 813-328-1796

Midcoast Yacht Sales
3957 Barcelona St.
Stuart, FL 34997
407-288-4886

Northside Marine Sales
400 NW Alice Ave.
Stuart, FL 34994
407-692-3052, Fax: 407-692-4006
Post, Mainship, Blackfin

Stuart Hatteras
110 N. Federal Hwy.
Stuart, FL 34994
407-692-1122, Fax: 407-692-1341
Hatteras, Tiara

Stuart Yacht
450 SW Salerno Rd.
Stuart, FL 34997
407-283-1947, Fax: 407-286-9800

Flammer Viking Yachts,
650 U.S. 19 North
Tarpon Springs, FL 34689
813-733-9289, Fax: 813-733-8876
Viking, Cabo

Complete Yacht Services
3599 E. Indian River Dr.
Vero Beach, FL 32963
407-231-2111, Fax: 407-231-4465
Grand Banks, Sabreline

Palm Beach Yacht Club Brokerage
800 N. Flagler Dr.
West Palm Beach, FL 33401
407-833-8633, Fax: 407-833-8639

Rybovich-Spencer Group
4200 N. Dixie
West Palm Beach, FL 33407
407-844-4331, Fax: 407-844-8393

GEORGIA

Robert P. Minis
102 McIntosh Dr.
Savannah, GA 31406
912-354-6589

Golden Isles Yacht Sales
PO Box 21715
St. Simons Island, GA 31522
912-638-5678, Fax: 912-638-8532

ILLINOIS

Class Sea Yachts
207 N. Hager
Barrington, IL 60010
708-382-2100, Fax: 708-381-1265

Larsen Marine Service
1663 N. Elston Ave.
Chicago, IL 60614
312-993-7711, Fax: 312772-0891
Tiara

Sailboat Sales Co.
2500 S. Corbett St.
Chicago, IL 60608
312-225-2046, Fax: 312-225-6354

Spring Brook Marina
623 W. River Dr., Box 379
Seneca, IL 61360
815-357-8666, Fax: 815-357-8678
Carver, Viking, Harbor Master, Californian

Riverview Marine
515 S. Spaulding St.
Spring Valley, IL 61362
815-663-1000, Fax: 815-663-2628
Fountain. Powerquest

Larsen Marine Service
625 Sea Horse Dr.
Waukegan, IL 60085
708-336-5456, Fax: 708-336-5530
Tiara

Skipper Bud's at North Point Marina
215 N. Point Dr.
Winthrop Harbor, IL 60096
708-872-3200, Fax: 708-872-3230
Hatteras, Chris Craft, Sea Ray

INDIANA

B&E Marine
Washington Park
Michigan City, IN 46360
219-879-8301, Fax: 219-879-8388
Sea Ray, Rinker

H&M Yacht Brokerage
1 Newport Dr.
Michigan City, IN 46360
219-879-7152

KENTUCKY

Kentuckiana Yacht Sales
Hwy. 641 South
Gilbertville, KY 42044
502-362-8343

LOUISIANA

A&M Yacht Sales/New Orleans Hatteras
126 South Roadway
New Orleans, LA 70124
504-282-6800
Hatteras, Viking

Prestige Yachts
6701 South Shore Harbor Blvd.
New Orleans, LA 70126
504-242-9000, Fax: 504-246-3908
Tiara, Silverton

MAINE

Duffy & Duffy Yacht Sales
HC 63, Box 333
Brooklin, ME 04616
207-359-4658, Fax: 207-359-8948

Camden Harbor Yachts
PO Box 880
Camden, ME 04843
207-236-7112, Fax: 207-236-7113

Casco Bay Yacht Exchange
P.O. Box 413, Freeport, ME 04032
207-865-4016, Fax: 207-865-0759

Steedman & Gray,
PO Box 1094
Kennebunkport, ME 04046
207-967-4211, Fax: 207-967-8428

Indian Point Yachts
HCR 62, Box 63
Mt. Desert, ME 04660
207-288-5258, Fax: 207-288-3093

North Star Yacht Sales
DiMillo's Marina, Long Wharf
Portland, ME 04101
207-879-7678, Fax: 207-879-1471

Robinhood Marine Center
PO Box 460
Robinhood, ME 04530
207-371-2343, Fax: 207-371-2899

Michael Waters Yacht Brokers
112 Beech St.
Rockland, ME 04841
207-594-4234, Fax: 207-596-0726
Lien Hwa Motoryachts

Atlantic Yacht Brokerage
PO Box 2277
South Portland, ME 04016
207-767-3254, Fax: 207-767-5940

The Yacht Connection
Marine East Marina
South Portland, ME 04106
207-799-3600, Fax: 207-767-5937

Hinckley Yacht Brokerage
Box 699, Shore Rd
Southwest Harbor, ME 04679
207-244-5531, Fax: 207-244-9833

Newman Marine
HC 33, Box 5
Southwest Harbor, ME 04679
207-244-5560

Midcoast Yacht Sales
PO Box 221
Wiscasset, ME 04567
207-882-6445, Fax: 207-882-4250

East Coast Yacht Sales
38 Lafayette St., Rt. 88
Yarmouth, ME 04096
207-846-4545, Fax: 207-846-6088
Grand Banks, Sabreline, J Boats

MARYLAND

Annapolis Landing Boat Sales
922 Klakring Rd.
Annapolis, MD 21403
410-263-0090, Fax: 410-626-1857

Annapolis Motor Yachts
P.O. Box 2193
Annapolis, MD 21404
410-268-7171, Fax: 410-268-6921

Annapolis Yacht Sales
7416 Edgewood Rd.
Annapolis, MD 21403
301-267-8181, Fax: 301-267-7409

Atlantic Coast Yacht Sales
Box 5042 - 326 First St.
Annapolis, MD 21403
410-268-5449, Fax: 410-267-6127

Bay Yacht Agency
326 First St.
Annapolis, MD 21403
410-263-2311, Fax: 410-263-2967

Bristol Yacht Sales
623 Sixth St.
Annapolis, MD 21403
410-280-6611, Fax: 410-280-0170
Black Watch, Bristol

Interyacht
7076 Bembe Beach Rd.
Annapolis, MD 21403
410-269-5200, Fax: 410-269-0571

Martin Bird & Associates
326 First St.
Annapolis, MD 21403
410-268-1086, Fax: 410-268-0942

Passport Yachts East
326 First St., #14
Annapolis, MD 21403
410-263-0008, Fax: 410-263-5705

Wilkins Yacht Sales
PO Box 787
Annapolis, MD 21404
410-266-8585, Fax: 410-266-9745
Hatteras

Yacht Net
1912 Forest Dr.
Annapolis, MD 21401
410-263-0993, Fax: 410-267-7967

Fred Quimby's Marine Services
9296 Ocean Gateway
Easton, MD 21601
410-822-8107
Mako, Fountain

Anchor Yacht Basin
1048 Turkey Point Rd.
Edgewater, MD 21037
410-269-6674, Fax: 410-798-6782
Phoenix, Dawson brokerage

Burr Yacht Sales, Inc
1106 Turkey Point Rd
Edgewater, MD 21037
410-798-5900, Fax: 410-798-5911
Fleming, Bertram

Cherry Yachts
2830 Solomons Island Rd.
Edgewater, MD 21037
410-266-3801, Fax: 410-266-3805

Free State Yachts
64 Old River Rd.
Edgewater, MD 21037
410-266-9060, Fax: 410-266-8309

Tidewater Yacht Sales
64A Old South River Rd.
Edgewater, MD 21307
800-899-2799, Fax: 410-224-6919
Bayliner

Anchor Bay Yacht Sales
202 Nanticoke Rd.
Essex, MD 21221
410-574-0777, Fax: 410-574-8364

Harbour Yacht Agency
PO Box 10
Friendship, MD 20758
410-855-4250, Fax: 410-855-4485

Hartge Yacht Sales
Church Lane
Galesville, MD 20765
410-867-7240, Fax: 410-867-7139

Nautilus Yacht Sales
150 Skipjack Rd., Box 56
Georgetown, MD 21930
410-275-1100, Fax: 410-275-1133

Bayport Yachts
Rt. 50 & Kent Narrows
Grasonville, MD 21638
410-827-5500, Fax: 410-827-5481
Carver

Harrison Yacht Sales
PO Box 98
Grasonville, MD 21638
410-827-6600
Sea Ray, Carver, Viking

Lippincott Marine
Rt. 2, Box 545
Grasonville, MD 21638
410-827-9300, Fax: 410-827-9303

Havre de Grace Yacht Sales
723 Water St.
Havre de Grace, MD 21078
410-939-2161, Fax: 410-939-0220

Tidewater Marine, Foot of Burbon St.
Havre de Grace, MD 21078
410-939-0950, Fax: 410-939-0955

Gunpowder Cove Marina
510 Riviera Dr.
Joppa, MD 21085
410-679-5454
Sea Ray

Jackson Marine Sales
PO Box 483, Hances Point
North East, MD 21901
410-287-9400, Fax: 410-287-9043
Onset

McDaniel Yacht Basin
PO Box E
North East, MD 21901
410-287-8121, Fax: 410-287-8127
Carver

Chesapeake Motoryacht Sales
Tilghman St. @ Town Creek, Box 417
Oxford, MD 21654
410-226-0002, Fax: 410-226-5699
Albin, President

Maryland Yachts
PO Box 216
Oxford, MD 21654
410-226-5571, Fax: 410-226-5080

Oxford Yacht Agency,
317 S. Morris St.
Oxford, MD 21654
410-226-5454, Fax: 410-226-5244
Grand Banks

Arnold C. Gay Yacht Sales
"C" Street, Box 538
Solomons, MD 20688
410-326-2011, Fax: 410-326-2012

Solomons Yacht Brokerage
PO Box 380, 255 "A" Street
Solomons, MD 20688
410-326-6748, Fax: 410-326-2149

William Magness Yachts
301 Pier One Rd., #103
Stevensville, MD 21666
301-643-8434, Fax: 301-643-8437

Warehouse Creek Yacht Sales
301 Pier One Rd.
Stevensville, MD 21666
410-643-7878, Fax: 410-643-7877
Egg Harbor, Cruisers

Clipper Bay Yacht Sales
389 Deale Rd.
Tracys Landing, MD 20779
410-261-5775, Fax: 410-261-5775

Shady Oaks Yacht Sales
846 Shady Oaks Dr.
West River, MD 20778
410-867-7700, Fax: 410-867-1563
Silverton,Tiara

MASSACHUSETTS

Northrop & Johnson
43 Water St.
Beverly, MA 01915
617-569-6900, Fax: 617-569-9247

John G. Alden & Co.
89 Commercial Wharf
Boston, MA 02110
617-227-9480, Fax: 617-523-5465

Onset Bay Yacht Sales
RFD #3, Green St.
Buzzards Bay, MA 02532
508-295-2300, Fax: 508-295-8873
Onset

Carl Bettano Yacht Brokerage
1000 Justin Dr., Admirals Hill Marina
Chelsea, MA 02150
617-889-4849, Fax: 617-889-4814

Danversport Marine
128 Water St.
Danvers, MA 01923
508-777-3822, Fax: 508-777-5478

Norwood Marine
R-24 Ericsson St.
Dorchester, MA 02122
617-288-1000, Fax: 617-282-5728
Silverton, Wellcraft

Yacht Listings
PO Box 465
East Sandwich, MA 02537
508-833-8591, Fax: 508-833-8592

Capt. O'Connell
180 River St., Fall River, MA 02720
508-672-6303, Fax: 508-672-0922
Silverton

Jameson Yacht Sales
PO Box 548, Falmouth, MA 02541
508-540-4750, Fax: 508-564-5940

Eastern Yacht Sales
349 Lincoln St.
Hingham, MA 02043
617-749-8600, Fax: 617-740-4149

Worldwide Yachts
350 Lincoln St., #105
Hingham, MA 02043
617-740-2628, Fax: 617-740-1325

Cape Cod Marine Group
PO Box 220
Hyannis, MA 02601
508-775-6002, Fax: 508-790-1099

Hyannis Marine
21 Arlington St.
Hyannis, MA 02601
508-775-5662, Fax: 508-775-0851

Able Yacht Brokerage
42 Doaks Lane, Little Harbor
Marblehead, MA 01945
617-639-4280, Fax: 617-639-4233

Wells Yachts
91 Front St.
Marblehead, MA 01945
617-631-3003, Fax: 617-639-2503
Luhrs, Phoenix, Pursuit

Powerbrokers International
PO Box 1015
Marion, MA 02738
508-748-3100, Fax: 508-748-3100

Rose Yacht Sales
PO Box 923
Marion, MA 02738
508-748-2211, Fax: 508-748-3773

Bosun's Marine
100 Falmouth Rd./Rte. 28
Mashpee, MA 02649
508-477-4626
Mako

Yacht Broker & Dealer Directory

Cape Yacht Brokers
Box 70, Seabrook Village
Mashpee, MA 02649
508-477-2422, Fax: 508-394-1660

Russo Marine
357 Mystic Ave.
Medford, MA 02155
617-395-0050, Fax: 617-396-8536

Yankee Yacht Sales
23 Low St.
Newburyport, MA 01950
508-462-2781, Fax: 508-465-8847

Dudley Yacht Sales
42 Fiddler Cove Rd.
North Falmouth, MA 02556
508-564-4100, Fax: 508-564-4129

Bay View Yacht Sales
304 Victory Rd.
North Quincy, MA 02171
617-328-1800

Boston Yacht Sales
PO Box 76, Tern Harbor Marina
North Weymouth, MA 02191
617-331-2400, Fax: 617-331-8215
Hatteras, Viking

Nauset Marine
Box 357, Route 6A
Orleans, MA 02653
508-255-0777, Fax: 508-255-0373
Grady-White

Crosby Yacht Yard
72 Crosby Circle
Osterville, MA 02655
508-428-6958, Fax: 508-428-0323

Oyster Harbor Marine
122 Bridge Street
Osterville, MA 02655
508-428-2017, Fax: 508-420-5398
Blackfin, Limestone

Gary Voller's Yacht Sales
3828 Riverside Ave.
Somerset, MA 02726
508-678-0404, Fax: 508-678-0990

Concordia Yacht Sales
South Wharf, Box P203
South Dartmouth, MA 02748
508-999-1381, Fax: 508-992-4682

Buzzards Bay Yacht Sales
PO Box 369
Westport Point, MA 02791
508-636-4010

MICHIGAN

Colony Marine
6509 M-29 Hwy., Box 388
Algonac, MI 48001
313-794-4932, Fax: 313-794-2147
Sea Ray

Bay Harbor Yacht Brokerage
5309 E. Wilder Rd.
Bay City, MI 48706
517-684-3593, Fax: 517-684-5920
Cruisers, Wellcraft, Silverton

Dilworth & Lally Yacht Brokers
100 North Lake Dr.
Boyne City, MI 49712
616-582-6886, Fax: 616-582-6891

Charlevoix Boat Shop
101 E. Mason (Harborside)
Charlevoix, MI 49720
616-547-2710, Fax: 616-547-2444

Irish Boat Shop
1300 Stover Rd.
Charlevoix, MI 49720
616-547-9967, Fax: 616-547-4129
Boston Whaler, Sea Ray

Diamond Boat Sales
28853 N. Gibraltar Rd.
Gibraltar, MI 48173
313-675-3575
Robolo

Grand Isle Marina
1 Grand Isle Dr.
Grand Haven, MI 49417
800-854-2628, Fax: 616-842-8783
Regal

Walstrom Marine
105 Bay Rd.
Harbor Springs, MI 49740
616-526-2141, Fax: 616-526-7527
Hatteras, Tiara

Toledo Beach Yacht Sales
11840 Toledo Beach Rd.
LaSalle, MI 48145
313-243-3830, Fax: 313-243-3815
Hatteras, Silverton

Eldean Boat Sales, Ltd.
2223 South Shore Dr.
Macatawa, MI 49434
616-335-5843, Fax: 616-335-5848
Grand Banks, Bertram, Ocean

Active Marine
31785 S. River Rd.
Mt. Clemens, MI 48045
810-463-7441, Fax: 810-468-7080

John B. Slaven,
Box 864, 31300 N. River Rd.
Mt. Clemens, MI 48046
810-463-0000, Fax: 810-463-4317

McMachen Sea Ray
30099 South River Rd.
Mt. Clemens, MI 48045
810-469-0223, Fax: 810-469-1646
Tiara, Sea Ray

Sun & Sail
31040 N. River Rd.
Mt. Clemens, MI 48045
313-463-4800

Oselka Marina
514 Oselka Dr.
New Buffalo, MI 49117
616-469-2600, Fax: 616-469-0988
Carver

Onekama Marine
Portage Lake
Onekama, MI 49675
616-889-4218, Fax: 616-889-3398
Cruisers, Silverton, Larson

Colony Marine
60 S. Telegraph Rd.
Pontiac, MI 48053
313-683-2500
Sea Ray

Barrett Boat Works
821 W. Savidge St.
Spring Lake, MI 49456
616-842-1202, Fax: 616-842-5735
Zodiac

Keenan Marine
526 Pine St.
Spring Lake, MI 49456
616-846-3830, Fax: 616-846-3821
Chris Craft, Baja

North Shore Marina
18275 Berwyck
Spring Lake, MI 49456
616-842-1488, Fax: 616-842-0143
Silverton, Chaparral

Colony Marine
24530 Jefferson Ave.
St. Clair Shores, MI 48080
810-772-1550
Sea Ray

Jefferson Beach Marina
24400 E. Jefferson
St. Clair Shores, MI 48080
810-778-7600, Fax: 810-778-4766
Viking, Sunseeker, Silverton, Fountain,
Cruisers, Formula

Pier 33 Yacht Sales
250 Anchors Way
St. Joseph, MI 49085
616-983-0677
Bayliner, Fountain, Hatteras, Silverton,
Wellcraft

Superbrokers of Traverse City
12719 SW Bayshore Dr., #9
Traverse City, MI 49684
616-922-3002, Fax: 616-922-3013

Yacht Broker & Dealer Directory

MINNESOTA

Owens Yacht Sales
371 Canal Park Dr.
Duluth, MN 55802
218-722-9212, Fax: 218-722-4730

MISSISSIPPI

Atlantic Marine Brokers
105 Highway 90
Waveland, MS 39576
800-748-9925, Fax: 601-467-9429
Sea Cat, Answer

NEW JERSEY

Twin Lights
197 Princeton Ave.
Brick, NJ 08724
908-295-3500, Fax: 908-295-0230
Bluewater

Comstock Yacht Sales
704 Princeton Ave
Brick Town, NJ 08724
908-899-2500, Fax: 908-892-3763
Post, Silverton, Blackfin, Regulator

Yacht Quest
197 Princeton Ave.
Brick Town, NJ 08724
908-295-0200, Fax: 908-295-0230

South Jersey Marine Brokers
602 Green Ave.
Brielle, NJ 08730
908-223-2200, Fax: 908-223-0211
Viking

Sportside Marine
201 Union St.
Brielle, NJ 08730
908-223-6677, Fax: 908-223-1215

Clark's Landing Marina
1224 Hwy. 109, Box 2170
Cape May, NJ 08204
609-898-9889, Fax: 609-898-1635
Luhrs, Pursuit, Pro-Line

South Jersey Yacht Sales
PO Box 641
Cape May, NJ 08204
609-884-0880, Fax: 609-884-2995
Viking

Integrity Marine
9401 Amherst Ave.
Margate City, NJ 08402
609-898-0801, Fax: 609-898-0785
Jersey

Olson/Weidman Int'l Yacht Brokers
PO Box 2182
Ocean City, NJ 08226
609-390-2288, Fax: 609-390-1260

Bob Massey Yacht Sales
1668 Beaver Dam Rd.
Pt. Pleasant, NJ 08742
908-295-3700, Fax: 908-892-0649
Jefferson, Onset

Clark's Landing Marina
847 Arnold Ave.
Pt. Pleasant, NJ 08742
908-899-5559, Fax: 908-899-5572
Luhrs, Pursuit, Pro-Line

Northeast Sportfishing
406 Channel Dr.
Pt. Pleasant Beach, NJ 08742
908-899-2600, Fax: 908-899-2701

Catskill Classic Yachts
1 Cherry Lane
Ramsey, NJ 07446
201-327-5000, Fax: 201-327-6848

Sandy Hook Yacht Sales
1246 Ocean Ave.
Sea Bright, NJ 07760
201-530-5500, Fax: 908-530-1323

Cape Island Yacht Sales
Bay & Decatur
Summers Point, NJ 08244
609-927-8886, Fax: 609-927-9707

Caribe Yachts
333 Marc Drive
Toms River, NJ 08753
908-914-1224
Ocean Master

North Sea Yachts
1 Robbins Parkway
Toms River, NJ 08753
908-286-6100, Fax: 908-286-2096
Monk 36

Total Marine
411 Great Bay Blvd.
Tuckerton, NJ 08087
609-294-0480
Phoenix, Powerplay

NEW YORK

City Island Yacht Sales
673 City Island Ave.
City Island, NY 10464
212-885-2300, Fax: 212-885-2385
Egg Harbor

Van Schaick Island Marina
South Delaware Ave.
Cohoes, NY 12047
518-237-2681, Fax: 518-233-8355
Carver, Trojan

Fred Chall Marine
1160 Merrick Rd.
Copaigue, NY 11726
516-842-7777
Hatteras, Wellcraft

Patchogue Shores Marina
28 Cornell Rd.
East Patchogue, NY 11772
516-475-0790, Fax: 516-475-0791

Lakes Yacht Sales,
P.O. Box 512
Freeport, NY 11520
516-378-6070, Fax: 516-546-9457

New York Yacht Corp.
102 Woodcleft Ave.
Freeport, NY 11520
516-546-3377, Fax: 516-223-8393

Star Island Yacht Club
116 Woodcleft Ave.
Freeport, NY 11520
516-623-6256, Fax: 516-868-7332
Tiara

Brewer Yacht Sales
500 Beach Rd.
Greenport, NY 11944
516-477-0770

Higgins Yacht Sales
229 6th St.
Greenport, NY 11944
516-477-2404, Fax: 516-477-8112

Islander Boat Center
555 W. Montauk Hwy.
Lindenhurst, NY 11757
516-957-8721, Fax: 516-957-8744
Bayliner, Regal

Surfside 3 Marina
846 S. Wellwood Ave.
Lindenhurst, NY 11757
516-957-5900, Fax: 516-957-5972
Carver, Sea Ray

McMichael Yacht Brokers
447 E. Boston Post Rd.
Mamaorneck, NY 10543
914-381-5900, Fax: 914-381-5060
Nauticat, J-Boats, Sweden Yachts

McMichael Yacht Brokers
700 Rushmore Ave.
Mamaroneck, NY 10543
914-381-2100, Fax: 914-381-2184
Nauticat, J-Boats, Sweden Yachts

Total Marine, Ltd.
622 Rushmore Ave.
Mamaroneck, NY 10543
914-698-2700, Fax: 914-698-8872
Phoenix, Powerplay

Mattituck Inlet Marina
Mill Road
Mattituck, NY 11952
516-298-4480, Fax: 516-298-4126
Viking, Post

Ocean Outboard
2976 Whaleneck Dr.
Merrick, NY 11566
516-378-6400, Fax: 516-378-1609
Mako, Fountain, Formula

Star Island Yacht Club
P.O. Box 2180
Montauk Point, NY 11954
516-668-5052, Fax: 516-668-5503
Tiara

Le Comte Company
101 Harbor Lane W.
New Rochelle, NY 10805
914-636-1524, Fax: 914-636-1359

Orange Boat Sales
51-57 Route 9W
New Windsor, NY 12553
914-565-8530, Fax: 914-565-2706
Baja, Thompson, Regal, Rinker, Bayliner,
Mainship

Solidmark North America
393 South End Ave.
New York, NY 10280
212-938-0883, Fax: 212-488-6053

Sparkman & Stevens
79 Madison Avenue
New York, NY 10016
212-689-9292, Fax: 212-689-3884

Prime Power Marine
2 Washington St.
Newburgh, NY 12550
914-565-7110, Fax: 914-569-8337
Regal, Pursuit

Smith Boys
278 River Rd.
North Tonawanda, NY 14120
716-695-3472
Sea Ray

Oyster Bay Marine Center
5 Bay Ave.
Oyster Bay, NY 11771
516-922-6331, Fax: 516-922-3542

Ventura Yacht Services
15 Orchard Beach Blvd.
Port Washington, NY 11050
516-944-8415, Fax: 516-944-8415

Shumway Yacht Sales
70 Pattonwood Dr.
Rochester, NY 14617
716-342-3030, Fax: 716-266-4722

Bruce Taite Yacht Sales
PO Box 1928
Sag Harbor, NY 11963
516-725-4222, Fax: 516-725-9886

Maritime Yacht
50 W. Water St., PO Box 1981
Sag Harbor, NY 11963
516-725-2878, Fax: 516-725-2878

White River Marine
5500 Sunrise Hwy.
Sayville, NY 11782
516-589-2502
Grady-White

Krenzer Marine
8495 Greig Street
Sodius Point, NY 14555
315-483-6986, Fax: 315-483-6986
Silverton, Cruisers

Dave Bofill Marine
1810 North Sea Rd.
Southampton, NY 11968
516-283-6736, Fax: 516-283-7041
Robolo, Formula

Port of Egypt Marine
Main Road
Southold, NY 11971
516-765-2445
Albemarle, Grady-White

Canyon Yacht Sales
870 Jericoh Turnpike
St. James, NY 11780
516-724-2424
Bertram, Cabo

Staten Island Boat Sales
222 Mansion Ave.
Staten Island, NY 10308
718-984-7676, Fax: 718-317-8338
Viking

Northeast Yachts,
3451 Burnett Ave.
Syracuse, NY 13206
315-437-1438, Fax: 315-437-2501
Bluewater

Hudson Boat Sales
Beach Road
West Haverstraw, NY 10993
914-429-5100
Bayliner

South Shore Boats of Suffolk
Box 1706, Library Ave.
Westhampton Beach, NY 11978
516-288-2400
Rampage

RCR Yachts
PO Box 399
Youngstown, NY 14174
716-745-3862, Fax: 716-745-9671

NORTH CAROLINA

Causeway Marina
300 Morehead Ave., Box 2366
Atlantic Beach, NC 28512
919-726-6977, Fax: 919-726-7089
Stamas

Beaufort Yacht Sales
328 Front St.
Beaufort, NC 28516
919-728-3155, Fax: 919-728-6715
Viking, Freedom, Valient

Nelson Yacht Sales
103 Hill St., Box 1129
Beaufort, NC 28516
919-728-3663, Fax: 919-728-5333
Island Packet, Cabo Rico

Pembroke Yacht Sales
PO Box 384
Edenton, NC 27932
919-482-5151, Fax: 919-482-8754

New Hope Marine
3717 S. New Hope Rd.
Gastonia, NC 28056
704-824-7653
Grady-White

Slane Marine
PO Box 6687
High Point, NC 27262
919-861-6100, Fax: 919-861-8329

70 West Marina
Highway 70
Morehead City, NC 28557
919-726-5171, Fax: 919-726-9993
Tiara, Jersey, Albemarle

Spooners Creek Yacht Sales
Rt. 2, Lands End Rd.
Morehead City, NC 28557
919-726-8082, Fax: 919-726-9806

Quay & Associates
PO Box 563
Oriental, NC 28571
919-249-1825, Fax: 919-249-2240

Whittaker Creek Yacht Sales
PO Box 357
Oriental, NC 28571
919-249-0666, Fax: 919-249-2222

Baker Marine
3410 River Rd.
Wilmington, NC 28412
910-256-8300, Fax: 910-256-9542
Grand Banks, Hatteras, Tiara

Bennett Brothers Yachts
8118 Market St.
Wilmington, NC 28405
919-686-9535, Fax: 919-686-1332

Carolina Yacht Sales
1322 Airlie Rd.
Wilmington, NC 28403
919-256-9901, Fax: 919-256-8526

Pages Creek Marina
7000 Market St.
Wilmington, NC 28405
919-799-7179, Fax: 919-799-1096
Mako

Yacht Broker & Dealer Directory

Harbourside Yachts
PO Drawer 896
Wrightsville Beach, NC 28480
910-350-0660, Fax: 910-350-0506
Carver, Blackfin, Luhrs, Trojan

OHIO

Captain's Cove Marina
4241 Kellogg Ave.
Cincinnati, OH 45226
513-321-1111, Fax: 513-654-2466
Baja, Formula, Fountain

North Shore Boat Brokerage
1787 Merwin
Cleveland, OH 44113
216-241-2237

Anchor Yacht Brokerage
10905 Corduroy Rd.
Curtice, OH 43412
419-836-8985

Bolton's Marine Sales
160 Forest Dr.
Eastlake, OH 44095
216-942-7426, Fax: 216-942-7404

South Shore Yacht Supply
36355 Lakeshore Blvd.
Eastlake, OH 44095
216-946-2266

Lakeside Marine
Erie Beach Rd.
Lakeside, OH 43440
419-798-4406, Fax: 419-798-4089
Tiara

Island Yacht Sales
4236 E. Moore's Dock Rd.
Port Clinton, OH 43452
419-797-9003, Fax: 419-797-6846

Riverdale
1805 W. Lakeshore Dr.
Port Clinton, OH 43452
419-732-2150, Fax: 419-732-8820
Tollycraft

OKLAHOMA

Ugly John's Custom Boats
Route 1, Box 50
Cleveland, OK 74020
918-243-5220, Fax: 918-243-5238
Bluewater, Carver, Celebrity, Fountain,
Gibson, Harbor Master

OREGON

Irwin Yacht Sales
865 NE Tomahawk Island Dr.
Portland, OR 97211
503-298-0074, Fax: 503-286-2213
Wellcraft

Oregon Yacht Sales
2305 NW 133rd Place
Portland, OR 97229
503-629-0717
Tollycraft, Tierra

Seaward Yacht Sales
0315 SW Montgomery, #200
Portland, OR 97201
503-224-2628, Fax: 503-224-5210
Grand Banks

RHODE ISLAND

Shaw Yachts
305 Oliphant Lane
Middletown, RI 02840
401-848-2900, Fax: 401-848-2904

Bartram & Brakenhoff
2 Marine Plaza, Goat Island
Newport, RI 02840
401-846-7355, Fax: 401-847-6329

Bass Harbor Marine
49 Americas Cup Ave.
Newport, RI 02840
401-849-0240, Fax: 401-849-0620
Mason, Taswell, Sabre, Nordhavn

Newport Yacht Services
PO Box 149
Newport, RI 02840
401-846-7720, Fax: 401-846-6850

Alden Yacht Brokerage
1909 Alden Landing
Portsmouth, RI 02871
401-683-4285, Fax: 401-683-3668

Alden Yachts, Power & Sail
Brewer's Yacht Sales
222 Narragansett Blvd.
Portsmouth, RI 02871
401-683-3977, Fax: 401-683-0696

Eastern Yacht Sales
One Lagoon Rd.
Portsmouth, RI 02871
401-683-2200, Fax: 401-683-0961

Little Harbor Yacht Sales
One Little Harbor Landing
Portsmouth, RI 02871
401-683-7000, Fax: 401-683-7029
Little Harbor Custom Yachts, Grand Banks,
Black Watch

SOUTH CAROLINA

Charleston Yacht Sales
3 Lockwood Dr., #201
Charleston, SC 29402
803-577-5050, Fax: 803-723-9829
Hunter

Pilot Yacht Sales
3 Lockwood Dr., #301
Charleston, SC 29401
803-723-8356, Fax: 803-723-2102

Sea Island Yacht Sales
105 Wappoo Creek Dr., #3A
Charleston, SC 29412
803762-2610, Fax: 803-762-2615

Yacht Brokerage USA
2345 Tall Sail Dr., #E
Charleston, SC 29414
803-763-1224, Fax: 803-763-4215

Ashley Marina Yacht Sales
33 Lockwood Drive
Charleston, SC 29401
803-722-1996, Fax: 803-720-3623

DYB Charters & Yacht Sales
14 New Orleans Rd., Suite 14
Hilton Head Island, SC 29928
803-785-4740, Fax: 803-785-4827
Catalina

Hilton Head Yachts, Ltd.
PO Box 22488
Hilton Head Island, SC 29925
803-686-6860, Fax: 803-681-5093

American Yacht Sales
1880 Andell Buffs Blvd.
Johns Island, SC 29455
800-234-8814, Fax: 803-768-7300
Luhrs, Mainship, Ocean

Berry-Boger Yacht Sales
Box 36, Harbour Place, #101
N. Myrtle Beach, SC 29597
803-249-6167, Fax: 803-249-0105
Marine Trader

Wilkins Boat & Yacht Co.
1 Harbour Place
N. Myrtle Beach, SC 29582
803-249-6032, Fax: 803-249-6523

TENNESSEE

Phil's Marine Sales
4935 Highway 58, Suite C
Chattanooga, TN 37416
615-892-0058, Fax: 615-894-3281

Leader Marine
720 E. College St.
Dickson, TN 37055
615-446-3422, Fax: 615-446-9819
Cruisers

Jim Bennett Yacht Sales
Route 4, Box 532
Iuka, TN 38852
601-423-9999, Fax: 601-423-3339
Bluewater, Carver

Fox Road Marina
1100 Fox Rd.
Knoxville, TN 37922
615-966-9422, Fax: 615-966-9475

Nashville Yacht Brokers
1 Vantage Way, Suite B-100
Nashville, TN 37228
615-259-9444, Fax: 615-259-9481

TEXAS

Coastal Yacht Brokers
715 Holiday Dr. North
Galveston, TX 77550
409-763-3474, Fax: 713-488-8782

HoustonYacht Sales
585 Bradford Ave., Suite B
Kemah, TX 77565
713-334-7094, Fax: 713-334-4936
Hatteras, Marlin, Ocean

Ship and Sail
300 Admiralty Way
Kemah, TX 77565
713-334-0573, Fax: 713-334-2697
Luhrs, Mainship, Carver

Delhomme Marine
2551 S. Shore Blvd., #C
League City, TX 77573
713-334-3335, Fax: 713-334-1402

Fox Yacht Sales
Box 772, Island Moorings Marina
Port Aransas, TX 78373
512-749-4870, Fax: 512-749-4859

Jay Bettis & Company
2509 NASA Road 1
Seabrook, TX 77586
713-474-4101, Fax: 713-532-1305
DeFever, Shamrock, Mainship

VIRGINIA

Doziers Dockyard
PO Box 388
Deltaville, VA 23043
804-776-6711, Fax: 804-776-6998

Norton's Yacht Sales
PO Box 220
Deltaville, VA 23043
804-776-9211, Fax: 804-776-9044
Luhrs, Hunter, Silverton

Commonwealth Yachts
PO Box 1070
Gloucester Point, VA 23062
804-642-2156, Fax: 804-642-4766

Bluewater Yacht Sales
25 Marina Rd.
Hampton, VA 23669
804-723-0793, Fax: 804-723-3320
Hatteras, Viking, Tiara

Casey Marine
1021 W. Mercury Blvd.
Hampton, VA 23666
804-591-1500, Fax: 804-244-7805
Pro-Line, Baja, Robolo, Maxum, Luhrs

Virginia Yacht Brokers
4503 Ericcson Dr.
Hampton, VA 23669
804-722-3500, Fax: 804-722-7909

Norview Yacht Sales
PO Box 740
Hayes, VA 23072
804-776-7233, Fax: 804-776-7940

Bay Harbor Brokerage
1553 Bayville St.
Norfolk, VA 23503
804-480-1073, Fax: 804-587-4612

Prince William Marine Sales
207 Mill St.
Occoquan, VA 22125
703-494-6611
Sea Ray

Tidewater Yacht Sales
10A Crawford Parkway
Portsmouth, VA 23704
804-393-6200, Fax: 804-397-1193
Bayliner

Atlantic Yacht Brokers
932 Laskin St., Suite 200
Virginia Beach, VA 23451
804-428-9000, Fax: 804-491-8632
Ocean, Cabo

Casey Marine
4417 Shore Dr.
Virginia Beach, VA 23455
Pro-Line, Baja, Robolo, Maxum, Luhrs

VERMONT

Bruce Hill Yacht Sales
219 Harbor Rd.
Shelburne, VT 05482
802-985-3336, Fax: 802-985-3337

WASHINGTON

Anacortes Yacht Sales
P.O. Box 855
Anacortes, WA 98221
206-293-0631, Fax: 206-293-0633

Skipper Cress Yacht Sales
1019 Q Ave., Suite B
Anacortes, WA 98221
800-996-9991, Fax: 206-293-7874
Nordic Tugs

Bellingham Yacht Sales
1801 Roeder Ave.
Bellingham, WA 98225
800-671-4244, Fax: 206-671-0992
Sabreline

Padden Creek Marine
809 Harris Ave.
Bellingham, WA 98225
206-733-6248, Fax: 206-733-6251

Edmonds Yacht Sales
300 Admiral Way
Edmonds, WA 98020
206-774-8878, Fax: 206-771-7277
Riviera

Superior Yacht Sales
628 Daley St., Unit 1
Edmonds, WA 98020
206-771-3786, Fax: 206-771-3786
Vitesse

Northwest Yachts
PO Box915, Friday Harbor, WA 98250
206-378-7196, Fax: 206-378-7197

Northwest Yachts
3805 Harborview Dr.
Gig Harbor, WA 98335
206-858-7700, Fax: 206-851-8649
Krogen

Sunset Yacht Sales
2905 Harborview Dr.
Gig Harbor, WA 98335
206-858-8811, Fax: 206-858-7373

Sailboats & Yachts Northwest
11207 101st Ave. NE
Kirkland, WA 98033
206-623-9011, Fax: 206-282-8815

Yacht Doc
8031 NE 112th St.
Kirkland, WA 98034
206-820-9659, Fax: 206-823-8913

La Conner Yacht Sales
612 Dunlap, #C
La Conner, WA 98257
206-466-3300, Fax: 206-466-3533

Adventure Yacht Sales
2400 Westlake Ave. North, #1
Seattle, WA 98109
206-283-3010, Fax: 206-283-8611

Alliance Yacht Sales
2130 Westlake Ave. North
Seattle, WA 98109
206-283-8111
Offshore

American Yacht Sales
2144 Westlake Ave. N.
Seattle, WA 98109
206-284-6354, Fax: 206-285-8772

Brigadoon Yacht Sales
1111 Fairview Ave. North
Seattle, WA 98109
206-282-6500, Fax: 206-282-2410

Yacht Broker & Dealer Directory

Cruising Yachts
927 N. Northlake Way
Seattle, WA 98103
206-632-4819, Fax: 206-548-1050
Nordhavn, Lord Nelson

Dave Maples Yacht Sales
1530 Westlake North
Seattle, WA 98109
206-284-0880, Fax: 206-285-7903
Canoe Cove

Elliott Bay Yachting Center
2601 West Marina Pl., #E
Seattle, WA 98199
206-285-9499, Fax: 206-281-7636

Fraser Yachts
1500 Westlake Ave. N.
Seattle, WA 98109
206-282-4943, Fax: 206-285-4956

Intrepid Yacht Sales
2000 Westlake Ave. North
Seattle, WA 98109
206-282-0211
Grand Banks

Lager Yacht Brokerage Corp.
2601 W. Marine Place
Seattle, WA 98199
206-283-6440, Fax: 206-283-4707

Lake Union Yacht Sales
3245 Fairview Ave. E. #103
Seattle, WA 98102
206-323-3505, Fax: 206-323-4751
Island Gypsy, Catalina

Maple Bay Boat Co.
1333 N. Northlake Way
Seattle, WA 98103
206-547-4780

Ocean Alexander Yacht Sales
1001 Fairview Ave. North
Seattle, WA 98109
206-223-0809, Fax: 206-223-0812
Ocean Alexander, Nordlund

Ray Rairdon Yacht Sales
1800 Westlake Ave. N., #101
Seattle, WA 98103
206-284-5527, Fax: 206-284-5537

Tatoosh Marine
809 Fairview Place N., #150
Seattle, WA 98109
206-625-1580, Fax: 206-682-1473

Tradewind Yacht Sales
2470 Westlake Ave. N.
Seattle, WA 98109
206-285-0926

Trans Coastal Yacht
1800 Westlake Avenue North, #201
Seattle, WA 98109
206-284-4547, Fax: 206-284-4337

West Coast Yachts
1836 Westlake Ave. N., #201
Seattle, WA 98109
206-298-3724, Fax: 206-298-0227

Yacht Sales International
1220 Westlake Ave. North
Seattle, WA 98109
206-282-0052, Fax: 206-283-2297
Tollycraft, Tiara, Ocean

River City Marina
E. 6326 Trent
Spokane, WA 99212
509-534-5444, Fax: 509-534-3179
Silverton

Murray Wasson Marine Sales
4224 Marine View Dr.
Tacoma, WA 98422
206-927-9036, Fax: 206-927-9034
Shamrock, Blackfin

Picks Cove Marine Center
1940 East D Street
Tacoma, WA 98421
206-572-3625
Symbol

Preferred Yacht & Ship Brokers
1802 East D Street
Tacoma, WA 98421
206-272-4550, Fax: 206-272-4804

WISCONSIN

Capt. Jim's Yacht Sales
5136 Sheridan Rd.
Kenosha, WI 53140
414-652-8866, Fax: 414-652-5453
Mainship, Silverton

Kewaunee Marina
77 N. Main St., Box 261
Kewaunee, WI 54216
414-388-4550
Pro-Line

Emerald Yacht Ship Mid America
759 N. Milwaukee Street
Milwaukee, WI 53202
414-271-2595, Fax: 414-271-4743

Professional Yacht Brokerage
9501 W. Morgan Ave.
Milwaukee, WI 53228
414-321-8880, Fax: 414-321-7411

Fox River Marina
P.O. Box 1006
Oshkosh, WI 54902
414-235-2340
Wellcraft, Cruisers

Lakeside Marina
902 Taft Ave.
Oshkosh, WI 54901
414-231-4321
Bayliner, Carver, Doral, Chaparral

Professional Yacht Sales
451 S. Second St.
Prescott, WI 54021
715-262-5762, Fax: 715-262-5658

Palmer Johnson Yacht Sales
811 Ontario St.
Racine, WI 53402
414-633-8883, Fax: 414-633-4681

Cal Marine
1024 Bay Shore Dr.
Sister Bay, WI 54234
414-854-4521, Fax: 414-854-5137
Tiara, Powerquest

Sturgeon Bay Yacht Harbor
306 Nautical Drive
Sturgeon Bay, WI 54235
414-743-3311, Fax: 414-743-4298
Alexander, Formula, Mako

Marine Surveyor Directory

Professional Surveyor Associations

ABYC ....American Boat & Yacht Council
ASA..American Society of Appraisors
AIMS ....American Institute of Marine Surveyors
MTAM..........................Marine Trade Association of Maryland
NAMI ....National Association of Marine Investigators
NAMS....................National Association of Marine Surveyors
NFPA ....National Fire Protection Association
SAMS........................Society of Accredited Marine Surveyors
SNAME........Society of Naval Architects & Marine Surveyors

ALABAMA

Donald Smith
Port City Marine Services
PO Box 190321
Mobile, AL 36619
205-661-5426
SAMS, ABYC

Michael Schiehl
M.J. Schiehl & Assoc.
PO Box 1990
Orange Beach, AL 36561-1990
NAMS

ALASKA

George Sepel
Sepel & Son Marine Surveying
PO Box 32223
Juneau, AK 99803
907-790-2628
SAMS

ARKANSAS

Angus Rankin
Marine Surveyor
PO Box 264
Maynard, AR 72444
501-892-8300
SAMS

CALIFORNIA

Kurt Holland
R.J. Whitfield & Assoc.
One Pacific Marina, Apt. 807
Alameda, CA 94501
800-344-1838
SAMS

Stanley Wild
Stan Wild & Associates
1912 Stanford
Alameda, CA 94501
510-521-8527
NAMS

Mare Colomb
Colomb Yacht Surveyor
2619 Willow Lane
Costa Mesa, CA 92627
714-646-7807
SAMS

Ronald Grant
Grant Marine Surveys
25611-114 Quail Run
Dana Point, CA 92629
714-240-8353
SAMS

Michael Whitfield
R.J. Whitfield & Associates
4471 Amador Rd.
Fremont, CA 94538-1201
800-344-1838
SAMS

Douglas Malin
Malin Marine Surveyors
5942 Edinger Ave., #113
Huntington Beach, CA 92649
714-897-6769
SAMS

Hans Anderson
Anderson Int'l. Marine Surveyors
433 North H St., Ste. G
Lompoc, CA 93436
805-737-3770
SAMS

Clark Barthol, CMS
Clark Barthol Marine Surveyors
27 Buccaneer St.
Marina del Rey, CA 90292
310-823-3350
NAMS, ABYC

William Butler
Marine Surveyor
PO Box 11914
Marina Del Rey, CA 90295
310-396-1791
SAMS

Terrence O'Herren
Marine Surveyor
2021 Ashton Ave.
Menlo Park, CA 94025
415-854-8380
SAMS

Donald Young
Donru Marine Surveyors & Adjusters
32 Cannery Row
Monterey, CA 93940
408-372-8604
SAMS, ABYC

Richard Christopher
Marine Surveyor
14705 Watsonville
Morgan Hill, CA 95037
415-368-8711
SAMS, ABYC

James Wood
Marine Surveyor
PO Box 968
Morro Bay, CA 93443
805-772-0110
SAMS

Marine Surveyor Directory

John Kelly
Kelly & Associates
PO Box 1031
Napa, CA 94581
707-641-1061
SAMS, ABYC

Bill Beck
Marine Surveyor
444-A N. Newport Blvd.
Newport Beach, CA 92663
714-642-6673
SAMS

Don Parish
Marine Surveyor
4140 Oceanside Blvd., #159-320
Oceanside, CA 92056
619-721-9410
ABYC

Richard Quinn
Oceanside Marine Surveyors
425 Calle Corazon
Oceanside, CA 92057
619-757-5586
SAMS

Mike Pierce
Mike Pierce Industries
1811 Diego Way
Oxnard, CA 93030
805-657-9490
SAMS

Skip Riley
Maritime Surveyors
3203 S. Victoria Ave., Ste. B
Oxnard, CA 93035
805-984-8889
NAMS, SAMS

Donald Brandmeyer
Brandmeyer International
2447 Sparta Dr.
Rancho Palos Verdes, CA 90274-6538
310-519-1979
NAMS

Marine Survey Group
1310 Rosecrans St., #K
San Diego, CA 92106
619-224-2944
NAMS

Anthony Tillett
A.N. Tillett & Associates
663 Switzer St.
San Diego, CA 92101
619-235-0766
NAMS, SAMS

Charles Driscoll
Frank Wyatt Marine Surveyors
1967 Shaffer St.
San Diego, CA 92106
619-223-8167
NAMS

Leroy Lester
Lester & Lester Marine Survey
1310 Rosecrans St., #K
San Diego, CA 92106
619-224-2944
SAMS

Marvin Henderson
Marvin Henderson Marine Surveyors
2727 Shelter Island Dr., #C
San Diego,CA 92106
619-224-3164
NAMS, ABYC, NFPA, SNAME

Todd Schwede
Todd & Associates
2390 Shelter Island Dr., #220
San Diego, CA 92106
619-226-1895
SAMS

Bruce Sherburne
Sherburne & Associates
6130 Monterey Rd., #23
San Jose, CA 95138
800-882-7124
SAMS

Jack Mackinnon
Marine Surveyor
PO Box 335
San Lorenzo, CA 94580-0335
415-276-4351
SAMS

Mike Pyzel
Marine Surveyor
PO Box 4217
Santa Barbara, CA 93140
805-640-0900
SAMS

Thomas Bell
Thomas Bell & Associates
1323 Berkeley Street
Santa Monica, CA 90404
310-306-1895
SAMS, ABYC

Archibald Campbell
Campbell's Marine Survey
340 Countryside Drive
Santa Rosa, CA 95401
707-542-8812
SAMS, ABYC, ASME, SNAME

Michael Wilson
Marine Surveyor
1001 Bridgeway, Suite 722
Sausalito, CA 94965
415-332-8928
SAMS

Peggy Feakes
R.J. Whitfield & Associates
7011 Bridgeport Circle
Stockton, CA 95207-2357
209-956-8488
SAMS

Rod Whitfield
R.J. Whitfield & Associates
7011 Bridgeport Circle
Stockton, CA 95207
209-956-8488
SAMS

Robert Downing
Marine Surveyor
PO Box 4154
Vallejo, CA 94590
707-642-6346
SAMS

Basil Dalseme
Marine Surveyor
PO Box 24353
Ventura, CA 93001
805-643-6407
SAMS

CONNECTICUT

J. Mitchell DePalma
Connecticut Yacht Survey Corp.
PO Box 842
Branford, CT 06405
203-488-0265
SAMS, ABYC

Richard Tudan
Bosun's Yacht Survey
26 Hickory Hill Lane
Branford, CT 06405
203-481-5099
SAMS

Grant Westerson
New England Marine Surveyors
PO Box 533, 19 Commerce St.
Clinton, CT 06413
203-669-4018
SAMS

William Robbins
New England Marine Surveyors
19 Commerce St., Box 533
Clinton, CT 06413
203-669-4018
SAMS

Harry Hartzell
Hartzell Marine Surveys
92 Willard Dr.
Enfield, CT 06082
203-292-7179
SAMS

Albert Truslow
Truslow Marine Surveying
PO Box 9185
Forestville, CT 06011-9185
203-583-6503
SAMS

Marine Surveyor Directory

George Stafford
Aetna Casualty
One Civic Ctr. Plaza, Box 2954
Hartford, CT 06143
203-240-6765
SAMS

Welles Worthen
Marine Surveyors, Inc.
102 Milford Point Rd.
Milford, CT 06460
203-874-2445
NAMS

Marine Surveyors Bureau
1440 Whalley Ave, #128
New Haven, CT 06515
203-323-0225
NAMS, SAMS, ABYC, NFPA

Robert Keaney, Jr.
Marine Surveyor
7 Candlewood Heights
New Milford, CT 06776
203-354-1372
SAMS

Kenneth Johnson
Johnson Marine Survey
2 Haley Farm Lane
Noank, CT 06340
203-444-8576
SAMS

Robert Krauss
Connecticut Compass Service
3 Anchorage Lane
Old Saybrook, CT 06475
203-388-2019
SAMS

William Stadel
Marine Surveyor
1088 Shippan Ave.
Stamford, CT 06902
203-324-2610
SAMS

Thomas Greaves
Greaves Yacht Service
30 Toby Hill Road
Westbrook, CT 06498
203-399-6966
SAMS

David Robotham
Robotham Marine Surveyors
PO Box 2143
Westport, CT 06880
203-227-9640
NAMS, SAMS

FLORIDA

Larry Vanscoy
Accredited Marine Surveys
PO Box 331162
Atlantic Beach, FL 32233
904-636-4382
SAMS

Dean Greger
Coastal Marine Surveyors
23 Winston Dr.
Belleair, FL 34616
813-581-0914

Kermit Naylor
Southern Yacht Surveyors
2895 Del Rio Dr.
Belleair Bluffs, FL 34640
813-585-8949
NAMS

Dick Williamson
Professional Marine Surveys, Inc.
7491-C5 N. Federal Hwy, #232
Boca Raton, FL 33487
407-272-1053
SAMS, ABYC, NFPA

John Greeley
Marine Surveyor
22177 Thomas Terrace
Boca Raton, FL 33433
305-360-3330
SAMS

Jeff Brown
JGB Corporation
8716 54th Ave. West
Bradenton, FL 34210
813-794-3998
SAMS

Stephen Fredrick
Preferred Claims Adjusters
PO Box 10265
Bradenton, FL 34282
813-794-3552
SAMS

James Hughes
Capt. J. R. Hughes Marine Services
368 Harbor Drive
Cape Canaveral, FL 32920
407-783-3832
SAMS

Lawrence O'Pezio
Canaveral Marine Consultants
677 George King Blvd., #112
Cape Canaveral, FL 32920
407-783-1771
NAMS, ABYC, NFPA

Ralph Strauss
Island Marine Service
PO Box 10636
Clearwater, FL 34617
813-581-0942
SAMS

Channing Chapman
Clyde Eaton & Assoc., Inc.
PO Box 231862
Cocoa, FL 32923-1862
407-633-0860
ABYC, NFPA

Anthony Pavlo
Alp's Marine Surveying, Inc.
281 NW 42nd Ave.
Coconut Creek, FL 33066
305-973-1135
SAMS

Jeffrey Turner
Turner & Associates
801 NE 3rd Street
Dania, FL 33004
305-922-3333
SAMS

Stephen Rhodes
Boating Services
6 Sunset Terrace
Daytona Beach, FL 32118
904-257-5112
SAMS

H. Jack MacDonald
H. Jack MacDonald, Inc.
23 NW 18th Street
Delray Beach, FL 33444
407-731-0471
SAMS, ABYC, NFPA

James Sanislo
C&J Marine Surveyors
4163 Frances Dr.
Delray Beach, FL 33445
407-495-4920
SAMS

Rollie Tallman
American Boat Brokerage
2548 Alton Rd.
Deltona, FL 32738
904-789-0971
SAMS

John Marrocco
Marine Surveyor
PO Box 891
Edgewater, FL 32132
904-426-0368
SAMS

Marine Surveyor Directory

Capt. Michael McGhee
Black Pearl Marine Specialities
6695 NW 25th Terrace
Ft. Lauderdale, FL 33309
305-970-8305
SAMS

Drew Kwederas
Global Adventure Marine Associates
4120 NE 26th Ave.
Ft. Lauderdale, FL 33308
305-566-4800
ABYC, NFPA, SNAME

Edward Rowe
Ed Rowe & Associates
1821 SW 22nd Ave.
Ft. Lauderdale, FL 33312
305-792-6062
SAMS

Gene Thornton
Gene Thornton Diesel Survey
4564 NE 11th Ave.
Ft. Lauderdale, FL 33334
305-776-7242
SAMS (Diesel Specialist)

Gerald Slakoff
Slakoff & Associates
1525 S. Andrews Ave.
Ft. Lauderdale, FL 33316
305-525-7930
SAMS

Gregory Mitchell
Marine Surveyor
1007 N. Federal Hwy., #84
Ft. Lauderdale, FL 33304
407-286-3924
SAMS

Gregory Newton
Marine Evaluation Service
1323 SE 17th St., #119
Ft. Lauderdale, FL 33316
305-763-9562
NAMS

Jerome Cramer
Gerald Slakoff & Associates
1524 S. Andrews Ave.
Ft. Lauderdale, FL 33316
305-525-7930
SAMS

Junko Pascoe
Marine Surveyor
501 SW 14th St.
Ft. Lauderdale, FL 33315
305-527-5741
SAMS

Kurt Merolla
Merolla Marine Surveyors & Consultants
4761 NE 29th Ave.
Ft. Lauderdale, FL 33308
305-772-8090
NAMS, SAMS, ASA SNAME, ABYC, NFPA

Marc Slakoff
Slakoff & Associates
1525 S. Andrews Ave.
Ft. Lauderdale, FL 33316
305-525-7930
SAMS

Norman Schreiber II
Transtech—Marine Division
PO Box 350247
Ft. Lauderdale, FL 33335
305-537-1423
NAMS, SNAME, ABYC, NFPA

Randal Roden
The Marine Surveyors
PO Box 100145
Ft. Lauderdale, FL 33310
800-522-5119
SAMS

Robert Heekin
The Marine Surveyors
PO Box 100145
Ft. Lauderdal, FL 33310
800-522-5119
SAMS

William Casey
SCS & Associates
3215 NW 10th Terrace, #209
Ft. Lauderdale, FL 33315
305-563-6900
SAMS

Steven Berlin
Independent Marine Surveyors
18400 San Carlos Blvd.
Ft. Myers Beach, FL 33931
813-466-4544
SAMS

Richard Cain
Independent Marine Surveyors
144 Bay Mar Dr.
Ft. Myers Beach, FL 33931
813-466-4544
SAMS

Donna Summerlin
Summerlin's Marine Survey
200 Naco Rd., Suite C
Ft. Pierce, FL 34949
407-461-3244
SAMS

John McCulley
McCulley Marine Services
101 Sea Way Dr., Suite A
Ft. Pierce, FL 34950
407-489-6069
SAMS

Thomas Price
Price Marine Services, Inc.
9418 Sharon St. SE
Hobe Sound, FL 33455
407-546-0928
SAMS, ABYC, NFPA

William King
Atlantic Marine Survey
6201 SE Monticello Terrace
Hobe Sound, FL 33455-7383
407-545-0011
SAMS

James Macefield
Macefield Marine Services, Inc.
3389 Sheridan St., #178
Hollywood, FL 33021
305-784-9188

Capt. Larry C. Dukehart
Marine Surveyor & Consultant
PO Box 1172
Islamorada, FL 33036-1172
305-664-9452
SAMS, ABYC, NFPA, NAMI

Downing Nightingale, Jr.
North Florida Marine Services
3360 Lake Shore Blvd.
Jacksonville, FL 32210-5348
904-384-4356
SAMS, AMS

Mickey Strocchi
Strocchi & Company
PO Box 16541
Jacksonville, FL 32245-6541
904-398-1862
SAMS

Ted Willandt
Marine Network
2771-25 Monument Rd., Box 210
Jacksonville, FL 32225-3547
904-641-3334
SAMS, ABYC, NAMI

Ted Stevens
Stevens & Stevens, Ltd.
3250 Candice Ave., #132
Jensen Beach, FL 34957
407-229-6394
SAMS

Michael Bennett
Marine Surveyor
12129 181st Court North
Jupiter, FL 33478
407-744-0213
SAMS

Robert Camuccio
Master Marine of South Florida
101425 Overseas Highway, Ste. 710
Key Largo, FL 33037
305-662-6644
SAMS

Edwin Crusoe
Key West Marine Services
PO Box 4854
Key West, FL 33040
305-872-9073
NAMS

Marine Surveyor Directory

George Stuck
Marine Surveyor
PO Box 5481
Key West, FL 33045
305-294-4959

Mark Perkins
Marine Surveyor
901 Fleming Street
Key West, FL 33040
305-294-7635
SAMS

William Colby
Florida Keys Community College
5901 W. Junior College Rd.
Key West, FL 33040
305-296-9081
SAMS

Ed Stanton
Rhodes Marine Surveyors
4701 N. Federal Hwy., Ste. 340, Box C-8
Lighthouse Point, FL 33064-6563
305-9466779
SAMS, ABYC, NFPA

Mark Rhodes
Rhodes Marine Surveyors
4701 N. Federal Hwy., Ste. 340, Box C-8
Lighthouse Point, FL 33064-6563
305-9466779
SAMS, ABYC, NFPA

Melvin Wamsley
Accurate Marine Surveying
2130 NE 42nd St., Apt. #3
Lighthouse Point, FL 4802133064
305-942-9206
SAMS

Mike Rhodes
Rhodes Marine Surveyors
4701 N. Federal Hwy., Ste. 340, Box C-8
Lighthouse Point, FL 33064-6563
305-9466779
SAMS, ABYC, NFPA

L. Frank Hamlin
L.F. Hamlin, Inc.
14085 E. Parsley Dr.
Madeira Beach, FL 33708
813-393-1905
NAMS, SNAME

Dewey Acker
Acker Marine Surveyors
551 61st St. Gulf
Marathon, FL 33050
305-743-3434
SAMS, ABYC

Brough Treffer
Treffer Marine Survey, Inc.
2865 S. Tropical Trail
Merritt Island, FL 32952
407-453-6046
SAMS, NFPA, ABYC

James Robbins
Marine Surveyor
7701 Pine Lake Dr.
Merritt Island, FL 32953
407-459-1196
SAMS

Joanna Bailey
Brevard Marine Service
150 E. Merritt Island Causeway
Merritt Island, FL 32952
407-452-8250
SAMS

Dave Alter
Dave Alter & Associates
6500 SW 129th Terrace
Miami, FL 33156
305-667-0326
SAMS

William Ballard
Ballard & Associates
18845 SW 93rd Ave.
Miami, FL 33157
305-378-9674
SAMS

Brett Carlson
Carlson Marine Surveyors & Adjusters
1002 NE 105th St.
Miami Shores, FL 33138
305-891-0445
SAMS

Allen Perry
Ocean Adventures
453 Spinnaker Dr.
Naples, FL 33940
813-261-5466
SAMS, ABYC, NAMS

Donald Walwer
D&G Marine Company
58 Ocean Blvd.
Naples, FL 33942
813-643-0028
SAMS

Eugene Sipe, Jr.
Nautical Services Technologies
424 Production Blvd., #70
Naples, FL 33940
813-434-7445
SAMS

Veronica Lawson
Veronica M. Lawson & Associates
PO Box 1201
Naples, FL 33939
813-434-6960
NAMS

Vikki Hughes
Marine Surveyor
236 Polk Place
Naples, FL 33942
813-643-5101
SAMS

Bobby Crawford
Professional Marine Surveys
6823 Tidewater Dr.
Navarre, FL 32566
904-939-1848
SAMS

Richard Jacobs
Gulf Coast Yacht Service
3444 Marinatown Lane, #8
North Ft. Myers, FL 33903
813-997-8822
SAMS

Richard Koogle
Marine Surveyor
5849 Millay Ct.
North Ft. Myers, FL 33903
813-997-5146
SAMS

Ronald Silvera
R.E. Silvera & Associates
1904 SW 86th Ave.
North Lauderdale, FL 33068
305-720-8660
SAMS, SNAME, ABYC

Tom Drennan
Continental Marine Consultants, Inc.
700 North U.S. Highway 1
North Palm Beach, FL 33408
305-844-6111
NAMS

Tony Uselis
Maritime Yachting Services
30 Turtle Creek Circle
Oldsmar, FL 34677
813-789-4226
SAMS

Jerry Wheeler
Wheeler Marine Surveying
60 Canterbury Court
Orange Park, FL 32065
904-269-2171
SAMS

Charles Akers
Marine Surveyor
2816 Ahern Dr.
Orlando, FL 32817
407-658-0622
SAMS

William Streeter
B&S Marine Inc.
PO Box 690082
Orlando, FL 32869-0082

Russell Thomas
Thomas Marine Surveyors
737 Bywood Dr., NE
Palm Bay, FL 32905
800-352-6287
NAMS, SAMS, SNAME

Marine Surveyor Directory

Richard Thompson
Lakes/Coastal Marine Surveys
235 E. Tall Oaks Circle
Palm Beach Gardens, FL 33410
407-622-9283
SAMS

William Slattum
The Marine Surveyors
3450 Northlake Blvd., #207
Palm Beach Gardens, FL 33403
407-627-4639
SAMS

David Wyman
Marine Surveyor
798 Wood Ave.
Panama City, FL 32401
904-769-6280
SAMS

Doug Wagner
Wagner & Associates
7231 LaFitte Reef
Pensacola, FL 32507
904-492-3475
SAMS

Eugene Briggs
Gene Briggs & Associates
505 Decatur Ave.
Pensacola, FL 32507
904-456-4968
SAMS

Richard Everett
Marine Surveyor
PO Box 13512
Pensacola, FL 32591
904-435-9026
SAMS, ABYC, NFPA

Elaine Miranda
Marine Surveyor
9400 Mainlands Blvd. W.
Pinellas Park, FL 34666
813-577-4128
SAMS

Robert Zimmerman
Integrity Marine Surveying
PO Box 543
Placida, FL 33946
813-697-4799
SAMS

Arthur Buchman, Jr.
Marine Surveyor
12118 Chancellor Blvd.
Port Charlotte, FL 33953
813-743-2198

Pat Guckian
Aquarius Marine Systems
160 SE Duxbury Ave.
Port St. Lucie, FL34983
407-871-0364
SAMS

Adrian Volney
Ardian J. Volney & Co.
5806 Whistlewood Circle
Sarasota, FL 34232
813-371-8781
SAMS

Roy Bowen
Bowen Enterprises
1114 Sylvan Rd.
Sarasota, FL 34234
813-350-3123
SAMS

Roy Pesta
Darling & Co., Marine Surveyors
6336 Brentwood Ave.
Sarasota, FL 34231
813-922-5341
SAMS

William Willien
W.F. Willien Associates
15 Crossroads, Suite 250
Sarasota, FL 34239
813-951-6138
SAMS

Gary Flack
Flack Marine Survey Service
9276 Elm Circle
Seminole, FL 34646
813-398-2267
SAMS

Chris Ramsdell
Marine Consultants, Inc.
13060 Gandy Blvd.
St. Petersburg, FL 33702
813-577-2033
SAMS

Alvin Kushner
Yacht Services
275 SE Salerno Rd.
Stuart, FL 34997
407-286-7961
SAMS

Charles Corder
Chapman School of Seamanship
4343 SE St. Lucie Blvd.
Stuart, FL 34997
407-283-8130
SAMS

Douglas Newbigin
Stuart Yacht Design
450 SW Salerno Rd.
Stuart, FL 34997
407-283-1947
SAMS

Marty Merolla
Independent Marine Surveyor
4300 SE St. Lucie Blvd., #128
Stuart, FL 34997
407-286-4880
NAMS

T. Richard Garlington
Garlington Marine Services
1083 SE St. Lucie Blvd.
Stuart, FL 34996
407-283-5102
SAMS

Tom Fexas
Tom Fexas Yacht Design
333 Tressler Dr., Suites B&C
Stuart, FL 34994
407-287-6558
NAMS

James Garrett
Garrett Marine Survey & Consultants
PO Box 333
Summerland Key, FL 33042
305-745-9989
SAMS

John Reynolds
Jack Reynolds International
11172 NW 35th St.
Sunrise, FL 33351
800-833-9698
SAMS

Sidney Kaufman
Surfside Harbor Associates
PO Box 54-6514
Surfside, FL 33154
305-358-1414
ABYC

Capt. E. Bay Hansen
Capt. E. Bay Hansen, Inc.
1302 N. 19th St., #101
Tampa, FL 33605
813-248-6897
NAMS

Charles Harden
Harden Marine Associates, Inc.
P.O. Box 13256
Tampa, FL 33681-3256
813-254-4273
SAMS

Henry Pickersgill
Henry W. Pickersgill & Co., Inc.
4118 W. Euclid Ave.
Tampa, FL 33629
800-348-8105
NAMS

Robert Buckles
USCG Marine Safety Office
155 Columbia Dr.
Tampa, FL 33606-3598
813-228-2196

Melvin Allen
Allen's Boat Surveying & Consulting
638 North U.S. Hwy. 1, Suite 207
Tequesta, FL 33469-2397
407-747-2433
SAMS, ABYC, NFPA

Marine Surveyor Directory

Omar Sultan
Maro Marine
610 Cheney Highway
Titusville, FL 32780
407-268-2655
SAMS

Richard Fortin
Marine Surveyor & Consultant
1405 19th St., SW
Vero Beach, FL 32962
407-567-9286
ABYC, SNAME

Capt. A.T. Kyle
Marine Consultants & Surveyors
6428 Heather Way
West Palm Beach, FL 33406
407-964-6189
SAMS

Robert Despres
Despres & Associates
332 Pine St.
West Palm Beach, FL 33407
407-820-9290
SAMS

GEORGIA

John Woodside III
Woodside Surveys
15 Howell Mill Plantation
Atlanta, GA 30327
404-355-3732
SAMS

Wilbur Wennersten
Wentek Associates
2137 Tully Wren
Marietta, GA 30066
404-516-5623
SAMS

HAWAII

Dennis Smith
Marine Surveyors & Consultants
677 Ala Moana Blvd., Ste. 812
Honolulu, HI 96813
808-545-1333
SAMS

E.H. "Chip" Gunther
All Ship & Cargo Surveys, Ltd.
965-A2 Nimitz Highway
Honolulu, HI 96817
808-538-3260
NAMS

John Mihlbauer
All Ship & Cargo Surveys, Ltd.
965-A2 Nimitz Highway
Honolulu, HI 96817
808-538-3260
NAMS

Michael Doyle
Mike Doyle, Ltd.
575 Cooke St., #B
Honolulu, HI 96813
808-521-9881
NAMS

IDAHO

Kirk Marshall
Accurate Marine Surveys
1906 North 9th Street
Coeur D'Alene, ID 83814
208-667-2610
SAMS

ILLINOIS

John Boltz
Inland Surveyors, Inc.
307 N. Michigan Ave., #1008
Chicago, IL 60601
312-329-9881
NAMS

Lee H. Asbridge
Marine Surveyor
480 N. McClurg Ct., #1002
Chicago, IL 60611
312-527-4860
SAMS

James Singer
Marine Surveyor
1854 York Lane
Highland Park, IL 60035
708-831-9157
SAMS, ABYC

Kenneth Martin
Professional Development Assoc.
PO Box 712
Mt. Prospect, IL 60056
708-476-7321
SAMS

Paul Petersen
Great Lakes Marine Surveys
710 E. Camp McDonald Rd.
Prospect Heights, IL 60070
708-253-3102
SAMS

INDIANA

Tim Kleihege
Great Lakes Marine Surveying, Inc.
2831 Lakewood Trail
Porter Beach, IN 46304
312-663-2503
SAMS, ABYC

Robert Craig
Marine Surveyor
323 West Main St.
Richmond, IN 47374-4161
317-966-9807
SAMS

KENTUCKY

Jim Hill
RR 1, Box 306
Gilbertsville, KY 42044-9801

Gregory Weeter
Riverlands Marine Surveyors
935 Riverside Dr.
Louisville, KY 40207
502-897-9900
NAMS, ABYC

Robert Urso
Urso Marine Surveying
PO Box 765
Prospect, KY 40059-0765
502-426-3997
SAMS, ABYC

LOUISIANA

Brendan O'Connor
Celtic Marine Corp.
357 Dunstan Circle
Baton Rouge, LA 70815
504-275-5320
SAMS

Kenneth Firm
Celtic Marine Corp.
357 Dunstan Circle
Baton Rouge, LA 70815
504-275-5320
SAMS

Michael O'Connor
Celtic Marine Corp.
357 Dunstan Circle
Baton Rouge, LA 70815
504-275-5320
SAMS

Roger Cheek
Celtic Marine Corp.
357 Dunstan Circle
Baton Rouge, LA 70815
504-275-5320
SAMS

John Illg
Summit Design Services
6444 Jefferson Hwy.
Harahan, LA 70123
504-737-3267
NAMS

Frank Basile
Entech & Associates
PO Box 1470
Houma, LA 70361
504-868-5524
SAMS

Cesar Lurati
Argos Marine Surveyors
PO Box 640191
Kenner, LA 70062
504-466-7333
SAMS

Marine Surveyor Directory

Alfred Cutno
Celtic Marine Corp.
1532 Natchez Lane
LaPlace, LA 70068
504-275-5320
SAMS

Curtley Boudreaux
Marine Surveyor
PO Box 321
Lockport, LA 70374
504-787-2391
SAMS

Chander Gorowara
Maritech Commercial, Inc.
4605 Alexander Dr.
Metairie, LA 70003-2809
504-455-7372
NAMS, SAMS

Pete Peters
Bachrach & Wood/Peters Assoc.
PO Box 7415
Metairie, LA 70010-7415
504-454-0001
SAMS

Andre Chauvin
Chauvin & Associates
PO Box 788
Morgan City, LA 70381
504-385-1043
SAMS

J. Anthony Brown
A.B. Marine Consulting
1397 E. Stephensville Rd.
Morgan City, LA 70380
504-384-5184
SAMS

Douglass Westgate
Westocean Marine, Inc.
PO Box 57446
New Orleans, LA 70157
504-895-7388
SAMS

Hjalmer Breit
Breit Marine Surveying
1311 Leonidas St.
New Orleans, LA 70118
504-866-1814
NAMS, SAMS

Sewell "Si" Williams
Arthur H. Terry & Co.
101 W. Robt. E. Lee Blvd., #200
New Orleans, LA 70124
504-283-1514
NAMS, SAMS, ASA, SNAME

Hubert Gallagher
Marine Surveyor
52246 Highway 90, Apt. 2
Slidell, LA 70461
504-641-2921

MAINE

Marvin Curtis
Marine Surveyor
HC 64, Box 355
Blue Hill, ME 04614
207-374-5342
SAMS

Bob Cartwright
North American Marine Surveying, Ltd.
PO Box 205
Boothbay, ME 04537
207-633-5062
NAMS, SNAME

Jeffrey Johnson
Marine Surveyor
PO Box 1305, Suite 130
Brunswick, ME 04011
207-729-6711
SAMS

Malcolm Harriman
Marine Surveyor
8 Country Club Rd.
Manchester, ME 04351
207-622-2049
SAMS

Jesus Artiaga
North Atlantic Marine
65 W. Commercial St.
Portland, ME 04530
207-775-7317
SAMS

William Leavitt
Chase, Leavitt & Company
10 Dana St.
Portland, ME 04112
207-772-3751
NAMS

MARYLAND

Ernie Leeger
Independent Marine Surveyor
2506 Buckingham Court
Abingdon, MD 21009
410-515-0155
SAMS, ABYC

Hartoft Marine Survey
PO, Box 3188
Annapolis, MD 21403
410-263-3609
ABYC, NAMS, MTAM

C. Robert Skord, Jr.
Skord & Company
400 Forest Beach Rd.
Annapolis, MD 21401
410-757-7454
NAMS, SAMS

Clyde Eaton
Clyde Eaton & Assoc., Inc.
PO Box 4609
Annapolis, MD 21403
800-347-7331
ABYC, NFPA

Frederick Hecklinger
Frederick E. Hecklinger, Inc.
17 Hull Ave.
Annapolis, MD 21403
410-268-3018
NAMS

Michael Kaufman III
Kaufman Design, Inc.
222 Severn Ave., Box 4219
Annapolis, MD 21403
410-263-8900
NAMS

Patricia Kearns
Marine Associates
PO Box 3441, 2 Leeward Ct.
Annapolis, MD 21403
410-263-2419
NAMS, SNAME

Terence Fitzsimmons
Kaufman Design, Inc.
222 Severn Ave., Box 4219
Annapolis, MD 21403
410-263-8900
NAMS

Anthony Eversmier
Marine Surveyor
8110 Woodhaven Rd.
Baltimore, MD 21237
410-391-4200
SAMS

Michael Wright
KIS Marine
5830 Hudson Wharf Rd.
Cambridge, MD 21613
410-228-1448
SAMS

Don Miller
Beacon Marine Surveys
2916 Cox Neck Rd. E.
Chester, MD 21619
410-643-4390
SAMS

Roy Beers
Full Circle Marine Surveyors
PO Box 835
Chestertown, MD 21620
410-778-0247
SAMS

Woodrow Loller
Woodrow W. Loller, Inc.
204 Washington Ave.
Chestertown, MD 21620
410-778-5357
NAMS, ABYC

Marine Surveyor Directory

Steve Sanders
East Coast Surveying
6375 Genoa Rd.
Dunkirk, MD 20754
410-257-3134
SAMS

John Griffiths
John R. Griffiths, Inc.
785 Knight Island Rd.
Earleville (Eastern Shore), MD 21919
410-275-8750
NAMS, ABYC

Kenneth Henry
McHenry Marine Services
38 Oak Hill Lane
Elkton, MD 21921
410-287-2028
SAMS

Charles Wilson
C.R. Wilson, Inc.
3912 Earon Drive
Jarrettsville, MD 21084-1314
410-692-6718
SAMS

Catherine C. McLaughlin
Marine Surveyor
29142 Belchester Rd.
Kennedyville, MD 21645
410-348-5188
SAMS

Marvin Dawson
Chesapeake Marine Surveyors
PO Box 322
Mayo, MD 21106-0322
301-798-5077
NAMS, NFPA

Rick Hall
Marine Surveyor
272 Hance Point Rd.
North East, MD 21901
410-287-2516
SAMS

Thomas Lucke
Oxford Marine Survey
4383 Holly Harbor Rd.
Oxford, MD 21654
410-226-5616
NAMS, SAMS

Marc Cruder
Marine Surveyor
514 Heavitree Garth
Severna Park, MD 21146
202-267-1055
SAMS

Harry Langley
Marine Surveyor
PO Box 220
Solomons, MD 20688
410-326-2001
SAMS

William Thomte
Atlantic Marine Surveyors
PO Box 299
St. Michaels, MD 21663
410-745-3080
NAMS, SNAME

MASSACHUSETTS

Edwin Boice
Robert N. Kershaw, Inc.
25 Garden Park, Box 285
Braintree, MA 02184
617-843-4550
SAMS

Robert Kershaw
Robert N. Kershaw, Inc.
PO Box 285
Braintree, MA 02184
617-843-4550
NAMS, SAMS

Allen Perry
Ocean Adventures
419 Sippewissett Rd.
Falmouth, MA 02540
508-540-5395
SAMS, ABYC, NAMS

Tom Hill
Atlantic & Pacific Marine Surveyors
27 Ferry St.
Gloucester, MA 01930
508-283-7006
SAMS, ABYC, NFPA

Norman Schreiber II
Transtech—Marine Division
140 Wendward Way
Hyannis, MA 02601
508-776-1670
NAMS, SNAME, ABYC, NFPA

Ralph Merrill
Certified Marine Surveyors
48 19th Street
Lowell, MA 01850
508-459-3082
ABYC

William Kirby
Coastal Associates
51 Bowman St.
Malden, MA 02148
617-322-5458
SAMS

Joseph Lombardi
Manchester Yacht Survey
PO Box 1576
Manchester, MA 01944
508-526-1894
SAMS

Capt. Guilford Full
Capt. G.W. Full & Associates
46 Cedar St.
Marblehead, MA 01945
617-631-4902
NAMS

Arnold Cestari
Metropolitan Property & Casualty
PO Box 821
Mattapoisett, MA 02739
800-634-9740
SAMS

Donald Walwer
D&G Marine Company
PO Box 635
North Eastham, MA 02651
508-255-2406
SAMS

Chris Leahy
Leahy Associates
PO Box 6313
North Plymouth, MA 02362
508-846-1725
SAMS

Donald Linde
Marine Surveyor
Old Centre St.
Pembroke, MA 02359
617-294-1919
SAMS

Capt. Norman LeBlanc
Marine Surveyor
23 Congress St.
Salem, MA 01970
508-744-8289
SAMS

Donald Pray
Marine Surveyor
91 Blanchard Rd.
South Weymouth, MA 02190
617-335-3033
SAMS, ABYC, NFPA

Morris Johnson
Marine Surveyor
PO Box 531
West Yarmouth, MA 02673
508-771-8054
SAMS

Wayne Robinson
Admiralty Consulting & Surveying
50 Dunster Lane
Winchester, MA 01890
617-721-7307
SAMS

Marine Surveyor Directory

MICHIGAN

Jeff Amesbury
Independant Marine Surveyor
213 Franklin St.
Boyne City, MI 49712
616-582-7329

Harry Canoles
Marine Appraisal Survey Service, Inc.
4888 Sherman Church Ave. SW
Canton, MI 44706-3966
216-484-0144

John M. Dionne
South Arm International
508 North Lake St.
East Jordan, MI 49727
616-536-7343
SAMS, ABYC

Jim Cukrowicz
Personal Marine Services
52671 CR 388
Grand Junction, MI 49056
616-434-6396
SAMS

Steve Zinner
Zinner Marine Services
38400 Elmite
Mt. Clemens, MI 48045
313-465-4898
SAMS

Capt. A. John Lobbezoo
Great Lakes Marine Surveyors, Inc.
Box 466, 16100 Highland Dr.
Spring Lake, MI 49456-0466
616-842-9400
SAMS, ABYC, NFPA

Donald Rzeppa
Rzeppa Brothers, Inc.
22418 LaVon Rd.
St. Clair Shores, MI 48081
313-778-0123
SAMS

Michael Koch
R.M. Jay Marine
3665 E. 11 Mile Rd.
Warren, MI 48092
313-573-2563
SAMS

MINNESOTA

Paul Liedl
Croix Marine Consultants
531 Mariner Dr.
Bayport, MN 55003
612-439-7748
SAMS, ABYC

John Rantala, Jr.
Rantala Marine Surveys & Services
1671 10th Ave, #2
Newport, MN 55055
612-458-5842
SAMS

A. William Fredell
Marine Surveyor
408 Quarry Lane
Stillwater, MN 55082
612-439-5795
SAMS

MISSISSIPPI

Rush Andre, AMS
Marine Surveyor & Consultant
414 McGuire Circle
Gulfport, MS 39507
601-863-5962
SAMS, ABYC, NFPA, NAMI

Clarence Hamilton
Hamilton, Inc.
PO Box 378
Ocean Springs, MS 39564
601-875-5800
MSPG, IAAI, ASA

Robert Payne
Marine Management, Inc.
PO Box 1803
Ocean Springs, MS 39564
601-872-2846
NAMS, ABYC

MISSOURI

Richard Thompson
Gay & Taylor—THK Marine & Aviation
1721 W. Elfindale St., Ste. 109
Springfield, MO 65807-8400
417-883-7053
SAMS

NEW HAMPSHIRE

Gerald Poliskey
Independent Marine Surveyors & Adjusters
819 2nd St., #B281
Manchester, NH 03102
603-644-4545
NAMS, SAMS

Capt. David Page
Associated Marine Services
2456 LaFayette Rd.
Portsmouth, NH 03801
603-433-1568; 603-431-6150
SAMS, ABYC, NAMI, NFPA

Patrick Enright
Vessel Management Group
PO Box 6579
Portsmouth, NH 03802
603-433-8914
SAMS

NEW JERSEY

John Klose
Bayview Associates
PO Box 368
Barnegat Light, NJ 08006
609-494-7450
SAMS

Dennis Kelly
Teal Yacht Services
668 Main Ave.
Bay Head, NJ 08742
908-295-8225
SAMS

A. William Gross III
Mid Atlantic Marine Consulting
39 Waterford/Blue Anchor Rd.
Blue Anchor, NJ 08037
609-694-6099
SAMS

Richard Thompson
R. T. Marine Associates
275 Shepherd Avenue
Bound Brook, NJ 08805
908-563-0615
SAMS

Robert Gibble
Robert Gibble, Inc.
25 Black Oak Dr.
Ocean View, NJ 08230
609-390-3708
NAMS, SAMS

William Campbell
W.J. Campbell, Marine Surveyor
9 Gate Rd.
Tabernacle, NJ 08088
609-268-7476
NAMS, SNAME

Terry Randolph
East Coast Marine Surveying
126 Emerald Ave.
West Cape May, NJ 08204
609-884-4668
SAMS

NEW YORK

Walter Lawrence
Lawrence Marine Services
PO Box 219
Alton, NY 14413
315-483-6680
SAMS

John Robertson
Fire Traders, Inc.
One Washington Place
Amityville, NY 11701
516-598-2824
NAMS

Marine Surveyor Directory

Joseph Connelly
All Points Marine
417 E. 2nd Street
Brooklyn, NY 11218-3905
718-851-0736

Thomas Crowley
Upstate Marine Consultants, Inc.
8840 New Country Dr.
Cicero, NY 13039
315-699-0024
ABYC, NFPA

Frederic Hamburg
Marine Surveyor
65 Buckley Street
City Island, NY 10464
212-885-1866
SAMS

Marine Surveyors Bureau
30 S. Ocean Ave.
Freeport, NY 11520
516-683-1199
NAMS, SAMS, ABYC, NFPA

Manuel Rebelo
Keel to Rafter
PO Box 1025
Greenwood Lake, NY 10925
914-477-9422
SAMS

Gerald Van Wart
Marine Surveyor
PO Box 795
Hampton Bays, NY 11946
516-728-5706
SAMS

Steve Maddick
Clyde Eaton & Assoc.
PO Box 796
Hampton Bays, NY 11946-0701
516-728-7970
ABYC, NFPA

Chris Garvey
Garvey & Scott Marine
15 Trail Rd.
Hampton Bays, L.I., NY 11946
516-728-5429
SAMS

Shawn Bartnett
Bartnett Marine Services, Inc.
52 Ontario St.
Honeoye Falls (Rochester), NY
14472
716-624-1380
NAMS, ABYC, NFPA, SNAME

Edward Viola
Edward J. Viola Marine Surveying
PO Box 430
Mattituck, NY 11952
516-298-9518
NAMS

Arnold Gaba
Gaba Marine Survey
PO Box 727
Merrick, NY 11566
516-868-1266
SAMS

Melvin Black
Black Marine Enterprise
753 Webster Ave.
New Rochelle, NY 10804
914-633-5499
SAMS

David McClay
Quality Boat Carpentry
57 Maple Ave.
Northport, NY 11768
516-757-9415
SAMS

Paul Robinson
Marifax Marine Services
21 Swanview Dr.
Patchogu, NY 11772
516-654-3300
SAMS, ABYC

Capt. Henry Olsen
Marine Surveyor
PO Box 283
Port Jefferson, NY 11777
516-928-0711
SNAME

Victor Baum
Marine Surveyor
1540 Middle Neck Rd.
Port Washington, NY 11050
516-358-3489
SAMS

Jerry Masters, Jr.
Marine Surveyor
PO Box 727
Poughkeepsie, NY 12602
800-982-6466
SAMS

Herbert Andrews
Marine Surveyor
308 Riverheights Circle
Rochester, NY 14612
716-663-2342
SAMS

James Gambino
Marine Surveyor
66 Browns Blvd.
Ronkonkoma, NY 11779
516-588-5308
SAMS, ABYC, NFPA, NAMI

Gerald LaMarque
LaMarque Marine Services
6 Red Oak Dr.
Rye, NY 10580
914-967-7731
NAMS, ABYC, NFPA

Long Island Marine Surveyor, Inc.
PO Box 542
Sayville, NY 11782
516-589-6154
ABYC, NFPA

Donald Cunningham
McGroder Marine Surveyors
Box 405, 228 Central Ave.
Silver Creek, NY 14136
716934-7848
NAMS, ABYC, NFPA

John Fitzgibbon
McGroder Marine Surveyors
Box 405, 228 Central Ave.
Silver Creek, NY 14136
716-934-7848
NAMS, ABYC, NFPA

Edwin Fleming
Marine Surveyor
21 Coolidge Ave.
Spencerport, NY 14559
716-352-8832
SAMS

Joseph Gaigal
Suffolk Marine Surveying
RFD 1, Box 174G
St. James, NY 11780
516-584-6297
SAMS, ABYC, NFPA, NAMI

William Foster
Marine Surveyor
185 Harrison Place
Staten Island, NY 10310
718-816-0588
SAMS

James Olsen
Marine Surveyor
101 Atlantic Ave.
West Sayville, NY 11796
516-563-8160
SAMS

William Matthews
Admiralty Marine Surveyors & Adjusters
PO Box 183
Westhampton, NY 11977-0183
516-288-3263
NAMS, SNAME. ABYC

Capt. Jim Dias, CMS
Marine Surveyors Bureau
221 Central Ave.
White Plains, NY 10606
914-684-9889
NAMS, SAMS, ABYC, NFPA

Kenneth Weinbrecht
Ocean Bay Marine Services
PO Box 668
Yaphank, NY 11980
516-924-4362
SAMS

Marine Surveyor Directory

NORTH CAROLINA

Carl Foxworth
Industrial Marine Claims Service
9805 White Cascade Dr.
Charlotte, NC 28269
704-536-7511
SAMS, ABYC, NAMI, NFPA

Michael Burns
Industrial Marine Claims
PO Box 1873
Davidson, NC 28036
704-536-7511
SAMS

Bert Quay
Quay Carolina Marine Surveys
PO Box 809
Oriental, NC 28571
919-249-2275
SAMS

Ron Reeves
Atlantic Maritime Services
PO Box 344
Oriental, NC 28571
919-249-1830
SAMS

W. Thomas Suggs
Marine Surveyor & Consultant
PO Box 400
Oriental, NC 28571
919-249-0374
NAMS, SAMS

Lloyd Moore
Moore Marine Surveying
11516 Hardwick Ct.
Raleigh, NC 27614
919-847-1786
SAMS

T. Fred Wright
M.B. Ward & Son, Inc.
PO Box 3632
Wilmington, NC 28406
919-392-1425
NAMS, ABYC

OHIO

Donald Blum
Neptune Marine Surveys
6603 Gracely Dr.
Cincinnati, OH 45233
513-941-4700
SAMS

George Jeffords
Davis & Company
4367 Rocky River Dr., #5
Cleveland, OH 44135
216-671-5181
SAMS

Ray McLeod
Douglas & McLeod, Inc.
209 River St., Box 398
Grand River, OH 44045
216-352-6156
SAMS, ABYC

Capt. Darrell Walton
West Sister Marine Survey
2260 S. Harris Salem Rd.
Oak Harbor, OH 43449-9339
419-898-1118
SAMS

Leroy Wenger
Wenger Enterprises
526 46th Street
Sandusky, OH 44870
419-626-3103
SAMS

Robert Walsh
Marine Survey Professionals
14532 Pearl Rd., #102
Strongsville, OH 44136
216-572-0866
SAMS

Ted Polgar
Marine Surveyor & Consultant
2745 Pine Knoll Dr.
Toledo, OH 43617
419-841-3600
ABYC

Lawrence Imhoff
Ideal Watercraft
PO Box 8027
Toledo,OH 43605
419-691-1600
SAMS

OREGON

Charles Thompson
Marine Surveyor
450 W. Lexington Ave.
Astoria, OR 97103
503-325-4062
SAMS

Peter Kelleher
Marine Surveyor
450 West Lexington
Astoria, OR 97103
503-325-4062
SAMS

PENNSYLVANIA

William Major
Bristol Yacht Services, Inc.
110 Mill St.
Bristol, PA 19007
215-788-0870
SAMS, ABYC

A.S. Impagliazzo
Chesapeake Marine Services
PO Box 218
New London, PA 19360
215-255-4411
SAMS

Charles Limbruner
Anchor's Away Marine Appraisals
3412 Harrisburg St.
Pittsburgh, PA 15204
412-922-3340
SAMS

PUERTO RICO

Julian Ducat
Octagon Marine Services
PO Box 3209, Old San Juan Station
San Juan, PR 00902-3209
809-722-8785

RHODE ISLAND

Charles Morvillo
Star Marine Surveyors
1700 Smith St.
N. Providence, RI 02911
401-353-1960
SAMS

Robert Daigle
Marine Surveyor
141 Plain Road
North Kingstown, RI 02852
401-295-8061
SAMS

Steve Dolloff
Marine Surveyor
38 Dorr Avenue
Riverside, RI 02915
401-433-4155
SAMS

SOUTH CAROLINA

George Lee
Independent Marine Surveyor
PO Box 30040
Charleston, SC 29417
803-571-2526
SAMS

George Barth
Barth Canvass
755 River Rd.
Columbia, SC 29212
803-781-0031
SAMS

John Peeples
Marine Surveyor
614 Regatta Road
Columbia, SC 29212
803-781-2250
SAMS

Mason Draper
Industrial Marine Claims
Rt. 2, Box 542
Marion, SC 29571
803-423-7624
SAMS

TENNESSEE

David Timpani
Marine Surveyor
PO Box 948
Goodlettsville, TN 37072
615-851-9456
SAMS

John Walker
Walker Marine Services
2845 Lebanon Rd.
Nashville, TN 37214
615-859-2337
SAMS

TEXAS

James Merritt
Tangent Development Co.
1715 Harlequin Run
Austin, TX 78758
512-266-9248
SAMS

Robert Hanson
Gulf Coast Surveyors
PO Box 5267
Beaumont, TX 77726-5267
409-866-4403
NAMS, SAMS

Marc McAllister
McAllister Marine Surveying Co.
PO Box 6375
Corpus Christi, TX 78466-6375
512-992-6633
NAMS, ABYC, NFPA

Peter Davidson
Able Seaman Marine Surveyors
341 Melrose Ave.
Corpus Christi, TX 78404
512-884-7245
SAMS

Richard Frenzel
Dixieland Marine, Inc.
PO Box 2408
Corpus Christi, TX 78403
512-946-5566
SAMS, ABYC

Kurtis Samples
Marine Surveyors of North Texas
3401 St. Johns
Dallas, TX 75205
903-786-6082
SAMS, ABYC, NFPA

J.K. Martens
J.K.M. Consulting
Route 1, Box 674
Dickinson, TX 77539
713-339-1267
SAMS

J.B. Oliveros
J.B. Oliveros, Inc.
127 Marlin St.
Galveston, TX 77550
409-763-3123
NAMS, ABYC

Charles Harrison
Russell Brierly & Assoc.
1712 Mercury Dr.
Houston, TX 77029
713-671-2163
SAMS

Fred Struben
The Dutchman Co.
604 Pebbleshire Dr.
Houston, TX 77062
713-480-7096
NAMS, SNAME, ASA

John Kingston
John L. Kingston & Associates
14425 Torry Chase Blvd., #240
Houston, TX 77014
713-537-7770
NAMS, SAMS

Lee Pearson
Pearson Enterprises
PO Box 301169
Houston, TX 77030-1169
713-622-8802
SAMS, ABYC, SNAME

Robert Cwalenski
Russell Brierly & Assoc.
1712 Mercury Dr.
Houston, TX 77029
713-671-2163
SAMS

Ron Ridgeway
Ridgeway Marine Survey
329 Piper Dr., Box 826
Port Aransas, TX 78373
SAMS

Drake Epple
Perry's Marine Survey Co.
1902 Bayport Blvd., #109
Seabrook, TX 77586
713-474-5273
NAMS, ABYC

Michael Firestone
Newberry & Associates
PO Box 998
Seabrook, TX 77586
713-326-6672
SAMS

Roy Newberry
Newberry & Associates
PO Box 998
Seabrook, TX 77586
713-326-6672
SAMS

Terry Moore
Newberry & Associates
PO Box 998
Seabrook, TX 77586
713-326-6672
SAMS

David Boyd
Marine Surveyor
P.O. Box 1416
Victoria, TX 77901
512-578-2708
SAMS

VIRGINIA

Timothy Warren
Bay Yacht Survey
PO Box 300
Carrollton, VA 23314
804-238-3833
SAMS

Edward Harbour
Harbour Marine Services
217 Silver Maple Dr.
Chesapeake, VA 23320
804-482-9119
SAMS

George Zahn, Jr.
Ware River Associates
Rt. 3, Box 1050
Gloucester, VA 23061
804-693-4329
SAMS, SNAME, ABYC, NFPA

Bill Coker
Entre Nous Marine Services
15 Marina Road
Hampton, VA 23669
804723-2883
ABYC, NFPA, SAMS

Gary Naigle
American Yacht Surveys, Inc.
PO Box 3214
Norfolk, VA 23514
804-622-7859
SAMS

Richard Radius
RHR Computer Services
105 Rens Road, #13
Poquoson, VA 23662
804-868-7355
SAMS

Marine Surveyor Directory

Steven Knox
Knox Marine Consultants
355 Crawford St., #601
Portsmouth, VA 23704
804-393-9788
NAMS

Ralph Brown
Marine Surveyor
11337 Orchard Lane
Reston, VA 22090-4431
703-435-1258
SAMS

Richard Geisel
Hoffman Geisel Surveying
8800 Three Chopt Rd., #301
Richmond, VA 23229
804-257-4140
SAMS

WASHINGTON

Matthew Harris, CMS
Reisner, McEwen & Harris
1333 Lincoln St., #323
Bellingham, WA 98226
206-647-6966
NAMS, SAMS, ABYC

Joe Stevens
Sound Surveyors
9651 South 206th Place
Kent, WA 98031
206-854-4375
SAMS

Steve Belzer
North Latitude Marine
26833 Border Way
Kingston, WA 98346
206-282-8806
SAMS

Kenneth Rider
Rider Associates
338 E. Cascade Place
Oak Harbor, WA 98277
206-675-8475

Barrie Arnett
Arnett & Berg Marine Surveyors
PO Box 70424
Seattle, WA 98107-0424
206-283-8884
SAMS

Carl Anderson
Carl A. Anderson,Inc.
8048 9th Ave. NW
Seattle, WA 98117
206-789-2315
SAMS, ABYC

David Berg
Arnett & Berg Marine Surveyors
PO Box 70424
Seattle, WA 98107-0424
206-283-8884
SAMS

Dennis Johnson
Dennis C. Johnson Marine Surveyor, Inc.
15734 Greenwood Ave. North
Seattle, WA 98133
206-365-6591

Robert McEwen
Reisner, McEwen & Associates
2500 Westlake Avenue North, Suite D
Seattle, WA 98109
206-285-8194
NAMS, ABYC

Ronald Reisner
Reisner, McEwen & Associates
2500 Westlake Ave. N., Suite D
Seattle, WA 98109
206-285-8194
NAMS, SAMS

William L. Hockett
Marine Surveyor
3415 NW 66th
Seattle, WA 98117
206-783-7617
NAMS

Martin Braune
NOR-PAC Marine Surveyors
East 570 Strong Rd.
Shelton, WA 98584
206-426-9118
SAMS

Doug McNeill
Tillikum Marine Services
7305 24th Street West
Tacoma, WA 98466
206-566-0737
SAMS

WISCONSIN

Christopher Kelly
Professional Yacht Services
2132–89th Street
Kenosha, WI 53143
414-694-6603
SAMS

Earl Shaw
Rice Adjustment Company
11422 N. Port Washington Rd.
Milwaukee, WI 53217-0529
414-241-6060
NAMS

CANADA

Ivan Herbert
Universal Marine Consultants, Ltd.
5 Carriageway Ct.
Bedford, Nova Scotia
Canada B4A 3V4
902-835-2283
NAMS

Peter Larkins
Larkins Marine Surveyors
6570 68th St.
Delta, B.C.
Canada V4K 4E2
604-940-1221

Wallace Nisbet
Nisbet Marine Surveyors
345 Lakeshore Rd., #301
Oakville, Ontario
Canada L6J 1J5
416-844-6670
NAMS, ASA, ABYC

Geoffrey Gould
Quality Marine Surveyors, Ltd.
PO Box 1105
Prince Ruppert, B.C.
Canada V8J 4H6
604-624-4138

Kelvin Colbourne
Kelvin Colbourne & Associates
PO Box 24 FP
Washago, Ontario
Canada L0K 2B0
705-689-8820
ABYC

Chris Small
Chris Small Marine Surveyors
15219 Royal Ave.
White Rock, B.C.
Canada V4B 1M4
604-681-8825
NAMS

ABOUT THE AUTHORS

Ed McKnew has been a yacht broker and powerboat design enthusiast for many years. He holds a business degree from Oakland University in Rochester, Michigan, and worked for several years in the solid waste business before becoming a yacht broker in 1977. Moving to the Houston area in 1984, he operated a yacht brokerage office in Clear Lake, Texas, before leaving the business in 1987 to work on the manuscript for the original *PowerBoat Guide*. Ed currently works full time on several publishing projects while spending his spare time pursuing his interest in Civil War literature. He is single and lives in Palm Beach Gardens, Florida.

Mark Parker has been a powerboat enthusiast since before he can remember. A graduate of Southwest Texas State University with a business degree in marketing, Mark also holds a Master's license and has captained several large sportfishing boats. He is a native Texan and worked as a broker in both Texas and Florida for twelve years. Mark currently works full time with American Marine Publishing. He and his wife, Sherri, reside in Palm Beach Gardens, Florida.

NO DEPOSIT.   NO RETURN.

INVEST IN THE FUTURE OF BILLFISH TODAY!

Billfish are being withdrawn from our oceans faster than they can multiply. Commercial longlines and gillnets are now the greatest threat to the survival of billfish and their marine environment. For that reason, The Billfish Foundation has spent the last 5 years investing member dollars in studying the biology and behavior of the world's billfish species. Now, TBF is the world's leading billfish conservation organization, delivering the hard scientific facts required to rebuild the oceans' billfish stocks. By earning substantial returns on your investment, we will ensure future prosperity for billfish and their ecosystems.

WITH YOUR HELP, THEY WILL RETURN.
JOIN THE BILLFISH FOUNDATION TODAY!

The BILLFISH
FOUNDATION
CONSERVATION THROUGH RESEARCH

The Billfish Foundation • 2419 E. Commercial Blvd., Suite 303 • Fort Lauderdale, FL 33308
800-438-8257 • Ph. 305-938-0150 • Fax 305-938-5311

ALBEMARLE 27 EXPRESS

SPECIFICATIONS

Length	27'1"	Fuel	230 gals.
Beam	9'6"	Cockpit	115 sq. ft.
Draft	3'0"	Hull Type	Deep-V
Weight	9,500#	Deadrise Aft	24°
Clearance	NA	Designer	Albemarle
Water	30 gals.	Production	1983–Current

A popular East Coast fisherman with a spacious cockpit and a choice of inboard or jackshaft power, the 27 Express is the oldest and best-known model in the Albemarle fleet. No lightweight, she's heavily constructed on a solid fiberglass deep-V hull with a steep 24° of deadrise aft, moderate beam, and a low center of gravity. Anglers will appreciate the single-level cockpit with its built-in rod storage, washdowns, baitwells, and tackle cabinets. The belowdecks accommodations are basic and functional: convertible dinette forward, compact galley, and a stand-up head with shower. The unusual jackshaft drive system—basically a drive shaft connecting an inboard motor to an outdrive (thus eliminating the space-wasting I/O box at the transom)—is unique, and only Albemarle and Dorado (a small Florida builder) use this setup. Combined with a pair of Volvo 350-cid gas Duoprops, the 27 Express will cruise efficiently at a brisk 24 knots and reach about 37 knots top. With straight inboard 350-cid Volvos, the cruising speed is about 21 knots (33 top). ❏

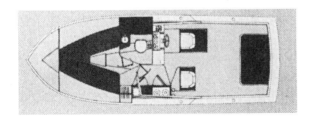

See Page 219 for Pricing Information

ALBEMARLE 32 FLYBRIDGE

SPECIFICATIONS

Length	32'2"	Fuel	309 gals.
Beam	10'11"	Cockpit	85 sq. ft.
Draft	3'0"	Hull Type	Deep-V
Weight	18,000#	Deadrise Aft	18°
Clearance	NA	Designer	Albemarle
Water	49 gals.	Production	1988–Current

From a distance, the Albemarle 32 has the bold and aggressive profile of a larger boat. Those who have been aboard the smaller Albemarle 27 will not be surprised with the quality engineering built into the 32 Flybridge. Her deep-V hull (18° transom deadrise) is solid fiberglass and reinforced on the bottom with a grid stringer system. The unobstructed cockpit is set up for serious fishing and includes two fish boxes under the sole. Inside, there's a real salon with room for a sofa and chairs—very unusual in just a 32-foot fishing boat. A double berth is fitted in the stateroom of early models (V-berths are now standard), and a stall shower is located in the head. Attractively decorated and featuring plenty of teak cabinetry and trim, this is a surprisingly spacious interior. Standard (but less popular) 454-cid gas engines will cruise the Albemarle 32 Flybridge at 22 knots and reach 32 knots top. Optional 300-hp Cummins diesels will cruise at a fast 27 knots and deliver 31–32 knots wide open.❏

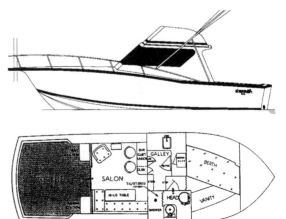

See Page 219 for Pricing Information

ALBEMARLE 32 EXPRESS

SPECIFICATIONS

Length	32'2"	Fuel	320 gals.
Beam	10'11"	Cockpit	NA
Draft	3'0"	Hull Type	Deep-V
Weight	13,500#	Deadrise Aft	18°
Clearance	NA	Designer	Albemarle
Water	50 gals.	Production	1990–Current

Sharing the same all-glass deep-V hull as the original 32 Flybridge, the Albemarle 32 Express is a dedicated offshore sportfisherman with a well-arranged and efficient cockpit layout to go with her basic, no-frills cabin accommodations. Albemarle has a history of building no-nonsense fishing boats, and the 32 Express is a very substantial platform indeed. Aside from her good looks and solid construction, she's loaded with practical features. The cockpit is large and completely unobstructed—no protruding cleats or hatches anywhere. The raised helm provides excellent visibility, and the sidedecks are wide enough to allow safe passage forward. There are two large in-deck fish boxes with macerator pumps and washdowns under the gunwales. For engine access, the entire bridgedeck can be hydraulically raised at the flick of a switch. If the belowdecks accommodations are limited, they're tastefully finished and include berths for four and a stand-up head. Cat or Cummins 300-hp diesels will cruise the Albemarle 32 Express at a fast 27–28 knots and reach 32 knots top. ❑

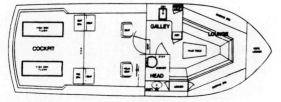

See Page 219 for Pricing Information

ALBIN 28 TOURNAMENT EXPRESS

SPECIFICATIONS

LOA	29'11"	Water	36 gals.
Hull Length	28'4"	Fuel, std	132 gals.
Beam	9'9"	Fuel, opt	192 gals.
Draft, I/Os	1'10"	Hull Type	Modified-V
Draft, Inboard	3'2"	Deadrise Aft	16°
Weight	7,500#	Designer	T. Compton
Clearance	8'6"	Production	1993–Current

The Albin 28 is a practical coastal fisherman with a large cockpit, wide sidedecks, and a roomy interior with accommodations for four. A traditional-looking boat with her Downeast styling, her balsa-cored hull boasts a prop-protecting skeg for increased tracking and stability. A centerline engine box completely dominates the cockpit (standard power is a single V-drive inboard), but there's still plenty of working space for anglers. An optional molded hard-top with sliding side windows makes the helm a semi-enclosed area. Inside, the look is straightforward and basic—white gel-coated bulkheads, snap-out carpeting, and a few pieces of teak trim. A quarter berth extends beneath the bridgedeck, and the cabin headroom is adequate thanks to the raised foredeck. Additional features include a side-dumping exhaust, stainless steel radar arch, transom livewell, and a nav station at the helm. A bow thruster is a popular option. A single 280-hp GM diesel will cruise the Albin 28 at an efficient 18–19 knots with a top speed of about 22 knots. ❑

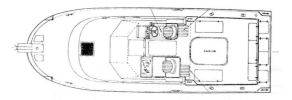

See Page 219 for Pricing Information

ALBIN 32 SPORTFISHER

SPECIFICATIONS

Length	32'4"	Fuel	280 gals.
Beam	12'3"	Cockpit	92 sq. ft.
Draft	3'10"	Hull Type	Modified-V
Weight	13,500#	Deadrise Aft	14°
Clearance	8'10"	Designer	T. Compton
Water	96 gals.	Production	1989–Current

In the past, the Albin nameplate has been associated with imported trawlers. The 32 Sportfisher represented a departure from that heritage when she came out in 1989—an attempt to crack the sport fishing market with a practical and fuel-efficient trunk cabin express cruiser. Built on a modified-V hull with a full-length keel and moderate deadrise aft, the Albin 32 features a large fishing cockpit with livewell, bait rigging center, transom door, seawater washdown, and lockable rod storage as standard. The sidedecks are wide, and high bulwarks provide secure footing in rough seas. Below, the U-shaped dinette will sleep two, and a unique mid-cabin fitted beneath the bridgedeck has a double berth and a single berth to port. Headroom is excellent thanks to the raised foredeck, and hatches in the cockpit sole provide good access to the engine and V-drive unit. With the standard single 300-hp Cummins diesel, she'll cruise around 18 knots with an outstanding 700 miles-plus range. Note that a bow thruster is standard with single-screw installations. ❏

AQUASPORT 290 TOURNAMENT MASTER

SPECIFICATIONS

Length w/Pulpit	31'0"	Fuel	300 gals.
Beam	11'0"	Cockpit	120 sq. ft.
Draft	2'6"	Hull Type	Modified-V
Weight	9,500#	Deadrise Aft	15°
Clearance	8'0"	Designer	Aquasport
Water	32 gals.	Production	1984–90

Still a popular model with anglers, the Aquasport 290 is a good-looking express with a notably big fishing cockpit and surprisingly spacious cabin accommodations. With her wide beam, molded pulpit, and trunk cabin profile, the 290 has the dockside appearance of a much larger boat. Construction is solid fiberglass, and she carries a moderate 15° of deadrise at the transom. The bi-level cockpit of the Aquasport 290 is a full 120 sq. ft.—very large for a 29-footer and came with an in-deck fish box, tackle center, transom door, and fresh and salt washdowns standard. Visibility from the raised helm is excellent, and a factory tower was standard. Inside, the dinette can be converted into four single berths (the hinged seatbacks swing up to become upper bunks). Rod racks were placed in the overhead, and the head compartment is quite large. Most Aquasport 290s were fitted with twin 350-cid gas inboards. A good performer (but a hard ride in a chop), she'll cruise around 25 knots and reach a top speed of 34 knots. ❏

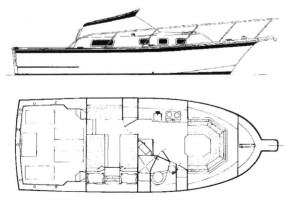

See Page 219 for Pricing Information

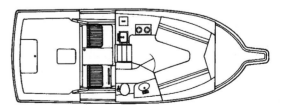

See Page 219 for Pricing Information

ATLANTIC 34 SPORTSMAN

SPECIFICATIONS

Length..........................34'0"	Fuel........................300 gals.
Beam ....12'0"	Cockpit ....NA
Draft.............................3'0"	Hull Type........Modified-V
Weight....................13,500#	Deadrise Aft..................16°
Clearance.......................8'0"	Designer..........J. Scopinich
Water......................40 gals.	Production.............1988–92

Until the 34 Sportsman came along, Atlantic Yachts had been known primarily for their line of trawler-style cruisers and motor yachts. It came as a surprise, then, to see their first new design in years fall into the sportfisherman category. A popular model with good handling qualities, she was built on a solid fiberglass hull with a modified-V bottom and generous flare at the bow. Her large bi-level cockpit was offered in several deck configurations for use as an express cruiser or sportfisherman. A centerline hatch on the bridgedeck provides decent access to the motors. Below, the cabin accommodations are laid out in the conventional manner with V-berths forward, an enclosed head with shower, small galley, and a dinette seating area. Standard gas 454-cid engines cruise the Sportsman at 25 knots and reach a top speed of 31–32 knots. Optional 300-hp GM 8.2 diesels cruise around 27 knots and reach 31 knots top. Of the 75 built, about 15 were customized by R.C. Ritchie in Stratford, CT, for East Coast anglers. ❑

BAYLINER 2502 TROPHY

SPECIFICATIONS

Length..........................24'7"	Water......................30 gals.
Beam ....9'6"	Fuel........................190 gals.
Draft, drive up..............1'4"	Hull Type..............Deep-V
Draft, drive down ......1'10"	Deadrise Aft..................20°
Weight.....................4,765#	Designer...............Bayliner
Clearance....................6'11"	Production ...1992-Current

With her modest price tag and spacious interior dimensions, the 2502 Trophy is clearly aimed at those seeking an afford-able walkaround fisherman with good accommodations. Her nine-foot-six beam is wide for a 25-footer and results in a good deal of cockpit space. Standard fishing equipment includes two in-deck fish boxes with macerators, an aerated livewell, tackle center with sink and storage, baitboxes at the transom, and rod storage under the gunwales. A pair of jump seats at the corners can be removed for added space. The helm console is well-arranged, but getting between the helm and companion seats to go below is a little tight. The roomy cabin features a small galley area, convertible dinette, enclosed head, and good headroom. A second double berth is fitted below the helm. With standard 150-hp Force outboards, the 2502 Trophy cruises at 26 knots and reaches a top speed of about 36 knots. Optional 175-hp Mercs cruise at 30 knots and reach 40+ knots top. Note that a molded hardtop is a popular option. ❑

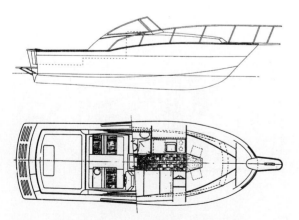

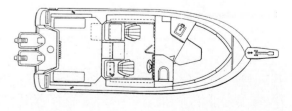

See Page 220 for Pricing Information

See Page 220 for Pricing Information

4

BAYLINER 2860 TROPHY

SPECIFICATIONS

Length..........................27'5"	Fuel........................144 gals.
Beam ....10'0"	Cockpit ....100 sq. ft.
Draft..............................2'4"	Hull Type........Modified-V
Weight......................6,000#	Deadrise Aft..................NA
Clearance......................7'8"	Designer................Bayliner
Water......................30 gals.	Production.............1984–87

The 2860 Trophy was built on the same basic hull used in the production of the earlier 2850 Contessa. Since the Trophy was to be an inboard model (although the base boat featured a single 260-hp stern drive), prop pockets were added to reduce shaft angles and big rudders were utilized for improved handling. The result turned out to be a competent low-cost fisherman with overnight cabin accommodations and plenty of fishing space. There are berths for three below (V berths forward and a portside quarter berth), a stand-up head with shower, and a compact galley. Outside, a convertible dinette is opposite the helm, and a complete bait station is aft of the captain's seat. Aside from the engine boxes, the single-level cockpit is completely uncluttered and comes with a pair of in-deck fish boxes and inwale padding. The standard 260-hp Volvo I/O will cruise efficiently at 17–18 knots and reach a top speed of around 25 knots. Optional 225-hp Volvo inboards cruise at 21 knots and deliver 28-30 knots wide open. ❏

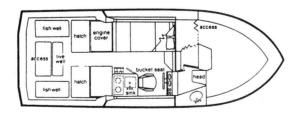

See Page 220 for Pricing Information

THIRTY-FOUR YEARS AFTER THE START OF OUR FIRST RACE, OUR LEAD CONTINUES.

The 1960 Miami-Nassau powerboat race. Winds gusted to thirty-five knots. Seas reached twelve feet.

But despite the conditions, "Moppie," a 31 Bertram, didn't just finish her first race. She won. Finishing two hours ahead of the second-place boat, another Bertram. And, a full day before the rest of the fleet.

But the race wasn't really over for "Moppie."

Her revolutionary, wave-taming, deep-v hull was used to make the mold for the Bertram 31 series. And she became the mother, the grand-mother, the great-grandmother of the Bertrams. Including the cult-classic 31, the heart-stopping 54, and the 42-mph Bertram 60; boats that are revered the world over.

Bertram is not content, however, to merely set standards. We continue to raise them.•A new man-agement team is in place, committed to ongoing in-novations in design and performance. A team of life-long boatbuilders, dedicated to the philosophy that if you can't build it *strong*, *fast*, and *beautiful*, you shouldn't build it at all.

Bertram's new president is Carl Herndon, our plant production manager in the sixties and

The man at the controls of this racing Bertram in 1969 is at the controls of the company today.

seventies, the man in charge of dissecting those early race-battered boats, finding what broke, and making sure it didn't happen again. Ever. Later, Carl created another of the world's most successful and respected boat building companies. Today, he's back, at the helm of Bertram.

The boat you see below is the culmination of our 34 years of experience and passion: the Bertram 60, al-ready becoming a legend. She embodies the qualities we build into every boat in our line - speed, comfort, fishability and resale value - qualities re-cognized as Bertram attributes around the world. Every Bertram from 28 to 72 feet is in production for timely delivery. What's more, they're backed by the finest full-service dealers in the world.

For a close-up look at any new Bertram, call 305-633-8011, or fax 305-635-1388 for the name and number of the dealer nearest you.

We've done our best to put a Bertram within your reach. And yet, still out of reach of the competition.

BERTRAM

The Dynasty Continues.

BERTRAM 28 FLYBRIDGE CRUISER

SPECIFICATIONS

Length	28'6"	Fuel	165/185/240 gals.
Beam	11'0"	Cockpit	85 sq. ft.
Draft	2'8"	Hull Type	Deep-V
Weight	12,060#	Deadrise Aft	23°
Clearance	9'4"	Designer	D. Napier
Water	54 gals.	Production	1971–Current

With over 2,800 built, the 28 Flybridge Cruiser is the best-selling Bertram ever. Designed along the lines of the classic Bertram 31, the 28 quickly established her reputation as a durable and rugged offshore fisherman. An excellent sea boat, she's built on a deep-V hull with a steep 23° of deadrise at the transom. Her cabin layout includes berths for four with a convertible dinette, an efficient galley and a stand-up head with shower. The mica interior was dropped in 1983 and replaced with a contemporary light oak woodwork. Updates in 1990 included a rearranged interior with a more open floorplan and an enlarged flybridge. An optional teak interior became available in 1991. Superior workmanship and constant engineering updates and refinements have kept her in the forefront of small fishing boat designs. Twin 228/230-hp gas engines (21 knots cruise/30 knots top) were standard until 1986 when they were replaced with the current 260-hp MerCruisers (23 cruise/32 top). Updates in 1992 include optional 230-hp Volvo diesels (27-knots cruise). Fuel increases came in 1980 and 1986. ❏

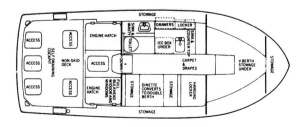

See Page 220 for Pricing Information

BERTRAM 28 SPORT FISHERMAN

SPECIFICATIONS

Length	28'6"	Fuel	185 gals.
Beam	11'0"	Cockpit	85 sq. ft.
Draft	2'8"	Hull Type	Deep-V
Weight	11,320#	Deadrise Aft	23°
Clearance	9'4"	Designer	D. Napier
Water	27 gals.	Production	1971–83

The Bertram 28 Sport Fisherman has the same deep-V hull and superstructure profile of her sistership, the 28 Flybridge Cruiser, but with an open deckhouse (no salon bulkhead) for improved fishability. A galley and dinette were optional (although most were so equipped), and the head is fitted below the forward berths in the cabin. Simple and easy to clean, this type of basic open-air deck layout is ideal in a sportfishing day boat. Few changes were made to the 28 SF during her long production run, and while she never attained the level of popularity enjoyed by the more versatile Flybridge Cruiser, used models are still valued today by knowledgeable anglers. From the standpoint of construction and design, few production fishing boats in this size range can match the performance of the Bertram 28s in bad weather. Indeed, her seakeeping qualities are phenomenal for such a small flybridge boat. Note the unique grabrails which serve to divide the cockpit from spectators. Most were powered with 230-hp MerCruiser engines for a cruising speed of around 20–21 knots and a top speed of 30. ❏

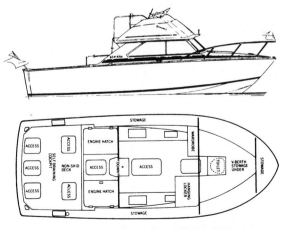

See Page 220 for Pricing Information

7

BERTRAM 28 BAHIA MAR

SPECIFICATIONS

Length	28'6"	Fuel	185/240 gals.
Beam	11'0"	Cockpit	85 sq. ft.
Draft	2'8"	Hull Type	Deep-V
Weight	11,700#	Deadrise Aft	23°
Clearance	7'10"	Designer	D. Napier
Water	48 gals.	Production	1985–92

The Bertram 28 Bahia Mar shares the same hull as the Bertram 28 FBC and SF models. Easily recognized in a crowd, her low-profile deckhouse and wraparound windshield reflect a distinctive European styling influence. The Bahia Mar is a superb sea boat, and her deep-V hull and low center of gravity result in superior offshore performance and handling characteristics. A no-compromise fishing boat at heart, she features a large, unobstructed cockpit with low freeboard and a basic (but well-finished) cabin layout offering overnight accommodations for two. Visibility from the helm position is good, and sightlines are excellent in all directions. The original raised engine boxes were eliminated in the 1986 models in favor of a flush deck; either way, service access to the motors is good. An impressive performer, standard 260-hp MerCruiser gas engines will cruise the 28 Bahia Mar around 23 knots and reach a top speed of 32–33 knots. Twin 230-hp Volvo diesels (28 knots cruise) became optional in 1992. The fuel capacity was increased in 1986 to 240 gallons. ❏

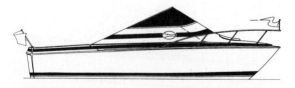

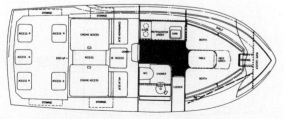

See Page 220 for Pricing Information

BERTRAM 28 MOPPIE

SPECIFICATIONS

Length	28'6"	Fuel	234 gals.
Beam	11'0"	Cockpit	85 sq. ft.
Draft	2'7"	Hull Type	Deep-V
Weight	10,400#	Deadrise Aft	23°
Clearance	7'1"	Designer	D. Napier
Water	27 gals.	Production	1987–Current

The latest in a long string of Bertram 28-footers, the Moppie is a very stylish inboard runabout with the quality engineering expected of a Bertram product. Her sleek profile is attractively accented with painted windshield frame and bowrails, and the Moppie has the modern sportboat "look" popular with many of today's performance-boat buyers. She's built on the standard Bertram 28 deep-V hull with solid fiberglass construction and a steep 23° of transom deadrise. Aside from her superb handling characteristics, the Moppie's primary attraction is her expansive and versatile bi-level cockpit layout. The lower level has a generous 85 sq. ft. of fishing space with plenty of room for a fighting chair. In a practical design application, the galley is concealed in molded lockers abaft the helm and companion seats in the cockpit. The cabin accommodations are basic with a head and V-berths. A good performer with standard 260-hp MerCruiser gas engines, the 28 Moppie will cruise around 24 knots and reach 31–32 knots top. Optional 230-hp Volvo diesels cruise at 28 knots. ❏

See Page 220 for Pricing Information

BERTRAM 30 FLYBRIDGE CRUISER

SPECIFICATIONS

Length	30'7"	Fuel	220 gals.
Beam	11'4"	Cockpit	101 sq. ft.
Draft	3'0"	Hull Type	Deep-V
Weight	16,500#	Deadrise Aft	18.5°
Clearance	8'5"	Designer	D. Napier
Water	61 gals.	Production	1984–85

Bertram rarely misfires when it comes to new model introductions, so it's notable when one of their designs fails to catch on with the public. Such was the case with the Bertram 30 Flybridge Cruiser--a boat that some (including a lot of industry professionals) thought destined to replace the classic Bertram 31 in the hearts of serious anglers. She's exactly the same length as the Bertram 31, but with slightly smaller cockpit dimensions, less transom deadrise (18.5° vs. 23°), improved trolling stability, and a notably dryer ride. The improvements carried into the interior as well, where the Bertram 30's stylish oak-paneled accommodations provide luxuries undreamed of in the old Bertram 31. Lasting only two years in production, the Bertram 30 Flybridge Cruiser proved too expensive for the market, and she was withdrawn in 1985. With standard MerCruiser 340-hp gas engines, she'll cruise at 22 knots and reach a top speed of about 30 knots. Note that the equally short-lived Bertram 30 Express Cruiser (1984–85) is the same boat without the flybridge. ❏

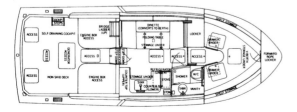

See Page 220 for Pricing Information

BERTRAM 30 MOPPIE

SPECIFICATIONS

Length	30'6"	Fuel	275 gals.
Beam	11'3"	Cockpit	50 sq. ft.
Draft	2'11"	Hull Type	Deep-V
Weight	12,500#	Deadrise Aft	18.5
Clearance	NA	Designer	Bertram
Water	40 gals.	Production	1994–Current

Designed to appeal to anglers as well as cruisers, the already-popular Bertram 30 Moppie is a good-looking inboard express with a sleek profile to go with her rugged construction. Employing the hull from the Bertran 30 FBC (1984–85), the Moppie's clean lines offer plenty of sex appeal without the integral swim platform and molded pulpit common in other modern express boats. Three deck plans make her adaptable to fishing, cruising or daytime activities. The Sport Cruiser layout (pictured above) features a large L-shaped settee opposite the helm, while the Sportfish arrangement comes with a companion seat and tackle centers. Below, the interior is the same for all three versions, with a double berth forward, generous galley space, and a stand-up head with shower. The engines are below the bridgedeck, and access to the motors is very good. Standard 454-cid gas engines will cruise the Moppie at 23 knots and reach 31 top. Optional 291 Cummins will cruise at 27 knots (31 top), and 340-hp Cats will cruise about 30 knots and reach 33 wide open. ❏

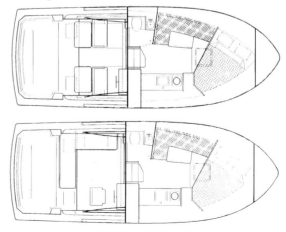

See Page 220 for Pricing Information

BERTRAM 31 FLYBRIDGE CRUISER

SPECIFICATIONS

Length	30'7"	Fuel	170/222 gals.
Beam	11'2"	Cockpit	110 sq. ft.
Draft	3'1"	Hull Type	Deep-V
Weight	10,600#	Deadrise Aft	23°
Clearance	11'0"	Designer	Ray Hunt
Water	18 gals.	Production	1961–83

Nothing in powerboating has equaled the continued worldwide popularity of the original deep-V boat—the Bertram 31. One of several Bertram 31 models, nearly 2,000 Flybridge Cruisers were built over the years, and used models are continually in demand regardless of age or condition. Unquestionably, the chief attribute of any Bertram 31 is her legendary deep-V hull design. In addition to her superb seakeeping characteristics (and a sometimes wet ride), the 31 FBC has a large fishing cockpit and comfortable (if Spartan) cabin accommodations with berths for four. Regular production ended in 1983, but 23 "Silver Anniversary" models were built in 1986 with oak interiors and custom hull striping. Twin 330-hp MerCruiser gas engines have powered the majority of the Bertram 31s, with several GM, Cat, or Cummins diesels offered as options. The Mercs cruise around 23 knots with a top speed of 32+ knots. Diesel powered 31 FBCs have less speed and horsepower but greatly improved range (300+ miles). Note that the fuel capacity increased in 1972 from 170 to 222 gallons. ❑

BERTRAM 31 SPORT FISHERMAN

SPECIFICATIONS

Length	30'7"	Fuel	170/222 gals.
Beam	11'2"	Cockpit	110 sq. ft.
Draft	3'1"	Hull Type	Deep-V
Weight	10,600#	Deadrise Aft	23°
Clearance	11'0"	Designer	Ray Hunt
Water	18 gals.	Production	1961–82

The Bertram 31 Sport Fisherman is the quintessential American fishing machine—a genuine classic that gave birth to the deep-V hull design and (not incidentally) to the Bertram company as well. This is one of the few small boats that can compete in bluewater tournament events without being at all out of place. Performance in head and following seas is outstanding, and her open cabin layout and ease of maintenance quickly earned the 31 SF a loyal and dedicated following among serious anglers and charter boat operators. Over 500 changes were made in the Bertram 31 during her long production run (mainly cosmetic or hardware-related), but the only significant design modification consisted of widening the hull chines in the early days. Standard 330-hp MerCruiser gas engines will cruise around 23 knots and reach a top speed of 33 knots. Many diesel options were offered over the years. The fuel capacity was increased in 1972 from the original 170 gallons to 222 gallons. A stable and highly maneuverable sportfisherman, used Bertram 31s are always in demand despite her reputation for being a wet ride.❑

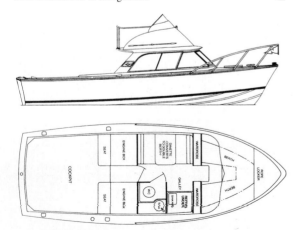

See Page 220 for Pricing Information

See Page 220 for Pricing Information

BERTRAM 31 BAHIA MAR

SPECIFICATIONS

Length	30'7"	Fuel	222 gals.
Beam	11'2"	Cockpit	147 sq. ft.
Draft	2'9"	Hull Type	Deep-V
Weight	9,400#	Deadrise Aft	23°
Clearance	8'3"	Designer	Ray Hunt
Water	18 gals.	Production	1966–81

Built on the legendary Bertram 31 deep-V hull with a steep 23° of deadrise at the transom, the 31 Bahia Mar is an open sport-cruiser design with a large fishing cockpit and basic interior accommodations for two. Bahia Mars have attracted a remarkable following among serious anglers who have come to appreciate her numerous fishing attributes. The 31 Bahia Mar is a stable fishing platform and ranks with the best modern designs when it comes to overall fishability. Her completely open cockpit arrangement puts the helm close to the action, and the cockpit itself is much larger than in most other sportfishermen of her size. Visibility from the helm is another feature fisherman have come to admire—sightlines are excellent in all directions. The Bahia Mar is considered a superb all-round utility boat, and many have seen years of operation in charter and dive-boat fleets. Engine boxes provide easy access to the motors. Standard 330-hp gas engines cruise around 23 knots and reach about 33 knots top. Several diesel options were offered over the years. ❑

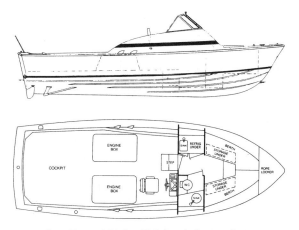

See Page 220 for Pricing Information

BERTRAM 33 FLYBRIDGE CRUISER

SPECIFICATIONS

Length	33'0"	Fuel, Gas	250/315 gals.
Beam	12'6"	Fuel, Dsl	255 gals.
Draft	3'0"	Cockpit	72 sq. ft.
Weight	22,800#	Hull Type	Deep-V
Clearance	12'6"	Deadrise Aft	17°
Fresh Water	70 gals.	Production	1977–92

The Bertram 33 FB Cruiser is a particularly flexible boat that can provide adequate service as a weekend fisherman while still offering excellent cruising accommodations. Combined with her deep-V hull, the 33 FBC's high deckhouse makes for a tender boat offshore. She was originally offered with a single-stateroom layout until a more popular two-stateroom interior became standard in 1980. In 1981 a new tournament flybridge was added, and in 1984 a teak interior decor replaced the woodgrain mica cabinetry. The Bertram 33 II version (introduced in 1988) has a restyled flybridge and an oak interior. Changes in 1990 included a revised layout with a stall shower in the head. In 1992 a varnished maple interior became standard (teak is optional). Twin 454-cid gas engines will cruise the Bertram 33 around 19 knots. Optional 260-hp Cats cruise at 22 knots, and the newer 320-hp Cats cruise at 25–26 knots (30 knots top). Note that the fuel capacity was increased for the gas models in 1980, although late diesel-powered 33s were still fitted with a 255-gallon tank. ❑

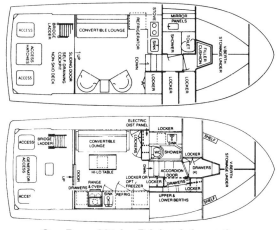

See Page 221 for Pricing Information

11

BERTRAM 33 SPORT FISHERMAN

SPECIFICATIONS

Length	33'0"	Fuel, Gas	250/310 gals.
Beam	12'6"	Fuel, Dsl	250 gals.
Draft	3'0"	Cockpit	116 sq. ft.
Weight	22,400#	Hull Type	Deep-V
Clearance	11'6"	Deadrise Aft	17°
Water	70 gals.	Production	1979–1992

The Bertram 33 SF is a big boat for her size with good styling, superior construction, and proven offshore performance. Built on the same hull as the 33 FB Cruiser, she has a larger cockpit than her sistership but no salon. Her aggressive low-profile lines, spacious flybridge, and top-quality engineering have made the 33 a favorite with deep-water fishermen. The interior accommodations were enlarged and rearranged in 1986 by moving the cabin bulkhead aft a few inches and replacing the dinette with a settee. The loss in cockpit space (122 to 116 sq. ft.) is negligible. A light oak interior was added in 1985, and the flybridge was restyled in 1988. Engines are located under raised boxes in the cockpit for easy access. Twin 330-hp gas engines were standard (20 knots cruise/29 knots top), and optional 260-hp 3208T Cat diesels were optional (23 knots cruise/27 knots top). Optional 320-hp Cats (1992 only) cruise at 27 knots and reach 31 knots top. Note that the fuel capacity for gas models was increased to 310 gallons in 1980. ❏

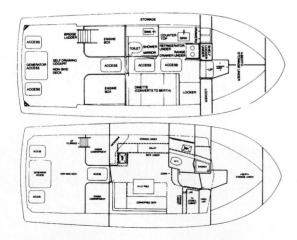

See Page 221 for Pricing Information

BERTRAM 35 CONVERTIBLE

SPECIFICATIONS

Length	35'4"	Fuel	285/273 gals.
Beam	13'3"	Cockpit	92 sq. ft.
Draft	3'2"	Hull Type	Deep-V
Weight	22,500#	Deadrise Aft	19°
Clearance	12'6"	Designer	D. Napier
Water	50/75 gals.	Production	1970–86

Few boats can rival the 15-year production run enjoyed by the Bertram 35 Convertible. For many, thirty-five feet is the ideal size for a sportfisherman, short of going into serious debt. Although the Bertram 35's interior layout is suitable for family cruising, she's most at home as a fishing boat, where her large cockpit, precise handling, and enviable seakeeping qualities are most appreciated. In 1981 a Mk II model came out with an updated tournament-style flybridge, and in 1984 a teak interior replaced the original woodgrain mica decor. Note that the vinyl cockpit sole of early models was replaced in 1982 with fiberglass—a notable improvement. Twin 350-hp Crusader gas engines were standard (19–20 knots cruise/28 top) during her production run, with 215-hp Cummins (around 18 knots cruise/22 knots top) or 300-hp Cat (23 knots cruise/27 knots top) diesels available as options. With the 300-hp Cats (1981–85 models), the Bertram 35 becomes a much-improved performer. A popular and good-looking convertible, these boats are nearly always in demand. ❏

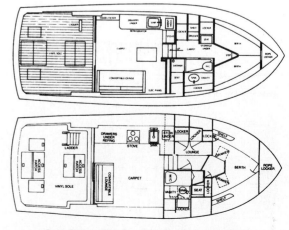

See Page 221 for Pricing Information

12

BERTRAM 37 CONVERTIBLE

SPECIFICATIONS

Length	37'9"	Fuel	473 gals.
Beam	13'3"	Cockpit	93 sq. ft.
Draft	3'9"	Hull Type	Deep-V
Weight	32,410#	Deadrise Aft	18°
Clearance	12'11"	Designer	D. Napier
Water	100 gals.	Production	1986–Current

Beautifully styled and designed for the rigors of tournament-level activities, the 37 Convertible has been a very popular boat for Bertram since her introduction in 1986. She's built on a deep-V hull (cored from the waterline up) using modern unidirectional fabrics and carbon fiber composites throughout. Below, her upscale two-stateroom layout includes overhead rod storage in the salon, over/under bunks in the (very) small guest cabin, a walkaround island berth forward, and light oak cabinetry and woodwork throughout. Note that maple woodwork became standard beginning in 1993. Considered by many to be among the best in her class, the Bertram 37 receives high marks for her superb handling and exceptional performance. A good-running boat, 450-hp 6V92s will cruise at 27 knots (31 knots top), and the more recent 550-hp 6V92s will cruise at 30 knots and reach 34+ knots wide open. Cat 375-hp diesels will cruise the Bertram 37 at 22–23 knots (27 knots top), and 435-hp 6V71s (1986–88 only) cruise at 24–25 knots. Resales values are excellent. ❑

See Page 221 for Pricing Information

BERTRAM 38 CONVERTIBLE

SPECIFICATIONS

Length	37'8"	Fuel	350 gals.
Beam	14'5"	Cockpit	109 sq. ft.
Draft	3'6"	Hull Type	Deep-V
Weight	26,000#	Deadrise Aft	22°
Clearance	NA	Designer	Ray Hunt
Water	100 gals.	Production	1970–76

The Bertram 38 Convertible was the second of three 38-foot Bertram models built over the years, the first being a Hunt-designed flybridge cruiser produced for the family market back in the early 1960s. In the case of the 38 Convertible, the emphasis was on fishability, pure and simple. Her deep-V hull was designed along the lines of the original Bertram 31, and her extra-wide beam provides the stability often missing in an early deep-V designs. Long out of production but still popular with budget-minded anglers, her large and uncluttered fishing cockpit and practical cabin accommodations continue to have wide appeal in spite of her age. The interior is efficiently arranged with the galley up, V-berths in the forward stateroom, and over/under berths in the guest cabin. By any standard, the woodgrain mica interior of the Bertram 38 is plain, but clean-up is easy. Twin 325-hp gas engines were standard (18 knots cruise/27 knots top), however most of the Bertram 38 Convertibles were delivered with the GM 8V53 or Cummins V903 diesels and cruise around 17–18 knots. ❑

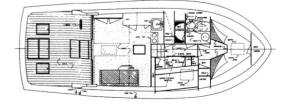

See Page 221 for Pricing Information

BERTRAM 38 III CONVERTIBLE

SPECIFICATIONS

Length..........................38'5"	Fuel.........................395 gals.
Beam ....13'3"	Cockpit.................100 sq. ft.
Draft...............................4'2"	Hull Type..............Deep-V
Weight....................30,400#	Deadrise Aft...................17°
Clearance....................13'0"	Designer.............D. Napier
Water.....................100 gals.	Production.............1978–86

The Bertram 38 III is an entirely different boat from the earlier Bertram 38 Convertible (1970–76). She has a more graceful profile, less beam, a shallower "V" bottom—from 22° of transom deadrise to a more moderate 17°—and generally improved handling characteristics. Aimed at the sportfishing market, the 38 III's large cockpit and tournament style flybridge make her well suited for serious bluewater events. Inside, her two-stateroom layout is efficient and well organized. In 1982 Bertram replaced the original Nautilex cockpit sole with a fiberglass deck (a major improvement), and a teak interior became standard. A little wet at times, the 38 III is otherwise known as a capable sea boat. Nearly all were diesel powered. Cat 300-hp diesels (19–20 knots cruise) were popular as were the Cat 355-hp and Cummins 380-hp VT903 engines, both of which cruise around 23 knots. Production ceased in 1987 with the introduction of the Bertram 37. A total of 331 Bertram 38 IIIs were built making her one of the best-selling 38-foot sportfishing boats ever. ❏

See Page 221 for Pricing Information

BERTRAM 38 SPECIAL

SPECIFICATIONS

Length..........................38'5"	Fuel.........................395 gals.
Beam ....13'3"	Cockpit...................97 sq. ft.
Draft...............................4'2"	Hull Type..............Deep-V
Weight....................27,000#	Deadrise Aft...................17°
Clearance....................9'11"	Designer...............Bertram
Water.....................100 gals.	Production.............1986–87

The Bertram 38 Special is a high quality, fast action sportfisherman with a huge fishing cockpit for serious tournament-level pursuits. Her hull is the same as that used in the 38 III Convertible but with balsa coring placed in the hullsides forward of the engine bulkhead. The design philosophy behind the 38 Special was to give the bluewater angler a pure, no-nonsense fishing machine with good performance and plenty of range. Although the interior is limited in size, the rounded bulkheads and radiused corners make the most of the available space. Visibility from the raised helm position is very good. A small hatch provides routine access to the engines, and the entire bridgedeck sole is removable for major work. Caterpillar 375-hp diesels were standard (23 knots cruise/27 knots wide open). GM 6V71TAs rated at 435-hp were optional and increased the cruising speed to about 25 knots and the top speed to 30 knots. A popular boat in resale markets, the Bertram 38 Special enjoyed limited market success due to her high cost and production ended after just two years. ❏

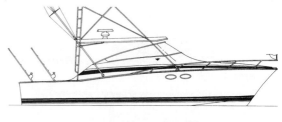

See Page 222 for Pricing Information

BERTRAM 42 CONVERTIBLE

SPECIFICATIONS

Length	42'6"	Fuel	488 gals.
Beam	14'10"	Cockpit	108 sq. ft.
Draft	4'0"	Hull Type	Deep-V
Weight	39,400#	Deadrise Aft	17°
Clearance	14'11"	Designer	Bertram
Water	150 gals.	Production	1976–87

One of Bertram's most successful boats, the 42 Convertible needs no introduction to anglers on either coast. A total of 329 of these boats were built, and her exceptional seakeeping abilities, superb fishability, long range, and top quality construction have earned for the Bertram 42 a reputation as a classic design. Heavily built on a deep-V hull, numerous updates were made during her long production run. In 1981, the twin sliding salon doors were replaced with a single door, and the flybridge helm position was moved from portside to the centerline. In 1982, a teak interior replaced the earlier woodgrain mica decor (a welcome improvement). In another major upgrade, the original vinyl cockpit sole was replaced with fiberglass in 1982. In 1983, a queen bed became standard in the master stateroom. A restyled flybridge in 1986 added much to her profile, and an oak interior became standard in 1987. Cummins 420-hp diesels (popular through 1979) and 435-hp GM 6V92TAs (1980–84 models) cruise around 23–24 knots, and the more recent 475-hp 6V92TAs cruise at 25+ knots. ❑

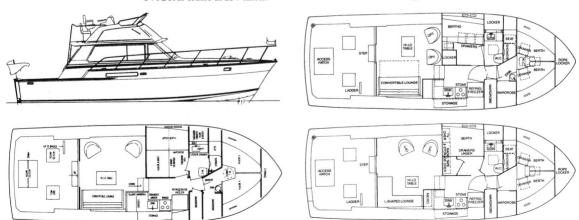

See Page 222 for Pricing Information

BERTRAM 43 CONVERTIBLE

SPECIFICATIONS

Length.........................43'4"	Fuel.......................567 gals.
Beam ....14'11"	Cockpit ....120 sq. ft.
Draft..............................4'4"	Hull Type...............Deep-V
Weight....................41,890#	Deadrise Aft...................17°
Clearance....................13'5"	Designer ....Bertram
Water....................160 gals.	Production...1988–Current

A popular model for Bertram with an excellent reputation for fishability, the 43 Convertible is built on a modified-V hull design with balsa coring in the sides, considerable flare at the bow, and a classic Bertram step-down sheer. Not surprisingly, she handles and performs like the thoroughbred sportfisherman she is: agile, dry, and fast. Her elegant two-stateroom interior is luxuriously appointed and finished with light oak or—beginning in 1993—maple wood-work. First offered with a galley-up layout and two heads, an alternate galley-down floorplan became available in 1989 (at the expense of one of the heads). Other significant updates in 1993 include a great new galley-up arrangement (the galley-down layout is still available) and direct cockpit access to the engine room. A well-designed console at the helm eliminates the need for an overhead electronics cabinet. Standard 550-hp 6V92TA diesels will cruise the Bertram 43 Convertible around 25 knots with a top speed of 28+. Range at a hard cruise is an impressive 300 nautical miles. ❑

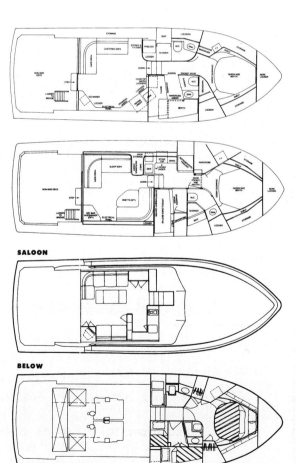

SALOON

BELOW

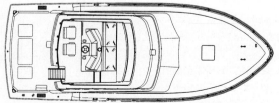

See Page 222 for Pricing Information

16

BERTRAM 46 CONVERTIBLE

SPECIFICATIONS

Length	46'6"	Fuel	620/720 gals.
Beam	16'0"	Cockpit	117/130 sq. ft.
Draft	4'6"	Hull Type	Deep-V
Weight	44,900#	Deadrise Aft	19°
Clearance	15'6"	Designer	Bertram
Water	230/246 gals.	Production	1971–87

The Bertram 46 Convertible was for many years the standard by which other production sportfishing boats her size were measured. Her popularity has much to do with the precise handling and impressive seakeeping characteristics of the 46's deep-V hull design. Originally a two-stateroom boat with the galley down, a three-stateroom model (the 46 II) was available during 1983–85. Significant design changes include a single sliding salon door (replacing double doors) in 1981, a fiberglass cockpit sole (replacing the Nautilex liner) and a new teak interior in 1982, and a standard transom door in 1985. The 46 III model (1986–87) features an updated layout with oak woodwork and a centerline queen forward. Prior to 1981, the most popular engines were the 435-hp 8V71TIs, which will cruise around 20 knots and reach 23 knots top. In 1981, the 570-hp 8V92TIs became available (around 24 knots cruise), and the 600-hp versions (1985–87) added another knot of speed. Note that the fuel capacity was increased to 720 gallons in 1983. ❏

See Page 222 for Pricing Information

18

BERTRAM 46 MOPPIE

SPECIFICATIONS

Length	46'0"	Fuel	650 gals.
Beam	14'11"	Cockpit	106 sq. ft.
Draft	4'8"	Hull Type	Deep-V
Weight	42,000#	Deadrise Aft	17°
Clearance	9'1"	Designer	Dave Napier
Water	135 gals.	Production	1993–Current

One of two new models for 1993, the Bertram 46 Moppie is built on a stretched 43 Convertible hull with cored hullsides and a fairly steep 17° of transom deadrise. This is one of the bigger express cruisers to be found, and she's designed to meet the needs of fishermen and sportcruisers alike. Offered with a choice of two floorplans (the single-stateroom layout has *two* heads), the interior woodwork is varnished maple throughout. There's plenty of space in the cockpit for a full-size chair, and an L-lounge opposite the helm provides adequate guest seating. Although the engines are located beneath the bridgedeck, they are reversed and power is delivered thru V-drive-like shaft couplers—a system that hard core anglers may question. Too, the generator (at least in early models) is located beneath the cockpit sole where it's always exposed to salt air. A good running boat, a pair of 735-hp 8V-92s will cruise the 46 Moppie at 28–29 knots and reach a top speed of 32 knots. ❑

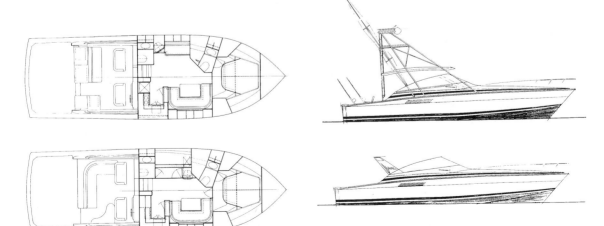

See Page 222 for Pricing Information

BERTRAM 50 CONVERTIBLE

SPECIFICATIONS

Length	50'0"	Fuel	1,046 gals.
Beam	16'0"	Cockpit	108 sq. ft.
Draft	5'0"	Hull Type	Deep-V
Weight	56,531#	Deadrise Aft	17°
Clearance	15'9"	Designer	Bertram
Water	175 gals.	Production	1987–Current

It isn't how fast you go, it's how you go fast that counts. In the case of the Bertram 50 that means big and beautiful and at no small expense. Introduced in 1987, the Bertram 50 follows in the high-tech footsteps of the Bertram 54 and 37 Convertibles. A beautifully styled boat with a truly aggressive profile, she's still considered by many to represent the state of the art in production sportfishermen of her size. Initially offered in a three-stateroom layout with the galley up, a spacious two-stateroom galley-down interior with an enormous salon became available in 1988. A transom door and tackle center are standard in the cockpit, and a wraparound helm console eliminates the need for an overhead electronics box on the bridge. A good performer, standard 735-hp 8V92 diesels will cruise at 24–25 knots (29 top) with a range of over 400 miles. Twin 820-hp MAN diesels introduced in 1989 provide cruising speeds of 27+ knots (31 knots top). This has been a popular model for Bertram, with good resale vales. ❑

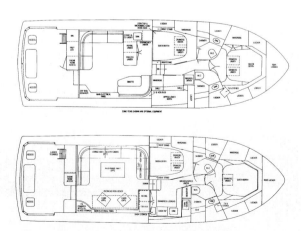

See Page 222 for Pricing Information

BERTRAM 54 CONVERTIBLE

SPECIFICATIONS

Length...........................54'0"	Fuel ....1,200/1,419 gals.
Beam ....16'11"	Cockpit ....144 sq. ft.
Draft ....5'2"	Hull Type ....Deep-V
Weight.....................65,000#	Deadrise Aft...................17°
Clearance.....................16'8"	Designer ....D. Napier
Water.....................250 gals.	Production.............1981–93

A proven tournament winner and sportfishing superstar, the Bertram 54 Convertible is built on a rugged deep-V hull with balsa coring above the waterline. With her near-perfect blend of design, engineering, and construction, she delivers absolutely outstanding rough water performance. Indeed, few production (or custom) boats her size can touch the Bertram 54 when it comes to heavy weather handling. Several three-stateroom/three-head interiors were offered (see below). Note that the generators were relocated from under the cockpit sole to the engine room in 1984. The front deckhouse windshield was eliminated in 1986, and updates for 1987 included a restyled flybridge, a queen berth forward, increased fuel capacity, and a new oak interior. The 800-hp 12V71 diesels were a popular option (over the standard 675-hp units) and cruise the Bertram 54 at 24–25 knots (29 knots top). The 900-hp 12V71s (1985–86) cruise at a fast 26 knots (31 knots top), and the 1,080-hp 12V92s cruise at an honest 29–30 knots and reach 33 knots wide open. ❑

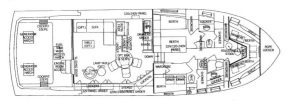

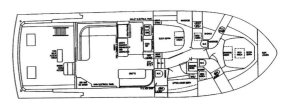

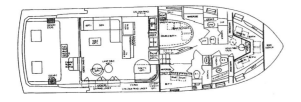

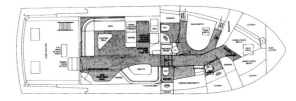

See Page 222 for Pricing Information

BERTRAM 58 CONVERTIBLE

SPECIFICATIONS

Length...........................58'3"	Fuel, Std.............1,300 gals.
Beam ....17'11"	Fuel, Opt.............2,020 gals.
Draft...............................5'6"	Cockpit................168 sq. ft.
Weight....................90,000#	Hull Type........Modified-V
Clearance....................19'5"	Deadrise Aft..................15°
Water.....................300 gals.	Production.............1977–83

The Bertram brochures hardly overstated the matter when they referred to the 58 Convertible as a "hugely elegant machine." Huge indeed—only the Hatteras 60 Convertible exceeded her in size among production sportfishing yachts of her era. The 58 Convertible's hull is solid fiberglass with a full keel below and just 15° of deadrise aft (the least amount of "V" in any Bertram hull). Notably, the decks and superstructure were built of aluminum. Among her many attributes is a ride that many consider to be the best in this size range. Designed for serious tournament level competition and comfortable offshore cruising, the Bertram 58's massive cockpit dimensions will accommodate *two* full size fighting chairs. Her luxurious three-stateroom/three-head teak interior features a huge salon with extravagant entertaining potential. The flybridge is arranged with two helm stations—one well forward and one aft to view the cockpit action. At 90,000 lbs., the Bertram 58 Convertible is no lightweight, but her performance with 675-hp 12V71 diesels is a respectable 18 knots at cruise and around 21 knots top. ❏

See Page 222 for Pricing Information

BERTRAM 60 CONVERTIBLE

SPECIFICATIONS

Length..........................60'0"	Fuel.....................1,630 gals.
Beam ....16'11"	Cockpit................144 sq. ft.
Draft...............................5'4"	Hull Type...............Deep-V
Weight....................85,000#	Deadrise Aft..................17°
Clearance....................16'8"	Designer ....D. Napier
Water....................250 gals.	Production ...1990-Current

A popular model, the Bertram 60 Convertible projects the classic styling and aggressive good looks common to all modern Bertram designs. Credit for her striking profile goes to designer Dave Napier, who stretched and reworked the existing Bertram 54 hull to create one of the finest 60-foot convertibles yet seen from a production yard. Her modified-V hull is cored from the waterline up. Construction and engineering are state-of-the-art. The original galley-up, three-stateroom floorplan is similar to that found in the Bertram 54 with the extra length used to enlarge the salon. A stall shower in the starboard guest head has been added, and the entire layout is finished with maple paneling since 1993. A new four-stateroom layout became available in 1994. The cockpit comes complete with an oversized transom door, tackle center, and direct engine room access. The flybridge helm is a work of art. Powered with 1,400-hp 16V92 diesels, she'll cruise at an honest 31 knots and reach 34–35 knots wide open. Over twenty have been built to date. ❏

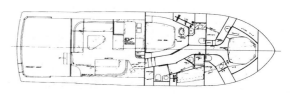

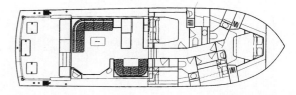

See Page 222 for Pricing Information

BERTRAM 72 CONVERTIBLE

SPECIFICATIONS

Length	72'6"	Fuel	2,570 gals.
Beam	18'5"	Cockpit	193 sq. ft.
Draft	6'9"	Hull Type	Deep-V
Weight	120,000#	Deadrise Aft	17°
Clearance	19'10"	Designer	Bertram
Water	300 gals.	Production	1990-Current

Designed to be one of the fastest yachts of her kind in the world, the Bertram 72 makes extensive use of balsa coring throughout the hull, including the bottom—a first for any Bertram yacht. The all-new hull is a deep-V design with 17° of deadrise and a sweeping sheer stepped just forward of the cockpit. The interior can be customized to an owner's specifications, however the three-stateroom, three-head layout with the galley up should prove to be popular among sportfishermen. (Note the full-width master stateroom below the galley.) The bridge is enclosed and air conditioned, and a second outside helm overlooks the massive cockpit. A convenient day head is provided on a small deck abaft the salon bulkhead. Additional features include a huge walk-in engine room, a sea chest to eliminate thru-hulls, trolling valves, and an optional bow thruster. The first hulls were fitted with 1,960-hp MTUs, although 1,440-hp 16V92s are standard. Speeds with the MTUs are reportedly 30 knots at cruise and 34 knots wide open. ❏

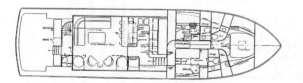

See Page 222 for Pricing Information

BIMINI 245 TOURNAMENT

SPECIFICATIONS

Length	24'4"	Fuel	140 gals.
Beam	8'0"	Cockpit	45 sq. ft.
Draft	2'2"	Hull Type	Modified-V
Weight	5,000#	Deadrise Aft	17°
Clearance	NA	Designer	P. Patterson
Water	None	Production	1991–Current

With the North Coast 24 now out of production, the Bimini 245 is the *only* twin-inboard trailerable model available in this size range. Built on the deep-V hull of the earlier Topaz 24 (a single-inboard design whose molds were acquired by Bimini Marine a few years ago), the 245 Tournament is otherwise a completely different boat with a raised deckhouse, prominent wraparound windshield, and single-level cockpit layout with room for a small chair and a couple of anglers. Indeed, the cockpit is among the largest in its class and comes with two in-deck fish boxes, cockpit coaming, and removable engine boxes that double as baitwatching seats. A well-arranged helm console provides space for flush-mounting basic electronics. Since the Bimini is a dedicated fisherman, the cabin accommodations are basic but attractively finished and adequate for weekend expeditions. An agile and good-running boat, twin 140-hp (4-cyl.) Volvo gas engines will cruise around 23 knots (at better than 2 mpg!) and deliver a top speed of about 30 knots. ❏

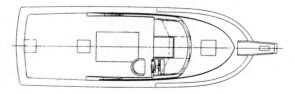

See Page 222 for Pricing Information

BIMINI 29

SPECIFICATIONS

Length..........................29'0"	Fuel........................225 gals.
Beam ....10'3"	Cockpit.................65 sq. ft.
Draft..............................2'6"	Hull Type........Modified-V
Weight.......................8,100#	Deadrise Aft.................NA
Clearance.......................NA	Designer ....P. Patterson
Water.......................30 gals.	Production...1989–Current

Bimini Marine acquired molds to the Topaz 29 SF in 1989 following that company's demise and reintroduced her the same year as the Bimini 29. Hull construction is solid fiberglass, and the layout of the Bimini is basically the same as the earlier Topaz model. A large hatch on the bridgedeck provides access to the engines, and visibility from the helm is excellent. The lower level of the cockpit is large enough for a mounted chair, and a large in-deck fish box and below-deck storage area keep the cockpit free of clutter. Inside, there are berths for three in the cabin along with a compact galley and a roomy stand-up head with shower. Most have been sold with the optional factory tower. Several gas and diesel engines have been offered in the Bimini 29 over the years. The popular 200-hp Volvo diesels will cruise at a fast 26–27 knots with a top speed of around 30 knots. Note that a 29 Sport model with an enlarged bridgedeck and smaller cabin is also available. ❏

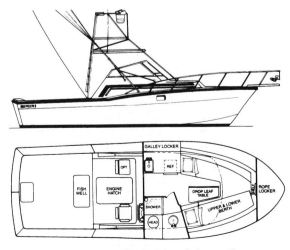

See Page 222 for Pricing Information

BLACK WATCH 26 SPORTFISHERMAN

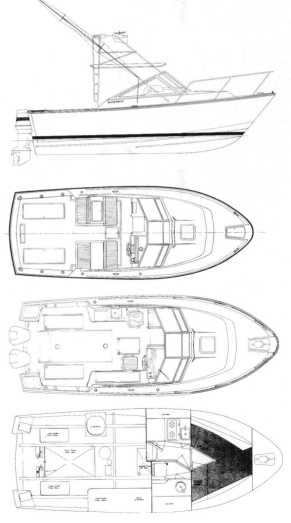

SPECIFICATIONS

Length	26'1"	Fuel	200/240 gals.
Beam	9'8"	Cockpit	102 sq. ft.
Draft	2'6"	Hull Type	Deep-V
Weight, O/B	7,140#	Deadrise Aft	19°
Weight, Inbd	8,300#	Designer	Hunt Assoc.
Water	25 gals.	Production	1988–Current

The Black Watch 26 is a solidly built day boat meant for the kind of offshore work that keeps most boats this size tied up at the docks in bad weather. She's built on a balsa-cored deep-V hull with a wide beam and a flush cockpit layout. Available with inboard or outboard power (inboard models are fitted with engine boxes), the Black Watch 26 provides anglers with a big fishing cockpit with two in-deck fish boxes and (in the outboard version) a nifty starboardside 7' rod locker. A 30-gallon livewell is standard, and there's space in the helm console for flush-mounting electronics. Inside, the accommodations include over/under V-berths, a small galley, and an enclosed head compartment with shower—not bad for a small fishing boat. Those powered with twin 200-hp outboards will cruise at a fast 24–25 knots and reach a top speed of about 42 knots. Inboard models (available since 1990) with 240-hp gas engines cruise at about 25 knots and deliver 35 knots wide open. ❑

See Page 222 for Pricing Information

BLACK WATCH 30 SPORTFISHERMAN

SPECIFICATIONS

Length..........................30'1"	Fuel........................240 gals.
Beam ....10'11"	Cockpit................120 sq. ft.
Draft.............................2'10"	Hull Type..............Deep-V
Weight.......................9,000#	Deadrise Aft..................18°
Clearance......................7'0"	Designer.........Hunt Assoc.
Water.......................50 gals.	Production...1986–Current

Introduced in 1986, the Black Watch 30 has been well-received among anglers for her extraordinary handling abilities, handsome profile, and high-tech construction. Her balsa-cored deep-V hull is capable of slugging it out in some pretty mean seas. Not surprisingly, the layout is dedicated to serious fishing activities, and her large unobstructed cockpit is set low to the water. A transom door is offset to starboard, and a pair of fish boxes are built into the cockpit sole. Engine boxes make access to the engines easy, and the entire cockpit liner is removable for major service work. Inside, the cabin accommodations are fairly basic with berths for four (the backrests of the convertible dinette forward swing up to create single berths), an enclosed head with shower, and a small galley area. Headroom is adequate throughout. A good performer, 454-cid gas engines will cruise around 26 knots (34 knots top), and the 300-hp Cummins (or Cat) diesels will cruise economically at a fast 28–29 knots and reach 33 knots wide open. ❏

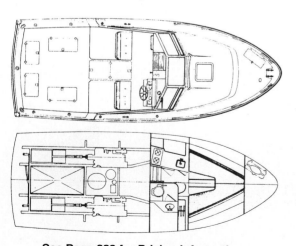

See Page 223 for Pricing Information

BLACK WATCH 30 FLYBRIDGE

SPECIFICATIONS

Length..........................30'1"	Fuel........................270 gals.
Length WL ....25'7"	Cockpit..................80 sq. ft.
Beam ....10'11"	Hull Type..............Deep-V
Draft.............................3'0"	Deadrise Aft..................18°
Weight....................12,000#	Designer.........Hunt Assoc.
Clearance......................9'6"	Production...1989–Current
Water.......................40 gals.	

Serious anglers, whose lust for a high-performance sportfisherman often conflicts with the family's demand for a comfortable interior, will quickly appreciate the Black Watch 30 Flybridge. A little top-heavy in appearance (thanks to an oversize flybridge) but an otherwise rugged-looking boat, she's built on the same balsa-cored deep-V hull as the Sportfisherman model. The interior is surprisingly roomy for a 30-footer and features V-berths forward, a convertible dinette, compact galley, and an enclosed head. The headroom is very good, and the teak trim, quality fabrics, and teak and holly cabin sole add an upscale feel to the interior. Outside, a big fish box runs athwartships across the after part of the cockpit, and clever roll-back engine boxes provide excellent access to the engines. Standard 454-cid gas engines will cruise the Black Watch 30 Flybridge around 24–25 knots (about 33 knots top), and optional 300-hp Cummins diesels provide outstanding performance and economy at a hard 28-knot cruise. Top speed with these engines is about 32–33 knots. ❏

See Page 223 for Pricing Information

BLACK WATCH 36 FLYBRIDGE

SPECIFICATIONS

Length	36'2"	Water	60 gals.
Beam	11'4"	Fuel	300 gals.
Draft	2'7"	Hull Type	Deep-V
Weight	13,900#	Deadrise Aft	18°
Clearance	11'0"	Designer	Hunt Assoc.
Cockpit	150 sq. ft.	Production	1991–Current

Built on a semi-custom basis, the Black Watch 36 is a light-weight, high-tech flybridge fisherman with top-quality construction and superb offshore performance. Her hull—a relatively narrow deep-V—is fully balsa cored, vacuum-bagged, and reinforced on the bottom with Kevlar. Aside from her graceful appearance and meticulous detailing, perhaps the most striking feature of the Black Watch 36 is her oversized fishing cockpit. Indeed, it's so big that the cabin layout is necessarily compact compared with other boats her size. With V-bunks, galley, dinette, and head, the Black Watch 36 provides accommodations for four with good headroom, overhead rod storage, and a stylish teak-and-holly sole. Note the absence of a stall shower in the head. The motors are easily accessed via engine boxes in the cockpit, and the bridge is arranged with a wraparound helm console, Panish controls, and guest seating forward. A economical boat with optional 291-hp Cummins diesels, she'll cruise at 24 knots (18–20 gph) and reach a top speed of 27–28 knots. ❏

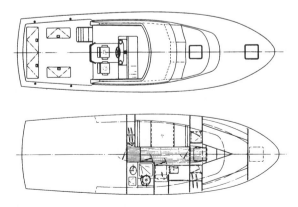

See Page 223 for Pricing Information

29

Everything you hear is true.

Walk down any dock and ask the serious fishermen about the Blackfin Flybridge Series. You'll find out why these boats have redefined "sportfishing."

There are reasons for this.

Years ago the designers and engineers at Blackfin followed a simple premise. Form follows function. What you need is an exceptionally dry and extraordinarily smooth riding boat that will flatten rough seas. A boat with a large, uncluttered cockpit. An interior that affords sumptuous comfort. The power and seakeeping ability to get you where you want to go. The reassurance that your boat can withstand anything the sea has to offer. This is what a Blackfin is about.

Nothing is left to chance. Every detail, no matter how insignificant it might seem, is intelligently thought out and executed to perfection.

This is what you'll hear. Now experience it for yourself.

For more information write: Blackfin Yacht Corp., P.O. Box 22982, Ft. Lauderdale, FL 33335 (305) 525-6314

BLACKFIN

Overbuilt By Any Standard Except The Sea's

BLACKFIN 27 FISHERMAN

SPECIFICATIONS

Length	27'9"	Water	30 gals.
Beam	10'0"	Fuel	230 gals.
Draft, Inbd.	2'5"	Hull Type	Deep-V
Draft, O/B	2'10"	Deadrise Aft	24°
Weight, Inbd.	8,780#	Designer	C. Jannace
Weight, O/B	7,840#	Production	1985–91

A well-built boat with a wide beam and a seriously deep-V hull, the Blackfin 27 will handle the kind of rough-water conditions that other center consoles her size can only fantasize about. No lightweight, she's built on a solid fiberglass hull, and a full-length inner liner only adds to her strength. At heart, this is a practical and functional boat with a great profile, lots of deck space, and a minimum of gingerbread. There's room at the helm for two pedestal seats (or a wide leaning post), and bench seating is forward of the console. The cuddy cabin comes with adult-size V-berths, a sink, and marine toilet. Additional features include under-gunwale rod racks, bow pulpit, rod holders, and excellent storage. Most 27 Fishermen were sold with outboards, although a single 350-cid gas engine (about 15 knots cruise/25 top) or 200-hp Volvo diesel (20 knots cruise/24 top) were available as well. Popular 200-hp Yamahas will cruise at 25 knots and reach a top speed of around 35 knots. ❏

BLACKFIN 27 COMBI

SPECIFICATIONS

Length	27'8"	Fuel	230 gals.
Beam	10'0"	Cockpit	61 sq. ft.
Draft	2'5"	Hull Type	Deep-V
Weight	8,780#	Deadrise Aft	24°
Clearance	7'10"	Designer	C. Jannace
Water	30 gals.	Production	1985–92

L ike all Blackfin models, the 27 Combi is built on a solid fiber-glass, seriously deep-V hull with a sharp entry, reverse outer chines, and plenty of bow flare. An inner liner is used to add stiffness to the hull, and the cockpit contains some 60 sq. ft. of usable space. Raised engine boxes provide excellent access to the motors while doubling as convenient seats for watching the baits. Forward, the nicely appointed V-berth cuddy features a marine head, sink, and standing headroom. While the majority of 27 Combis have been powered with outboards, Blackfin offered an inboard version of this rugged dayboat for those who prefer the dependability and ease of maintenance of inboards and an unobstructed transom. Inboard 350-cid gas engines will cruise at 25 knots and reach around 34 knots top. (A pair of factory-rigged 200-hp Yamaha O/Bs will cruise easily at 25 knots.) A great rough-water boat, the 27 Combi's superb seakeeping characteristics have made her a desirable boat on the used market. Note that a dual console model was also available. ❏

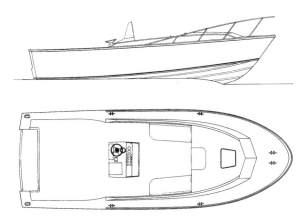

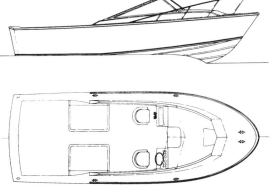

See Page 223 for Pricing Information

See Page 223 for Pricing Information

BLACKFIN 29 COMBI

SPECIFICATIONS

Length	29'4"	Water	30 gals.
Beam	10'6"	Fuel	250 gals.
Draft	2'5"	Cockpit	62 sq. ft.
Weight, Gas	10,025#	Hull Type	Deep-V
Weight, Dsl	12,120#	Deadrise Aft	22°
Clearance	7'5"	Production	1983–Current

A no-nonsense offshore fisherman in spite of her small size, the Blackfin 29 Combi is built on a solid fiberglass deep-V hull with moderate beam and plenty of flare at the bow. Her relatively wide beam and low center of gravity make her a surprisingly stable trolling platform. Below, the small cabin features a convertible dinette forward, together with a mini-galley and a stand-up head with shower—adequate accommodations for a couple of overnight anglers but certainly not designed with extended cruising in mind. The raised engine boxes in the cockpit provide easy access to the motors and also serve as a convenient seating area for watching the baits. Probably overbuilt by current production standards, the 29 Combi's ride is remarkably soft in a headsea and her downsea tracking ability is tops. Transom-mounted outboard rudders provide precise steering and reduced shaft angles. Standard 454-cid gas engines cruise the Blackfin 29 Combi at 25–26 knots, and optional 300-hp Cummins (or Cat) diesels cruise at an economical 28–29 knots. ❏

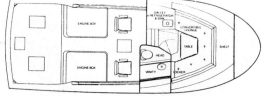

See Page 223 for Pricing Information

BLACKFIN 29 FLYBRIDGE SF

SPECIFICATIONS

Length	29'4"	Water	50 gals.
Beam	10'9"	Fuel	250 gals.
Draft	2'6"	Cockpit	56 sq. ft.
Weight, Gas	11,109#	Hull Type	Deep-V
Weight, Dsl	13,604#	Deadrise Aft	22°
Clearance	9'4"	Production	1986–Current

The Blackfin 29 Flybridge Sportfisherman is a great looking small convertible and one of the few under-30' boats of her type capable of running with the heavy hitters in offshore tournament events. She shares the same rugged deep-V hull as the 29 Combi with generous flare at the bow and outboard-mounted rudders. The Blackfin 29 is considered a superb small fisherman with a clean, unobstructed cockpit and an easy-to-reach flybridge. The fact that she has a stylish and comfortable interior only adds to her appeal. Finished with white mica countertops and cabinetry and trimmed in teak, the Blackfin 29's cabin accommodations allow her to serve as a practical weekend family cruiser. Raised engine boxes in the cockpit provide excellent access to the motors and a generator—or an extra 39 gallons of fuel, but not both—is optional. Standard 454-cid Crusader gas engines will cruise around 22–23 knots and turn a top speed of 32 knots. Optional 300-hp Cat 3116 diesels cruise at an economical 25–26 knots and reach about 29 knots wide open. ❏

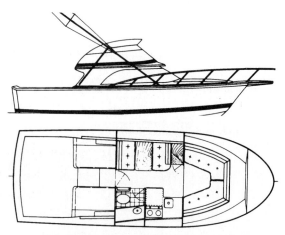

See Page 223 for Pricing Information

BLACKFIN 31 COMBI

SPECIFICATIONS

Length..........................30'8"	Water.......................70 gals.
Beam ....12'0"	Fuel........................300 gals.
Draft.............................2'11"	Cockpit ....75 sq. ft.
Weight, Gas............13,300#	Hull Type...............Deep-V
Weight, Dsl.............15,500#	Deadrise Aft...................23°
Clearance......................7'3"	Production...1993–Current

If the Blackfin 31 Combi has a different *look* than previous Combi models, it's because she's a remake of the earlier North Coast 31 (1988–90), a highly regarded deep-V fisherman from Massachusetts. (Interestingly, the North Coast hull was originally drawn by Charlie Jannace, the same designer who's been creating Blackfins for years.) In developing the 31 Combi, Blackfin engineers replaced the original strictly fishing North Coast floorplan with a new dinette layout which is more open and suitable for family cruising. Lounge seating has also been added opposite the helm. The result is a proven offshore fisherman with civilized (almost upscale) cruising accommodations—a rarity in a serious fishboat. Additional features of the 31 Combi include unusually wide sidedecks, hydraulically operated engine room hatches, a redesigned helm console, removable in-deck fish boxes, and transom door. An excellent sea boat with a notably sharp entry, standard 3116 Cats (340-hp) will cruise in the neighborhood of 27–28 knots. Optional 3208 Cats (412-hp) will cruise at 30 knots and reach 34 knots wide open. ❑

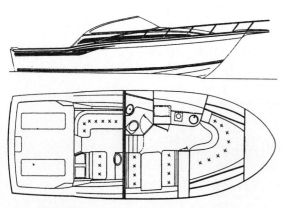

See Page 224 for Pricing Information

BLACKFIN 32 SPORTFISHERMAN

SPECIFICATIONS

Length..........................31'9"	Fuel........................304 gals.
Beam ....11'11"	Cockpit ....71 sq. ft.
Draft, Dsl.....................2'8"	Hull Type...............Deep-V
Weight....................17,800#	Deadrise Aft...................21°
Clearance......................NA	Designer ....C. Jannace
Water.......................60 gals.	Production.............1980–91

With her low and purposely aggressive profile, the Blackfin 32 SF has the unmistakable look of a serious bluewater tournament machine. Like all Blackfins, she was built on a solid fiberglass deep-V hull, and her wide beam adds stability not always found in deep-V boats this size. Not surprisingly, the good looks of the Blackfin 32 are backed up by solid construction, good open-water performance, and strong resale values. The cabin is attractively finished with off-white mica laminates trimmed in teak and offers comfortable—if basic—overnight accommodations for four. There's room in the cockpit for a full-size tuna chair. The raised (and dangerously heavy) engine boxes provide cockpit seating as well as good access to the motors. Standard 454-cid gas engines will cruise the Blackfin 32 around 18 knots and reach 27 knots top. Several diesel engine options were offered over the years. The popular 300-hp Cats will cruise about 23–24 knots, and the 375-hp versions cruise at 29 knots and reach around 33 knots wide open. ❑

See Page 224 for Pricing Information

34

BLACKFIN 32 COMBI

SPECIFICATIONS

Length...........................31'9"	Fuel..........................304 gals.
Beam ....11'11"	Cockpit ....80 sq. ft.
Draft................................2'8"	Hull Type...............Deep-V
Weight, Gas............15,081#	Deadrise Aft....................21°
Weight, Dsl.............17,788#	Designer ....C. Jannace
Water.......................50 gals.	Production.............1988–92

The Blackfin marketing people once dubbed the 32 Combi the "944 Turbo of sportfishing boats"—a fair description for what many anglers regard as one of the premium day boats in the market. She was built using the already proven deep-V hull of the Blackfin 32 Sportfisherman with plenty of flare at the bow and a sharp 21° of transom deadrise. Like other Combi models, the 32 is a beamy, low profile day boat that almost begs for a tower. Blackfins aren't inexpensive, and they're clearly aimed at the upscale end of the market. While the 32 Combi is designed for fishing, her accommodations below are surprisingly plush. Indeed, with berths for four inside and lounge seating opposite the helm on the bridgedeck, she can easily double as a weekend cruiser. A transom door was standard, and the cockpit can easily handle a full-size chair. Standard 454-cid Crusader gas engines will cruise the 32 Combi at 24 knots (31+ top), and the optional 300-hp Cat 3116 diesels will cruise economically at around 26 knots and reach 29–30 knots wide open. ❑

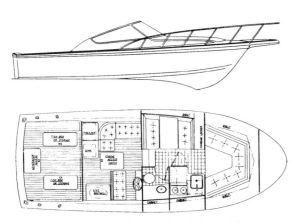

See Page 224 for Pricing Information

BLACKFIN 33 SPORTFISHERMAN

SPECIFICATIONS

Length..........................32'6"	Fuel.......................225 gals.
Beam ....9'9"	Cockpit ....NA
Draft................................2'8"	Hull Type...............Deep-V
Weight....................10,470#	Deadrise Aft..................24°
Clearance....................10'8"	Designer.............John Bird
Water.......................30 gals.	Production.............1978–84

When Blackfin acquired the assets of Cary Marine back in the 1970s, included in the package was this 32'6" hull originally designed as an offshore racer. Long and slender with a drooped nose and low freeboard, Blackfin engineers took this hull, modified it for a sportfishing application, and introduced her in 1978 as the Blackfin 32 (later changed to 33) Sportfisherman. At the time, one writer referred to her as the Rolls Royce of open fishing boats. Serious anglers were impressed with the fishability of the Blackfin 33's large and unobstructed cockpit, and she soon became recognized as a rugged, hard-core sportfishing boat. She also has a reputation for truly awesome performance in nasty seas. Definitely a no-frills ride, the cuddy cabin consists only of two 7' berths and a marine toilet. Used Blackfin 33s are found today with a wide range of power, including outboards. The standard 454-cid gas engines cruise at a fast 26–27 knots and run at 36+ wide open. The optional 210-hp Cat diesels will cruise at 21–22 knots and reach 26 knots top. ❑

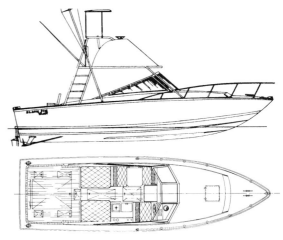

See Page 224 for Pricing Information

35

BLACKFIN 33 FLYBRIDGE

SPECIFICATIONS

Length	32'11"	Fuel	340 gals.
Beam	12'0"	Cockpit	75 sq. ft.
Draft	2'11"	Hull Type	Deep-V
Weight	20,169#	Deadrise Aft	21°
Clearance	10'0"	Designer	Blackfin
Water	80 gals.	Production	1990–Current

Replacing the classic Blackfin 32 in 1990, the 33 Flybridge is a better-handling boat in just about every respect. Blackfin doesn't use coring in their hulls, so there's nothing high-tech here in the way of construction. Indeed, the 33 is a straightforward deep-V design with a relatively wide beam. Anyone who ever fished a 32 will appreciate the 33's enlarged cockpit and standard transom door. Engine boxes are retained in the new 33, and access to the motors is excellent. Interior space has been dramatically increased, thanks to the additional beam. The white cabinetry and teak trim are appealing, and the separate stall shower is a pleasant surprise. In 1993, a floorplan option has the dinette forward and an L-lounge in the cabin. The flybridge is large for a 33-footer with bench seating forward of the helm and a large console for flush-mounting electronics. Standard 454-cid gas engines will cruise around 24 knots. Optional 320-hp or 375-hp Cats cruise at a fast 25 and 28 knots respectively and reach 30+ wide open. ❏

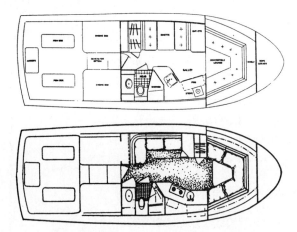

See Page 224 for Pricing Information

BLACKFIN 33 COMBI

SPECIFICATIONS

Length	32'11"	Water	80 gals.
Beam	12'0"	Fuel	340 gals.
Draft	2'11"	Cockpit	75 sq. ft.
Weight, Gas	16,428#	Hull Type	Deep-V
Weight, Dsl	19,132#	Deadrise Aft	22°
Clearance	8'6"	Production	1994–Current

A good-looking boat with an upscale price tag to go with her strictly business appearance, the 33 Combi is about as good as it gets in a mid-size express fisherman. Like all Blackfins, she's built on a solid fiberglass deep-V hull (borrowed from the 33 FB) with considerably more transom deadrise than other production boats. Her profile is low, the beam is wide, and the ride is superb. Inside, the lush well-appointed interior will come as a surprise to those expecting the plain-Jane cabin accommodations common to most thoroughbred fishing machines. Indeed, the light ash woodwork, off-white cabinetry, Avonite countertops and halogen lighting present a warm and completely inviting appearance. The Combi's bi-level cockpit is ideally arranged with lounge seating opposite the helm and a big fishing platform aft. The helm and companion seats can be raised hydraulically for access to the engines, and the sidedecks are notably wide and well-secured. The finish work is excellent. Optional 425-hp Cats will cruise at a fast 28 knots and reach 33 knots wide open. ❏

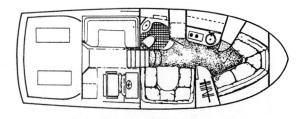

See Page 224 for Pricing Information

BLACKFIN 38 COMBI

SPECIFICATIONS

Length..........................38'3"	Fuel........................514 gals.
Beam ....14'5"	Cockpit ....122 sq. ft.
Draft...............................3'9"	Hull Type.............Deep-V
Weight...................34,170#	Deadrise Aft..................18°
Clearance......................9'6"	Designer ....C. Jannace
Water....................135 gals.	Production...1989–Current

The 38 Combi is a hard-core express fisherman with the rugged good looks and built-in fishability one expects of a Blackfin product. She's actually a stretched version of the earlier Blackfin 36 Combi (1987–88) the difference being the larger cockpit of the 38 model. The Combi makes a great first impression on those who enjoy the open helm and bi-level cockpit layout of an express-type fishing boat. There's a full 120 sq. ft. of fishing platform on the lower level and L-shaped passenger seating opposite the helm on the raised deck. While the 38 may have less living space below than other day boats her size, the cabin nonetheless manages to include the necessities. First offered with a queen berth forward, a dinette floorplan with V-berths became standard in 1991, and in 1993 an optional layout with a U-shaped dinette became available. Optional 485-hp 6-71s will cruise at 27 knots (30 top) and 550-hp 6V92s cruise around 29–30 knots and reach 33 knots wide open. ❏

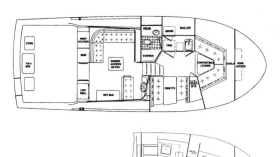

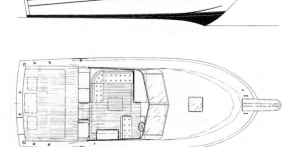

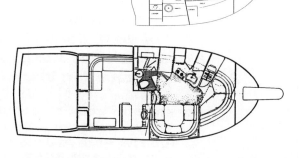

See Page 224 for Pricing Information

BLACKFIN 38 CONVERTIBLE

BOSTON WHALER 31L

SPECIFICATIONS

Length	38'3"	Fuel	514 gals.
Beam	14'5"	Cockpit	122 sq. ft.
Draft	4'0"	Hull Type	Deep-V
Weight	35,970#	Deadrise Aft	18°
Clearance	13'0"	Designer	C. Jannace
Water	135 gals.	Production	1989–Current

The 38 Convertible pictured above is actually a stretched version of the earlier Blackfin 36 Convertible (1987–88), a heavy deep-V fisherman with a solid fiberglass hull and a reputation for exceptional all-weather performance. A better sea boat than the 36, the extra length went into the cockpit dimensions—a big improvement. A sportfisherman at heart, her upscale cabin accommodations allow the 38 to easily double as a weekend cruiser. The original two-stateroom, galley-up layout was replaced in 1990 with a new mid-level galley floorplan offering a choice of either a dinette or second stateroom. Where the early interiors were finished with teak, recent models use light oak woodwork. A good performer, twin 425-hp Cats will cruise the Blackfin 38 Convertible around 23 knots and reach 26 knots top. The 485-hp 6-71 diesels will deliver a cruising speed of about 28 knots and 31+ knots at full throttle, and the 550-hp 6V92s will produce an honest 28-knot cruise and a top speed of around 31–32 knots. ❏

SPECIFICATIONS

Length	31'9"	Fuel	313 gals.
Beam	11'10"	Cockpit	74 sq. ft.
Draft	2'8"	Hull Type	Deep-V
Weight	12,500#	Deadrise Aft	20°
Clearance	7'6"	Designer	Whaler
Water	40 gals.	Production	1988–92

The fact that you can't sink the Boston Whaler 31 will appeal to safety-conscious anglers who can afford to own this well-built inboard sportfisherman. Constructed on a rugged deep-V hull, a layer of urethane foam bonds the inner liner to the outer hull acting as a stiffener and providing enough flotation to keep the 31 afloat even when fully swamped! This is a proven offshore design with good trolling stability and better-than-average performance in rough water. Introduced in 1988, she was redesigned in 1991 with a new deckhouse profile, relocated engines, and fresh interior and cockpit layouts. (The private stateroom in early models was a rarity in a fishing boat this size.) The revised bi-level cockpit features an in-deck fish box, bait-prep center, lockable rod storage, and a fold-down jumpseat. The hinged bridgedeck tilts up for excellent engine access. Most early 31s were powered with 250-hp Cummins diesels (23 knots cruise/27 top). Later models with 300-hp Cummins cruise at 25 knots and deliver around 29 knots top. ❏

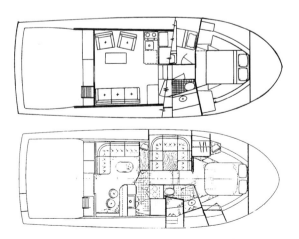

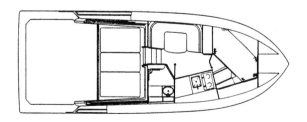

See Page 224 for Pricing Information

See Page 224 for Pricing Information

CABO 35 Express

Although this edition is the first to include the CABO 35 Express, as this book goes to print over 20 of these high performance and extraordinarily well-engineered Sportfishers have been delivered. The CABO 35 Express has become the choice of hot anglers and seasoned cruisers from Nantucket sound to the Gulf of Mexico. One reason for their choice is the excellent reputation earned by the highly regarded CABO 35 Flybridge. Another is the fact that few builders in this country, or any other for that matter, have the level of quality the guys at Cat Harbor build into the CABO 35. But then, few builders have been able to assemble the team of designers, engineers and craftsmen that have made the CABO what it is today. Cat Harbor founders Henry Mohrschladt and Michael Howarth have formed a team that have literally made the CABO 35 the new standard of quality for mid-sized sportfishing boats.

For over 25 years Mohrschladt and Howarth have been building boats hailed as America's best. Even the most critical eye will appreciate the care taken to carefully align screw heads in deck fittings and in the stainless strip on the rugged molded rub rail. Such attention to detail is rare, even among the best custom builders. All of the hardware is extra heavy and highly polished. The transom door hinges are massive and beautiful, allowing the flawless one-piece door to open outboard, for clear access to two large insulated fish boxes built into the deck. The cockpit features a built-in sink and bait prep area, as well as an insulated chest. Tackle and rod storage are abundant and exceptionally well thought out. All of this and still over 120 sq. ft. left to fish. There is so much to say and to appreciate about this boat that every time you look at it, you notice something even more outstanding.

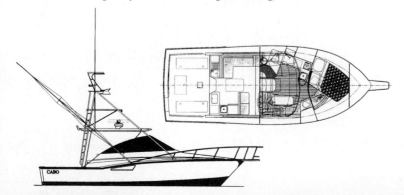

For a complete brochure package including unedited reprints of six Cabo 35 boat tests, write, call or fax:

CABO™ Sportfishers
by **Cat Harbor Boats, Inc.**
9780 Rancho Road
Adelanto, Ca. 92301
Fax. (619) 246-8970
Tel. (619) 246-8917

CABO 35 FLYBRIDGE SF

SPECIFICATIONS

LOA w/Pulpit	37'6"	Water	80 gals.
Hull Length	34'6"	Fuel	420 gals.
Beam	13'0"	Cockpit	130 sq. ft.
Draft	2'6"	Hull Type	Deep-V
Weight	21,000#	Deadrise Aft	17°
Clearance	11'3"	Production	1992–Current

A good-looking boat with a low-slung appearance and a huge cockpit, the Cabo 35 is a rugged West Coast fisherman with a growing following among anglers nationwide. She's constructed on a deep-V hull with a relatively wide beam and Airex coring above the waterline. Her low profile is the result of placing the motors in cockpit engine boxes, thus allowing the salon sole to be set low in the hull. Considering her oversized cockpit, the Cabo's interior is surprisingly spacious. The galley-up layout includes an 8' settee with hidden rod storage in the salon and an island berth in the stateroom, while the galley-down floorplan has a stall shower in the head. (There's a large storage area beneath the salon sole.) Additional features include two in-deck fish boxes, transom door and gate, good cabin headroom, single-lever helm controls, and wide sidedecks with sturdy rails. A good performer, optional 375-hp Cats will cruise the Cabo 35 efficiently at 27 knots and reach around 32 knots top. Note the generous 420-gallon fuel capacity. ❏

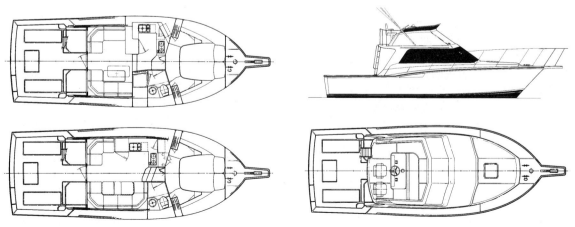

See Page 224 for Pricing Information

CABO 35 EXPRESS SF

SPECIFICATIONS

LOA w/ Pulpit	37'6"	Water	188 gals.
Hull Length	34'6"	Fuel	400 gals.
Beam	13'0'	Cockpit	130 sq. ft.
Draft	2'6"	Hull Type	Deep-V
Weight	18,000#	Deadrise Aft	17.5°
Clearance	11'3"	Production	1993–Current

Using the hull of the highly regarded Cabo 35 Flybridge, the Cabo 35 Express is a rugged offshore fisherman with the kind of family-style interior accommodations that most dedicated fish-boats lack. She's constructed on a deep-V hull with a relatively wide beam and Airex coring above the waterline. The Cabo's cockpit is big for a 35-footer and comes standard with a bait prep center, tackle drawers, two in-deck fish boxes, cockpit coaming and washdowns. An L-shaped setee is opposite the helm, and the entire bridgedeck lifts hydraulically for exellent access to the motors. Several floorplan configurations are offered, including a two-stateroom arrangement with V-berths forward. There's a shower stall in the head, and the Corian countertops, teak joinerwork, and upscale appliances combine to present an attractive interior decor. Indeed, the reason the Cabo 35 stands out among most other express boats her size is quality—this is an extremely well-crafted boat inside and out. A good performer, optional 375-hp Cats will cruise at 29 knots and reach around 33 knots top. ❑

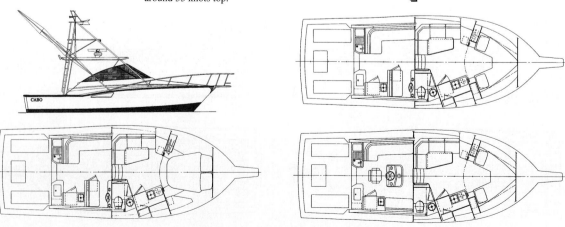

See Page 224 for Pricing Information

CALIFORNIAN 48 CONVERTIBLE

SPECIFICATIONS

Length	48'5"	Fuel	760 gals.
Beam	15'2"	Cockpit	NA
Draft	4'8"	Hull Type	Modified-V
Weight	40,000#	Deadrise Aft	NA
Clearance	14'1"	Designer	B. Collier
Water	210 gals.	Production	1986–89

Built on the standard hull used for the entire Californian line in the late 80s, the 48 was the largest convertible model the company ever built. The contemporary styling is accented by a glassed-over deckhouse windshield. Her attractive three-stateroom interior is visually impressive and finished throughout with well-crafted teak paneling (walnut in pre-1988 models). The salon dimensions are on the narrow side due to the wide sidedecks and relatively narrow beam of the 48's hull. Unlike a lot of other floorplans in convertibles this size, the Californian 48 has the master stateroom located amidships rather than forward in the bow—certainly a more comfortable place to sleep underway. Standard features included separate stall showers in both heads, a molded pulpit, transom door, and tackle center in the cockpit. Among several engine options, 550-hp 6V92s will cruise at 21 knots with a top speed of around 24 knots. The 650-hp 8V92s improve those speeds to 24 knots cruise and 27 knots top. Never a big seller, the 48 Convertible was withdrawn from production in 1989. ❏

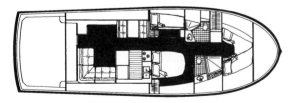

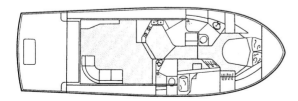

See Page 224 for Pricing Information

CHASE 38 SPORTFISHERMAN

SPECIFICATIONS

Length	38'0"	Fuel	500 gals.
Beam	13'9"	Cockpit	108 sq. ft.
Draft	4'9"	Hull Type	Deep V
Weight	28,000#	Deadrise Aft	18°
Clearance	NA	Designer	Hunt & Assoc.
Water	130 gals.	Production	1988–92

A distinctive boat, the Chase 38 is an upscale express fisherman with a very unusual layout. She was built in Costa Rica on a fully cored deep-V hull, and at 28,000 lbs the Chase is no lightweight. Stepping below from the elevated bridgedeck, one is immediately confronted with an abundance of varnished teak woodwork and brass accessories more common to a sailboat than a serious sportfishing boat. (Too much teak in the eyes of a lot of anglers who'd rather invest in more practical fishing features.) The interior isn't notably spacious but includes a stall shower in the head and an island berth forward. Topsides, the huge bridgedeck features wraparound seating for a crowd—a superb entertaining platform several steps above the cockpit with a walk-thru to the foredeck. Access to the large engine room is from the cockpit. Cat diesels were standard, and GM 6-71s and 6V92s were optional. Cat 375-hp diesels will cruise a loaded Chase 38 around 23 knots, while the larger 550-hp 6V92s will cruise about 28 knots. ❏

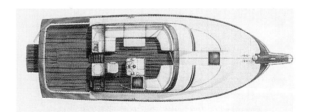

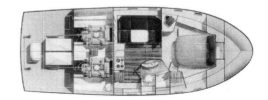

See Page 225 for Pricing Information

CHEOY LEE 48 SPORT YACHT

SPECIFICATIONS

Length	48'0"	Fuel	1,000 gals.
Beam	15'0"	Cockpit	140 sq. ft.
Draft	4'0"	Hull Type	Modified-V
Weight	37,000#	Designer	Tom Fexas
Clearance	16'6"	Production	1980–1986
Water	200 gals.		

The 48 Sport Yacht was the first modern sportfishing boat ever offered by the Cheoy Lee yard. She's built on a lightweight fully cored hull with a relatively flat bottom and moderate beam. Big and dramatic with a flat black mask running around the deckhouse and a rakish flybridge, her long foredeck gives the 48 Sport Yacht a dramatic appearance. Conceived as a competent sportfisherman with elegant interior comforts, the European decor (painted walls) found in early models was quickly replaced with a more traditional teak interior. The innovative two-stateroom floorplan of the 48 Sport Yacht has the galley aft in the salon, and a unique curved corridor leads from the salon to the master stateroom. The cockpit, with a full 140 sq. ft. of space, is huge, but the raised deck along the salon bulkhead restricts the installation of a full-size tackle center. A good performer with 8V92 diesels, the Cheoy Lee 48 Sport Yacht will cruise around 27 knots and reach a top speed of 30+ knots. Definitely not for everyone. ❏

See Page 225 for Pricing Information

CHEOY LEE 50 SPORT YACHT

SPECIFICATIONS

Length	50'8"	Fuel	1,000 gals.
Beam	16'1"	Cockpit	115 sq. ft.
Draft	3'2"	Hull Type	Modified-V
Weight	36,000#	Designer	Tom Fexas
Clearance	14'0"	Production	1987–Current
Water	200 gals.		

Introduced in 1987 as a replacement for the 48 Sport Yacht, the Cheoy Lee 50 features greater beam, a third stateroom, and more conservative styling than her predecessor. Airex coring is used extensively in the construction of the hull, deck, and superstructure, resulting in a strong lightweight fisherman with a very good turn of speed. At only 36,000 lbs.—very light indeed—the 50 Sport Yacht has the displacement of a much smaller boat. Her three-stateroom floorplan is efficiently arranged with the U-shaped galley forward and separated from the salon by a serving counter. A walkaround double berth is fitted in the master stateroom, and both heads are equipped with separate stall showers. Outside, the sidedecks are wide, and the uncluttered cockpit is designed for serious fishing activities. The tournament-style flybridge is large for a 50-foot convertible and features a built-in table and seating for eight. With standard 720-hp 8V92 diesels, the Cheoy Lee 50 Sport Yacht cruises at 25–26 knots and reaches a top speed of around 28 knots. ❏

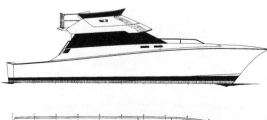

See Page 225 for Pricing Information

CHEOY LEE 58 SPORT YACHT

SPECIFICATIONS

Length............................58'5"	Fuel......................1,000 gals.
Beam ....17'10"	Cockpit................138 sq. ft.
Draft................................4'3"	Hull Type........Modified-V
Weight......................58,500#	Designer............Tom Fexas
Clearance...................15'10"	Production...1986–Current
Water.....................150 gals.	

Distinctively styled and featuring a unique underwater profile, the Cheoy Lee 58 Sport Yacht is certainly one of the more dramatic boats to be found among the ranks of big offshore production sportfishermen. This yacht is meant to go fast—construction is high-tech with lightweight Airex and Divinycell coring and unidirectional laminates throughout. The wide open cockpit includes direct engine room access, molded tackle centers, flush fish boxes and built-in storage. The flybridge is huge with the helm console set well aft and circular guest seating forward. Inside, the innovative salon of the Cheoy Lee 58 is arranged with two facing sectional sofas forward and the dinette and galley aft—a practical arrangement that eliminates a good deal of traffic through the boat. There are three staterooms on the lower level, two with walkaround double berths. The interior is completely paneled and finished with varnished teak or ash woodwork. A fast boat with standard 870-hp 12V71 diesels, the 58 Sport Yacht will cruise fully loaded at 28 knots and reach a top speed of 30–31 knots. ❑

See Page 225 for Pricing Information

CHEOY LEE 66 SPORT YACHT

SPECIFICATIONS

Length.........................66'0"	Fuel......................1670 gals.
Beam ....19'0"	Cockpit................176 sq. ft.
Draft................................4'6"	Hull Type........Modified-V
Weight......................65,000#	Designer............Tom Fexas
Clearance...................19'10"	Production.........1984–1987
Water.....................370 gals.	

The Cheoy Lee 66 Sport Yacht is more than a little different from most other production yachts of her size. Dramatic in appearance, her high-tech construction and extensive coring materials have resulted in a lightweight hull with excellent performance. The Sport Yacht's unusual four-stateroom floorplan includes full crew quarters forward and features an opulent master stateroom *beneath* the salon an arrangement made possible by placing the motors well aft in the hull (and increasing the shaft angles to the max). That the salon isn't especially roomy is due primarily to the very wide side-decks. Outside, an aft deck overlooks the cockpit, giving the 66 a distinct "yachtfish" profile. Additional features include cockpit access to the (small) engine room, foredeck lounge, and a full teak interior. The cockpit can easily handle a tuna chair, and a tackle center with cockpit controls was standard. A good performer with standard 870-hp 12V71 diesels, the Cheoy Lee 66 Sport Yacht will cruise at 20–21 knots and reach a top speed of 24 knots. ❑

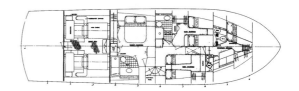

See Page 225 for Pricing Information

45

CHRIS CRAFT 30 TOURNAMENT SF

SPECIFICATIONS

Length.........................30'2"	Fuel.......................184 gals.
Beam ....11'11"	Cockpit................120 sq. ft.
Draft..............................2'6"	Hull Type..............Deep-V
Weight...................13,500#	Designer.........Hunt Assoc.
Clearance....................11'8"	Production.............1975–77
Water.......................45 gals.	

Sporting a handsome profile and a notably wide beam, the Chris 30 Tournament Fisherman has the distinction of being the only Chris Craft ever built on a deep-V, Hunt-designed offshore hull. With a steep 21° of deadrise at the transom and six lifting strakes, this boat is clearly built to run in rough weather. Hull construction is solid fiberglass, and the engines rest on inverted aluminum mounts —a very heavy-duty installation. Inside, the wide beam provides for a roomy cabin with berths for four and a stand-up head. A privacy curtain separates the V-berths from the salon, and the woodwork is teak. Hinged engine boxes are forward in the cockpit, and with a full 120 sq. ft. of space, the cockpit is exceptionally large and easily fished. The flybridge is big, and the backrest on the aft bench seat folds down so the helmsman can get a view of the cockpit. Twin 250-hp gas engines will cruise the Chris 30 Tournament SF at 18 knots and reach a top speed of 25–26 knots.   ❏

CHRIS CRAFT 315 SPORT SEDAN

SPECIFICATIONS

Length........................30'10"	Fuel.......................250 gals.
Beam ....11'10"	Cockpit..........................NA
Draft..............................2'4"	Hull Type........Modified-V
Weight...................11,400#	Deadrise Aft.....................5°
Clearance......................9'6"	Designer...........Chris Craft
Water.......................40 gals.	Production.............1983–90

The 315 Sport Sedan is a handsome flybridge fisherman with a big cockpit and basic cabin accommodations. She was built on the same flat-bottom hull used to build the 310 Catalina. To say that she's a hard ride in a chop is charitable; she'll knock your fillings out in a headsea. Her interior is rather cheery for a sportfishing boat with berths for four persons and room to store most of the things that cruising families will need for a few days away from home. Note that in 1988 Chris Craft designers replaced the engine boxes and flush cockpit sole with a raised bridgedeck arrangement—a definite improvement. The floorplan was redesigned at the same time by moving the head aft. Standard features included teak covering boards in the cockpit, a spacious flybridge with bench seating in front of the helm console and wide sidedecks for secure foredeck access. With the optional 330-hp gas engines, the 315 Sport Sedan will cruise around 22–23 knots and reach a top speed of 30+.   ❏

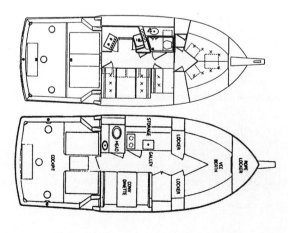

See Page 225 for Pricing Information

See Page 225 for Pricing Information

CHRIS CRAFT 360 SPORT SEDAN

1973–84

1985–86

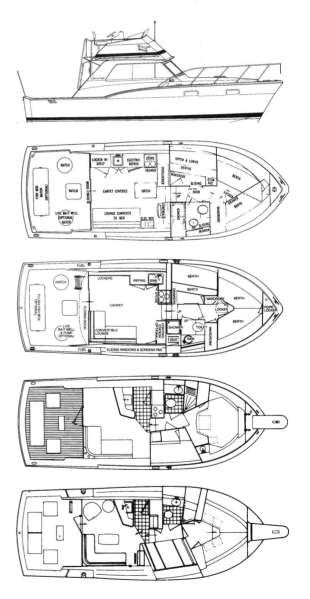

SPECIFICATIONS

Length	36'0"	Fuel	300/400 gals.
Beam	13'0"	Cockpit	NA
Draft	3'2"	Hull Type	Modified-V
Weight	22,600#	Designer	Chris Craft
Clearance	11'11"	Production	1973–86
Water	75/100 gals.		

A long-time favorite with fishermen and family cruisers alike, the Chris 360 Sport Sedan enjoyed an unusually long production run (for a Chris Craft), and they remain reasonably popular today on the used markets. Introduced in 1973 as a Tournament (she became the 360 Commander in 1981), she had a practical two-stateroom, galley-up interior until 1984 when a single-stateroom floorplan with a dinette became standard. Construction is solid fiberglass, and her low deadrise hull can be a harsh ride when the seas pick up. The profile of the original 360 Commander (pictured above) remained the same until 1985, when the deckhouse and flybridge were dramatically restyled. An increase in fuel capacity (to 400 gallons) in 1983 improved the range considerably. Standard 454-cid gas engines will cruise at about 18 knots with a top speed of 27–28 knots. Among numerous diesel options, the 300-hp Cat (or 320-hp Cummins) diesels bring the cruising speed up to approximately 23 knots and the top speed to 26–27 knots. ❏

See Page 225 for Pricing Information

CHRIS CRAFT 382/392 COMMANDER

1985

1986–90

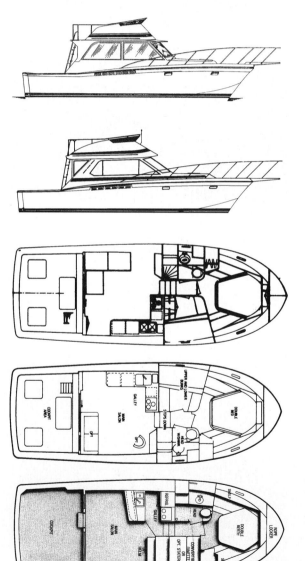

SPECIFICATIONS

Length	38'0"	Water	100 gals.
Length WL	33'0"	Fuel	350 gals.
Beam	13'11"	Cockpit	92 sq. ft.
Draft	3'9"	Hull Type	Modified-V
Weight	28,000#	Designer	Uniflite
Clearance	12'0"	Production	1985–90

The Chris 392 Commander Sport Sedan is actually the old Uniflite 38 Convertible dressed up in a modern package. Chris Craft first marketed this boat in 1985 as the 382 Commander Sport Sedan—basically the late Uniflite 38 with a new name. The following year (1986) Chris Craft redesigned the deckhouse and flybridge resulting in a much-improved profile. Several two-stateroom floorplans were offered during her production run, and in 1990 (the final year) a single-stateroom floorplan with a mid-level galley and oak paneling became standard. While the Chris 392 is light-years ahead of the old Uniflite in appearance and decor, the well-known seakeeping properties of the original hull have been retained. The cockpit is large enough for a fighting chair; sidedecks are wide; and the bridge is arranged with bench seating forward of the helm. Standard 454-cid gas engines will cruise at 17–18 knots and reach 27 knots at full throttle. Optional 375-hp Cats will cruise at 24 knots and turn a top speed of 28 knots. ❑

See Page 225 for Pricing Information

48

CHRIS CRAFT 422 SPORT SEDAN

1974–84

1985–90

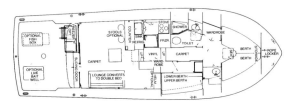

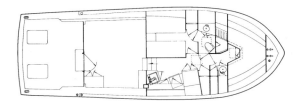

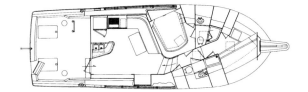

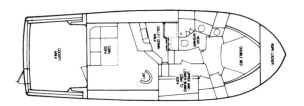

SPECIFICATIONS

Length	42'4"	Fuel	400/525 gals.
Beam	14'0"	Cockpit	110 sq. ft.
Draft	3'11"	Hull Type	Modified-V
Weight	33,000#	Designer	Chris Craft
Clearance	13'7"	Production	1974–90
Water	125 gals.		

The Chris 422 Commander enjoyed the longest production run of any modern Chris Craft model. She was introduced as the 42 Tournament Fisherman in 1974, and critics were impressed with her comfortably dry ride and 24-knot cruising speed with then-new 8V71TIs. She was built on a shallow deadrise hull with a wide beam and a big fishing cockpit to go with her roomy two-stateroom interior. The 421 models (1983–84) are remembered for their gaudy hull graphics and cheap interiors. Chris Craft engineers thoroughly redesigned the boat in 1985 (new house, enlarged flybridge, glassed-over windshield, teak interior, etc.) with the introduction on the final 422 model. Throughout all the model changes the basic two-stateroom layout has been retained in one fashion or another. Retained too were the excellent seakeeping qualities that made her such a good performer. With either the original 8V71s or the later 485-hp 6-71s, the Chris 42 is a reasonably fast boat for her size with a cruising speed of 24 knots and a top speed of 27 knots. ❏

See Page 225 for Pricing Information

CHRIS CRAFT 45 COMMANDER SF

SPECIFICATIONS

Length	45'6"	Fuel	600 gals.
Beam	16'0"	Cockpit	NA
Draft	3'11"	Hull Type	Modified-V
Weight	38,700#	Designer	Chris Craft
Clearance	13'7"	Production	1972–81
Water	150 gals.		

Although the Chris 45 Commander Sportfisherman was in production for nearly a decade, she never achieved the widespread popularity among hard-core anglers of the Hatteras 45 and 46 convertibles or the Bertram 46. The 45 Commander went into production in 1972 on a heavy, broad-beamed hull with a sharp entry and a nearly flat bottom at the transom. A conventional two-stateroom, galley-down interior was standard and a three-stateroom layout was also available (one of the first three-stateroom arrangements ever offered in a production boat of this size). Notable features include overhead rod storage in the salon, a big tournament-style flybridge, and good storage throughout. The large and well-organized cockpit includes two fish boxes, a livewell on the centerline, and a wide transom door. After playing around with the idea of gas turbines in early production models, a variety of optional diesel engines were offered over the years. Among them, the popular 425-hp GM 8V71s will cruise the Chris 45 Commander SF at a respectable 20 knots and reach 23 knots wide open. ❏

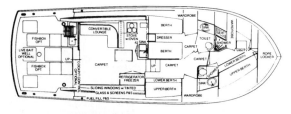

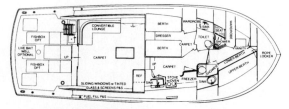

See Page 225 for Pricing Information

CHRIS CRAFT 482 CONVERTIBLE

SPECIFICATIONS

Length	48'10"	Fuel	780 gals.
Beam	15'9"	Cockpit	133 sq. ft.
Draft	4'9"	Hull Type	Modified-V
Weight	48,000#	Deadrise Aft	14°
Clearance	13'9"	Designer	A. Nordtvedt
Water	200 gals.	Production	1985–1988

Originally introduced in 1980 as the Uniflite 48 Convertible, the Chris 482 Commander was built on a rugged modified-V hull with moderate transom deadrise and balsa coring in the hullsides. Her long foredeck and huge cockpit mark her as a tournament-style fisherman although the luxurious interior of the 48 Commander is certainly one of her more desirable features. Various floorplans were offered when she was built by Uniflite, but Chris Craft settled on the popular three-stateroom arrangement with a queen berth in the starboard master stateroom. Rich teak paneling and a modern decor highlight the spacious salon. Chris Craft offered an optional glassed-in front windshield in later models in keeping with current design trends. With good offshore performance and 780 gallons of fuel, the Chris Craft 482 is a heavyweight tournament contender. With standard 8V92 diesels (600-hp), she can cruise at a steady 25 knots and reach a top speed of about 28 knots. Note that the Chris Craft 502 Convertible (1989 only) was built on a stretched 482 hull. ❏

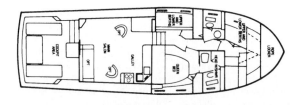

See Page 225 for Pricing Information

CONTENDER 35

SPECIFICATIONS

Length	35'0'	Fuel	250 gals.
Beam	10'0"	Cockpit	NA
Draft	2'0"	Hull Type	Deep-V
Weight w/o power	5,200#	Deadrise Aft	24°
Clearance	NA	Designer	J. Nebber
Water	45 gals.	Production	1989–Current

The Contender 35 is a high performance tournament-class fishing boat designed for serious offshore anglers. She's built on a narrow deep-V hull with balsa coring from the waterline up and a unique integral swim platform extension. A good-looking boat, the Contender is available with three separate cockpit configurations, however the aft-console/L-shaped settee layout (pictured above) is said to be the most popular. (Twin helm consoles can also be fitted aft, or the helm can be aft and midships.) Inside fold-up bunks provide berths for four with a stand-up head, high-low table and small galley. Notable features include good access to the engines on inboard models (the whole center section of the deck raises hydraulically), a well-arranged helm console with tilt wheel, livewell, removable fish boxes, and rod storage below. Available with inboard or outboard power (most late models have had the outboards), twin 250-hp Yamahas will deliver a top speed of 42+ knots while the 250-hp Cummins inboard diesels will cruise at a fast 32 knots (about 36 knots top). ❏

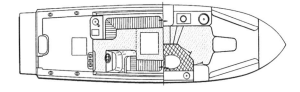

CRUISERS 3210 SEA DEVIL

SPECIFICATIONS

Length	30'10"	Water	45 gals.
Beam	10'10"	Fuel	250 gals.
Draft	2'10"	Hull Type	Modified-V
Weight	9,500#	Designer	Jim Wynne
Clearance	7'0"	Production	1988–90

The 3210 Sea Devil isn't noted for her long production run; she was dropped from the line after just three years. Construction was solid fiberglass and she was built on the same 31-foot hull used in the production of the 3260 Esprit— a deep-V with moderate beam and prop pockets at the transom. The Sea Devil is a stylish design for anglers who like their boats with a little sex appeal. The cockpit is fitted with rod holders, built-in livewells, and a big fish box, and the transom door and integral swim platform are big pluses. Visibility from the raised helm console is excellent, and the instrument panel is very well arranged. The interior layout is nearly identical to that in the 3260 Esprit—very upscale and ideal for family cruising with berths for four. A good-running boat with standard 260-hp gas engines, she'll cruise easily at 19–20 knots and reach a top speed of about 30 knots. The Sea Devil is admittedly no tournament monster, but she certainly is easy on the eye. ❏

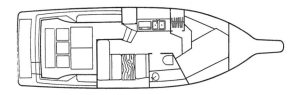

See Page 226 for Pricing Information

See Page 226 for Pricing Information

DAVIS 44 SPORTFISHERMAN

SPECIFICATIONS

Length ....44'5"	Fuel........................650 gals.
Beam ....15'3"	Cockpit................100 sq. ft.
Draft..............................4'0"	Hull Type........Modified-V
Weight ....35,000#	Deadrise Aft.................NA
Clearance.......................NA	Designer ....Davis
Water.....................135 gals.	Production.............1991–93

Designed as an affordable alternative to the Davis 47, the 44 Sportfisherman displays the same incredibly well-proportioned profile of larger Davis models along with the smooth ride and proven offshore performance expected in a design from this highly regarded North Carolina builder. Her modified-V hull is constructed on a solid fiberglass bottom with cored hullsides, a fine entry, and greatly flared bow sections—the so-called "Carolina Flare." Several floorplans were offered, and each of the four 44s delivered had at least a few custom interior features. Not surprisingly, the cockpit is set up for tournament-level fishing activities, with plenty of workspace, direct engine room access, a huge in-deck fish box, and modular tackle centers. Note the extended flybridge overhang in the cockpit. Topside, the varnished teak helm console features Panish controls and a pop-up instrument pod. Standard engines in the Davis 44 SF were 485-hp 6-71s which cruise at 23 knots and reach 26–27 knots wide open. Optional 550-hp 6V92s cruise at 26 knots and deliver 30 knots wide open. ❏

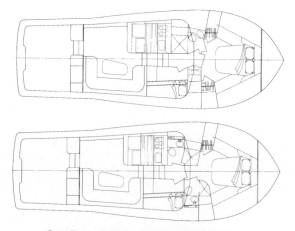

See Page 226 for Pricing Information

DAVIS 44 EXPRESS SF

SPECIFICATIONS

Length ....44'5"	Fuel........................500 gals.
Beam ....15'3"	Cockpit................100 sq. ft.
Draft..............................4'0"	Hull Type........Modified-V
Weight ....35,000#	Deadrise Aft.................NA
Clearance.......................NA	Designer ....Davis
Water.....................135 gals.	Production.............1992–93

A good-looking boat, the Davis 44 Express is an upscale fisherman with the look and feel of a custom-made boat. A total of four were built on an easy-riding modified-V hull with a greatly flared bow and moderate deadrise at the transom. The spacious cockpit (three steps below the bridgedeck level) is designed with low-freeboard gunwales and features a complete set of molded tackle centers, livewell, in-deck fish boxes, an offset transom door, and direct access to the large engine room. The helm is located on the centerline, and the varnished teak console and single-lever controls are impressive. There were also two interior floorplans offered, and both include an island berth forward, a small galley, and a separate stall shower in the head. Not surprisingly, handling characteristics are excellent, and the flared bow results in a dry ride. Optional 550-hp 6V92 diesels will cruise the 44 Express at 27 knots (about 30 knots top) and the 675-hp MANs will cruise at 29 knots and reach 33+ wide open. ❏

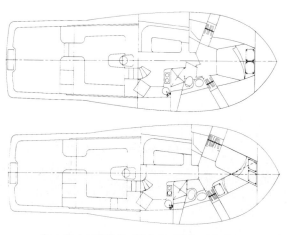

See Page 226 for Pricing Information

DAVIS 47 FLYBRIDGE SF

SPECIFICATIONS

Length	47'0"	Fuel	750/840 gals.
Beam	16'0"	Cockpit	NA
Draft	4'0"	Hull Type	Modified-V
Weight	45,000#	Deadrise Aft	NA
Clearance	12'10"	Designer	Davis
Water	150 gals.	Production	1986–93

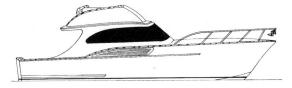

While she has the distinctive appearance of a custom design, the Davis 47 was a full production boat and remains one of the more popular sportfishing boats of her size in the market. She's built on a modified-V hull with Divinycell coring in the hullsides from the waterline up. (The first six hulls were fully cored.) After experimenting with several floorplans, Davis in 1990 introduced two layouts (see below) that remained standard until she went out of production in 1993. The popular galley-down, two-stateroom version features a huge salon, and the galley-up floorplan has three staterooms—rare on a 47-footer. Access to the engine room is through a door in the cockpit. A teak console with single-lever controls dominates the flybridge. The cockpit features a molded tackle center, teak covering boards, transom door, and two in-deck storage boxes. Standard 735-hp 8V92s will cruise around 24 knots (29 knots top), and optional 820-hp MANs cruise around 28 knots (33 top). Fuel was increased for 1990. A total of 88 Davis 47s were built. ❏

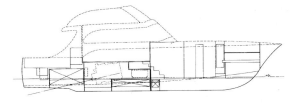

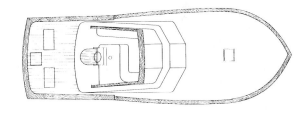

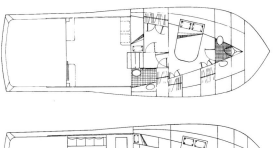

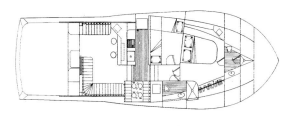

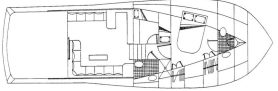

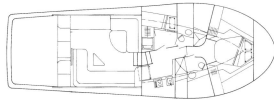

See Page 226 for Pricing Information

DAVIS 61 FLYBRIDGE SF

SPECIFICATIONS

Length	61'0"	Fuel	1,550 gals.
Beam	17'6"	Cockpit	185 sq. ft.
Draft	5'8"	Hull Type	Modified-V
Weight	80,000#	Deadrise Aft	NA
Clearance	18'0"	Designer	G. Van Tassel
Water	250 gals.	Production	1987–93

Behind the classic profile and aggressive styling of the Davis 61 lurks the heart of a proven big-game tournament-winner with truly outstanding performance capabilities. Indeed, it's been said many times that her ability to run into a head sea is better than any other boat in her class. In the Davis 61, a buyer can get the look and feel of an expensive custom boat for the price of a high-quality production model. The result is an opulent and completely upscale sportfisherman with an elegant teak interior, four staterooms (two with double berths), and a huge fishing cockpit with a teak sole and teak covering boards. Other features include direct cockpit access to the engine room, a custom teak helm console on the flybridge with Panish controls and pop-up electronics display, and the availability of huge 1,400-hp 16V92s for an honest 30-knot cruising speed. Standard 1,040-hp 12V92s cruise at 26 knots (with a tower and full fuel) and reach a top speed of 31 knots. A total of 34 were built.❏

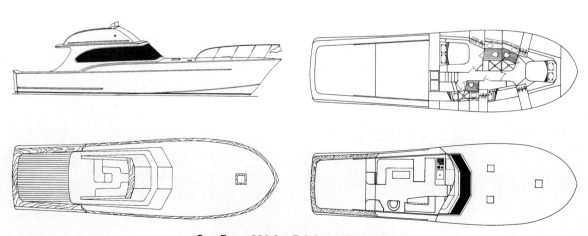

See Page 226 for Pricing Information

54

DAWSON 38 SPORTFISHERMAN

DELTA 36 SFX

SPECIFICATIONS

Length	38'0"	Fuel	400 gals.
Beam	13'8"	Cockpit	100 sq. ft.
Draft	3'6"	Hull Type	Deep-V
Weight	28,000#	Deadrise Aft	24°
Clearance	NA	Designer	T. Dawson
Water	90 gals.	Production	1987-Current

SPECIFICATIONS

Length	36'3"	Fuel	400 gals.
Beam	12'2"	Cockpit	98 sq. ft.
Draft	3'0"	Hull Type	Deep-V
Weight	17,200#	Deadrise Aft	NA
Clearance	NA	Designer	Delta
Water	50 gals.	Production	1987–Current

The Dawson 38 is a limited production fisherman designed to appeal to the tournament-level angler. The hull is not a new design; it was first developed back in 1975 in Pensacola and has since been used for commercial and charter service. The hulls are purchased and shipped to New Jersey where the Dawson 38 is finished out at the old Pacemaker yard. With a steep 24° of deadrise aft, the Dawson has more "V" than any other boat of her type on the market. An attractive design, her styling is on the conservative side, and most will view the Dawson as a strictly business sportfisherman in spite of her comfortable interior. The two-stateroom, galley-up floorplan includes a centerline double bed forward, a separate stall shower, and bunk berths in the guest cabin. Standard 375-hp Cats will cruise the Dawson 38 around 25 knots (30 knots top) and optional 485-hp 6-71s cruise at a fast 30 knots (33–34 knots wide open). Note that an express model became available in 1991. ❏

Delta boats are well known in the charter boat trade for their no-nonsense approach to the basics. The hulls are generally Coast Guard certified and the construction is rugged with the emphasis on reliability. In the Delta 36 SFX, however, there's more than just a tough deep-V hull and a big fishing cockpit. This is truly an innovative and practical boat with an outright aggressive appearance. What sets her apart from most other sportfishers in the mid-range market is her unique raised command bridge—a spacious platform that splits the difference between a true flybridge and the raised bridgedeck used in open express boats. Positioned about three feet above the cockpit level, this sensible concept provides a stand-up engine room (virtually unheard of in a small fisherman), with direct cockpit access and extraordinary headroom below. Inside, the layout is modern and very attractive with a circular pit-style dinette, linear galley, and double berth forward. A good seaboat, she'll cruise around 24–26 knots with optional 425-hp Cat (or 400-hp Cummins) diesels. ❏

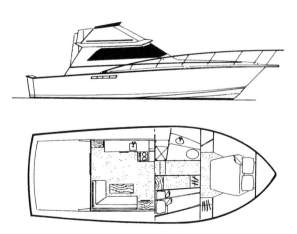

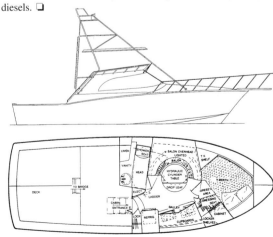

See Page 226 for Pricing Information

See Page 226 for Pricing Information

DELTA 38 SPORTFISHERMAN

SPECIFICATIONS

Length	38'0"	Fuel	300 gals.
Beam	12'5"	Cockpit	120 sq. ft.
Draft	3'0"	Hull Type	Modified-V
Weight	19,500#	Deadrise Aft	13°
Clearance	NA	Designer	Delta
Water	50 gals.	Production	1984—Current

The first Delta 38s were commercial dive and charter boats, where they earned a reputation for dependability and offshore stability. A semi-custom model, about 70 have been built (most to USCG specifications), and while the majority are used commercially, there are many that are privately owned as well. Her modified-V hull is narrow with moderate deadrise aft and a spray rail forward—a no-nonsense fishing platform with solid fiberglass construction and proven offshore performance. The cockpit in this boat is huge with low freeboard and plenty of space for tackle centers and a full-size chair. The interior dimensions are limited due to the oversize cockpit and the unique 4' collision bulkhead forward (a watertight compartment required by the CG in certified boats). A lower helm is standard, and V-berths are below, along with a galley and small head. The Delta 38 has been offered with a wide variety of power options including GM, Cat, Volvo, and Cummins diesels to 425-hp. A good-running boat, she'll appeal to anglers seeking simplicity and durability. ❏

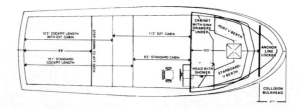

See Page 226 for Pricing Information

DONZI 65 SPORTFISHERMAN

SPECIFICATIONS

Length	65'0"	Fuel	2,000 gals.
Beam	18'8"	Cockpit	NA
Draft	5'2"	Hull Type	Modified-V
Weight	72,000#	Deadrise Aft	12°
Clearance	14'4"	Designer	J. Garland
Water	350 gals.	Production	1987–Current

Built on a semi-custom basis by Roscioli International, the Donzi 65 is a magnificent display of big-time sportfishing elegance. The beauty is more than skin deep: construction of the Donzi 65 is state-of-the-art with Divinycell hull coring and a long list of exotic materials used to create a strong and relatively lightweight structure. The hull is a modified-V design with a sharp entry forward and 12° of transom deadrise. The Donzi's cockpit is huge, and the full-width flybridge above can accommodate a dozen people. Several three- and four-stateroom layouts are offered, and all feature a wide-open salon with the galley forward. The teak (or oak) interior woodwork and decor appointments are opulent in the extreme. The stand-up engine room runs about a third of the boat's LOA and is accessed from the cockpit or through a door next to the crew quarters. Twin 12V92s are standard, but the engines of choice have been 1,440-hp 16V92s which cruise at a fast 27–28 knots and deliver 32 knots wide open. ❑

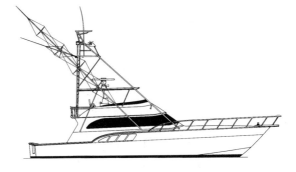

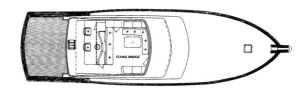

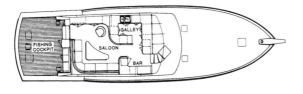

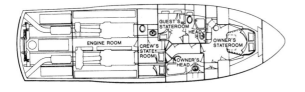

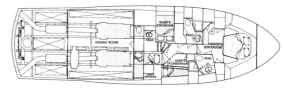

See Page 226 for Pricing Information

57

DORADO 30

SPECIFICATIONS

Length	30'0"	Fuel	90 gals.
Beam	8'8"	Cockpit	NA
Draft	1'6"	Hull Type	Modified-V
Weight	4,900#	Deadrise Aft	8°
Clearance	NA	Designer	C. Werebach
Water	25 gals.	Production	1988–Current

The Dorado 30 is a semi-custom center console fisherman with a relatively narrow flat-bottom hull and a unique jackshaft drive system. Weighing in at less than 5,000 lbs., the Dorado is light for her size (and extremely fuel efficient) thanks to her Divinycell-cored hull construction and single engine power. The hull was first designed back in the 1950s for tarpon fishing and has been built of fiberglass since 1988. Although the transom deadrise is marginal, the ability to adjust the outdrive to sea conditions provides a dryer and softer ride than might otherwise be expected. The uncluttered cockpit is arranged with an in-deck livewell and fish box on each side of the boat and bench seating forward of the console. Storage is excellent (superior, actually), and V-berths and dry storage are provided in the cuddy cabin. Among several engine options, most recent models have been fitted with a single 230-hp Volvo Duoprop diesel (28 knots cruise/36 knots top). Range (with diesel)—over 300 miles on a 90-gallon tank—is excellent. ❏

DUFFY 42 FLYBRIDGE CRUISER

SPECIFICATIONS

Length	42'0"	Fuel	500 gals.
Beam	14'6"	Cockpit	NA
Draft	4'6"	Hull Type	Semi-Disp.
Weight	24,000#	Designer	S. Lincoln
Clearance	NA	Production	1985–Current
Water	100 gals.		

A classic lobster boat profile and a high level of craftsmanship have made the Duffy 42 one of the more popular Downeast cruisers currently on the market. These are rugged semi-custom boats with cored hulls and a full length keel below—seaworthy designs with beautiful sheers, protected running gear, and generous cockpits. There are several versions of the Duffy 42, and each can be built to a buyer's specifications. The two-stateroom, galley-up floorplan of the FB Cruiser (pictured above) features an island berth forward and bunk berths in the guest cabin. A lower helm is standard, and the conservative interior decor is functional and well finished. Engine room access is very good, and a transom door and swim platform are standard. Most of the Duffy 42s built for private use (many are used commercially) have been powered with a single 375-hp Cat which delivers a 14–15 knot cruising speed and around 18 knots wide open. Cruising range is an impressive 500+ miles. A class act, used Duffy 42s are considered premium boats on the used markets. ❏

See Page 226 for Pricing Information

See Page 226 for Pricing Information

DYER 29

SPECIFICATIONS

Length..........................28'6"	Fuel.......................110 gals.
Beam ....9'5"	Cockpit ....NA
Draft..............................2'6"	Hull Type ....Semi-Disp.
Weight.....................6,700#	Designer ....Nick Potter
Clearance......................6'0"	Production...1955–Current
Water......................24 Gals	

Designed for cruising, fishing, or as a general utility boat, the durable Dyer 29 is an industry classic. Production began over 35 years ago making her the longest-running fiberglass design in the business. Each of the over 300 sold has been customized to some extent and the boat has seen many updates over the years. At only 6,700 lbs., the Dyer would be considered a light boat were it not for her narrow beam. She's built on a soft-chined hull with a fine entry, protected prop, and an uncommonly graceful sheer. The ability of the hull to tackle heavy sea conditions is legendary. Those who own Dyers tolerate her tight cabin quarters and inconvenient engine box and delight in the fingertip control and positive response of this easily driven hull. Among numerous engine options, a single 200-hp Volvo diesel will cruise the Dyer 29 around 16 knots and reach a top speed of approximately 20–21 knots. In addition to the popular Trunk Cabin model (pictured above), the 29 is available in a hardtop or open fishing version. ❑

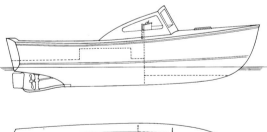

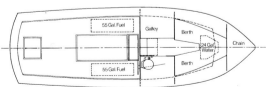

See Page 226 for Pricing Information

Assembly Lines Not Included.

 *EGG-HARBOR*

TIMELESS CRAFTSMANSHIP SINCE 1946.

For details on the Egg Harbor 34', 38', 42', 54' and 58' Golden Egg Convertibles, or your nearest dealer, call 609-965-2300. Or fax your request to 609-965-2870.

EGG HARBOR 33 SEDAN

1971–77

1978–81

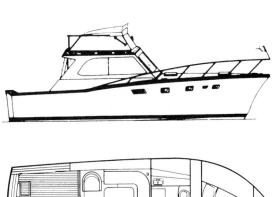

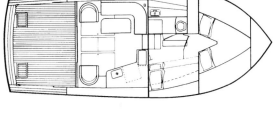

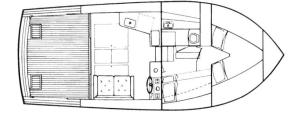

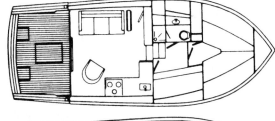

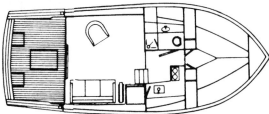

SPECIFICATIONS

Length	33'0"	Fuel	216 gals.
Beam	13'2"	Cockpit	NA
Draft	2'9"	Hull Type	Modified-V
Weight	13,000#	Deadrise Aft	8°
Clearance	NA	Designer	Egg Harbor
Water	50 gals.	Production	1971–81

The 33 Sedan was the first fiberglass hull ever built by the Egg Harbor Yacht Company. Designed primarily as a family cruiser, she was constructed with a mahogany deck and superstructure until 1978, when the switch was made to all-fiberglass construction. The standard floorplan arrangement has a two-stateroom layout with the galley in the salon. A galley-down version was offered in later models, and the head was also redesigned to accommodate a separate stall shower. Although the cockpit is small and the range is limited, the great appeal of the Egg Harbor 33 Sedan lies in her graceful profile, rich mahogany interior, and the extensive use of exterior teak, including teak covering boards and a solid teak cockpit sole. Her appearance improved dramatically when the fiberglass deck and house were introduced, and she remained in production until replaced in 1981 with the all-new Egg Harbor 33 Convertible. Twin 270-hp Crusader engines will cruise the Egg 33 at a modest 15–16 knots, and she'll reach a top speed of about 23 knots. ❏

See Page 226 for Pricing Information

61

EGG HARBOR 33 CONVERTIBLE

SPECIFICATIONS

Length	33'0"	Fuel	320 gals.
Beam	13'2"	Cockpit	70 sq. ft.
Draft	2'5"	Hull Type	Modified-V
Weight	17,000#	Deadrise Aft	8°
Clearance	NA	Designer	W. Nickerson
Water	50 gals.	Production	1982–89

The 33 Convertible was the first of the new-style Egg Harbor designs when she came out in 1982. She evolved from the Pacemaker 33 SF, a good-looking flybridge sedan that went into production in 1979 and ended when Pacemaker closed down the following year. Egg Harbor picked up the tooling, revised the interior layout, and reintroduced her as a replacement for the original 33 Sedan. In addition to the Convertible model, Egg Harbor also offered the 33 in an express fisherman version with no flybridge. Significantly, the fuel capacity of the newer Egg 33 is 320 gallons—a big improvement in range from the original 33 Sedan—and a teak interior replaced the original 33 Sedan's mahogany woodwork. From 1987 to 1989 a stretched version, the Egg Harbor 35 SF, was built with a larger cockpit and 400 gallons of fuel. Upgrades on both eliminated the front windshield in later models. Standard 350-hp gas engines cruise the Egg Harbor 33 around 19 knots with top speed of 28–29 knots. ❏

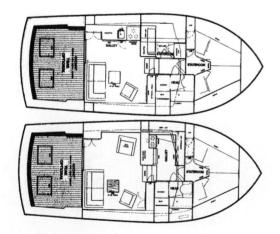

See Page 227 for Pricing Information

EGG HARBOR 34 GOLDEN EGG

SPECIFICATIONS

Length	34'6"	Fuel	400 gals.
Beam	13'2"	Cockpit	113 sq. ft.
Draft	3'2"	Hull Type	Modified-V
Weight	17,500#	Deadrise Aft	8°
Clearance	12'3"	Designer	W. Nickerson
Water	70 gals.	Production	1990-Current

Smallest of the current Egg Harbor lineup, the 34 Golden Egg employs the same hull used in the previous Egg Harbor 33 models but stretched to 34'6". The extra length has been used to give her a larger cockpit area as well as increased fuel capacity—features sure to appeal to serious anglers for whom the boat was designed. The most dramatic change, however, is in the crisp styling now incorporated throughout the Egg Harbor fleet. The styling of the 34 was again revised in 1994 with a new deckhouse profile and the addition of some attractice graphics. Two interior floorplans are offered: a two-stateroom, galley-up layout, and a single-stateroom version with a larger salon and the galley down. A walkaround double berth is set on the centerline in the spacious forward stateroom, and the head compartment is fitted with a stall shower. Standard features include a generator, tackle center with sink and icebox, transom door, and teak covering boards. Standard 454-cid gas engines will cruise at 19 knots and reach about 28 knots wide open. ❏

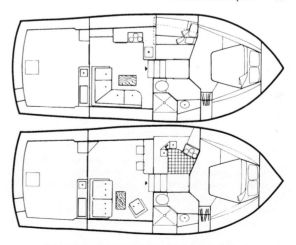

See Page 227 for Pricing Information

EGG HARBOR 36 SEDAN

SPECIFICATIONS

Length	36'0"	Cockpit	NA
Beam	13'3"	Hull Type	Modified-V
Draft	2'9"	Deadrise Aft	6°
Weight	17,000#	Designer	Egg Harbor
Water	75 gals.	Production	1976-1985
Fuel	260/320 gals.		

A good many fishermen find the 34–36-foot size range to be ideal in a sportfishing boat. The cockpit is usually large enough for serious fishing, and a good design will retain the maneuverability of a much smaller hull. Such a boat is the Egg Harbor 36 Sedan. She's built on a modified-V hull designed by Egg Harbor with a deep forefoot and flat aftersections for quick planing. Early models were built with a glassed-over mahogany deckhouse, but in 1978 construction became all-fiberglass. The Egg 36 has the teak cockpit sole and covering boards that many fishermen find appealing in spite of the maintanance. The interior can accommodate up to six depending on the floorplan (there were a total of four). A Tournament Fisherman model in 1978 featured an improved bridge layout with bench seating forward of the helm. The standard 350-hp gas engines will cruise at about 19 knots and reach 28 knots top. Note that the Taiwan-built Pace 36 SF (1988–92) used the old Egg Harbor 36 Sedan molds. ❏

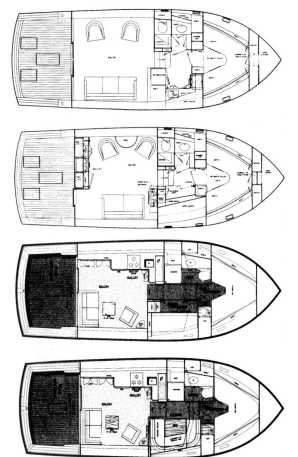

See Page 227 for Pricing Information

63

EGG HARBOR 37 CONVERTIBLE

SPECIFICATIONS

Length	37'5"	Fuel	340/400 gals.
Beam	14'5"	Cockpit	NA
Draft	3'0"	Hull Type	Modified-V
Weight	24,000#	Deadrise Aft	9°
Clearance	NA	Designer	W. Nickerson
Water	80 gals.	Production	1985–89

A scaled-down version of the Egg Harbor 41 SF, the 37 Convertible is a competent family cruiser with a smallish cockpit and a rather unattractive profile. She's built on a modified-V hull with balsa coring in the hullsides and a relatively flat bottom for lift and quick acceleration. Inside, the interior is every bit as impressive (and exactly the same size) as her bigger sister. The salon is clearly the centerpiece of the boat—a completely stylish and comfortable living area offered in a choice of two layouts. The 37's wide beam provides an interior volume seldom found on boats of her size, and the quality teak woodwork is typical of all Egg Harbor models. Outside, the sidedecks are wide enough to get forward, and the average-size bridge is arranged with guest seating forward of the helm. Twin 350-hp gas engines were standard in the Egg 37 for a cruising speed of 19 knots and a top speed of around 28 knots. The fuel was increased to 400 gallons in 1986 models. ❏

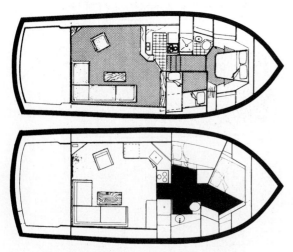

See Page 227 for Pricing Information

EGG HARBOR 38 GOLDEN EGG

SPECIFICATIONS

Length	38'6"	Fuel, Gas	400 gals.
Beam	15'0"	Fuel, Dsl	500 gals.
Draft	3'10"	Cockpit	108 sq. ft.
Weight	22,500#	Hull Type	Modified-V
Clearance	13'0"	Deadrise Aft	8°
Water	120 gals.	Production	1990-Current

The 38 Golden Egg replaced the 37 Convertible in the Egg Harbor fleet in 1990. She's built on a modified-V hull with moderate beam and a relatively flat 8° of transom deadrise—the same basic hull used in the construction of the larger 42 Golden Egg. The 38 Golden Egg is a good-looking yacht with a rakish profile and a wraparound black-mask window treatment. A choice of two interior configurations is available (a single-stateroom dinette version or two-stateroom layout), and both are arranged with the mid-level galley separated from the salon by a serving counter. The full-size cockpit is set up for serious fishing pursuits and includes a complete tackle center, livewell, transom door, fish box, and teak covering boards. Updates in 1994 include a revised window treatment and the addition of graphics to the superstructure. Crusader 454-cid gas engines are standard, but anglers are sure to favor the optional 375-hp Caterpillar or 400-hp 6V53 diesels, either of which should cruise around 22–23 knots and reach 25 knots wide open. ❏

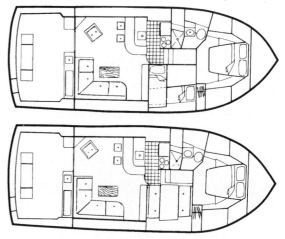

See Page 227 for Pricing Information

EGG HARBOR 40 SEDAN

SPECIFICATIONS

Length	40'0"	Fuel	338 gals.
Beam	14'0"	Cockpit	95 sq. ft.
Draft	2'9"	Hull Type	Modified-V
Weight	28,000#	Deadrise Aft	6°
Clearance	NA	Designer	D. Martin
Water	100 gals.	Production	1975–86

Introduced as a replacement for the Egg Harbor 38 Sedan in 1975, the principal difference between the Egg Harbor 40 Sedan and her predecessor is the 40's larger cockpit dimensions—something the Egg Harbor 38 sorely lacked. The original 38-foot hull was stretched, and the additional length adds much to her graceful profile. Her appearance was considerably enhanced when a new fiberglass deckhouse and flybridge replaced the wooden superstructure in 1978. Several interior floorplans were offered over the years with most of the recent models being two-stateroom layouts with a mid-level galley to port. In a significant production change, the original mahogany interiors were changed to teak in 1982. A large and unobstructed cockpit made the Egg Harbor 40 Sedan a popular and competent sportfisherman, and the teak sole and covering boards were standard. A Tournament Fisherman version introduced in 1978 moved the helm aft for better cockpit visibility. Optional 450-hp GM 6-71 diesels will cruise the Egg Harbor 40 Sedan around 24 knots and reach 27 knots wide open. ❏

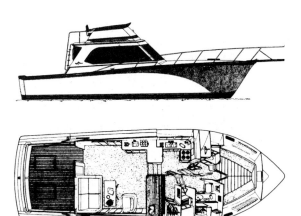

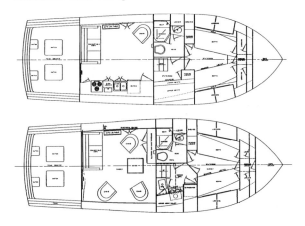

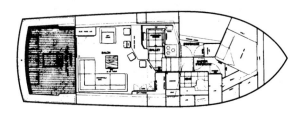

See Page 227 for Pricing Information

65

EGG HARBOR 41 SPORTFISHERMAN

SPECIFICATIONS

Length	40'10"	Fuel	500 gals.
Beam	14'5"	Cockpit	NA
Draft	3'0"	Hull Type	Modified-V
Weight	28,000#	Deadrise Aft	8°
Clearance	13'0"	Designer	W. Nickerson
Water	80 gals.	Production	1984–89

The Egg Harbor 41 SF stands out among most mid-sized convertible models because of her huge cockpit and elegant interior accommodations. She's designed around a reworked Pacemaker 38 hull acquired by Egg Harbor when Pacemaker went out of business in 1980. A good-running boat with quick acceleration, the hull is a modified-V affair with a flat 8° of transom deadrise and balsa coring in the hullsides. She was introduced in 1984 in both a Sportfisherman and a Convertible Sedan version, the difference being the larger salon and smaller cockpit of the Convertible. The upscale interiors of both boats are lush with furniture-quality teak cabinetry and paneling throughout. Outside, the exterior styling of the Egg Harbor 41 is very graceful, and when fitted with a full tower she has a decidedly serious appearance. Gas engines were standard, but optional GM and Caterpillar diesels were the engines of choice for most. A pair of 375-hp Cats will cruise about 22 knots, and the 6-71TIs cruise in the 26+ range. ❏

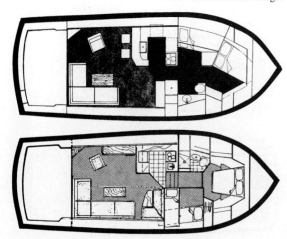

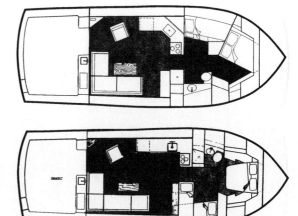

See Page 227 for Pricing Information

See Page 227 for Pricing Information

EGG HARBOR 42 GOLDEN EGG

SPECIFICATIONS

LOA	45'10"	Fuel, Gas	500 gals.
Hull Length	42'2"	Fuel, Dsl	600 gals.
Beam	15'0"	Cockpit	120 sq. ft.
Draft	3'10"	Hull Type	Modified-V
Weight	27,000#	Deadrise Aft	8°
Clearance	13'0"	Production	1990-Current
Water	120 gals.		

Introduced in 1990, the 42 Golden Egg replaced both the 41 and 43 Convertibles in the revised Egg Harbor fleet. She's built on the same hull used in thr current Egg 38 with balsa coring from the waterline up and 8° of deadrise at the transom. The lines of the 42 are particularly graceful, and the new deckhouse window and graphics treatments introduced in 1994 further enhance the appearance. The interior choices are both two-stateroom affairs with the difference found in the salon. The spacious interior is finished with teak and may be customized to some extent at the factory. The cockpit can handle a fighting chair and includes a tackle center, in-deck fish box, livewell, transom door and teak covering boards—all standard. Topside, the tournament flybridge is arranged with the helm well aft for a good view of the cockpit. Although 502-cid gas engines are standard, it's likely that 375-hp Cats (about 23–24 knots at cruise) or 485-hp 6-71 Detroits (26 knots cruise/29 knots top) will be found in most hulls. ❏

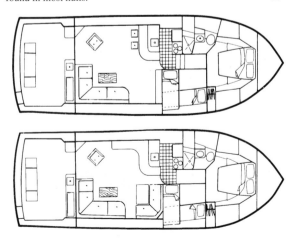

See Page 227 for Pricing Information

EGG HARBOR 43 SPORTFISHERMAN

SPECIFICATIONS

Length	43'0"	Fuel	600 gals.
Beam	14'5"	Cockpit	NA
Draft	3'0"	Hull Type	Modified-V
Weight	32,000#	Deadrise Aft	8°
Clearance	NA	Designer	W. Nickerson
Water	80 gals.	Production	1986–89

The Egg Harbor 43 Sportfisherman is easily one of the better-looking boats in her size class. She's built on a stretched version of the Egg 41 SF hull—a relatively flat-bottom affair with moderate beam and cored hullsides—and she carries an extra 100 gallons of fuel for increased range. (The extra two feet of length has been used to enlarge the salon dimensions. Indeed, the 43's interior appears to be that of a much larger boat.) Several two-stateroom floorplans were offered, and all feature a single head and mid-level galley. The teak cabinetry and paneling used throughout is impressive and very well crafted. Taken together, the upscale decor and luxurious accommodations make the Egg Harbor 43 a comfortable boat for family cruising. Like many modern sportfishermen the front windshield area is glassed-over and painted to create a distinctive wraparound black "mask" surrounding the deckhouse. A pair of 375-hp Cats will cruise the 43 SF around 22 knots, and the larger 6-71TIs will cruise at 26 knots. ❏

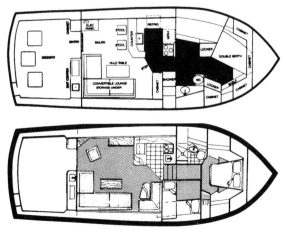

See Page 227 for Pricing Information

67

EGG HARBOR 46 SEDAN

SPECIFICATIONS

Length..........................46'8"	Fuel.......500/628/788 gals.
Beam ....15'0"	Cockpit ....NA
Draft..............................3'8"	Hull Type........Modified-V
Weight....................38,000#	Deadrise Aft....................2°
Clearance.......................NA	Designer ....D. Martin
Water.....................100 gals.	Production.............1973–83

Considered a handsome boat in her day with good all-around accommodations, the 46 Sedan was a popular model for Egg Harbor during her decade-plus in production. Originally built with a fiberglass hull and mahogany deck and superstructure, Egg Harbor went to all-fiberglass construction in 1978, and the new tooling considerably improved her appearance. As a fisherman, she had the cockpit space and handling qualities then demanded by serious anglers. Several interior arrangements were available over the years including a three-stateroom version—a rarity in just a 46-foot boat. More popular, however, was the two-stateroom layout with the galley down and a more open salon. As the Egg 46 matured, she received the additional fuel capacity necessary for offshore work, and a new teak interior in 1982 replaced the original mahogany woodwork used in the earlier models. GM 8V71TIs will cruise the Egg Harbor 46 Sedan around 20 knots and reach a top speed of 23. Note that this hull was stretched to create the Egg Harbor 48 in 1978. ❏

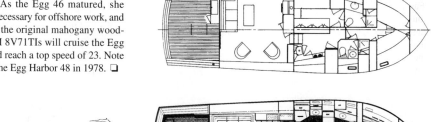

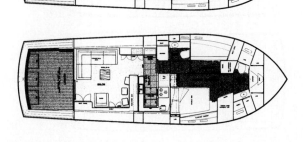

See Page 228 for Pricing Information

EGG HARBOR 48 SPORTFISHERMAN

SPECIFICATIONS

Length	48'2"	Fuel	788 gals.
Beam	15'0"	Cockpit	NA
Draft	4'4"	Hull Type	Modified-V
Weight	44,000#	Deadrise Aft	2°
Clearance	13'1"	Designer	D. Martin
Water	110/210 gals.	Production	1978–86

Built on a stretched version of the flat-bottom hull first used for the Egg 46 Sedan, the Egg 48 SF represented the last of the classic old-style Egg Harbor convertible designs. Aimed at the luxury end of the sportfishing market, she was originally offered in either a two- or three-stateroom layout with a large portside master stateroom. The floorplans were revised in 1982 when the galley became a permanent part of the salon, and a new teak interior replaced the mahogany woodwork found in earlier models. Notably, the Egg Harbor 48 was one of the first production boats fitted out with the early 550-hp 8V92 diesels resulting in a fast 25-knot cruising speed. (Fast indeed for 1978, and very few other production boats her size could run with her.) Additional features include a very spacious engine room with flooring all around the motors, teak cockpit sole and covering boards, a spacious main salon with overhead grabrails, and large wraparound cabin windows. (Note that late model Egg 48s have a solid front windshield.) ❏

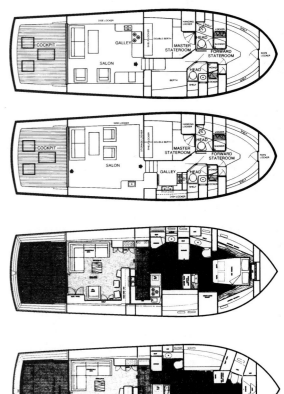

See Page 228 for Pricing Information

EGG HARBOR 54 CONVERTIBLE

SPECIFICATIONS

Length	54'6"	Fuel	1,000 gals.
Beam	17'6"	Cockpit	120 sq. ft.
Draft	5'3"	Hull Type	Modified-V
Weight	64,000#	Deadrise Aft	8°
Clearance	15'10"	Designer	D. Martin
Water	220 gals.	Production	1988–Current

The Egg 54 Convertible is essentially a scaled-down version of the company's 60-foot convertible introduced in 1986. Both share the same shallow deadrise hull design with balsa coring in the hullsides and modern high-tech composites in the laminate. With a wide 17'6" of beam, the interior accommodations of the 54 Convertible are very expansive, and the three-stateroom layout is unique. The owner's stateroom is to starboard of the companionway (rather than forward) and features a separate dressing room tucked beneath the salon sole and a tub/shower in the head. A second full head with shower serves the two guest staterooms. Outside, the cockpit can easily handle a full-size fighting chair and features direct access to the engine room (which is small, thanks to the interior layout), tackle center, in-deck fish box, and a transom door. Updates in 1994 include a restyled deckhouse with improved graphic and window treatments. A good-running boat, standard 8V92s will cruise the Egg Harbor 54 around 25 knots and deliver a top speed of 28 knots. ❏

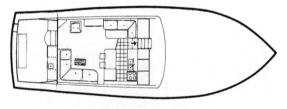

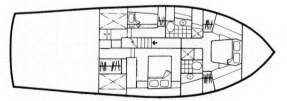

See Page 228 for Pricing Information

EGG HARBOR 58 GOLDEN EGG

SPECIFICATIONS

Length	59'6"	Fuel	1,200 gals.
Beam	17'6"	Cockpit	165 sq. ft.
Draft	5'3"	Hull Type	Modified-V
Weight	72,000#	Deadrise Aft	8°
Clearance	NA	Designer	D. Martin
Water	220 gals.	Production	1990-Current

The 58 Golden Egg replaced the 60 SF in the Egg Harbor fleet in 1990. She's built on the same high-tech hull as the 60 (with the same 59'6" LOA), although the deckhouse has been redesigned, and the interior is slightly rearranged on the lower level. A good-looking boat with her long foredeck and sweeping sheer, Egg Harbor updated the deckhouse with a window styling in 1994. Belowdecks, the three-stateroom, two-head floorplan is arranged with the galley and dinette forward in the salon. The spacious master stateroom—with its unique step-down dressing room tucked below the galley—is located to starboard, while the VIP guest stateroom is forward. The cockpit is huge with molded tackle centers, an in-deck fish box, transom door, etc., and direct access to the engine room (which turns out to be rather a tight fit). The 58 Golden Egg is a good performer for her size. With standard 1,080-hp 12V92 diesels, she'll cruise at a fast 27 knots and reach a top speed of around 30 knots. ❏

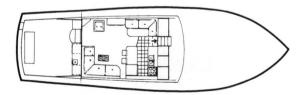

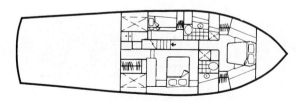

See Page 228 for Pricing Information

70

EGG HARBOR 60 CONVERTIBLE

SPECIFICATIONS

Length	59'6"	Fuel	1,200/1,500 gals.
Beam	17'6"	Cockpit	111 sq. ft.
Draft	5'3"	Hull Type	Modified-V
Weight	72,000#	Deadrise Aft	8°
Clearance	18'5"	Designer	D. Martin
Water	300 gals.	Production	1986–89

Egg Harbor made a clean break with the past when they introduced the 60 Sportfisherman in 1986. Her high-tech construction (balsa-cored hullsides, triaxial/Kevlar composites, etc.) represented an engineering first for Egg Harbor. This luxury sportfisherman features an innovative floorplan on the lower level: by moving the engines aft and tightening up the engine room, Martin was able to fit a unique dressing area into the master stateroom and a separate utility room to port. The huge salon/galley layout is impressive in both size and decor. So too is the rest of the interior, including the expansive master stateroom with walkaround queen berth and a forward stateroom with yet another walkaround queen—accommodations on a scale more often found on motor yachts. Outside, the profile of the Egg Harbor 60 is classic Jersey-style sportfish with a graceful sheer and generously flared bow. On the downside, the engine room is small for a 60-footer. A good performer, 1,080-hp 12V92 diesels will cruise around 27 knots with a top speed of 30 knots. ❏

GAMEFISHERMAN 40

SPECIFICATIONS

Length	40'0"	Fuel	400 gals.
Beam	13'0"	Cockpit	120 sq. ft.
Draft	3'1"	Hull Type	Modified-V
Weight	22,000#	Deadrise Aft	10°
Clearance	13'4"	Designer	B. Jackman
Water	50 gals.	Production	1986–Current

Seemingly a modern version of the Merritt 37 or 43, the Gamefisher 40 is a better sea boat with superior rough-water capabilities. She's an open bulkhead design with a flush deck layout from the transom to the forward cabin door. Hull construction is cold-molded mahogany planking with an epoxy glass outer covering. The flybridge and foredeck are laminated and epoxied, and the cockpit sole is teak. This hull is so well-balanced that trim tabs are not required (and not installed). The long narrow cockpit is excellent for all types of fishing and offers an in-deck livewell and fish box as well as a complete tackle center. The open deckhouse dinette and settee are slightly raised on engine boxes, and there are two big single berths below along with an enclosed head forward—the ideal day boat layout. Engine access is good, and there's space for a generator in the engine room. Volvo 380-hp diesels will cruise a tower-equipped Gamefisherman 40 at an economical 23 knots and reach a top speed of 27–28 knots. ❏

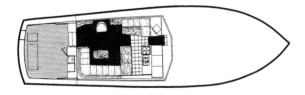

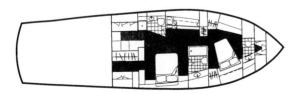

See Page 228 for Pricing Information

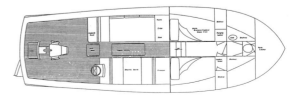

See Page 228 for Pricing Information

GARLINGTON 44

SPECIFICATIONS

Length	44'6"	Fuel	350–500 gals.
Beam	13'9"	Cockpit	100 sq. ft.
Draft	3'2"	Hull Type	Modified-V
Weight	22,000#	Deadrise Aft	16°
Clearance	NA	Designer	D. McCarthy
Water	75 gals.	Production	1990–Current

When custom boat builder Richard Garlington sat down to design a boat for himself, the Garlington 44 was the result, a good-looking express fisherman with classic South Florida custom styling. Rapidly growing in popularity (about ten have been built to date), the 44's state-of-the-art construction includes composite cores of Kevlar, carbon fiber, Airex foam and fiberglass. The hull is Awlgripped at the factory, and the sweeping sheer and flared bow make the Garlington 44 one of the most beautiful production fishermen available (and certainly one of the more expensive). The elegant teak interior includes a full dinette and galley along with a separate stall shower in the head. Outside, an L-shaped settee is opposite the helm on the raised bridgedeck, and there's over 100 sq. ft. of fishing space on the lower level. The engine room is tight. A superior sea boat with a great ride and incredible sex appeal (and resale), twin 460-hp Lugger diesels will cruise the Garlington 44 at 30 knots (at about 1 mpg!) and reach 34 knots top. ❏

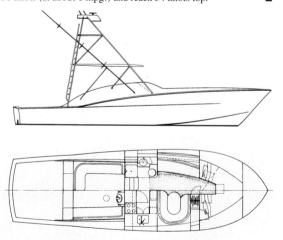

See Page 228 for Pricing Information

GRADY-WHITE SAILFISH 25

SPECIFICATIONS

Length	25'4"	Fuel	202 gals.
Beam	9'6"	Hull Type	Deep-V
Draft	1'6"	Deadrise Aft	20°
Weight	6,100#	Designer	In-House
Clearance	9'3"	Production	1980–Current
Water	32 gals.		

Based upon a design introduced back in 1980, the Grady-White Sailfish 25 is a rugged offshore fisherman with many years of fine-tuning and refinement. Like all Grady-White boats, the Sailfish is constructed of solid fiberglass, and cavities between the hull and deck are filled with foam to provide flotation. Her 9'6" beam is wide for a 25-footer, and there's more usable cockpit space than most other boats her size. While her walkaround cuddy layout has remained basically unchanged over the years, in 1990 the helm was elevated several inches (to provide better belowdeck accommodations), and the cabin hatch was repositioned to port to create a wider helm console. An integral bracket platform for 1994 adds considerably to her appearance. Prominent features include a well-arranged cockpit, wide sidedecks, livewell, and fish boxes. Most Sailfish 25s have been outboard-powered. Twin Yamaha 200-hp O/Bs will cruise at 24 knots and reach about 37 knots wide open. Note that the Grady-White Dolphin 25 is the same boat with a stripped-out interior and more fishing features. ❏

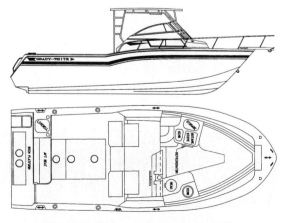

See Page 228 for Pricing Information

GRADY-WHITE MARLIN 28

SPECIFICATIONS

LOA	32'7"	Water	35 gals.
Hull Length	28'0"	Fuel	306 gals.
Beam	10'7"	Hull Type	Deep-V
Hull Draft	1'7"	Deadrise Aft	20°
Weight	7,000#	Designer	Hunt & Assoc.
Cockpit	60 sq. ft.	Production	1989–Current

The largest model in the Grady-White fleet, the Marlin 28 is a popular walkaround cuddy design with a surprisingly generous cabin to go with her strictly fishing cockpit layout. Hull construction is solid glass, and the Marlin's deep-V hull was specifically designed by Hunt & Associates for outboard V-6 power—not V-8s. (Note that below-deck cavities are filled with polyurethane flotation, which makes the Marlin unsinkable—an uncommon feature in a boat this size.) With her walkaround deck layout and big cockpit, the interior dimensions are necessarily limited but hardly confining. Indeed, there are comfortable berths for four (including a big quarter berth that extends below the bridgedeck), plus a stand-up head compartment with shower, excellent headroom, and a compact galley. Standard features include an integral engine bracket platform with transom door and swim ladder, fish box, 30-gallon livewell and tackle center. A good-running boat, twin 225 Yamaha O/Bs will cruise the Grady-White 28 at an easy 24 knots and deliver a top speed of 35–36 knots. ❏

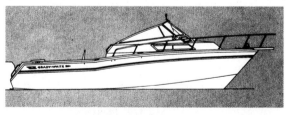

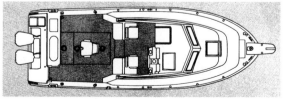

See Page 228 for Pricing Information

GRAND BANKS 42 SPORTS CRUISER

SPECIFICATIONS

Length	42'7"	Water	270 gals.
Length WL	40'9"	Fuel	600 gals.
Beam	13'7"	Cockpit	NA
Draft	4'2"	Hull Type	Semi-Disp.
Weight	34,000#	Designer	Ken Smith
Clearance	NA	Production	1989–Current

Sharing the same semi-displacement hull as the famous Grand Banks 42, the 42 Sports Cruiser is a beautifully styled flybridge sedan capable of serious sportfishing or economical family cruising. Her long forward trunk cabin and large house give the Sports Cruiser a distinctive and traditional profile. Like all Grand Banks boats, the keel provides grounding protection for the running gear, and the simulated planked hull is flawlessly finished and topped with a teak caprail. Her practical two-stateroom, galley-up floorplan includes one full head and a deck access door at the lower helm. Grain-matched teak paneling and a teak parquet sole join with the large wraparound cabin widows to create an open and very traditional salon. Twin teak-framed sliding doors open from the salon into a very large cockpit with a teak sole, transom door, and plenty of room for a tackle center and mounted chair. The sidedecks are wide and well secured with rails and raised bulwarks all around the house. A classy boat with tremendous eye appeal, engine options range from standard 135-hp Lehmans (8-knots cruise) to 375-hp Cats (16-knots cruise). ❏

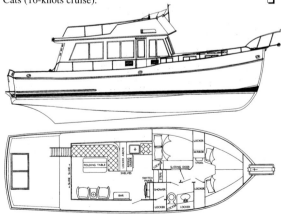

See Page 228 for Pricing Information

BEFORE BUYING YOUR NEW BOAT, MAKE SURE IT'S EQUIPPED WITH THIS ESSENTIAL PART.

HATTERAS 32 FLYBRIDGE SF

SPECIFICATIONS

Length	32'8"	Fuel	265 gals.
Beam	12'0"	Cockpit	95 sq. ft.
Draft	3'0"	Hull Type	Modified-V
Weight	18,000#	Deadrise Aft	18°
Clearance	10'6"	Designer	Jim Wynne
Water	50 gals.	Production	1982–86

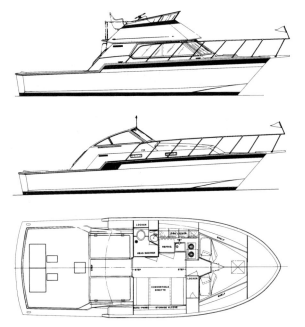

The Hatteras 32 Flybridge SF was built with the modern good looks and quality touches one expects in a Hatteras product. The hull is a Jim Wynne design with recessed propeller pockets and 18° of transom deadrise. The hullsides are balsa-cored from the waterline up, and considerable flare is used at the bow. Compared to other boats in her class, the Hatteras 32 is no lightweight. Inside, the cabin is arranged with a small galley, a roomy head compartment, and overnight berths for four. This is one of the more finely crafted and stylish interiors one is likely to find in a 32-foot fishing boat. The decor is bright and airy with only a modest amount of teak trim. Although not designed with any serious cruising in mind, the Hatteras 32 can provide comfortable accommodations for an extended weekend. Twin 300-hp Caterpillar diesels will cruise at 21–22 knots with a top speed of around 26 knots. Note that the Hatteras 32 Sport Fisherman (with no flybridge) has the same interior layout but smaller cabin windows. ❏

See Page 228 for Pricing Information

HATTERAS 36 CONVERTIBLE (EARLY)

SPECIFICATIONS

Length..........................36'1"	Fuel...............240/300 gals.
Beam.............................12'9"	Cockpit...........................NA
Draft................................3'0"	Hull Type........Modified-V
Weight.....................19,000#	Deadrise Aft..................NA
Clearance...................12'11"	Designer..........J. Hargrave
Water........................70 gals.	Production.............1969–77

The original Hatteras 36 Convertible is still a popular boat on the used market in spite of her obviously dated profile and over-built hull construction. Equally adept as an offshore fishing boat or comfortable family cruiser, the Hatteras 36 features an all-teak interior with the galley and stateroom three steps down from the salon. A two-stateroom floorplan with deckhouse galley was made available in 1975. While the accommodations are not considered spacious by today's standards, the mahogany woodwork and quality hardware, fixtures, and systems installed aboard the Hatteras 36 make renovations practical and reasonably cost-effective. The cockpit is large enough for a mounted chair and tackle center, but the flybridge and (especially) the engine room are both small. Never known for her blinding speed, standard 330-hp gas engines will cruise the Hatteras 36 Convertible at 18 knots (26–27 top) while the optional Caterpillar 3160 diesels cruise around 15 knots with a top speed of 18 knots. Significantly, the fuel capacity was increased in 1971 to 300 gallons.❑

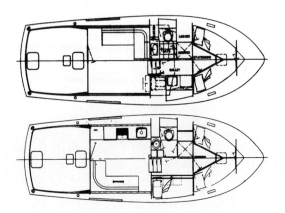

See Page 229 for Pricing Information

HATTERAS 36 CONVERTIBLE

SPECIFICATIONS

Length..........................36'6"	Fuel........................355 gals.
Beam.............................13'7"	Cockpit...........................NA
Draft................................3'9"	Hull Type...............Deep-V
Weight.....................26,500#	Deadrise Aft..................18°
Clearance....................12'6"	Designer...........Jim Wynne
Water......................115 gals.	Production.........1983–1987

The most recent Hatteras 36 Convertible (the original 36 Convertible ran 1969–77) was introduced in 1983. Designed as a replacement for the aging Hatteras 37, she's built on a heavy Jim Wynne-designed hull with a shallow keel and prop pockets. This is the same hull used in the Hatteras 36 SF—a good open-water design but not especially fuel efficient. Well-engineered and impressively finished, the Hatteras 36 makes an excellent family cruiser with her deluxe interior accommodations and stylish decor. Buyers can chose between a single-stateroom floorplan with an open salon and the galley down or a two-stateroom layout with the galley up. Note that her relatively small cockpit and unimpressive performance have resulted in mixed reviews among serious anglers. Standard 454-cid gas engines cruise at just 15 knots and the optional 390-hp 6-71 diesels cruise around 22 knots (26 knots wide open). Note that the Hatteras 36 Sedan Cruiser (1986–87) is the same boat with an enlarged interior and an even smaller cockpit.❑

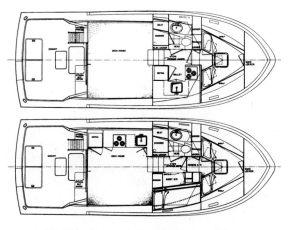

See Page 229 for Pricing Information

HATTERAS 36 SPORT FISHERMAN

SPECIFICATIONS

Length	36'6"	Fuel	355 gals.
Beam	13'7"	Cockpit	110 sq. ft.
Draft	3'9"	Hull Type	Deep-V
Weight	25,000#	Deadrise Aft	18°
Clearance	9'3"	Designer	Jim Wynne
Water	115 gals.	Production	1983–86

The Hatteras 36 Sport Fisherman is a heavy boat for her size, a fact that doubtless accounts for much of her somewhat sedate performance. Hull construction is solid fiberglass with balsa coring applied in the deck and superstructure. The 36 SF runs on a Jim Wynne-designed hull with recessed propeller pockets below for reduced shaft angles—the same hull used in the production of the Hatteras 36 Convertible (1983–87). Her open bi-level cockpit layout is well suited for serious deep-water fishing and comes standard with a transom door and a built-in fish box. Other features include wide walkaround sidedecks, an elevated helm position, a wraparound windshield, and easy cockpit access to the engines. Three steps down into the cabin reveals a practical layout with stylish fabrics, attractive high-pressure plastic laminates, and teak trim. Not only is this interior completely modern and appealing, it's easy to clean as well. The optional 390-hp GM 6-71s will cruise the Hatteras 36 Sport Fisherman around 24 knots and reach a top speed of 27–28 knots. ❏

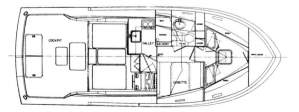

See Page 229 for Pricing Information

HATTERAS 37 CONVERTIBLE

SPECIFICATIONS

Length	37'0"	Fuel	330 gals.
Beam	14'0"	Cockpit	NA
Draft	3'3"	Hull Type	Modified-V
Weight	29,000#	Deadrise Aft	NA
Clearance	13'5"	Designer	J. Hargrave
Water	135 gals.	Production	1977–83

Introduced as a replacement for the very popular Hatteras 36 (1969–77), the 37 Convertible never achieved the widespread popularity of her predecessor among anglers in spite of her improved profile and roomier accommodations. She's built on a solid fiberglass hull with twin chines, a long keel, and moderate deadrise at the transom. With only 330 gallons of fuel, she's not a long-range boat. The interior is paneled in teak, and an offset double berth was offered in the forward stateroom beginning with the 1982 models. A stall shower is located in the double-entry head compartment. Large wraparound cabin windows give the salon a surprisingly spacious feeling for a 37-foot boat, and her tournament-style flybridge has seating for five. At 29,000 lbs., the Hatteras 37 Convertible is no lightweight. Those powered with the GM 6-71N diesels will cruise 18–19 knots with a top speed of about 21 knots. The optional 390-hp 6-71TIs will cruise the 37 Convertible around 21 knots and reach 23–24 knots wide open. ❏

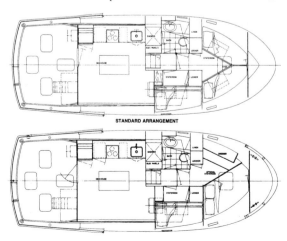

STANDARD ARRANGEMENT

See Page 229 for Pricing Information

HATTERAS 38 CONVERTIBLE (EARLY)

SPECIFICATIONS

Length	38'4"	Fuel	300 gals.
Beam	13'7"	Cockpit	NA
Draft	3'2"	Hull Type	Modified-V
Weight	29,000#	Deadrise Aft	NA
Clearance	13'4"	Designer	J. Hargrave
Water	148 gals.	Production	1968–74

The last of the original Hatteras 38 Convertibles were built some fifteen years ago, but used models are still seen regularly in most coastal markets. While only two feet longer than the 36 Convertible (1969–77), the Hatteras 38's interior, flybridge, and engine room dimensions are notably larger. The galley location is unique: arranged athwartships against the aft bulkhead, it's convenient and opens up the salon considerably but severely restricts any view of the cockpit. The salon is fully paneled in teak or mahogany and features a standard lower helm and space for a sofa-bed and a couple of chairs. V-berths are located in the forward stateroom and stacked single berths are fitted in the guest cabin. Outside, the cockpit is on the smallish side although suitable for sportfishing activities. Cockpit freeboard is only 3'4"—boating a fish should be easy. The tournament flybridge has bench seating forward of the console and good cockpit visibility. With the 8V53N diesels, the 38 Convertible models will cruise around 17 knots and reach 20 knots wide open. ❏

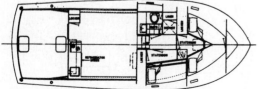

See Page 229 for Pricing Information

HATTERAS 38 CONVERTIBLE

SPECIFICATIONS

Length	38'10"	Fuel	490 gals.
Beam	13'5"	Cockpit	103 sq. ft.
Draft	4'8"	Hull Type	Modified-V
Weight	28,800#	Deadrise Aft	NA
Clearance	12'6"	Designer	Hatteras
Water	117 gals.	Production	1988–93

The 38 Convertible was one of a growing number of recent Hatteras models *not* designed by Jack Hargrave. A handsome boat with an aggressive profile, she's constructed on a modified-V hull with balsa coring in the hullsides and moderate transom deadrise. Aside from her stylish lines, the Hatteras 38 features a glassed-in front windshield and a luxurious two-stateroom teak interior layout with the galley in the salon. A centerline double berth is located in the master stateroom, and over/under single bunks are fitted in the guest cabin. While the cockpit dimensions are not notably deep, her beam is carried well aft, providing ample space for the installation of a full-size tuna chair. A molded tackle center and a transom door are standard, and the engine room air intakes are located under the coaming. The aft-raking flybridge windshield is particularly stylish. An average performer, standard 485-hp Detroit 6-71 diesels will cruise the Hatteras 38 Convertible at a steady 24 knots and reach a top speed of around 27 knots. ❏

See Page 229 for Pricing Information

HATTERAS 39 CONVERTIBLE

HATTERAS 41 CONVERTIBLE (EARLY)

SPECIFICATIONS

Length.......................38'10"	Fuel.......................490 gals.
Beam ....13'5"	Cockpit...............103 sq. ft.
Draft...............................4'8"	Hull Type........Modified-V
Weight....................28,800#	Deadrise Aft.................NA
Clearance....................12'6"	Designer ....Hatteras
Water....................117 gals.	Production...1994–Current

SPECIFICATIONS

Length.........................40'9"	Fuel.......................400 gals.
Beam ....14'0"	Cockpit...............105 sq. ft.
Draft............................2'11"	Hull Type........Modified-V
Weight....................23,000#	Deadrise Aft.................NA
Clearance....................13'6"	Designer ....J. Hargrave
Water....................150 gals.	Production.............1968–71

The Hatteras 39 Convertible is basically an updated version of the earlier 38 Convertible with a handsome new deckhouse and flybridge profile and a revised interior. She's built on a modified-V hull with cored hullsides and a relatively deep keel. While the interior dimensions of the Hatteras 39 are about average for a boat this size, the mid-level galley configuration opens up the salon considerably (the 38 had a more confining galley-up layout). Outside, the cockpit comes with a transom door and gate, molded tackle center, and in-deck fish box. Additional features include light oak interior woodwork, a well-arranged helm console, and expensive 5-bladed props. The real news about the Hatteras 39, however, is her low base price with standard 314-hp 4-71 diesels—a marketing choice that reduces cost at the expence of performance: 19 knots cruise/about 22–23 knots top. Optional (and more practical) 465-hp 6-71s will cruise the Hatteras 39 at a respectable 24–25 knots and reach a top speed of around 28 knots. ❏

Sharing the same hull as the Hatteras 41 Twin Cabin motor yacht, the old Hatteras 41 Convertible continues to be a highly visible and still-popular boat more than two decades after going out of production. Her chief attributes today remain her rugged all-fiberglass construction, a practical two-stateroom interior layout, a sizable fishing cockpit, and quality hardware and fixtures. A lower helm station was standard, and the interior is finished in mahogany. While the salon and staterooms aren't notably large, they're still comfortable and can easily be updated at a moderate cost. The Hatteras 41 is almost totally dated by today's standards—the flybridge is ancient, and the ride, while stable, is wet. Nonetheless, a used Hatteras 41 in top condition can still bring a strong resale value in spite of her age. Although 300-hp gas engines were standard, most of the early Hatteras 41s were powered with the 283-hp GM 8V53N diesels (a tight fit in the 41's small engine room). She'll cruise around 17 knots and reach a top speed of about 20 knots. ❏

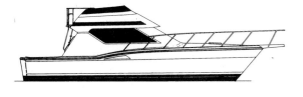

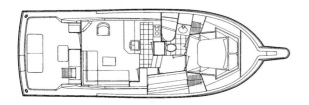

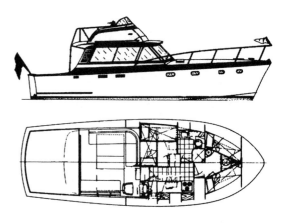

See Page 229 for Pricing Information

See Page 229 for Pricing Information

HATTERAS 41 CONVERTIBLE

SPECIFICATIONS

Length	41'9"	Fuel	400/500 gals.
Beam	14'3"	Cockpit	120 sq. ft.
Draft	4'4"	Hull Type	Modified-V
Weight	35,400#	Deadrise Aft	NA
Clearance	13'9"	Designer	J. Hargrave
Water	150 gals.	Production	1986–91

When the Hatteras 41 Convertible was introduced in 1986, she was widely hailed as the beginning of a new series of modern Hatteras designs. She was the first to have a fully cored hull (discontinued early in the production run), and vacuum-bagging was used extensively in the construction process. The "new look" window treatment, solid front windshield, stepped sheer, and rakish flybridge were the forerunners of today's Hatteras convertible styling. In the original two-stateroom layout, the in-line galley consumes a lot of the salon's living space. (A single-stateroom, galley-down floorplan was also offered.) In 1989, a revised two-stateroom floorplan greatly improved the original layout by moving the galley to starboard. A light ash interior became available in 1987. The transom door and tackle center were standard, and the engine air intakes are located under the gunwales. Fuel tankage was increased to 500 gallons in 1987. A good-running boat, standard 465-hp 6-71s diesels cruise at 23–24 knots, and the optional 535-hp 6V92s cruise at 26 knots with 29 knots top. ❑

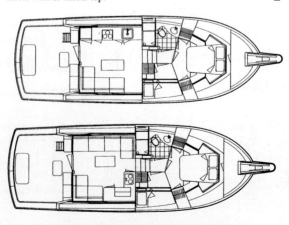

See Page 229 for Pricing Information

HATTERAS 42 CONVERTIBLE

SPECIFICATIONS

Length	42'8"	Fuel	400 gals.
Beam	13'10"	Cockpit	110 sq. ft.
Draft	3'5"	Hull Type	Modified-V
Weight	31,000#	Deadrise Aft	NA
Clearance	13'3"	Designer	J. Hargrave
Water	150 gals.	Production	1971–78

The long-awaited replacement boat for the aging 41 Convertible, the Hatteras 42 Convertible represented a big step forward in convertible design in 1971 with her full-width flybridge (the first in any Hatteras model) and her bold, more aggressive exterior profile. Construction was on the heavy side, and considerable flare was added at the bow. Her large 110 sq. ft. cockpit easily accommodates a mounted chair and complete tackle center. The Hatteras 42 was offered with only one floorplan: a two-stateroom arrangement with the galley down to starboard. A stall shower is fitted in the double-entry head, and teak paneling and cabinetry are used throughout. The engine room is tight, but routine access is satisfactory. In 1977, the flybridge was restyled, and the galley was rearranged with the refrigerator moved forward (thus opening the galley up to the salon)—big improvements when compared against the earlier models. A comfortable offshore boat, the 42 Convertible will cruise around 19–20 knots with either the GM 6-71TIs or the Cummins VT-903 diesels. Top speed is 22–23 knots. ❑

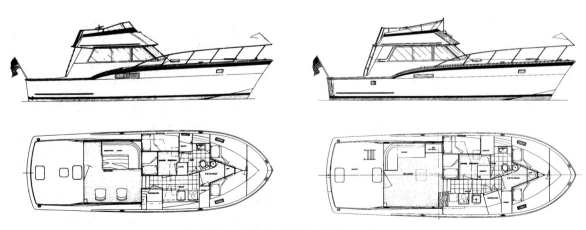

See Page 229 for Pricing Information
81

HATTERAS 43 CONVERTIBLE (EARLY)

SPECIFICATIONS

Length	43'8"	Fuel	470 gals.
Beam	14'6"	Cockpit	110 sq. ft.
Draft	4'2"	Hull Type	Modified-V
Weight	41,000#	Deadrise Aft	11°
Clearance	14'3"	Designer	J. Hargrave
Water	165 gals.	Production	1979–84

The Hatteras 43 Convertible was the replacement boat for the earlier Hatteras 42 Convertible. A good-looking boat, her new double-chined hull resulted in an enlarged engine room capable of handling the (then) recently introduced GM 6V92 diesels. In addition, her extra beam allowed for the installation of side-by-side berths in the master stateroom. (A double berth became available in 1982.) Other notable features of the Hatteras 43 include a spacious teak-paneled salon, an oversize flybridge with seating for eight, under-coaming air intakes in the cockpit, and a transom door with gate. The cockpit, while adequate for serious fishing activities, seems nonetheless small in an otherwise spacious boat. Note that a short-lived European arrangement (crew quarters forward with foredeck access) was offered in 1981–82 models. Never considered a particularly fast boat for her size, the early models with 450-hp 6V92s cruise around 20 knots. In 1981, the high-performance 6V92s (500-hp) were offered for a cruising speed of 22–23 knots and 26 knots at full throttle. ❏

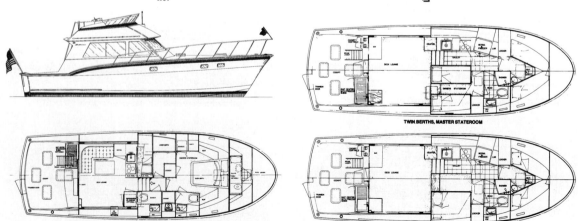

TWIN BERTHS, MASTER STATEROOM

See Page 229 for Pricing Information

HATTERAS 43 CONVERTIBLE

SPECIFICATIONS

Length	43'2"	Fuel	500 gals.
Beam	14'3"	Cockpit	120 sq. ft.
Draft	4'8"	Hull Type	Modified-V
Weight	40,000#	Deadrise Aft	10°
Clearance	12'4"	Designer	Hatteras
Water	154 gals.	Production	1991–Current

Sharing the same rakish profile and step-down sheer of her larger sisterships, the Hatteras 43 Convertible is a good-looking sportfisherman with the solid construction and improved performance typical of most recent Hatteras designs. She's built on a conventional modified-V hull with balsa coring in the hullsides, moderate beam, and a shallow keel below. A galley-down, two-stateroom layout is standard, and the optional single-stateroom floorplan trades out the guest cabin for a large U-shaped dinette. While the salon dimensions in both layouts are somewhat compact for a 43-footer, the light ash woodwork opens up the interior significantly. A washer/dryer is located in the companionway, and there's a stylish curved shower door in the head. Outside, the 43's large cockpit is tournament-grade all the way and includes direct access to the engine room—a feature seldom found in sportfisherman under 50 feet. A good running boat, standard 535-hp 6V92s will cruise the Hatteras 43 at 25 knots with a top speed of about 28 knots. ❏

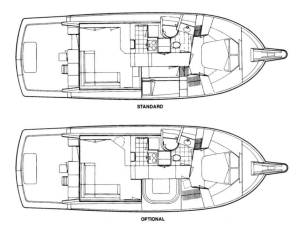

STANDARD

OPTIONAL

See Page 229 for Pricing Information

HATTERAS 45 CONVERTIBLE (EARLY)

SPECIFICATIONS

Length	45'2"	Fuel	650 gals.
Beam	14'7"	Cockpit	NA
Draft	3'6"	Hull Type	Modified-V
Weight	37,000#	Deadrise Aft	NA
Clearance	13'10"	Designer	J. Hargrave
Water	180 gals.	Production	1968–74

There always seems to be a market for the old Hatteras 45 Convertible. Her profile is that of a classic sportfisherman with a high foredeck and sweeping sheerline ending with a low-freeboard cockpit. Solid hull construction and good seakeeping qualities have made the 45 Convertible a favorite among tournament-minded anglers. Her conventional two-stateroom, galley-down interior includes a spacious main salon with a complete lower helm station and built-in lounge seating to port. A less popular galley-up model was also available with an open day berth replacing the galley in the companionway. A versatile boat, the spacious cockpit in the Hatteras 45 gets high marks for good all-around fishability. The old-style flybridge, however, is small. (Note that the original centerline pedestal bridge layout was revised in 1970 to a more versatile tournament-style design.) The popular engine choices were 8V71Ns (15–16 knots cruise) and 8V71TIs (around 20 knots at cruise and 23 knots at full throttle). A wet ride in a chop, the resale values of early Hatteras 45 Convertibles are surprisingly good. ❏

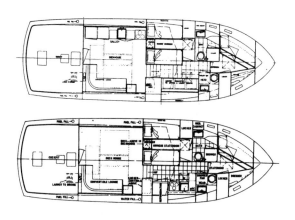

See Page 229 for Pricing Information

HATTERAS 45 CONVERTIBLE

1984–88

1989–91

SPECIFICATIONS

Length	45'8"	Fuel	590 gals.
Beam	14'6"	Cockpit	135 sq. ft.
Draft	4'6"	Hull Type	Modified-V
Weight	45,000#	Deadrise Aft	NA
Clearance	14'3"	Designer	J. Hargrave
Water	165 gals.	Production	1984–91

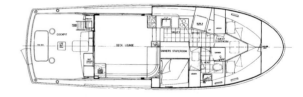

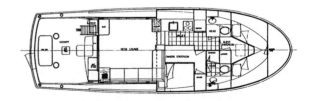

The Hatteras 45 Convertible began life in 1984 as simply an enlarged version of the previous Hatteras 43 Convertible (1979–84). The 45 kept the popular two-stateroom floorplan of the 43 intact (with its midships master stateroom and spacious salon) and used the additional hull length to create a bigger and much-improved fishing cockpit—something the 43 sorely lacked. A durable and popular boat, Hatteras dramatically updated her appearance in 1989 with a new deckhouse profile featuring the new-age Hatteras window treatment and a restyled flybridge. Note that a short-lived "Palm Beach" version of the 45 Convertible (1987 only) featured an optional two-stateroom, two-head layout with a glassed-in front windshield. In 1986 a contemporary light ash interior became available, and in 1988 the interior layout was revised to include an S-shaped forward companionway, a larger master stateroom, and two heads. Never known as a particularly fast boat, standard 535-hp 6V92s will cruise the Hatteras 45 Convertible at 23–24 knots and reach 27 knots wide open. ❏

See Page 229 for Pricing Information

HATTERAS 46 CONVERTIBLE (EARLY)

SPECIFICATIONS

Length..........................46'2"	Fuel ....650/710 gals.
Beam ....14'9"	Cockpit................125 sq. ft.
Draft..............................4'2"	Hull Type........Modified-V
Weight....................41,000#	Deadrise Aft.................NA
Clearance...................13'8"	Designer ....J. Hargrave
Water.....................180 gals.	Production.............1974–85

One of the most popular big-boat convertibles ever produced, the Hatteras 46 was heavily built on the original single-chine Hatteras 45 hull with a deep, full-length keel and moderate transom deadrise. Aside from being an excellent fisherman with good handling characteristics, her spacious cabin accommodations and upscale teak interior have made her a popular boat with cruisers. Revised two and three-stateroom floorplans were introduced in 1982 (each with two heads), and a new sliding door replaced the original hinged salon door in the same year. The original 46 Convertibles was powered with 8V71TIs and will cruise at 20 knots and deliver a top speed of 23-24 knots. In 1982, a high-performance version of the Hatteras 46 (with 650-hp 8V92TIs) featured a beefed-up hull with balsa coring in the hullsides and extra transverse frames in the bottom. (The keel was also shortened to improve handling and reduce wetted surface.) Speeds with the high-performance 8V92s are around 26 knots cruise and 29 knots top—not bad for any Hatteras of her era. ❏

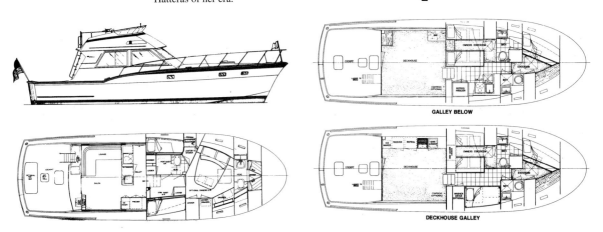

GALLEY BELOW

DECKHOUSE GALLEY

See Page 229 for Pricing Information

HATTERAS 46 CONVERTIBLE

SPECIFICATIONS

Length	46'10"	Fuel	775 gals.
Beam	15'7"	Cockpit	121 sq. ft.
Draft	411"	Hull Type	Modified-V
Weight	52,000#	Deadrise Aft	7°
Clearance	13'9"	Designer	Hatteras
Water	188 gals.	Production	1992–Current

Sharing the rakish profile and step-down sheer of all modern Hatteras sportfishermen, the 46 Convertible replaced the long-running 45 Convertible in the Hatteras fleet in 1992. She's heavily built on a beamy, low-deadrise hull with cored hullsides and a shallow keel—an in-house design with terrific lines and a lot of sex appeal. Inside, the two-stateroom ash interior is arranged with a mid-level dinette opposite the galley and a single head compartment. An alternate floorplan moves the dinette up into the salon and adds a second head with a stall shower. The cockpit—among the largest of any boat this size—comes with molded-in bait and tackle centers, an in-deck fish box, transom door, and direct access to a very well-engineered engine room with (wow!) standing headroom. (Note that the exhausts are underwater.) A good-running boat, a pair of 735-hp 8V-92s will cruise the Hatteras 46 at a steady 25 knots and reach 28–29 knots wide open. Hatteras also offers 780-hp MANs for the 46 Convertible. ❏

STANDARD ARRANGEMENT

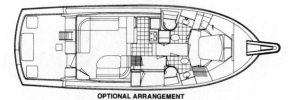

OPTIONAL ARRANGEMENT

See Page 229 for Pricing Information

HATTERAS 48 CONVERTIBLE

SPECIFICATIONS

Length	48'8"	Fuel	812 gals.
Beam	16'0"	Cockpit	135 sq. ft.
Draft	5'5"	Hull Type	Modified-V
Weight	51,500#	Deadrise Aft	8°
Clearance	14'0"	Designer	J. Hargrave
Water	184 gals.	Production	1987–91

Modern construction, contemporary styling and good seakeeping characteristics personify the Hatteras 48 Convertible—a striking design aimed at the upscale end of the sportfish market. Somehow, her weight wasn't kept down very much in spite of the Divinycell coring used in the hullsides and bulkheads. Her big tournament-size cockpit came with a wide transom door and molded tackle center along with an engine room access door and undercoaming air intakes. Below, the spacious salon is laid out with a complete entertainment center, stylish fabrics, and teak paneling and cabinetry (light ash woodwork was also available) but with no dinette. Both staterooms have roomy head compartments with stall showers, and a convenient raised serving counter divides the salon from the mid-level galley area. Additional features include a solid front windshield, side exhausts, wide sidedecks, and a huge flybridge with plenty of guest seating. Standard 720-hp 8V92 diesels will cruise the Hatteras 48 at 24–25 knots and turn a top speed of 28 knots. (Note that the current Hatteras 50 Convertible rides on the 48's stretched hull.) ❏

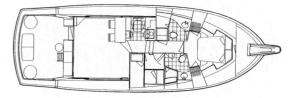

See Page 229 for Pricing Information

HATTERAS 50 CONVERTIBLE (EARLY)

SPECIFICATIONS

Length	50'0"	Fuel	950 gals.
Beam	15'10"	Cockpit	136 sq. ft.
Draft	4'0"	Hull Type	Modified-V
Weight	42,000#	Deadrise Aft	NA
Clearance	15'2"	Designer	J. Hargrave
Water	250 gals.	Production	1967–69

Obviously dated by today's standards, the old Hatteras 50 Convertible remains a fairly common occurrence on today's used boat market. She was a popular yacht in her day—the next step up from the legendary Hatteras 41 Convertible when she was introduced in 1967—and she retained her popularity among sportfishermen until the classic 53 Convertible came out in 1969. Like many early Hatteras single-chine hulls, the 50 can be a wet ride when the seas pick up. Below, the three-stateroom, three-head interior is arranged with twin berths in the owner's cabin and a shower stall in the adjoining head. Both of the guest staterooms are fitted with over/under berths. The salon is quite roomy in spite of the galley-up layout and broad sidedecks, and the interior is finished with mahogany woodwork throughout. The flybridge is very small compared to modern 50-footers. No racehorse, 8V71N diesels were standard in the early Hatteras 50 Convertibles (14 knots cruise/17 knots top) with 12V71Ns (17 knots cruise/20 top) offered as options. ❏

HATTERAS 50 CONVERTIBLE

SPECIFICATIONS

Length	50'0"	Fuel	1,065 gals.
Beam	16'4"	Cockpit	NA
Draft	4'6"	Hull Type	Modified-V
Weight	56,500#	Deadrise Aft	NA
Clearance	15'10"	Designer	J. Hargrave
Fresh Water	185 gals.	Production	1980–83

Introduced in 1980, this second Hatteras 50 Convertible was designed to handle the then-new GM 8V92 diesels. Constructed on a beamy modified-V hull with balsa coring from the waterline up and a long keel, the Hatteras 50 is still regarded as a good-looking convertible. Her wide beam provides interior accommodations that generous for a boat this size (especially considering the extra-wide sidedecks). Two floorplans were offered: a two-stateroom version with the galley down and a huge salon, and a more popular three-stateroom layout with a deckhouse galley. The cockpit (decidedly small for a 50-footer) came with a transom door, under-coaming air intakes, and direct engine room access. The flybridge is huge with bench seating for seven. The original 550-hp 8V92 diesels will cruise at 20 knots (22–23 top), while the high-performance 650-hp versions (introduced in 1982) cruise at 22 knots with a top speed of 25 knots. Note that the more recent Hatteras 52 Convertible (1984–91) is the same boat with a bigger cockpit. ❏

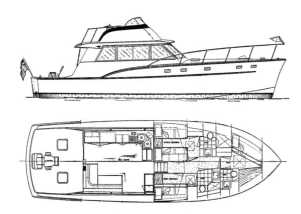

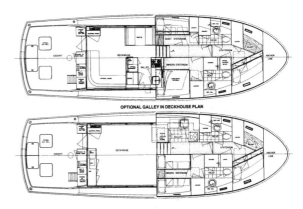

OPTIONAL GALLEY IN DECKHOUSE PLAN

See Page 229 for Pricing Information

See Page 230 for Pricing Information

HATTERAS 50 CONVERTIBLE (CURRENT)

SPECIFICATIONS

Length	50'10"	Fuel	890 gals.
Beam	16'1"	Cockpit	135 sq. ft.
Draft	5'9"	Hull Type	Modified-V
Weight	60,000#	Deadrise Aft	8°
Clearance	13'8"	Designer	J. Hargrave
Water	184 gals.	Production	1991–Current

The newest Hatteras 50—third in the company's history—replaced the popular 52 Convertible in the Hatteras lineup in 1991. The hull is a stretched version of the earlier 48 Convertible with a wide beam and modest transom deadrise. A handsome boat with her long foredeck, stepped sheer, and rakish flybridge, the Hatteras 50's standard three-stateroom, galley-up floorplan is arranged with the master stateroom amidships where the ride is most comfortable. By employing lighter woods and a cut-down galley, the salon has a surprisingly wide-open feeling. (A galley-down, two-stateroom floorplan is optional.) Additional features include cockpit access to the engine room (with near-standing headroom), a huge flybridge, underwater exhausts, and five-bladed props. A heavy boat for her size, performance is good but at a price. To achieve a competitive 26-knot cruising speed, the Hatteras 50 Convertible requires the optional 780-hp MANs or the 870-hp Detroit 12V71s. The standard 720-hp 8V92 diesels provide a modest 23–24 knots at cruise and 26 knots wide open. ❏

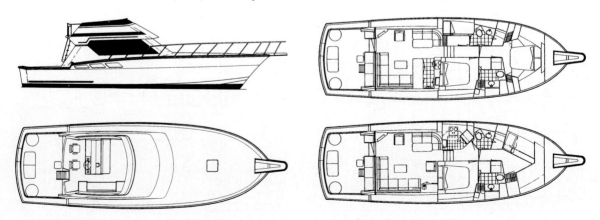

See Page 230 for Pricing Information

Hatteras
In The West !

The West Coasts only full service HATTERAS Dealership is proud to offer the new 1995 models. From the sleek new 39' Convertible to the custom 135' Tri-Deck Motoryacht, HATTERAS is truly America's premiere builder! The popular and successful **82' Convertible pictured at the left** is a prime example. This bluewater sportfisherman rules the seven seas worldwide in comfort and style. Other Convertibles: 39', 43', 46', 50', 54' & 65'.

The HATTERAS 50' Convertible pictured at the right is one of the finest mid-rangesportfisherman built today. She offers a choice of power options and layouts to customize your 50' to fit your needs. This model is seen frequentlyfrom Mexico to Alaska. HATTERAS is also the largest manufacturer of Motoryachts from 40' to 135'. **The 70' Cockpit Motor Yacht pictured below** is one of the most popular versions offerred today. Other Motor Yachts: 40', 42', 48', 52', 54', 60', 65' and 70'. Customs from 92' to 135'.

We at The Crow's Nest are celebrating our 20th years in business serving the boating community both here in the U.S. and throughout the Pacific Rim. We are export specialists and go to all means to serve our clients worldwide. In addition to the HATTERAS line, we are also proud to represent BERTRAM and TIARA Yachts. The Crow's Nest is also a major yacht brokerage firm on the west coast and offer a vast selection of quality used yachts. We have offices in both Newport Beach and San Diego with marina facilities. We invite your inquiry.

THE CROW'S NEST

NEWPORT BEACH
2801 W. Coast Highway, Suite #260
Newport Beach, California 92663
FAX: (714) 574-7610

(714) 574-7600

SAN DIEGO
2515 Shelter Island Drive
San Diego, California 92106
FAX: (619) 222-3851

(619) 222-1122

HATTERAS 52 CONVERTIBLE

1984–87

1987–91

SPECIFICATIONS

Length	52'0"	Fuel	1,068 gals.
Beam	16'4"	Cockpit	153 sq. ft.
Draft	5'0"	Hull Type	Modified-V
Weight	55,400#	Deadrise Aft	NA
Clearance	15'10"	Designer	J. Hargrave
Water	188 gals.	Production	1984–91

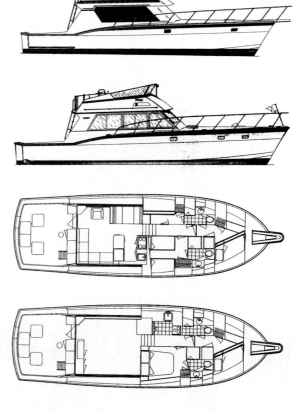

The Hatteras 52 Convertible is virtually identical to the earlier Hatteras 50 Convertible with the extra length going into a larger cockpit—a big improvement. A popular design (just over 200 were built), she's constructed on a modified-V bottom with a long keel below and balsa coring in the hullsides. In mid-1987, the Hatteras 52 was dramatically restyled on the outside with a fresh deckhouse window treatment, solid front windshield, and a redesigned flybridge. Two floorplans were available—a galley-down layout with two staterooms, and a more popular deckhouse galley arrangement with three staterooms. Both floorplans include two heads with stall showers. A teak interior was standard, and light ash woodwork became optional in 1987. The large cockpit features a molded-in tackle center, transom door with gate, and an access door to the spacious engine room. A good sea boat, the Hatteras 52 will cruise around 23 knots with 720-hp 8V92s and reach a top speed of 26 knots. Notably, this was the first Hatteras convertible to use side-dumping exhausts. ❑

See Page 230 for Pricing Information

HATTERAS 53 CONVERTIBLE

SPECIFICATIONS

Length	53'7"	Fuel	950/1,100 gals.
Beam	16'0"	Cockpit	147 sq. ft.
Draft	4'0"	Hull Type	Modified-V
Weight	61,000#	Deadrise Aft	NA
Clearance	15'2"	Designer	J. Hargrave
Water	250 gals.	Production	1969–80

Until she was retired from the fleet in 1980, the Hatteras 53 Convertible was the industry standard for over-50-foot sportfishing yachts. Her long foredeck and sweeping sheer combine to present the aggressive appearance of a thoroughbred sportfisherman, and her low-freeboard fishing cockpit has never been surpassed for sheer fishability. Indeed, this boat is so well proportioned that she must be seen up close to fully appreciate her size. There have been several three-stateroom, galley-up layouts used in the 53 including a popular U-shaped galley to port with separate under-counter refrigeration. An alternate two-stateroom floorplan has the galley located forward of the dinette in the companionway. Significant updates include increased fuel and prop pockets in 1976 and a restyled flybridge in 1977. A comfortable boat offshore (but a wet ride in weather), GM 12V71Ns (525-hp) will cruise the Hatteras 53 efficiently at 17 knots with a top speed of about 20 knots. The 8V92TIs (550-hp) will cruise around 19 knots and 12V71TIs (650-hp) cruise at 20 knots. ❏

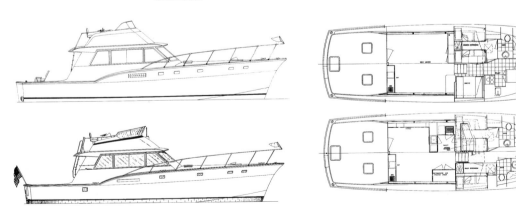

See Page 230 for Pricing Information

HATTERAS 54 CONVERTIBLE

SPECIFICATIONS

Length	54'11"	Fuel	1,320 gals.
Beam	17'4"	Cockpit	157 sq. ft.
Draft	5'10"	Hull Type	Modified-V
Weight	70,000#	Deadrise Aft	9°
Clearance	14'8"	Designer	Hatteras
Water	200 gals.	Production	1991–Current

The Hatteras 54—the replacement for the popular Hatteras 55 Convertible—is a completely impressive sportfisherman with the upscale interior accommodations of a fair-size motor yacht. A handsome boat with the aggressive profile and the rakish sheer found in all of the newer Hatteras convertibles, she's built on a new in-house hull design with a wide beam, shallow deadrise aft, and balsa-cored hullsides. Perhaps the most impressive feature of the Hatteras 54 is her innovative three-stateroom interior with an incredibly open deckhouse and the largest master stateroom seen in a convertible this size. The diagonal galley configuration *really* opens up the salon and adds considerable living and entertaining space. Additional features include an immense flybridge, a helm console designed to flush-mount all necessary electronics, and a spacious walk-in engine room with near-standing headroom. No racehorse, standard 870-hp 12V71s cruise the Hatteras 54 at 22 knots with a top speed of about 24–25 knots. Optional (and more popular) 1,040-hp 12V92s will cruise around 25 knots and reach 28+ knots top. ❏

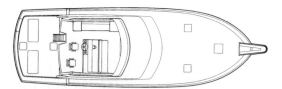

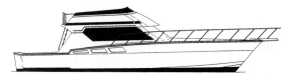

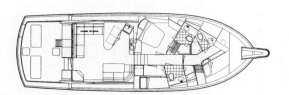

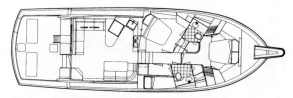

See Page 230 for Pricing Information

92

HATTERAS 55 CONVERTIBLE

1980–86

1987–89

SPECIFICATIONS

Length	55'8"	Fuel	1,285 gals.
Length WL	50'2"	Cockpit	158 sq. ft.
Beam	17'6"	Hull Type	Modified-V
Draft	4'10"	Deadrise Aft	NA
Weight	70,000#	Designer	J. Hargrave
Clearance	16'8"	Production	1980–89
Water	380 gals.		

Introduced in 1980 as the replacement for the Hatteras 53 Convertible, the 55 Convertible enjoyed a long and very successful production run. Her appearance was updated in 1987 when the front windshield was glassed over, and the cabin windows and flybridge were restyled in keeping with the current new look of the Hatteras convertibles. Two accommodation plans were offered with the three-stateroom, galley/dinette-up layout being the more popular. The huge cockpit came equipped with a molded tackle center, transom door, and direct access to the 55's spacious stand-up engine room. (Note that the air intakes for the engine room are located under the cockpit coaming.) The flybridge is huge with a superb helm layout and plenty of guest seating. No lightweight in spite of her cored hullsides, the Hatteras 55 is recognized as a stable fishing platform and a popular boat with anglers. Standard 650-hp 12V71TIs cruise at 19–20 knots (23 knots top), and 870-hp high-performance versions (available from 1982) cruise at 23+ knots (about 26 knots top). ❏

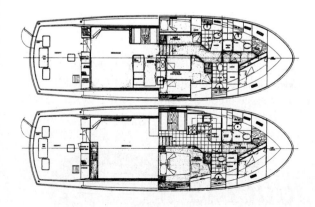

See Page 230 for Pricing Information

94

HATTERAS 58 CONVERTIBLE

SPECIFICATIONS

Length	58'10"	Fuel	1,660 gals.
Beam	17'9"	Cockpit	175 sq. ft.
Draft	5'11"	Hull Type	Modified-V
Weight	92,000#	Deadrise Aft	10°
Clearance	22'4"	Designer	Hatteras
Water	250 gals.	Production	1990–94

The Hatteras 58 Convertible is an in-house design built on a heavy modified-V hull with cored hullsides and a deep six-foot-deep keel. A good-looking boat, her three-stateroom, galley-up floorplan is arranged with the VIP guest suite equal in size and amenities to the master stateroom. The extravagant, high-style salon of the Hatteras 58 is impressive—closer to what one expects in a much bigger boat. Outside, the immense cockpit is set up for tournament-level fishing and includes an oversize transom door, live baitwell, molded tackle centers, engine room access, and a waist-level fish box built into the transom. The *two station* flybridge can be fully enclosed and features a centerline helm. The Hatteras 58 is a heavy boat, and the added drag of her deep keel results in disappointing performance: standard 1,040-hp 12V92s cruise at just 22 knots (26 knots top). More popular (also costlier, heavier, and thirstier) 1,350-hp 16V-92s will cruise at 28–29 knots (140 gph!) with a top speed of 32 knots. ❑

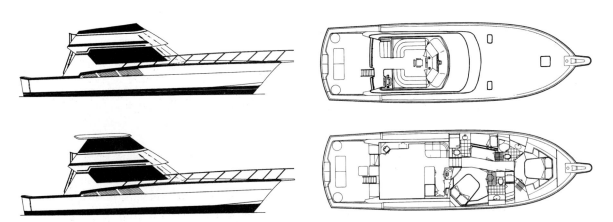

See Page 230 for Pricing Information

HATTERAS 60 CONVERTIBLE

SPECIFICATIONS

Length	60'11"	Fuel	1,555 gals.
Beam	18'0"	Cockpit	175 sq. ft.
Draft	4'11"	Hull Type	Modified-V
Weight	82,000#	Deadrise Aft	NA
Clearance	17'1"	Designer	J. Hargrave
Water	490 gals.	Production	1977–86

The 60 Convertible was a successful boat for Hatteras, and over 100 were built before she was replaced with the 65 Convertible in 1987. Offered with a fully enclosed and air conditioned flybridge, her three-stateroom, three-head floorplan is arranged with the galley and dinette on the deckhouse level and a midships master stateroom. A separate utility room forward of the engine compartment houses the air conditioning compressors, washer/dryer, etc., with room to spare. Additional features include a deep keel for prop protection, fore and aft flybridge helm stations, and a queen berth in the master stateroom. Her massive cockpit (175 sq. ft.) provides direct access to the well-arranged stand-up engine room. In 1968, the High-Performance model became available with more powerful motors, balsa coring in the hullsides, and beefed-up internal strengthening. A decent performer for her era, the standard 650-hp 12V71s will cruise the Hatteras 60 Convertible at 17–18 knots (about 20 knots top), and the high-performance 825-hp 12V71s cruise around 20 knots (23 knots top). ❏

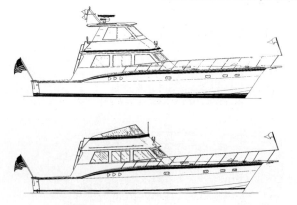

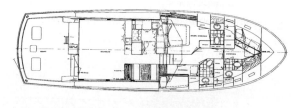

See Page 230 for Pricing Information

SPECIFICATIONS

Length	65'5"	Fuel	1,674 gals.
Beam	18'0"	Cockpit	183 sq. ft.
Draft	5'11"	Hull Type	Modified-V
Weight	102,000#	Deadrise Aft	NA
Clearance	16'4'	Designer	J. Hargrave
Water	460 gals.	Production	1987–Current

A good-selling boat (almost 90 have been sold to date), the Hatteras 65 Convertible is the most popular 60-foot-plus sportfisherman ever built. She's a step up from the earlier Hatteras 60 Convertible—not only are her lines more aggressive but the performance is improved as well. The 65's hull is derived from an extension of the mold used in the production of the Hatteras 60 with a finer entry and the addition of lightweight Baltec coring in the hullsides. Her spacious three-stateroom layout is highlighted by an extravagant salon that many consider to be the ultimate in a production sportfisherman. The 183 sq. ft. cockpit is the largest found in a production boat this size. Topside, a second helm station is aft of the bridge enclosure for cockpit visibility. Standard 1,035-hp Detroit 12V92s will cruise the Hatteras 65 Convertible around 23 knots. Optional 1,235-hp MTUs (or 1350-hp 16V92s) will cruise at 26–28 knots and reach a top speed of 30+ knots. Note the distinctive engine room air intakes on the hullsides. ❏

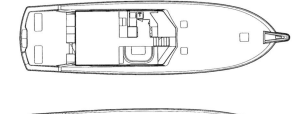

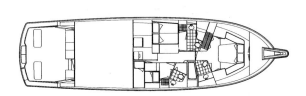

See Page 230 for Pricing Information

HATTERAS 82 CONVERTIBLE

SPECIFICATIONS

Length	82'8"	Water	840 gals.
Beam	21'5"	Fuel	4,075 gals.
Draft	6'6"	Hull Type	Modified-V
Weight	196,000#	Deadrise Aft	NA
Clearance	26'0"	Designer	Hatteras
Cockpit	NA	Production	1992–Current

To begin with, the Hatteras 82 is the largest production convertible available. A production fiberglass sportfisherman over eighty feet was just a dream a few years ago, and Hatteras is finding that there's a market for such a boat with some very well-heeled sport fishermen. Designed as a crewed yacht (with crew quarters are beneath the afterdeck, not forward), her extravagant triple-deck profile includes a two-station enclosed bridge, four staterooms with full heads, a vast salon/deckhouse galley living and entertainment area, and a huge tournament-style cockpit. Notable features of the Hatteras 82 include a circular stairwell in the salon for access to the bridge, a full-beam master suite with his-and-her heads, a utility/work room, a large observation deck overlooking the cockpit, and a convenient day head on the deckhouse level. The motors are almost lost in the huge stand-up engine room with its cockpit access. Powerful 16-cylinder Deutz diesels (2,540-hp each) are available in the Hatteras 82 Convertible as well as smaller 16V92s and 16V149s. ❏

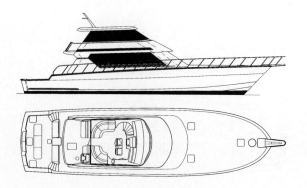

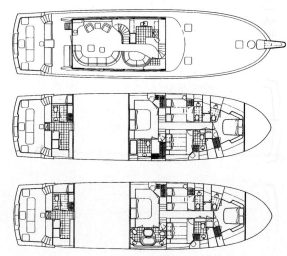

See Page 230 for Pricing Information

HENRIQUES 35 MAINE COASTER

HENRIQUES 38 SPORTFISHERMAN

SPECIFICATIONS

Length...........................35'4"	Fuel.......................320 gals.
Beam ....12'0"	Cockpit...............120 sq. ft.
Draft..............................3'1"	Hull Type.......Modified-V
Weight....................22,000#	Designer.........J. Henriques
Clearance.......................NA	Production...1977–Current
Water.......................60 gals.	

SPECIFICATIONS

Length...........................38'0"	Fuel.......................415 gals.
Beam ....13'10"	Cockpit...............140 sq. ft.
Draft.............................3'10"	Hull Type.......Modified-V
Weight....................28,000#	Deadrise Aft..................14°
Clearance....................21'0"	Designer.........J. Henriques
Water.......................75 gals.	Production...1988–Current

The Main Coaster 35 is a conservative long-range diesel sport-fisherman with good heavy-weather performance, a huge cockpit, and a practical interior layout with accommodations for four. The first production boat from the Henrique yard and their best-selling model ever (over 100 have been sold), she's a durable design that has remained essentially unchanged since her introduction in 1977. The hull is constructed the old-fashioned way—a solid fiberglass laminate with a fine entry, deep forefoot, and a flat run aft. The original floorplan had the galley on the deckhouse level, but by 1985 buyers were offered the option of having the galley down. The layout is basic but well finished with off-white laminate countertops and teak cabinetry throughout. The interior dimensions of the Maine Coaster are necessarily modest thanks to her huge 120 sq. ft. cockpit—an expansive fishing platform unmatched in size by any other production boat in her class. Standard 250-hp Cummins diesels will efficiently cruise the Henriques 35 at about 20 knots and reach 23 knots wide open. ❑

The Henriques 38 SF is a sturdy East Coast sportfisherman with a no-nonsense profile to go with her practical layout. She's built on a conventional modified-V hull with moderate beam, a flared bow, a gently curved sheer, and Divinycell-cored hullsides. The house, deck, and cockpit are constructed in a single mold (no leaks) and with a full 140 sq. ft. of cockpit space is among the largest to be found in a boat this size. Nearly all Henriques 38's have been built with the dinette (single-stateroom) layout, although a second stateroom can be added in place of the dinette. The somewhat dark interior is tastefully finished with traditional teak cabinetry and woodwork throughout. Outside, cockpit controls, transom door, tackle center, rod storage, and two 70-gallon recessed fish boxes are standard. Note the side-facing bridge ladder. A good-running boat, the Henriques 38 will cruise at 24–25 knots with the 375-hp Cat diesels (or 380-hp Volvos) and reach a top speed of about 30 knots. ❑

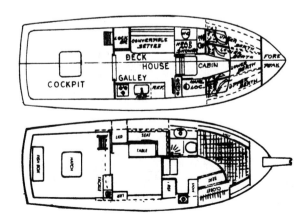

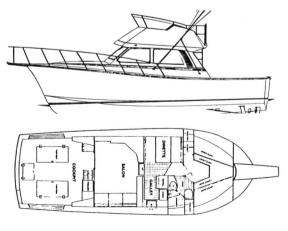

See Page 230 for Pricing Information

See Page 230 for Pricing Information

HENRIQUES 38 EL BRAVO

SPECIFICATIONS

Length	38'0"	Fuel	415 gals.
Beam	13'10"	Cockpit	130 sq. ft.
Draft	3'4"	Hull Type	Modified-V
Weight	28,000#	Deadrise Aft	14°
Clearance	9'3"	Designer	J. Henriques
Water	60 gals.	Production	1991–Current

Based on the proven hull of the Henriques 38 Sportfisherman with moderate beam and cored hullsides, the 38 El Bravo is a good-looking express fisherman with an array of features that serious anglers will appreciate. Foremost among her attributes is an absolutely huge fishing cockpit—only the Blackfin 38 rivals the El Bravo in cockpit space for a boat this size. Not surprisingly, the El Bravo's single-stateroom interior is small for a 38-footer since so much of the hull's LOA has been given over to the cockpit. A wrap-around helm console provides space for flush-mounting most electronics and a centerline hatch on the bridgedeck provides quick and easy access to the motors. Standard features include a tuna tower, generator, in-deck fish boxes, transom door, fresh- and salt-water washdowns, and lots of tackle and rod storage. Fully loaded with tower and gear, the 38 El Bravo will cruise economically at 25 knots with optional 425-hp Cats (375-hp Cats are standard) and reach a top speed of 29–30 knots. ❑

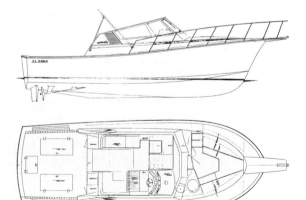

See Page 230 for Pricing Information

HENRIQUES 44 SPORTFISHERMAN

SPECIFICATIONS

Length	44'0"	Fuel	600 gals.
Beam	14'10"	Cockpit	170 sq. ft.
Draft	3'8"	Hull Type	Modified-V
Weight	37,000#	Deadrise Aft	12°
Clearance	NA	Designer	J. Henriques
Water	120 gals.	Production	1983–Current

The Henriques 44 SF is a dedicated Jersey-style sportfisherman with a conservative profile and the largest fishing cockpit in her class. She's built on a solid fiberglass hull with moderate beam, a shallow keel, and 12° of deadrise at the transom. While many convertible builders are quick to sacrifice cockpit space for a bigger interior, Henriques boats are well known in the trade for their big cockpits. In the case of the Henriques 44, that translates into a huge and completely uncluttered 12' x 14' cockpit—more than enough space to satisfy the requirements of the most demanding tournament activities. Insulated fish boxes, a transom door, tackle center, and teak covering boards are all standard. Several one- and two-stateroom floorplans have been offered over the years—the latest has an island berth in the forward stateroom—all fully paneled and finished with traditional teak woodwork. Most have been sold with the hard enclosure. Standard 550-hp 6V92s will cruise the Henriques 44 around 25 knots and reach 29 knots wide open. ❑

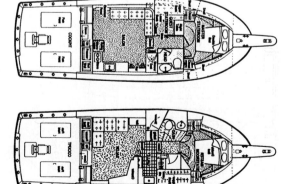

See Page 231 for Pricing Information

HYDRA-SPORTS 2550 WALKAROUND

SPECIFICATIONS

Length w/Pulpit ....27'1"	Fuel.......................200 gals.
Hull Length................25'5"	Cockpit ....NA
Beam ....9'5"	Hull Type..............Deep-V
Draft................................1'9'	Deadrise Aft..................20°
Weight.......................5,100#	Designer ....In-House
Clearance.......................NA	Production...1991–Current
Water.......................32 gals.	

The Hydra-Sports 2550 is a well-built fishing boat for anglers who appreciate the conveniences of a small cabin but still want full walkaround deck access to the bow. With her wide beam, the 2550 is a roomy boat, and the extra width allows the engines to be set further apart than most other 25-footers—a big asset when it comes to low speed handling. Bracket-mounted twin engines allows the 2550 to have a full-height transom with built-in storage bins and a bait prep center. Rod lockers are under both gunwales, and visibility from the elevated helm is excellent. Inside, the cuddy is set up with V-berths forward, a small galley, and a stand-up head with shower. A pull-out child-size bunk is hidden in a storage area across the aft end of the cuddy. Additional features include an in-deck fish box and cockpit washdowns. A good rough-water performer, twin 200-hp outboards will cruise the Hydra-Sports 2550 at 28 knots and reach 45–46 knots wide open. ❑

HYDRA-SPORTS 2800 SF

SPECIFICATIONS

Length w/Pulpit ....30'1"	Fuel.......................300 gals.
Beam ....10'7"	Cockpit ....NA
Draft................................2'3"	Hull Type..............Deep-V
Hull Weight..............7,900#	Deadrise Aft..................19°
Clearance.......................NA	Designer ....In-House
Water.......................31 gals.	Production...1991–Current

A good-running boat with an integrated transom and efficient deck plan, the Hydra-Sports 2800 manages to combine all the necessary elements of a good offshore fishing boat. Hull construction is solid fiberglass, and the wide 10'7" beam makes for a roomy layout both above and below. In the cockpit, a bait prep station and baitwell are built into the 2800's full-height transom, and a big lift-out fish box resides in the cockpit sole. Visibility from the raised bridgedeck is excellent, and a chart flat is built into the dash in front of the companion seat. Belowdecks is a well-arranged cabin with a private head, small galley area, and plenty of headroom. The dinette converts into a double bed, and a small aft cabin is placed below the bridgedeck. Additional features include trim tabs, walk-thru transom door, tackle drawers, molded pulpit, and cockpit washdowns. Designed to handle up to 500-hp, twin 225-hp outboards will cruise the Hydra-Sports 2800 SF at an easy 25 knots and hit 40+ knots top. ❑

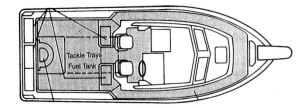

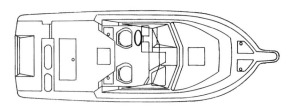

See Page 231 for Pricing Information

See Page 231 for Pricing Information

HYDRA-SPORTS 3300 SF

SPECIFICATIONS

Length	32'11"	Fuel	270 gals.
Beam	9'6"	Cockpit	75 sq. ft.
Draft	2'8"	Hull Type	Deep-V
Hull Weight	10,500#	Deadrise Aft	24°
Clearance	14'3"	Designer	In-House
Water	40 gals.	Production	1989–92

The Hydra-Sports 3300 Sportfisherman is a high-performance offshore fisherman with a versatile center console deck plan, a cuddy cabin forward, and bracket-mounted engines aft. Designed for offshore work, the 3300's deep-V hull is balsa-cored from the water-line up, and the relatively narrow 9'6" beam allows her to be trailer-able with a permit. A good-looking boat with an aggressive profile, the 3300 features a wide helm console with space for flush-mounting some electronics. Cockpit seating is excellent: a bench seat behind the helm seat faces aft, and a full-width bench seat folds flush against the transom for more cockpit space. Inside the small cuddy, a V-berth will sleep two adults, and the compact galley has a stove and sink. Note that the stand-up head/shower compartment is located inside the center console—a great convenience. No lightweight (and not particularly economical to operate), bracket-mounted 300-hp Evinrude V8 outboards will cruise the Hydra-Sports 3300 at 24 knots and reach a top speed of 36–37 knots. ❏

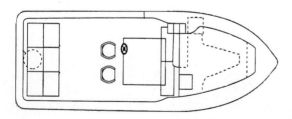

HYLAS 47 CONVERTIBLE

SPECIFICATIONS

Length	46'6"	Fuel	600 gals.
Length WL	40'5"	Cockpit	90 sq. ft.
Beam	16'9"	Hull Type	Modified-V
Draft	3'10"	Deadrise Aft	NA
Weight	38,000#	Designer	Jim Wynne
Clearance	13'4"	Production	1987–93
Water	160 gals.		

Built in Taiwan, the Hylas 47 is a rakish flybridge convertible with a Euro-style profile and a notably wide beam. The hull was drawn by Jim Wynne and features balsa-cored hullsides, prop pock-ets, and plenty of freeboard all around. The interior is incredibly expansive thanks to the super-wide beam, and the Hylas is the only boat in this size range to feature walkaround queen berths in *both* staterooms. (A three-stateroom layout with the galley up was optional.) The front windows are real, not glassed-over, and both heads have separate stall showers. The deep cockpit is large enough for a fighting chair, but the gunwales are abnormally high and not well-suited to fishing. Note the cockpit engine room access door. On balance, the main features of the Hylas are centered around her spa-cious accommodations and glitzy appearance, and, while she looks like a competent fisherman, she's really more suited to family cruis-ing. Twin 450-hp 6-71 diesels will cruise at 22–23 knots (26 top), and optional 550-hp 6V92s cruise about 24 knots and reach 27 knots top. ❏

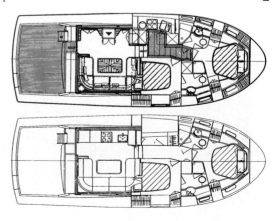

See Page 231 for Pricing Information

See Page 231 for Pricing Information

INNOVATOR 31

SPECIFICATIONS

Length........................30'10"	Cockpit..................75 sq. ft.
Beam ....10'4"	Hull Type........Modified-V
Weight....................11,000#	Deadrise Aft...................12°
Clearance......................9'0"	Designer ....Ed Monk, Jr.
Water.......................60 gals.	Production.............1988–91
Fuel........................265 gals.	

The Innovator 31 is a well-built West Coast design with a single-minded objective: catching fish. Introduced in 1988, she was
updated in late 1991 and re-introduced as the Innovator 30 (see
lower floorplan below). Only a few of the 30s were built, however,
and of the two models the original 31 sold better (about 35 were
built) and remains better-known today. The hull is solid glass, and
the deadrise at the transom is a modest 12°. Inside, the cabin is
arranged with berths for four along with a compact galley and a
stand-up head with shower.The cockpit comes with two in-deck
fish boxes along with washdowns and rod holders. Engine boxes
provide excellent access to the motors, and molded cockpit steps at
the cockpit corners lead to extra-wide sidedecks. Gas engines were
standard, but most Innovators were delivered with one of several
diesel options. Among them, Cummins 210-hp diesels will deliver
an impressive cruising speed of 23–24 knots and a top speed of
around 28 knots.   ❑

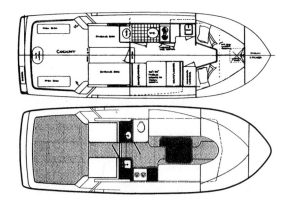

See Page 231 for Pricing Information

103

INTREPID 30

SPECIFICATIONS

Length w/Bracket	32'1"	Fuel	170 gals.
Beam	8'6"	Cockpit	NA
Draft	2'0"	Hull Type	Deep-V
Weight	3,250#	Deadrise Aft	22°
Clearance	5'5"	Designer	J. Wynne
Water	None	Production	1991–Current

The Intrepid 30 is a high-performance center console fisherman with the same lightweight, high-tech construction common to all modern Intrepid designs. Offered with or without a cuddy cabin, the Intrepid 30 is among the lightest and most fuel-efficient boats in her class. She's also an excellent rough-water boat thanks to her Jim Wynne-designed deep-V hull. The relatively narrow 8'6" beam adds to the performance but doesn't offer the cockpit dimensions of most competitive models. The console is arranged with space for flush-mounting a few pieces of electronics, and the bench seat forward of the helm has storage under. The fully integrated bracket brings the motors close to the transom and reduces the possibility of a snagged line while working a rodtip around the engines. It's worth noting that Intrepid has always been a semi-custom builder, and all of their models can be highly personalized. A fast ride, twin 250-hp Yamaha outboards will cruise the Intrepid 30 at a brisk 33 knots and reach a top speed of 46+ knots. ❏

INTREPID 33

SPECIFICATIONS

Length	35'6"	Fuel	250 gals.
Beam	10'6"	Cockpit	NA
Draft	2'0"	Hull Type	Deep-V
Weight	5,500#	Deadrise Aft	22°
Clearance	8'0"	Designer	M. Peters
Water	40 gals.	Production	1993–Current

An incredibly lightweight boat for her size, the Intrepid 33 is a high-performance day fisherman with plenty of sex appeal to go with her practical layout. Her raceboat-style stepped hull is built on a solid fiberglass bottom with Divinycell coring in the hullsides, and multidirectional pre-impregnated fabrics are used along with vacuum-bagging in the high-tech construction process. The 33's center console deck plan will appeal to those seeking plenty of guest seating in addition to good overall fishability. The layout features a semi-circular settee forward of the helm and a wide-open cockpit with three in-deck storage boxes and a below-deck livewell. There's room in the console for flush-mounting electronics and convenient swim steps are outboard of the integral engine bracket. Belowdecks, the cabin will sleep three and comes with a small galley and a private head with shower. A good sea boat, the Intrepid 32 will cruise economically at a fast 33 knots and reach a top speed of around 42 knots with twin 275-hp outboards. ❏

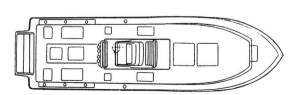

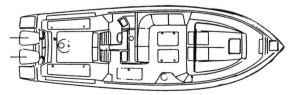

See Page 231 for Pricing Information

See Page 231 for Pricing Information

INTREPID 38

SPECIFICATIONS

Length ....37'6"
Beam ....12'0"
Draft.............................2'6"
Weight....................14,000#
Clearance......................NA
Water.......................52 gals.

Fuel.......................300 gals.
Cockpit ....108 sq. ft.
Hull Type...............Deep-V
Deadrise Aft..................NA
Designer..............M. Peters
Production.............1991–93

With her high-tech materials and state-of-the-art construction, the Intrepid 38 is a very specialized boat with a price tag to match. She's built on a stepped deep-V hull similar to that used by racing boats. Her primary purpose is offshore fishing, and she's the largest production inboard *center console* dayboat on the market. The walkaround deck layout will appeal to light-tackle and stand-up anglers. The cockpit will easily handle a full-size chair, and there are molded steps port and starboard. The helm is set well aft on the bridgedeck with seating forward—innovative but windy with no screen. The compact helm console provides space for flush mounting most electronics, and a hydraulically operated hatch provides excellent access to the motors below. Inside, the accommodations are basic with a small galley, king-size V-berths, a stand-up head, and a unique double berth below the helm. Twin 400-hp Merlin inboard diesels will cruise at 28–29 knots and reach 35 knots top, and 425-hp Cats are capable of 40 knots top. ❏

See Page 231 for Pricing Information

ISLAND GYPSY 32 FISHERMAN

SPECIFICATIONS

Length	32'1"	Water	120 gals.
Length WL	29'8"	Fuel	250 gals.
Beam	11'6"	Cockpit	110 sq. ft.
Draft	3'8"	Hull Type	Semi-Disp.
Weight	13,000#	Designer	H. Halvorsen
Clearance	NA	Production	1987–Current

A great-looking boat with a distinctive profile, the Island Gypsy 32 Fisherman uses the same two-piece semi-displacement hull mold used in the 32 Sedan model. Said to be based on a traditional Australian fishing boat design (yeah, sure), she's built at the Halvorsen yard in mainland China. This is a handsome little fisherman with a spacious cockpit and a straightforward, business-like appearance. The accommodations—basic overnight accommodations for two anglers—include V-berths forward, an enclosed head with stand-up shower, galley, and dinette. The lower helm (optional) is uniquely located just inside the cockpit door where forward and port-side visibility are limited. The flybridge is rather small with passenger seating aft of the helm. Engine access is from inside the cabin as well as via a raised cockpit hatch, and the transom door and swim platform are standard. A single 275-hp Sabre diesel will cruise the Island Gypsy 32 Fisherman at an economical 15 knots (17–18 knots top), and optional 210-hp Cummins will cruise at a brisk 20+ knots. ❑

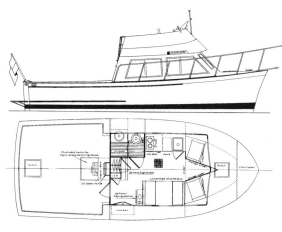

See Page 231 for Pricing Information

SPORTS FISHERMAN

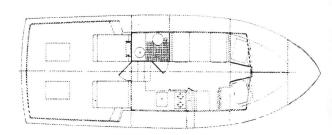

STANDARD TWIN ENGINE LAYOUT

SPECIFICATIONS

LOA ....39'4"	Fuel........................365 gals.
Hull Length................36'4"	Cockpit ....90 sq. ft.
Beam ....13'4"	Hull Type........Modified-V
Draft.............................2'6"	Deadrise Aft..................10°
Weight....................23,500#	Designer.........F. McCarthy
Clearance....................11'0"	Production...1986–Current
Water.......................75 gals.	

A handsome sportfisherman with flowing, almost custom lines, the Jersey 36 is built on a solid fiberglass hull with moderate beam and substantial flare at the bow. Her original single-stateroom interior (still available) is arranged with the galley down, a big head compartment with stall shower, and an offset double berth forward. A new floorplan introduced in 1991 offers a centerline double berth forward with the addition of a dinette (or second stateroom) at the expense of the stall shower and some engine room and salon space. The bridge layout was also rearranged in 1991 with the helm console now on the centerline rather than to starboard—a big improvement. The 36 comes with a long list of standard equipment including a factory hardtop. Her large fishing cockpit features very low freeboard with plenty of room for tackle centers and a mounted chair. With standard 350-hp gas engines, the Jersey 36 will cruise at 19–20 knots and reach 29 knots wide open. Optional 375-hp Cats cruise at 24–25 knots and top out around 28 knots. ❑

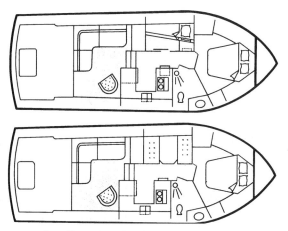

See Page 231 for Pricing Information

SPECIFICATIONS

Length..........................40'0"	Fuel........................400 gals.
Beam ....14'6"	Cockpit ....NA
Draft.............................3'5"	Hull Type........Modified-V
Weight....................28,000#	Deadrise Aft..................10°
Clearance.......................NA	Designer.........F. McCarthy
Water....................100 gals.	Production.............1973–88

No longer in production, the 40 Dawn is a classic East Coast fisherman with a low-deadrise bottom, a sweeping sheerline, and a greatly flared bow. Her wide beam and relatively deep keel insure stable handling characteristics in most weather conditions, and a spacious cockpit provides plenty of room for tournament-level fishing activities. Two interior floorplans were offered with the single-stateroom dinette layout proving more popular than the two-stateroom, galley-up version. The interior—which is a little dark—is completely finished with teak woodwork and cabinetry. (Note that the switch from woodgrain mica to an all-teak interior was made in 1979.) Standard features include bow pulpit, air conditioning, generator, stereo, and color TV. Still popular with experienced fishermen, many of the Jersey 40s were powered with economical 235-hp Volvo diesels which cruise around 18 knots at only 18 gph, or 1 mpg—very efficient indeed. Later models with the optional 325-hp Cats are capable of cruising around 20 knots and reaching 23–24 knots wide open. ❑

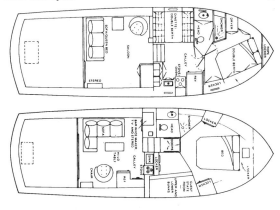

See Page 231 for Pricing Information

JERSEY DEVIL 44 SF

SPECIFICATIONS

Length..........................44'0"	Fuel........................400 gals.
Beam ....14'6"	Cockpit................154 sq. ft.
Draft.............................14'6"	Hull Type........Modified-V
Weight ....34,800#	Deadrise Aft...................10°
Clearance....................14'2"	Designer.........F. McCarthy
Water.....................100 gals.	Production.............1980–85

When it comes down to cockpit size, the Jersey Devil 44 is simply in a class by herself. Eight of these durable canyon runners were built during a 6-year production run and several can be found today operating as charter boats along the East Coast. She was built using a stretched version of the Jersey 40 hull with a deep entry and a slightly rounded bottom. Transom deadrise is a modest 10°. The basic two-stateroom interior is arranged with the galley up on the salon level. (The front windshield panels are glassed over.) Early interiors were finished with simulated teak laminates, but Jersey went to an all-teak interior in 1979. A very useful feature is the huge storage bin below the galley sole—large enough for an inflatable and extra ground tackle. The cockpit has lockable rod racks under the gunwales and a tackle center to port. A good-running boat, all Jersey Devil 44s were powered with 450-hp GM 6-71 diesels. She'll cruise around 24–25 knots and run 27 knots wide open. ❏

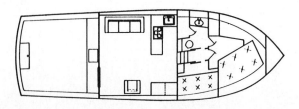

See Page 231 for Pricing Information

JERSEY 44 CONVERTIBLE SF

SPECIFICATIONS

LOA ....45'6"	Fuel ....400/476 gals.
Hull Length.................42'4"	Cockpit................114 sq. ft.
Beam ....15'8"	Hull Type........Modified-V
Draft.............................3'6"	Deadrise Aft...................10°
Weight ....30,500#	Designer.........F. McCarthy
Clearance....................17'0"	Production...1989–Current
Water.....................100 gals.	

Introduced as the Jersey 42, the 44 Convertible retains the distinctive styling characteristics—the long foredeck, sweeping sheer, and graceful profile—common to all Jersey boats. (The front windshield is almost a rarity on big convertibles these days). Construction is solid fiberglass, and the Jersey 44 carries more beam for her length than any of her predecessors. Aside from building a tough hull, the more recent Jersey boats have very tastefully finished interiors. Several accommodation plans have been offered during her production years and the now-standard dinette layout (two staterooms with the galley down to starboard) features upper/lower berths in the guest stateroom and a breakfast bar in the salon. Throughout, the interior is fully paneled with dark teak woodwork and cabinetry. The large fishing cockpit is free of obstructions, and a factory hardtop and flybridge enclosure are standard. Caterpillar 375-hp diesels will cruise the Jersey 42 around 22 knots with a top speed of 26. The optional 485-hp 6-71s cruise at a fast 27 knots and reach 30 knots wide open. ❏

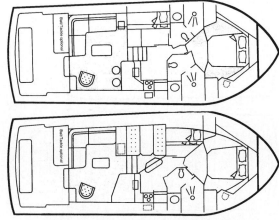

See Page 231 for Pricing Information

JERSEY 47 CONVERTIBLE

SPECIFICATIONS

Length	47'4"	Fuel	600 gals.
Beam	15'8"	Cockpit	124 sq. ft.
Draft	3'10"	Hull Type	Modified-V
Weight	36,000#	Deadrise Aft	10°
Clearance	17'0"	Designer	F. McCarthy
Water	150 gals.	Production	1987–Current

Introduced in 1989, the Jersey 47 Convertible is the largest boat currently offered by this small New Jersey manufacturer. Notably, Jersey is one of the few builders that hasn't abandoned single-skin fiberglass hull construction thus avoiding the complexities (and the benefits) of cored hulls. The graceful profile of the Jersey 47 is quite distinctive, and her extra-long foredeck and cockpit bridge overhang make her an easy boat to recognize. Note the use of front windows—most modern sportfisherman have glassed-over windshields (although that option is available from the factory). Three interior plans are offered with the three-stateroom, galley-up layout being the more popular. Both guest staterooms are small, but the heads are very large and fitted with shower stalls. Traditional teak woodwork is used extensively throughout the interior. Outside, the cockpit is arranged for serious fishing pursuits, and the flybridge is huge with seating for eight. Reliable 6-71 diesels (485-hp) are standard, and the Jersey 47 Convertible will cruise at a fast 26 knots with a top speed of 30 knots. ❑

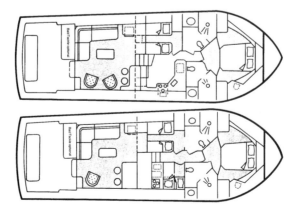

See Page 231 for Pricing Information

111

T-380 Open

T-350

T-320 Open

T-250 CC

Choose Your Favorite Fishing Luhrs

9 exciting choices from 25' to 38'

Sport Fishing is a growing sport and Luhrs has a boat just right for you. These are fishing yachts for the serious angler, equipped with all the right gear and powered with gasoline or diesel inboard engines.

The Luhrs Tournament Series features wide beam, deep-V hulls with a flared bows. All have towers or T-tops, electronics boxes and bait prep stations. Most have color TV, VCR, stereo and microwave as standard equipment. All feature a 5 year Limited Hull Warranty, offered at very competitive prices.

So visit your Luhrs dealer today to experience the incomparable design, performance and value of a Luhrs Tournament sportfisherman. You'll be hooked!

Luhrs®

5 YEAR Security Assurance Plan

U.S. CUSTOMER HOTLINE: 800-829-5847
Luhrs Corporation
255 Diesel Rd, St. Augustine, FL USA 32086
Phone: (904) 829-0500 FAX: (904) 829-0683

Luhrs reserves the right to change, without notice, any materials, specifications, equipment and/or accessories. See Dealer for details on the Luhrs five year limited warranty.

T-250 O/CC

T-290-O

T-300

T-320

T-320-O

T-350

T-380

T-380-O

SPECIFICATIONS

Length	25'1"	Fuel	196 gals.
Beam	9'3"	Cockpit	NA
Draft	2'3"	Hull Type	Modified-V
Weight	6,500#	Deadrise Aft	15°
Clearance	8'6"	Designer	Luhrs
Water	20 gals.	Production	1993–Current

The Luhrs 250 Open is an express fisherman with a big cockpit and surprisingly roomy cabin accommodations. Inboard-powered 25-footers are rare (most fishing boats this size are designed for outboards) and the 250 has few competitors in the marketplace. Hull construction is solid fiberglass, and her wide beam and moderate-deadrise hull allow the 250 to carry a tower without difficulty. Trim tabs are recessed into the hull to avoid snagging lines. The fold-away helm seat is unique: it rests on an arm extending from below the console. The bridgedeck lifts to reveal the engine compartment, and an oval in-deck livewell is located in the cockpit. (There's also a fish box built into the transom.) The biggest surprise is the cabin with berths for four, a compact galley, and head with shower. A single 454-cid gas engine (standard) will cruise the 250 Open at 16–17 knots (28 knots top), and optional twin 170-hp Yanmar diesels will cruise efficiently at 24 knots burning only 10 gph. A center console version is also available (see layout below). ❏

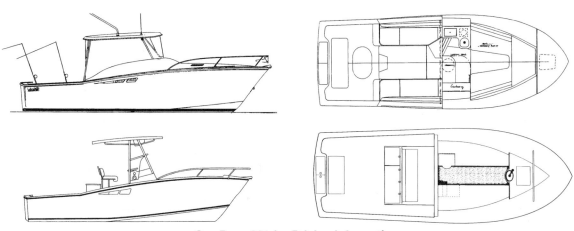

See Page 231 for Pricing Information

LUHRS TOURNAMENT 290 (EARLY)

SPECIFICATIONS

Length	29'0"	Fuel	200/260 gals.
Beam	10'9"	Cockpit	60 sq. ft.
Draft	2'5"	Hull Type	Modified Deep-V
Weight	9,000#	Deadrise Aft	17°
Clearance	14'6"	Designer	Mike Peters
Water	40 gals.	Production	1986–88

The first of three models to carry the same name, the Tournament 290 pictured above is notable for her ungainly and somewhat top-heavy bridgedeck profile. She's built on a modified-V hull with a double chine and a relatively steep 17° of deadrise at the transom. An out-and-out fishing boat, the Tournament 290 has a large bi-level cockpit with roughly 60 sq. ft. of fishing area on the lower level. All were delivered with a standard factory tower. Three lift-out fish boxes provide good access to the rudder posts and bilges, and a cockpit washdown and coaming padding were standard. The accommodations below are simple but nicely finished with oak paneling and a teak and holly sole. Cabin headroom is 6'2". The full-width of the cabin results in narrow sidedecks, and walking forward to the bow is difficult. Twin 270-hp Crusaders were standard with GM 6.2 diesels offered as an option. The 270s will cruise the Luhrs Tournament 290 around 24 knots with a top speed of 30+ knots. ❏

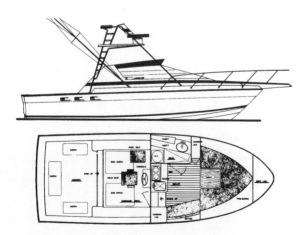

See Page 232 for Pricing Information

LUHRS TOURNAMENT 290

SPECIFICATIONS

Length	29'6"	Fuel	250 gals.
Beam	10'9"	Cockpit	NA
Draft	2'5"	Hull Type	Modified Deep-V
Weight	7,480#	Deadrise Aft	17°
Clearance	NA	Designer	Mike Peters
Water	40 gals.	Production	1989–91

With her large cockpit and walkaround decks, the Luhrs Tournament 290 will appeal to the fisherman who requires basic cabin accommodations to go with a good day boat layout. The second of three 290 express models from Luhrs, she was built on the same hull as the original Tournament 290 (1986–88) with steep deadrise at the transom and solid fiberglass construction. Dedicated anglers will appreciate the wide sidedecks and efficient cockpit. Fishing features include rod storage under the gunwales, a drop curtain to enclose the lower helm, standard bait center, a large livewell in the transom, and a standard factory tower with controls. Note the lack of a windshield at the helm. Below, the cabin is surprisingly spacious. The dinette converts to a double berth, and the galley and head are adequate for weekend service. The seat at the lower helm also folds out when two extra berths are required. A good-running boat with standard 350-cid gas engines, the Tournament 290 will cruise around 23 knots and reach 31–32 knots wide open. ❏

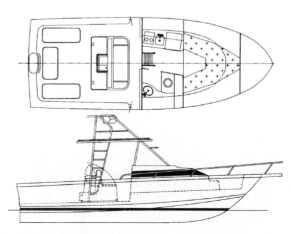

See Page 232 for Pricing Information

LUHRS TOURNAMENT 290 OPEN

SPECIFICATIONS

Length	29'10"	Fuel	300 gals.
Beam	11'6"	Cockpit	NA
Draft	2'9"	Hull Type	Deep-V
Weight	8,000#	Deadrise Aft	18°
Clearance	16'6"	Designer	Luhrs
Water	30 gals.	Production	1992–Current

The Tournament 290 Open is a scaled-down version of the Tournament 380 introduced in 1991. Luhrs is building some good-looking fishing boats these days, and the 290 Open will appeal to anglers seeking a capable offshore fishing platform at an affordable price. She's built on a lightweight deep-V hull with cored hull-sides and a wide 11'6" beam. Her cockpit is large enough for a full-size chair and includes two in-deck fish boxes, a unique lift-out transom door, and a smaller fish box built into the transom. The helm is located on the centerline, and the bridgedeck sole lifts up for easy access to the step-down engine compartment. There are overnight accommodations for four in the small cabin which is arranged with the head in the forepeak. Notable features include a full tower with buggy top and controls, electronics box, entertainment center, bait prep station, and side exhausts. Standard 350-cid gas engines will cruise at 16–17 knots and reach a top speed of about 27 knots. ❏

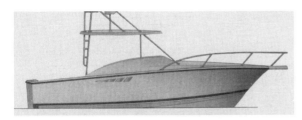

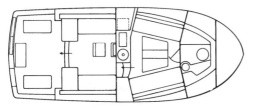

See Page 232 for Pricing Information

LUHRS ALURA 30

SPECIFICATIONS

Length	30'0"	Water	38 gals.
Length WL	28'0"	Fuel	196 gals.
Beam	10'3"	Cockpit	110 sq. ft.
Draft	2'11"	Hull Type	Semi-Disp.
Weight	7,800#	Designer	Luhrs
Clearance	NA	Production	1987–90

Featuring a distinctive Downeast profile, the Alura 30 is a versatile weekender with a large fishing cockpit and comfortable cabin accommodations. She's built of solid fiberglass on a semi-displacement hull with a sweeping sheer and moderate beam. A long keel provides a measure of prop protection while providing good handling characteristics at low speeds. Although not considered a beamy boat, the cockpit is exceptionally large and includes built-in baitwells and fish boxes. Helm visibility is good, and the windshield can be opened for ventilation. The wide sidedecks are notable. Inside, the cabin layout is clean and simple, and the teak and holly sole is especially attractive. Two people can cruise aboard this boat for a few days without problem. A good all-purpose design, the Alura 30 will do well as a dive boat or as an inexpensive fisherman and weekend cruiser. Note that the keel was redesigned in 1988 to reduce vibration problems. Her single 270-hp gas engine provides an efficient cruising speed of 14–15 knots and a top speed of around 22 knots. ❏

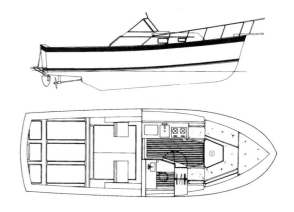

See Page 232 for Pricing Information

115

LUHRS TOURNAMENT 300

SPECIFICATIONS

LOA	34'6"	Water	40 gals.
Hull Length	31'6"	Fuel	250 gals.
Beam	10'9"	Hull Type	Deep-V
Draft	2'6"	Deadrise Aft	18°
Weight	12,000#	Designer	Luhrs
Clearance	11'6"	Production	1991–Current

The Tournament 300 SF is an updated version of the earlier Tournament 290 model with several improvements including a windshield and molded swim platform. A good-looking boat, she's built on a deep-V hull with average beam and cored hullsides. The cockpit is large enough to handle a fighting chair, and comes standard with an in-deck fish box, tackle drawers, bait prep center, and two built-in seats with rod gimbals. The helm is set behind a center-vent windshield, and there's space in the console for flush-mounting electronics. A baitwell is located on the transom platform and the full-length helm seat features a hydraulic lift mechanism for easy access to the (tight) engine compartment. Cabin accommodations include a dinette that converts to a double berth, a small galley, and a stand-up head with shower—a generous layout for a walkaround boat. Twin 350-cid gas engines are standard (21 knots cruise and 28 top), and 170-hp Yanmar diesels (21 knots at cruise and 24–25 knots wide open) are a popular option. ❏

See Page 232 for Pricing Information

LUHRS TOURNAMENT 320

SPECIFICATIONS

LOA	34'8"	Water	60 gals.
Hull Length	31'6"	Fuel	300 gals.
Beam	13'0"	Cockpit	NA
Draft	3'1"	Hull Type	Modified-V
Weight	15,000#	Deadrise Aft	15°
Clearance	NA	Production	1988–Current

The Luhrs Tournament 320 has the classic profile of a high-dollar South Florida custom fisherman. Indeed, her lines are very attractive, and the affordable price of the Tournament 320 has already made her a popular boat in a short period of time. She's built on a wide-beam modified-hull with lightweight balsa coring and a moderate 15° of deadrise at the transom. Primarily a fishing boat, her surprisingly roomy cabin can accommodate six in reasonable comfort. An island berth is fitted in the stateroom, and a complete galley and head compartment round out the floorplan. The flybridge is fitted with bench seating forward of the helm console. The 320's large, uncluttered fishing cockpit has enough room for a small mounted chair. Additional features include built-in fish boxes, livewell, tackle center with controls, fresh and saltwater washdowns, and a transom door. Standard 320-hp Crusader gas engines will cruise the Luhrs Tournament 320 around 20 knots and reach a top speed of 29–30 knots. Note that the dinette was eliminated in 1992. ❏

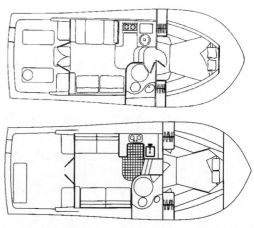

See Page 232 for Pricing Information

LUHRS 320 OPEN

SPECIFICATIONS

LOA ....34'8"	Water.......................60 gals.
Hull Length.................31'6"	Fuel.........................340 gals.
Beam ....13'0"	Cockpit ....NA
Draft..............................3'1"	Hull Type........Modified-V
Weight ....15,000#	Deadrise Aft...................15°
Clearance....................15'9"	Production...1994–Current

The Tournament 320 Open is a good-looking express fisherman with a good deal of value built into her affordable base price. Designed as a smaller alternative to the popular 380 Open, the 320 is built on a modified-V hull with cored hullsides, a wide beam, moderate transom deadrise, and considerable flare at the bow. The deck plan is arranged with a walkaround center console and flanking bench seats on the bridgedeck level and a big fishing cockpit aft with a transom door, molded tackle center, and stand-up livewell. Inside, the 320 Open has berths for five with a V-berth/dinette forward and a convertible settee whose hinged backrest becomes a pilot berth at night. The teak woodwork, Corian countertops, and upscale fabrics make this an attractive and easily cleaned interior. The list of standard equipment is impressive: full tower with controls, hardtop with electronics box, enclosure panels, and cockpit washdowns. Standard 320-hp Crusader gas engines will cruise the Luhrs Tournament 320 Open around 21 knots and reach a top speed of 30–31 knots. ❏

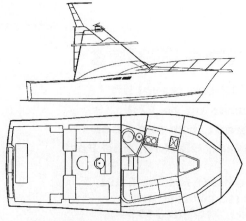

See Page 232 for Pricing Information

LUHRS 340 SPORTFISHERMAN

SPECIFICATIONS

Length.........................34'0"	Fuel........................260 gals.
Beam ....12'6"	Cockpit ....67 sq. ft.
Draft..............................3'0"	Hull Type........Modified-V
Weight ....12,300#	Deadrise Aft...................15°
Clearance....................11'5"	Designer.............J. Fielding
Water.......................60 gals.	Production.............1983–87

The Luhrs 340 Sportfisherman shares the same hull as the Silverton 34 Convertible—a proven and well-tested design with generous flare at the bow, plenty of beam, and moderate transom deadrise. She was marketed as an inexpensive and fully equipped fisherman with a marlin tower, fish boxes, salt and freshwater washdown, side exhausts, and recessed rod storage in the cabin—all standard. The Luhrs 340 has a large bi-level cockpit (the bridgedeck is raised two feet from the cockpit sole) resulting in good helm visibility and adequate working space in the engine compartment. The helm console is positioned on the centerline with the companionway offset to starboard. Below, the 340's cabin is arranged in the normal fashion with a convertible dinette and V-berths forward. Teak-trimmed white mica cabinetry and a teak and holly sole highlight the interior. Standard 454-cid gas engines will cruise at 21 knots (about 30 top), and optional 210-hp GM 8.2 diesels will cruise around 23 knots and reach 25–26 knots wide open. ❏

See Page 232 for Pricing Information

LUHRS TOURNAMENT 342

LUHRS ALURA 35

SPECIFICATIONS

Length	34'0"	Fuel	300 gals.
Beam	12'6"	Cockpit	67 sq. ft.
Draft	3'2"	Hull Type	Modified-V
Weight	13,500#	Deadrise Aft	15°
Clearance	11'5"	Designer	J. Fielding
Water	60 gals.	Production	1986–89

SPECIFICATIONS

Length	35'5"	Fuel	260 gals.
Beam	12'2"	Cockpit	NA
Draft	2'11"	Hull Type	Modified-V
Weight	12,800#	Designer	Luhrs
Clearance	NA	Production	1988–89
Water	55 gals.		

The Luhrs Tournament 342 shares the same hull as the Luhrs 340 but with a different superstructure and a much larger interior. She was sold as a fairly complete package in keeping with the long-standing Luhrs practice of marketing a well-equipped boat at an affordable price. Her cockpit will handle a mounted chair and comes equipped with fresh and saltwater washdowns, fish boxes (small), and padded coaming. The flybridge is particularly spacious with bench seating forward of the console. The original layout featured two staterooms, a deckhouse dinette, and oak woodwork. A much-revised layout was introduced in 1988 with only one stateroom, a more open salon/galley arrangement, and an updated decor with an absence of any wood. The 342 also has a unique cabin ventilation system with hidden air intakes located beneath the forward bridge overhang. A good-running boat with brisk acceleration, the Luhrs Tournament 342 will cruise at 21–22 knots with standard 454-cid Crusaders gas engines and reach a top speed of 30 knots. ❏

The appealing Downeast character of the original Alura 30 is missing from the more recent Alura 35. Here, the styling is more contemporary and the accent is on the "sportboat" image. As such, the Alura 35 was designed to appeal to the price-conscious buyer. This is a very straightforward design without the curved windshield, fancy radar arch, or elaborate swim platform found in many of today's modern sportboats. What the Alura 35 does provide is a lot of boat for the money. The interior accommodations are roomy and very comfortable with a mid-cabin stateroom fitted aft below the raised bridgedeck. The decor is light and airy, and the teak-and-holly cabin sole is especially attractive. Outside, the 35's large bi-level cockpit is well-suited for fishing, and anglers will appreciate the bait prep center with cutting board behind the helm seat. A practical and low maintenance family cruiser, twin 270-hp Crusader gas engines will cruise the Alura 35 at around 17 knots with a top speed of 25–26 knots. ❏

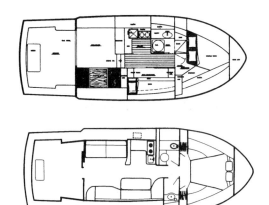

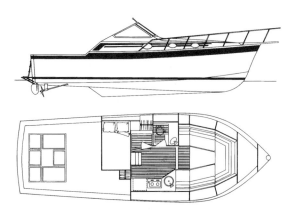

See Page 232 for Pricing Information

See Page 232 for Pricing Information

LUHRS TOURNAMENT 350

SPECIFICATIONS

LOA	38'6"	Water	93 gals.
Hull Length	35'0"	Fuel	390 gals.
Beam	12'10"	Cockpit	94 sq. ft.
Draft	3'4"	Hull Type	Modified Deep-V
Weight	19,000#	Deadrise Aft	17°
Clearance	16'0"	Production	1990–Current

Designed to fill the gap between the Tournament 320 and 380 models, the Luhrs Tournament 350 is built on an all-new hull design with balsa coring in the hullsides and a wide 12'10" beam. The aggressive profile and custom-style appearance of the 350 are accented by her darkly tinted wraparound windows and a rakish flybridge with its stylish cockpit overhang. Inside, the single-stateroom floorplan is arranged with the mid-level galley open to the salon. A centerline island berth is forward, and the head includes a separate stall shower. While the interior of the Tournament 350 seems large for only a 35-foot boat, the cockpit is still big enough for the installation of a fighting chair and a full tackle center. A transom door and in-deck fish boxes are standard. Twin 454-cid gas engines will cruise the Tournament 350 at an easy 17 knots with a top speed of around 25-26 knots. The optional 300-hp GM diesels cruise around 23 knots and reach 26 knots top. ❏

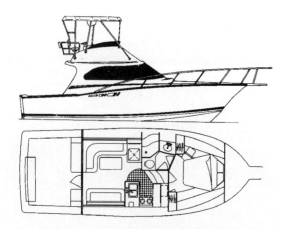

See Page 232 for Pricing Information

LUHRS TOURNAMENT 380

SPECIFICATIONS

LOA	40'10"	Water	100 gals.
Hull Length	37'9"	Fuel	450 gals.
Beam	14'11"	Cockpit	100 sq. ft.
Draft	3'7"	Hull Type	Deep-V
Weight	28,000#	Deadrise Aft	18°
Clearance	16'0"	Production	1989–Current

The Tournament 380 is a good-looking convertible with a classic sportfish profile and a surprisingly affordable price tag. She's built on a beamy deep-V hull designed with generous flare at the bow and balsa coring in the hullsides. The half-tower is standard, and her tournament-style flybridge and the large cockpit with molded tackle centers will satisfy the demands of most serious anglers. Inside, the original two-stateroom interior was arranged with the galley to port on the salon level. The floorplan was restyled in 1990 with an athwartships galley forward of the salon—an unusual but still-practical layout. Storage is excellent, and the head compartment is very large. Interestingly, the front windows are real and not fiberglassed-over, although the wraparound deckhouse mask does a good job of concealing them. A popular model with the lines of a custom boat, 454-cid gas engines were standard (15 knots cruise/about 25 knots top) in the 380 until 1991 when they were replaced by 425-hp J&T 6-71 diesels (22 knots cruise/27 knots top). ❏

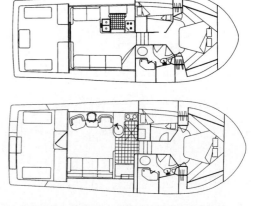

See Page 232 for Pricing Information

LUHRS TOURNAMENT 380 OPEN

SPECIFICATIONS

Length	37'10"	Fuel	600 gals.
Beam	14'11"	Cockpit	100 sq. ft.
Draft	3'7"	Hull Type	Deep-V
Weight	24,000#	Deadrise Aft	18°
Clearance	22'0"	Designer	Luhrs
Water	85 gals.	Production	1991–Current

Luhrs has come up with a real beauty in the Tournament 380 Open, a versatile and feature-packed fishing machine with a very inviting price tag. Open sportfishermen have been growing in length and popularity in recent years, and this is becoming a very competitive market. Built on a wide, low-profile hull with cored hullsides, the 380 Open is a roomy and capable offshore boat. Her large bi-level cockpit layout includes a unique centerline helm console, flanking full-length lounge seating with rod storage under, molded transom fish box, and P&S molded tackle centers which double as bait-watching seats. Below, the interior is notable for its spacious layout and stylish decor—impressive indeed for a serious fishboat. Additional features include a standard tuna tower, hydraulic bridgedeck lift mechanism for superb engine room access, pop-up electronics display at the helm, and side exhausts. A good-running boat with excellent range, standard 485-hp 6-71 diesels will cruise the Tournament 380 Open around 26 knots and deliver 29–30 knots wide open. ❏

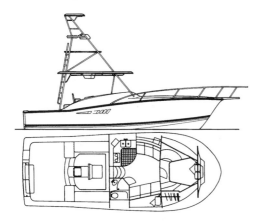

See Page 232 for Pricing Information

LUHRS TOURNAMENT 400

SPECIFICATIONS

Length	40'0"	Fuel	400 gals.
Beam	14'0"	Cockpit	NA
Draft	3'2"	Hull Type	Modified-V
Weight	25,500#	Deadrise Aft	14°
Clearance	14'0"	Designer	Bob Rioux
Water	100 gals.	Production	1987–90

Built on the same hull as the Silverton 40 Convertible, the Luhrs Tournament 400 was a moderately priced convertible sport-fisherman with aggressive lines and comfortable accommodations. With her rakish flybridge and black wraparound deckhouse mask, the Luhrs 400 has a very distinctive profile. Her two-stateroom interior is arranged with the galley down and an L-shaped dinette in the salon. The forward stateroom has an offset double berth, and over/under bunks are fitted in the guest cabin. The 400's interior originally featured oak paneling but was revised in 1988 with updated fabrics and off-white mica surfaces trimmed in teak. Fishing accessories in the cockpit include fresh- and salt-water washdowns, an in-deck fish box, rocket launchers, and flush rod holders. The half tower was standard, and the flybridge is notably large compared to other convertibles her size. The cruising speed with 454-cid gas engines is a sluggish 15–16 knots (around 25 knots top). Optional 375-hp Cats will cruise the Tournament 400 around 22 knots and reach 26 wide open. ❏

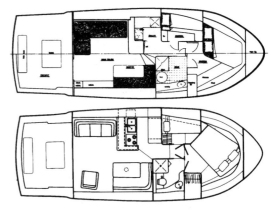

See Page 232 for Pricing Information

MAKO 263 WALKAROUND

SPECIFICATIONS

LOA w/Pulpit	30'10"	Water	25 gals.
Hull Length	28'7"	Fuel	240 gals.
Beam	9'6"	Hull Type	Deep-V
Draft	1'7"	Deadrise Aft	23°
Weight	5,000#	Designer	Mako
Clearance	8'0"	Production	1993–Current

The Mako 263's wide beam and integrated swim platform/engine bracket combine to make her one of the biggest 26-footers in the business. She's built on a deep-V hull with a solid fiberglass bottom and cored hullsides, and there's enough foam packed into the hull to provide positive floatation. The 263's walkaround deck layout boasts a full-height transom with a built-in livewell, shower, and two storage bins. (Note the absence of a transom door.) There are two big fish boxes in the cockpit sole, and tackle drawers are located behind the helm and companion seats. Rod storage is under the gunwales. The sidedecks are wide, deep, and well-secured, and bench seating is built into the forward part of the house. Inside, the midcabin floorplan sleeps four and includes a fair-size galley, good headroom, and a private head with shower. A good performer with better-than-average economy, the Mako 263 will cruise efficiently at 29 knots with a pair of 275-hp O/Bs and reach about 40 knots wide open. ❑

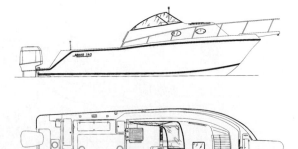

See Page 232 for Pricing Information

MAKO 286 INBOARD

SPECIFICATIONS

Length	28'5"	Fuel	213/230 gals.
Beam	9'10"	Cockpit	NA
Draft	2'6"	Hull Type	Deep-V
Weight	8,000#	Deadrise Aft	19°
Clearance	6'6"	Designer	Mako
Water	30 gals.	Production	1985–Current

A popular boat for Mako (and the largest boat in the fleet for several years), the 286 Inboard is a dual console fisherman with a practical deck layout and good overall performance. She's built on a rugged deep-V hull with a relatively wide beam and positive foam floatation. Like all of the larger Makos, the 286 performs well in rough weather and tracks nicely in a chop. The single-level cockpit is large enough to handle a full-size fighting chair, and there's a large fish box built into the cockpit sole near the transom. The portside console includes a sink with storage below, and there's built-in bench seating forward of the helm. Belowdecks, the lockable cuddy cabin contains adult-size V-berths, storage lockers, and a plumbed marine head. Additional features include teak covering boards, under-gunwale rod storage, companion seat, and very sturdy bow rails. An easy-riding boat with standard 350-cid gas inboards, the Mako 286 will cruise at 23 knots and reach a top speed of 30–31 knots. ❑

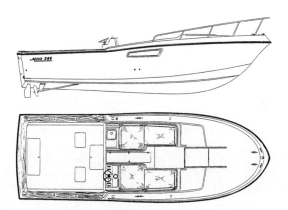

See Page 232 for Pricing Information

MAKO 295 DUAL CONSOLE

SPECIFICATIONS

LOA w/Bracket ....31'9"
Hull Length.................28'3"
Beam ....10'0"
Hull Draft....................1'11"
Hull Weight ....6,800#
Clearance......................6'0"
Water......................39 gals.

Fuel........................300 gals.
Cockpit ....56 sq. ft.
Hull Type...............Deep-V
Deadrise Aft.................19°
Designer ....Mako
Production...1993–Current

The largest Mako ever, the 295 is a long-range dayboat with a wide-open deck plan and a low-profile appearance. She's built on a deep-V hull with a full-length inner liner, cored hullsides, and a relatively wide beam. The cockpit is large enough for a mounted chair and features two 6' fish boxes in the sole, an in-deck 165-qt. livewell, bait prep station, and transom door. (A storage bin built into the full-height transom can also be plumbed as a livewell.) While the cabin is small, it can still sleep four in a pullman-type V-berth. There's also a private head with a sink. The sidedecks leading around the cuddy are narrow, and the low bow rails don't add much in the way of foredeck access. Notably, the outboards are mounted on 32" centers (rather than the 28" centers seen in most outboard this size), and low-speed handling is impressive. A heavy boat, twin 250-hp Yamahas will cruise efficiently at 26 knots (about 1 gpm) and reach 37–38 knots top. ❏

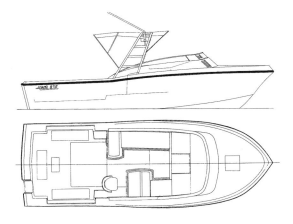

See Page 232 for Pricing Information

Built Like An Icebreaker, Moves Like A Jet.

With twin 225hp outboards, the Marlin 350 SF moves at speeds exceeding 50 mph yet offers its passengers the comfort of seaworthiness and superior handling.

Constructed with the world's strongest core material sprayed between hand-laid fiberglass and gel coat that includes ultra-violet inhibitors, these boats are built to handle the extremes of blue water fishing and last the test of a harsh environment.

Efficient use of space above and below deck provides comfort for fishing and relaxing not found in other boats of this size.

The Marlin 35 SF ia a complete blue water fishing machine at a price that offers supreme value.

For more information contact:

850 Northeast Third Street
Dania, Florida 33004
305-929.3800

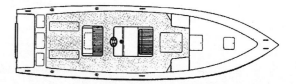
See Page 232 for Pricing Information

124

MATTHEWS 46 SPORTFISHERMAN

SPECIFICATIONS

Length	46'0"	Fuel	320/520 gals.
Beam	14'10"	Cockpit	NA
Draft	3'6"	Hull Type	Modified-V
Weight	34,000#	Deadrise Aft	8°
Clearance	14'2"	Designer	Hargrave
Water	100 gals.	Production	1970–75

Although many of the old wood-built Matthews boats have disappeared, the company's switch to fiberglass in 1970 insured that used Matthews products will be with us for a few more years. Designed by Jack Hargrave (then becoming famous for his work with Hatteras), the Matthews 46 SF is still admired for her classic convertible profile—a long foredeck, aggressive bow, and well-proportioned house. She shares the same Halmatic fiberglass hull used in the production of the 46 Motor Yacht with slack chines and a deep keel. She rolls a lot, and she's wet, but the ride is soft. Indeed, the hull is notably efficient and easily driven. Early models of the Matthews 46 SF (called a 45-footer in 1970–71) were built with a two-stateroom, galley-down layout. In 1973, a revised three-stateroom, galley-up floorplan became available. The cockpit is roomy, and the bridge (with the helm forward) is small. Optional 320-hp V-903 Cummins diesels cruise the 46 SF around 17–18 knots and provide a top speed of 21 knots. ❏

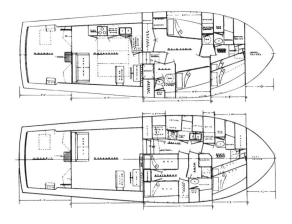

See Page 233 for Pricing Information

MATTHEWS 56 SPORTFISHERMAN

SPECIFICATIONS

Length	56'0"	Fuel	700 gals.
Beam	16'0"	Cockpit	NA
Draft	4'1"	Hull Type	Modified-V
Weight	63,000#	Deadrise Aft	8°
Clearance	14'5"	Designer	Hargrave
Water	300 gals.	Production	1972–75

Basically an enlarged version of the 46 Sportfisherman, the Matthews 56 SF is one of four different Matthews models built on the same 56-foot fiberglass hull during 1971–75 (the other three were motor yacht designs). These were heavily constructed modified-V hulls with tapered aftersections, slightly rounded bilges, and a deep keel for directional stability. The superstructure of the 56 SF is wood, and the decks are fiberglass over wood. Besides being a good fisherman, the 56 is a comfortable cruising yacht in spite of her slight rolling characteristics. The floorplan includes three staterooms with the large master stateroom located to starboard. The galley is on the salon level, and both head compartments are fitted with stall showers. Outside, the deep cockpit can easily accommodate a full-size fighting chair. The flybridge is equally spacious, although the helm console is located forward thus limiting cockpit sightlines. Supposedly, only three 56 Sportfisherman were built, and all were equipped with 8V71TI diesels. She'll cruise in the 18-knot range and reach a top speed of around 21 knots. ❏

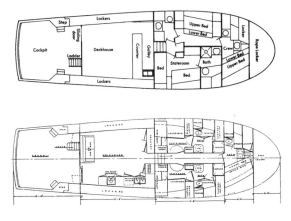

See Page 233 for Pricing Information

MEDITERRANEAN 38 CONVERTIBLE

SPECIFICATIONS

LOA w/Pulpit	42'10"	Water	100 gals.
Hull Length	38'4"	Fuel	300/450 gals.
Beam	12'6"	Cockpit	NA
Draft	3'2"	Hull Type	Deep-V
Weight	25,000#	Deadrise Aft	18°
Clearance	11'6"	Production	1985–Current

The Mediterranean 38 is a sturdy West Coast fisherman with a good deal of value packed into her low factory-direct price. She's built on a balsa-cored deep-V hull, and the construction involves some 65 individual molds resulting in a finished, gelcoated surface everywhere you look. Two interior layouts are offered with the single-stateroom floorplan being more popular. An overhead compartment in the salon can store six rods and reels. The interior is comprised of laminated teak cabinets and decorator fabrics. Outside, the sidedecks are very wide, and a cockpit tackle center, transom door, and fish box are standard. (Some anglers may not like the inward-opening transom door.) The step in the sheer was eliminated in 1987, and in 1988 the cockpit was rearranged and the fuel increased to 450 gallons. The flybridge can be ordered with the helm console forward or aft for East Coast owners. Cummins 300-hp diesels will cruise at an economical 22 knots (27 knots top), and the larger 388-hp Cummins will cruise at 24–25 knots and reach 30 knots wide open. ❑

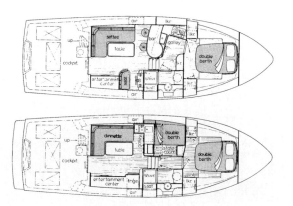

See Page 233 for Pricing Information

MIKELSON 50 SEDAN SF

SPECIFICATIONS

Length	48'6"	Fuel	1,000 gals.
Beam	16'8"	Cockpit	90 sq. ft.
Draft	3'6"	Hull Type	Modified-V
Weight	35,000#	Deadrise Aft	12°
Clearance	NA	Designer	Tom Fexas
Water	300 gals.	Production	1990–Current

The Mikelson 50 is a completely radical design whose innovations go beyond her distinctive profile. Designed by Tom Fexas, the 50 is constructed on a beamy fully cored hull with rounded bilges and a reverse transom. The result is a surprisingly fast boat (23-knots cruise/26 top) with just 425-hp Cat diesels and V-drives. (The V-drives are used to get the engines aft where they're accessed from the cockpit—a very unusual application in a boat this size.) The Mikelson comes with a spacious two-stateroom, galley-down teak interior with built-in settees in the salon and stall showers in both heads. A three-stateroom floorplan is also available. The cockpit isn't very deep, but it's still big enough for two or three anglers and their gear. (The Mikelson 48 SF—basically the same boat—has an integrated swim platform.) The flybridge is huge with *two* helm stations and a circular dinette aft of the helm. A good-selling boat with excellent range, the Mikelson 48 is usually found in West Coast markets. ❏

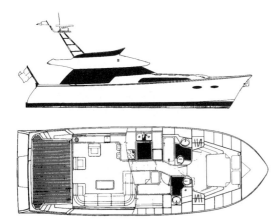

See Page 233 for Pricing Information

MIKELSON 60 SPORTFISHER

SPECIFICATIONS

Length	59'1"	Fuel	1,000 gals.
Beam	17'2"	Cockpit	NA
Draft	4'4"	Hull Type	Modified-V
Weight	55,000#	Deadrise Aft	14.4°
Clearance	NA	Designer	Tom Fexas
Water	300 gals.	Production	1992–Current

Designed by Tom Fexas and built in Taiwan, the Mikelson 60 is an innovative West Coast sedan fisherman with a dramatic profile and plenty of built-in sex appeal. She's built on a lightweight, fully cored hull with a wide beam, prop pockets, and moderate transom deadrise—a notably efficient hull requiring relatively small engines for her size. Two floorplans are available: the standard galley-down layout has three staterooms, and the alternate arrangement calls for two staterooms with an enlarged galley. Either way, the wide-open salon comes with built-in settees and plenty of teak cabinetry and woodwork. Stepping outside, an unusual aft deck platform overlooks the cockpit. The flybridge is huge with a wraparound helm console and seating for a crowd. The engines are located under the aft deck where they're accessed via hydraulically operated hatches in the sole. Note that the Mikelson has a rather unique underwater exhaust system with a transom bypass for quiet operation. A good performer with 735-hp 8V92s, she'll cruise at 23 knots and reach 26–27 knots wide open. ❏

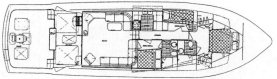

See Page 233 for Pricing Information

128

NORTH COAST 31 SPORTFISHERMAN

SPECIFICATIONS

Length	30'8"	Fuel, Opt	410 gals.
Beam	12'0"	Cockpit	77 sq. ft.
Draft	3'2"	Hull Type	Deep-V
Weight	11,300#	Deadrise Aft	23°
Clearance	8'0"	Designer	C. Jannace
Water	50 gals.	Production	1988–90
Fuel, Std	275 gals.		

Several builders inaccurately apply the "Deep-V" label to their hulls in an attempt to curry favor with offshore fishermen convinced of the superiority of a deep-V design. In the case of the North Coast 31 the claim is more than just advertising hype—the transom deadrise is a steep 23°. In a field crowded with small inboard sportfisherman, the North Coast 31 has several features that anglers will admire. The helm visibility is particularly good, and the unique console provides space for flush-mounting most electronics. The cockpit has molded steps for easy access to the recessed sidedecks, and there are two removable fish boxes in the sole. Below, the well-finished cabin has a teak-and-holly sole, attractive light ash trim work, and a head with stall shower. A good-running boat, twin 250-hp Cummins diesels will cruise the North Coast 31 at an economical 25 knots with a top speed of about 29 knots. Note that Blackfin recently acquired the molds to this model, and she's now marketed as the Blackfin 31 Combi. ❏

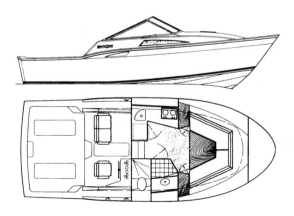

See Page 233 for Pricing Information

OCEAN 29 SUPER SPORT

OCEAN 32 SUPER SPORT

SPECIFICATIONS

Length	29'0"	Fuel	215 gals.
Beam	11'6"	Cockpit	68 sq. ft.
Draft	2'5"	Hull Type	Modified-V
Weight	13,500#	Deadrise Aft	14°
Clearance	10'6"	Designer	D. Martin
Water	35 gals.	Production	1990–92

The Ocean 29 SS is one of the smallest flybridge boats ever offered by a major builder. Even with her wide beam and relatively heavy displacement, however, she's a small boat, and the addition of a flybridge results in a little more weight up high than is desirable. Like the earlier 32 and 35 SS models, the 29 SS carries more transom deadrise than most previous Ocean hulls. Inside, the floorplan includes a small salon/dinette level with a step-down galley to starboard and an offset double berth in the stateroom. The interior is attractively furnished with varnished teak woodwork, wall-to-wall carpeting, mini-blinds, and decorator fabrics. The good-size cockpit is fitted out with an in-deck fish box, tackle centers, and rod lockers. Standard 350-cid gas engines deliver a cruising speed of around 22 knots and a top speed of 30 knots. Larger 454-cid gas engines will cruise around 25 knots (34 knots top). Optional 250-hp Cummins diesels deliver 26 knots at cruise (at only 16 gph) and 30 knots wide open. ❏

SPECIFICATIONS

Length	32'0"	Fuel	280 gals.
Beam	12'4"	Cockpit	NA
Draft	2'6"	Hull Type	Modified-V
Weight	17,043#	Deadrise Aft	13°
Clearance	11'1"	Designer	D. Martin
Water	60 gals.	Production	1989–92

The Ocean 32 Super Sport has the classic raked-back cabin profile and aggressive performance found in all of the larger Ocean models. Indeed, she's a good-looking boat with a roomy cockpit and a surprisingly open interior layout. The fact that she has a real salon—and a stylish one at that—is notable in a 32-footer, and the walkaround island berth in the stateroom is a comfort seldom found in a boat this size. There's plenty of room in the cockpit for a mounted chair, and the flybridge will seat six comfortably. Standard features included a central vacuum system, bimini with enclosure panels, basic electronics, and teak covering boards in the cockpit. Twin 320-hp Crusader gas engines were standard for the Ocean 32 (about 23 knots cruise/30 top). Optional 250-hp Cummins diesels will cruise economically at 22 knots (at 1 mpg) and reach 25–26 knots wide open. The larger 300-hp Cummins will cruise at a fast 25 knots (about 29 knots top). The engine room is a seriously tight fit. ❏

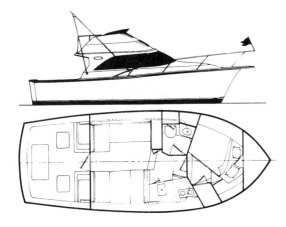

See Page 233 for Pricing Information

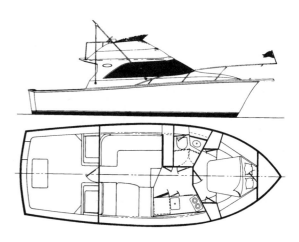

See Page 233 for Pricing Information

OCEAN 35 SUPER SPORT

SPECIFICATIONS

Length	35'0"	Fuel	320 gals.
Beam	13'0"	Cockpit	NA
Draft	2'5"	Hull Type	Modified-V
Weight	19,800#	Deadrise Aft	13°
Clearance	11'9"	Designer	D. Martin
Water	70 gals.	Production	1988–Current

The Ocean 35 SS is a fast convertible sportfisherman with the sleek Jersey-style profile of the larger Ocean yachts. She's built on a modified-V hull with considerable beam forward, Divinycell-cored hullsides, and more transom deadrise than earlier Ocean hulls. The interior is roomy for a 35-footer with the salon completely open to the galley and dinette. The list of standard equipment includes a generator, air conditioning, and central vacuum system. The use of interior teak woodwork is notably scaled-back in the 35 SS compared to other Ocean models. Outside, the cockpit is fitted with a standard transom door, molded-in tackle center, side lockers, and teak covering boards. The Ocean 35 does not have the teak cockpit sole or toe rail found in previous Ocean yachts. Standard 320-hp Crusaders will cruise at 21 knots and reach 30 knots wide open. The optional 300-hp Cummins diesels will cruise the Ocean 35 SS around 25 knots (at an economical 23 gph) and reach 30 knots top. The engine room is a tight fit. ❑

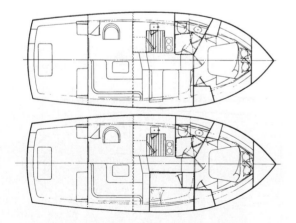

See Page 233 for Pricing Information

OCEAN 35 SPORT CRUISER/SF

SPECIFICATIONS

Length	35'0"	Fuel	280 gals.
Beam	13'0"	Cockpit	74 sq. ft.
Draft	2'11"	Hull Type	Modified-V
Weight	18,000#	Deadrise Aft	13°
Clearance	8'9"	Designer	D. Martin
Water	55 gals.	Production	1990–92

In general, the open dayboat-type sportfishermen offered by major builders tend to be at the high end of the price spectrum. The Ocean 35 Sport Fish and Sport Cruiser models fill this void rather nicely as both are priced moderately compared to the competition. Based on the Ocean 35 SS hull, the basic difference between these two express models is the additional cockpit seating and radar arch found in the Sport Cruiser and the teak covering boards, tackle lockers, and hinged transom gate of the SF. The interiors are identical in both boats with a centerline double berth in the forward stateroom, a nifty mid-cabin fitted beneath the bridgedeck, head with shower stall, and a portside galley with dinette opposite. Both models came with an impressive list of standard equipment including air conditioning, generator, washdowns, rod storage, and bimini with enclosure. Twin 320-hp gas engines will cruise at 22–23 knots and exceed 30 knots wide open. The optional 300-hp Cummins diesels cruise around 26 knots with a top speed of 29–30 knots. ❑

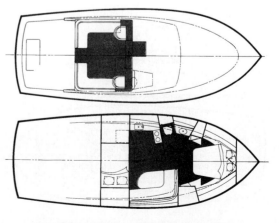

See Page 233 for Pricing Information

OCEAN 38 SUPER SPORT (EARLY)

SPECIFICATIONS

Length	38'4"	Fuel	354 gals.
Beam	13'8"	Cockpit	NA
Draft	3'2"	Hull Type	Modified-V
Weight	23,000#	Deadrise Aft	NA
Clearance	13'1"	Designer	D. Martin
Water	80 gals.	Production	1984–91

The 38 Super Sport was one of Ocean's best-selling models with 158 built during her long production run. She's a big boat for her length with the speed and performance of a sportfisherman and the upscale interior of a family cruiser. Indeed, the 38 SS has the aggressive good looks that many other convertibles her size can only admire. Note the glassed-over deckhouse windshield panels and wraparound black mask. Most 38s were delivered with the two-stateroom layout (the alternate single-stateroom floorplan has a more open salon), and the varnished teak woodwork is impressive. One of the more appealing aspects of the Ocean 38 is her serviceable engine room. The cockpit is set up for serious fishing and includes a tackle center, freezer, teak sole, and teak covering boards. A sistership—the Ocean 38 Super Sportfisherman (1984–87)—was also available with a larger cockpit and no fixed salon bulkhead. A stiff ride in a chop, 375-hp Caterpillar diesels will cruise at a fast 26–27 knots and reach 30+ knots top. ❏

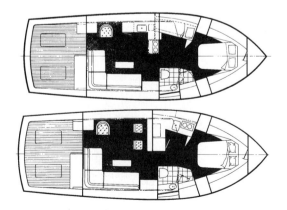

See Page 233 for Pricing Information

OCEAN 38 SUPER SPORT

SPECIFICATIONS

Length	38'9"	Fuel	400 gals.
Beam	14'2"	Cockpit	85 sq. ft.
Draft	3'8"	Hull Type	Modified-V
Weight	27,000#	Deadrise Aft	NA
Clearance	15'6"	Designer	D. Martin
Water	80 gals.	Production	1992–Current

The new Ocean 38 SS looks a lot like the original 38 SS on the outside, but she's an entirely different boat below. Built on a slightly wider (and heavier) hull with a sharper entry and cored hull-sides, the new 38 has a smaller cockpit than her predecessor but a much larger interior. Indeed, the two-stateroom floorplan is innovative and completely unique for a boat of this size. Stepping into the salon, one is confronted with a surprisingly spacious and efficient layout with the dinette positioned forward (beneath the windshield panels) and an open galley to starboard. The companionway is all the way to port (there's a 7' rod locker in the outside wall) and leads down to a *midships* master stateroom of truly remarkable proportions. The engine room, however, is a tight fit. Note that the hard-top is standard. The Ocean 38 SS comes standard with a choice of 425-hp Cats (22–23 knots cruise/28 knots top) or the new 430-hp Volvo diesels (26 knots cruise/31 top). ❏

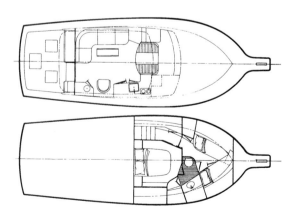

See Page 233 for Pricing Information

OCEAN 40 SUPER SPORT

SPECIFICATIONS

Length	40'2"	Fuel	450 gals.
Beam	14'4"	Cockpit	80 sq. ft.
Draft	3'0"	Hull Type	Modified-V
Weight	30,000#	Deadrise Aft	NA
Clearance	12'0"	Designer	D. Martin
Water	100 gals.	Production	1977–80

The Ocean 40 Super Sport was the first production design built by Ocean Yachts. Introduced to enthusiastic reviews in 1977, the 40 SS was a breakthrough boat capable of reaching a top speed of 30 knots—unheard-of performance back then in a production boat this size. The cockpit is adequate for serious fishing activities and came with a teak sole and teak covering boards. Delivered with a long list of standard equipment (generator, air conditioning, cockpit freezer, etc.), the Ocean 40 was available with a two-stateroom, galley-down floorplan or a two-stateroom, galley-up layout with a day berth in the companionway. The interior is a blend of varnished teak woodwork and vinyl wall coverings, and large cabin windows in the salon allow for plenty of natural lighting. A good-running boat, with the standard 410-hp 6-71 diesels, she'll cruise around 25 knots and reach a top speed of 28–29 knots. Stretched to 42 feet in 1980, the Ocean 40 SS marked the beginning of a long series of Ocean sportfishing designs. ❑

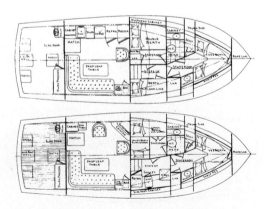

See Page 233 for Pricing Information

OCEAN 42 SUPER SPORT (EARLY)

SPECIFICATIONS

Length	42'0"	Fuel	480 gals.
Beam	14'4"	Cockpit	100 sq. ft.
Draft	3'4"	Hull Type	Modified-V
Weight	30,000#	Deadrise Aft	1.5°
Clearance	12'0"	Designer	D. Martin
Water	100 gals.	Production	1980–83

One of the best-selling Oceans ever, the 42 Super Sport is a stretched (and much-improved) version of the earlier 40 Super Sport with the additional length used to create a full 100 sq. ft. fishing cockpit. A good-looking boat with a clean-cut profile and excellent performance, her nearly flat bottom (just 1.5° of transom deadrise) provides a nice turn of speed with relatively small engines but makes for a hard ride in a chop. Oceans are noted for their attractive teak interiors, and the 42 is no exception. The standard two-stateroom layout is well arranged and suited to the needs of anglers and family cruisers alike. Additional features included a cockpit control station, tackle center, freezer, transom door, teak cockpit sole, central vacuum system, and a generator. On the downside, the engine room is a tight fit, and there's plenty of exterior teak trim to maintain. A good-running boat, the 42 SS will cruise at a fast 26 knots and reach a top speed of about 30 knots with standard 6-71 diesels. ❑

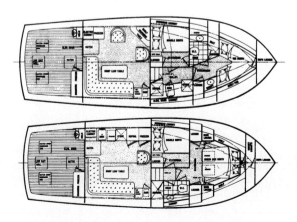

See Page 233 for Pricing Information

OCEAN 42 SUPER SPORT

SPECIFICATIONS

Length ....42'0"	Fuel.........................466 gals.
Beam ....15'0"	Cockpit ....100 sq. ft.
Draft..............................3'7"	Hull Type........Modified-V
Weight ....35,466#	Deadrise Aft.................NA
Clearance.....................12'0"	Designer ....D. Martin
Water.....................100 gals.	Production...1991–Current

One of the so-called "new generation" of Super Sport models, the Ocean 42 (note that an earlier Ocean 42 SS model ran from 1980–83) has a more streamlined deckhouse than earlier Ocean models together with an all-new hull design with additional transom deadrise and a shallower, slightly longer keel. Notably, most of the outside teak trim is gone. But the real story is below, where the Ocean 42 lays claim to one of the more impressive galley-up salon layouts to be found in a boat this size. It's an overused refrain, but this is a spacious floorplan. The master stateroom is very roomy, and a unique midships guest stateroom extends beneath the salon sole and includes a double *and* single berth. Additional features include a stylish hardtop, separate pump room below the galley sole, a huge fish box in the cockpit, and good engine access. Cat 425-hp diesels are standard in the Ocean 42 (24 knots cruise/27 knots top), and 485-hp 6-71s (26 knots cruise/30 top) are optional. ❑

OCEAN 44 SUPER SPORT

SPECIFICATIONS

Length..........................44'0"	Fuel.........................480 gals.
Beam ....15'2"	Cockpit ....130 sq. ft.
Draft..............................3'6"	Hull Type........Modified-V
Weight....................36,000#	Deadrise Aft.................1.5°
Clearance.....................13'3"	Designer ....D. Martin
Water.....................100 gals.	Production.............1985–91

The Ocean 44 Super Sport was built on a shortened 46 Super Sport hull with a restyled deck and superstructure. A popular boat (111 were built) with a particularly handsome profile, she was designed to replace the original 42 SS in 1985. With her flat bottom (1.5° transom deadrise) and narrow aftersections, the 44 is quick to accelerate but a hard ride in a chop. Below, the two-stateroom layout is arranged with the galley down from the salon. This is a notably wide-open and comfortable floorplan, and both heads have stall showers. Also notable is the more serviceable engine room in the Ocean 44—an improvement from that found in many earlier Ocean models. The large and unobstructed cockpit came standard with a tackle center, cockpit controls, washdown, a teak sole, and teak covering boards. Later models powered with the 485-hp versions of the GM 6-71s will cruise the Ocean 44 around 27 knots and reach 30+ knots top. Earlier 450-hp versions of the same engines are about a knot slower. ❑

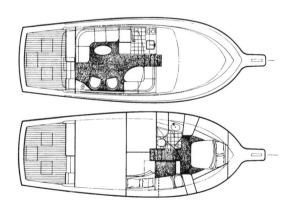

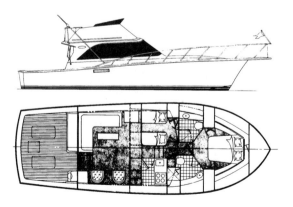

See Page 233 for Pricing Information

See Page 233 for Pricing Information

OCEAN 46 SUPER SPORT

SPECIFICATIONS

Length	46'0"	Fuel	580 gals.
Beam	15'2"	Cockpit	NA
Draft	3'6"	Hull Type	Modified-V
Weight	40,000#	Deadrise Aft	1.5°
Clearance	13'3"	Designer	D. Martin
Water	150 gals.	Production	1983–85

Introduced in 1983 as a bridge between the 42 and 50 Super Sport models, the Ocean 46 is a typical Jersey-style canyon runner with a relatively flat bottom and very quick performance. For a fishing boat, the interior was considered lush (by mid-'80s standards), and the attractive teak woodwork and cabinetry and high-style decors helped make this a very popular boat. While a conventional two-stateroom layout was available, the three-stateroom floorplan with mid-level galley is an unusual find in a 46-footer. The list of standard equipment was equally impressive—teak cockpit sole and covering boards, molded-in tackle center, freezer, vacuum system, etc. Most were sold with the optional factory hardtop. Access to the engines and generator is fair. A fast boat, the 46 SS will cruise at 25 knots and reach a top speed of 29–30 knots with standard 450-hp 6-71s. Optional 475-hp 6V92s cruise at 27 knots (about 30 top). With over 160 built, the 46 SS became one of Ocean's best-selling models.❏

OCEAN 48 SUPER SPORT (EARLY)

SPECIFICATIONS

Length	48'0"	Fuel	580 gals.
Beam	15'2"	Cockpit	152 sq. ft.
Draft	3'6"	Hull Type	Modified-V
Weight	40,000#	Deadrise Aft	2°
Clearance	13'3"	Designer	D. Martin
Water	150 gals.	Production	1986–90

A best-seller for Ocean, the 48 SS was built on a stretched 46 SS hull with all-new deck and superstructure styling. She's a good-looking boat with her stylish profile and aggressive appearance, but even more notable is the fact that she can turn an honest 30 knots with standard 485-hp 6-71 diesels. That spells economy: at a hard 27-knot cruising speed, she's burning only 44–46 gph. Built on a light-weight hull with a narrow beam and 2° of transom deadrise, she's quick to accelerate but a stiff ride in a chop thanks to her flat-bottom design. Ocean 48s were offered with a very popular three-stateroom, mid-galley interior (unusual in just a 48-footer) in addition to a conventional two-stateroom, galley-down floorplan. The interior cabinetry and woodwork are varnished teak, and the array of standard equipment included cockpit controls, tackle center with freezer, teak cockpit sole, and teak covering boards. A total of 167 Ocean 48 Super Sports were built during her 5-year production run.   ❏

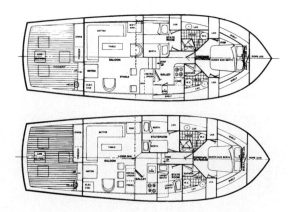

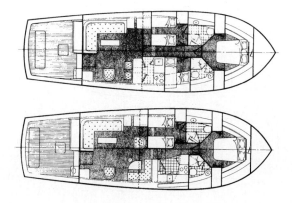

See Page 233 for Pricing Information

See Page 233 for Pricing Information

OCEAN 48 SUPER SPORT

SPECIFICATIONS

Length	48'0"	Fuel	580 gals.
Beam	15'2"	Cockpit	NA
Draft	3'6"	Hull Type	Modified-V
Weight	40,000#	Deadrise Aft	2°
Clearance	13'3"	Designer	D. Martin
Water	150 gals.	Production	1991–Current

The new Ocean 48 SS is basically a restyled version of the original 48 SS model (1986–90) with a more streamlined deck and superstructure, built-in hardtop with arch, less exterior teak, and a completely revised three-stateroom interior layout. The hull, tankage, power, and performance remain unchanged. The urethaned teak interior of the Ocean 48 is lush indeed and decorated with designer-style fabrics throughout. The galley is open to the salon in this floorplan, and the result is a very spacious and well-appointed living area with a built-in entertainment center and full dinette. The midships location of the master stateroom is ideal, although the deep overhead intrusion from the dinette above is discomforting. There's a double berth in the forward stateroom, and both heads are fitted with stall showers. Additional features include good engine room access, a new cockpit layout, and a long list of standard equipment. Priced well below the competition, she'll cruise at 26–27 knots with 485-hp 6-71 diesels and reach a top speed of 30+ knots. ❏

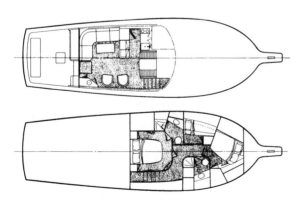

See Page 234 for Pricing Information

OCEAN 50 SUPER SPORT

SPECIFICATIONS

Length	50'0"	Fuel	750 gals.
Beam	16'0"	Cockpit	NA
Draft	4'2"	Hull Type	Modified-V
Weight	50,000#	Deadrise Aft	5°
Clearance	14'2"	Designer	D. Martin
Water	200 gals.	Production	1982–85

The Ocean 50 SS was built on a shortened 55 SS hull with balsa coring in the hullsides, a wide beam, and a flat 5° of deadrise at the transom. The result was a fast and easily powered yacht capable of a good turn of speed with standard 8V92 diesels. Unlike the earlier Ocean 55s with their see-thru front cabin windows, the windshield panels of the Ocean 50 are solid fiberglass. Below, two- and three-stateroom floorplans were offered with the two-stateroom version notable for its huge master stateroom dimensions. Both layouts feature an expansive salon with the galley down to starboard. The cockpit came standard with molded tackle centers, freezer, baitwell, transom door, and a teak sole. The engine room is entered directly from the cockpit, but access to the engines and generator is poor—a serious drawback. A hard-riding boat in a chop, the Ocean 50 SS will cruise at a brisk 25–26 knots with standard 675-hp 8V92 diesels and reach a top speed of about 29 knots. ❏

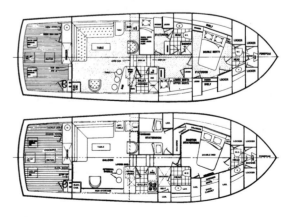

See Page 234 for Pricing Information

SPECIFICATIONS

Length	53'0"	Fuel	860 gals.
Beam	16'4"	Cockpit	118 sq. ft.
Draft	4'4"	Hull Type	Modified-V
Weight	52,000#	Deadrise Aft	8°
Clearance	16'3"	Designer	D. Martin
Water	200 gals.	Production	1991–Current

Replacing the *very* popular 55 Super Sport, the 53 SS is built on an all-new Ocean hull design with a sharper entry and slightly increased transom deadrise. The hull changes make the Ocean 53 a generally better headsea boat than her predecessor with a notably dryer ride. The standard three-stateroom, galley-up layout is arranged with a midships master suite and another double berth forward. The alternate (and less popular) two-stateroom floorplan has the galley down and a dinette in the salon. While the salon dimensions are slightly smaller than the 55 SS, the furnishings and decor are plush in the extreme. A transom door is standard in the cockpit, and the fish box has been repositioned behind the chair for improved access to the rudder posts. Competitively priced, additional features include a new-style factory hardtop, molded pulpit, enlarged tackle centers, and the elimination of exterior teak trim. A fast boat with just 760-hp 8V92s, the Ocean 53 Super Sport will cruise at 27 knots and reach a top speed of around 30 knots. ❏

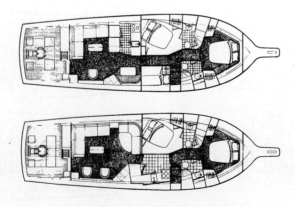

See Page 234 for Pricing Information

OCEAN 55 SUPER SPORT

SPECIFICATIONS

Length	55'8"	Fuel	1,000 gals.
Beam	16'4"	Cockpit	130 sq. ft.
Draft	4'4"	Hull Type	Modified-V
Weight	58,000#	Deadrise Aft	4°
Clearance	14'6"	Designer	D. Martin
Water	200 gals.	Production	1981–90

The Ocean 55 Super Sport combines two essential elements of any modern tournament fisherman: speed and beauty. Her long foredeck, unbroken sheerline, and sleek cabin profile are pure Jersey-style sportfish. Inside—luxury on a grand scale. The three-stateroom layout with three heads and deckhouse galley proved more popular than the mid-level galley version with two heads and a huge salon. The 55 SS was restyled in 1986 with a new flybridge, a solid front windshield, and a black mask running around the deckhouse. The foredeck seat was also eliminated in 1986 for a more streamlined appearance. Whereas most big sportfishermen in this size range require the heavier 12-cylinder diesels to reach (or even approach) the magic 30-knot number, the Ocean 55 SS gets the job done with lighter, more efficient (and far less expensive) 8V92s. Top speed with the 735-hp versions of the 8V92s is 31 knots, and she'll cruise at a fast 27 knots. A total of 170 were built, making her the most popular big Ocean model ever. ❏

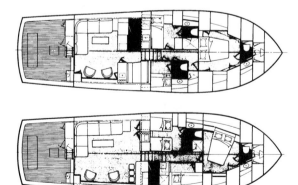

See Page 234 for Pricing Information

OCEAN 58 SUPER SPORT

SPECIFICATIONS

Length	58'0"	Fuel	1,100 gals.
Beam	17'6"	Cockpit	131 sq. ft.
Draft	4'10"	Hull Type	Modified-V
Weight	72,215#	Deadrise Aft	NA
Clearance	14'11"	Designer	D. Martin
Water	250 gals.	Production	1990–Current

First of the so-called "new generation" Ocean yachts in 1990, the muscular 58 Super Sport is built on an efficient modified-V hull design with cored hullsides, modest deadrise at the transom, and a good deal of flare at the bow. Belowdecks, her innovative three-stateroom, three-head layout is arranged with the huge full-width master stateroom located *beneath* the raised salon sole—a giant departure from conventional convertible floorplans. Like all Ocean models, the 58 features a beautiful varnished teak interior with upscale furnishings and color-coordinated fabrics throughout. The tournament-sized cockpit features molded tackle centers, cockpit controls, teak covering boards, transom door, and direct engine room access. The flybridge is extremely large with three helm chairs and U-shaped lounge seating forward of the helm console. A factory option allows the flybridge to be fully enclosed and air conditioned. A good-running boat with plenty of eye appeal, standard 1,080-hp 12V-92 diesels (or 1,100-hp MANs) will cruise the fully loaded Ocean 58 Super Sport at a fast 29–30 knots. ❏

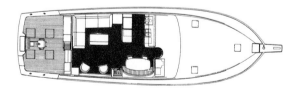

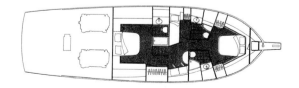

See Page 234 for Pricing Information

139

OCEAN 63 SUPER SPORT

SPECIFICATIONS

Length	63'0"	Fuel	1,200 gals.
Beam	17'8"	Cockpit	150 sq. ft.
Draft	4'8"	Hull Type	Modified-V
Weight	74,000#	Deadrise Aft	3°
Clearance	14'9"	Designer	D. Martin
Water	300 gals.	Production	1986–91

Once the largest boat in the Ocean fleet, the 63 SS was for a time one of the largest production sportfisherman built in the U.S. Constructed on a relatively lightweight flat-bottom hull with cored hullsides, the Ocean 63 is a classic Jersey-style tournament sport-fisherman with an opulent interior to go with her stylish profile. Inside, the innovative floorplan is arranged with four staterooms—two extending beneath the salon sole and two others with a queen bed. An eye-catching glass-enclosed rod locker is recessed into the wall in the forward passageway. Outside, the massive flybridge and equally spacious cockpit are fitted with an impressive array of standard features. A good performer for her size, standard 900-hp 12V71s will cruise the Ocean 63 Super Sport at 25 knots (about 29 knots top). Optional 1,050-hp 12V92s will cruise around 27–28 knots with a top speed of 32 knots. During 1990–91 MAN 1,050-hp diesels were also available (28 knots cruise/32–33 knots top). A total of 32 Ocean 63s were built. ❏

OCEAN 66 SUPER SPORT

SPECIFICATIONS

Length	66'0"	Fuel	1,400 gals.
Beam	17'8"	Cockpit	135 sq. ft.
Draft	5'0"	Hull Type	Modified-V
Weight	80,000#	Deadrise Aft	3°
Clearance	18'9"	Designer	D. Martin
Water	300 gals.	Production	1993–Current

Sportfishing luxury on a grand scale describes the 66 Super Sport, the largest boat yet from Ocean Yachts. She's basically an improved (easier riding) version of the previous 63 Super Sport with a deeper forefoot, a reshaped transom, additional fuel, and a newly configured flybridge. She's built on a tapered modified-V hull with cored hullsides and a nearly flat 3° of transom deadrise. Inside, the lavish (and innovative) floorplan is arranged with the galley and dinette forward and a step up from the huge salon. There are four staterooms on the lower level with the full-beam master suite located beneath the galley. The cockpit comes with molded tackle centers, cockpit controls, in-deck fish box, and direct engine room access. Topside, the factory hardtop and built-in radar arch are standard, and the massive flybridge includes three pedestal seats, a wet bar, and lounge seating for a crowd. A good-running boat with plenty of eye appeal, standard 1,040-hp 12V-92s will cruise the Ocean 66 at 25 knots and deliver a top speed of 28–29 knots. ❏

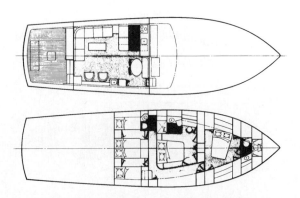

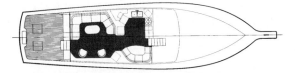

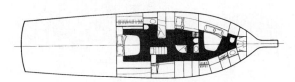

See Page 234 for Pricing Information

See Page 234 for Pricing Information

OCEAN MASTER 31 CENTER CONSOLE

SPECIFICATIONS

Length	30'7"	Fuel	300 gals.
Beam	10'3"	Cockpit	90 sq. ft.
Draft	1'4"	Hull Type	Modified-V
Hull Weight	5,140#	Deadrise Aft	16°
Clearance	NA	Designer	J. Hargrave
Water	None	Production	1975–Current

First of the big outboard-powered offshore day boats, the Ocean Master 31 is a classic center console fisherman with a production record (over 360 built) unmatched by the competition. These boats have a well-known reputation for being seriously overbuilt: the hull is laid up with *20* layers of solid fiberglass, and the inner liner is glassed directly to the stringers and hullsides. Designed for the serious angler, the deck layout boasts 90 sq. ft. of space aft of the console and 55 sq. ft. of elevated casting platform forward—enough room for four or five people to fish. Standard features include a 52-gallon livewell and an 850-gallon fish box, high gunwales with plenty of toe room beneath, and an excellent nonskid cockpit surface. Note that the hard chines were reconfigured in 1993, softening amidships and running all the way to the transom for a dryer ride. Aside from the center console, a walkaround version with a small cuddy is also offered. Twin 225-hp outboards will cruise around 26 knots and reach about 40 knots top. ❏

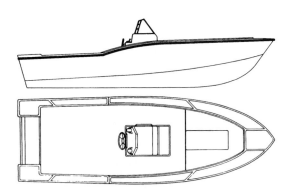

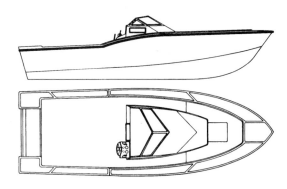

See Page 234 for Pricing Information

ORCA 36

SPECIFICATIONS

Length	36'0"	Fuel	500 gals.
Beam	13'0"	Cockpit	NA
Draft	3'0"	Hull Type	Deep-V
Weight	15,000#	Deadrise Aft	23°
Clearance	17'3"	Designer	C. Jannace
Water	50 gals.	Production	1990–Current

The Orca 36 is a West Coast stand-up fisherman with an unconventional profile and plenty of space-age engineering. Her deep-V hull (23° deadrise aft) is fully cored with Airex, reinforced with Kevlar and carbon fiber, and vacuum bagged with vinylester resins. The unique, aerodynamically shaped marlin tower permits true 360° walkaround fishing access, and the hardtop is canted down 4° to match the boat's running angle for reduced windage. The Orca's bottom is also clean—no thru-hulls, just a sea chest in the engine room fed from the transom. There are two fish boxes in the cockpit sole, and the helm seat module rolls aft to expose the engine compartment. The interior is one of the more spacious found in a boat of this type with good headroom, an oversized head, and berths for four. A superb performer, 300-hp Cummins diesels deliver a top speed of 34 knots—hard to believe in a 36' boat. At a steady 25 knot cruise (16 gph) the Orca's range is around 700 miles! ❏

PACE 36 SPORTFISHERMAN

SPECIFICATIONS

Length	36'0"	Fuel	400 gals.
Beam	13'3"	Cockpit	NA
Draft	2'9"	Hull Type	Modified-V
Weight	20,000#	Designer	Egg Harbor
Clearance	12'2"	Production	1988–92
Water	75 gals.		

The classic Egg Harbor 36 Sedan (1976–85) was reborn for a time in the Pace 36 Sportfisherman. Built in Taiwan using the original molds, the relatively flat-bottom Egg Harbor hull was first used some years ago in the Pacemaker 36 (1973–80) and only later served as the platform for the Egg 36 Sedan. The Pace 36 is a good-looking boat with her traditional Jersey-style profile accented with a black wraparound deckhouse mask. Two floorplans were offered: a two-stateroom layout with the galley up, and a single-stateroom, galley-down arrangement with a much more open salon plus an island berth forward. The interior woodwork is teak, of course, and the Pace 36 uses plenty of teak trim outside as well, just like the original Egg Harbors. Crusader 454-cid gas engines were standard and will cruise the Pace 36 at 18 knots with 27 knots top. The optional 320-hp Cat diesels will cruise around 22 knots and turn 26 knots wide open. She's a good-handling boat overall but a hard ride in a chop. ❏

See Page 234 for Pricing Information

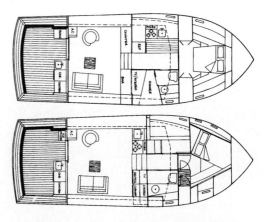

See Page 234 for Pricing Information

PACE 40 SPORTFISHERMAN

SPECIFICATIONS

Length	40'0"	Fuel	450 gals.
Beam	14'0"	Cockpit	95 sq. ft.
Draft	2'9"	Hull Type	Modified-V
Weight	28,000#	Deadrise Aft	NA
Clearance	NA	Designer	D. Martin
Water	100 gals.	Production	1988–92

The Pace 40 Sportfisherman is a re-creation of the earlier Egg Harbor 40 Sedan built from 1975 until early 1986. (The molds for five Egg Harbor designs were purchased and sent to Taiwan, where the Pace series was built by Nautique Yachts.) Aside from her solid front windshield and bold deckhouse mask, the Pace 40's styling remains very close to the original Egg Harbor 40 Sedan. The interior arrangement is also similar to that used in (later-model) Egg 40s with a mid-level galley, two staterooms below, and a single head compartment. The breakfast bar found in the original Egg 40 is eliminated in the Pace, thereby opening up the salon considerably. A generous amount of well-crafted teak cabinetry and paneling is applied throughout. The cockpit features a teak sole and covering boards, bait-prep center, and a transom door. Caterpillar 375-hp diesels will cruise around 22 knots, and the larger 485-hp 6-71s cruise about 25 knots. A handsome boat, the Pace 40 is a good reproduction of a classic Jersey-style sportfisherman. ❏

See Page 234 for Pricing Information

PACE 48 SPORTFISHERMAN

SPECIFICATIONS

Length	48'2"	Fuel	720 gals.
Beam	15'0"	Cockpit	NA
Draft	4'4"	Hull Type	Modified-V
Weight	40,000#	Deadrise Aft	2°
Clearance	NA	Designer	D. Martin
Water	200 gals.	Production	1987–92

Purists will recognize the familiar lines of the Pace 48 SF as those of the old Egg Harbor 48. Indeed, this is the same boat right down to the foredeck storage box and the teak cockpit, but with a new wraparound black mask and solid front windshield panels. Built in Taiwan, the original Egg Harbor molds were reworked for the new production run. Construction is identical to the earlier specifications with a solid fiberglass hull and balsa coring in the decks and superstructure. This is a narrow hull design with a fine entry and a nearly flat 2° of deadrise at the transom. Teak cabinetry is applied throughout the interior, and those who enjoy the ambience of a traditional interior will like the feel of the Pace 48's salon. The two-stateroom, two-head layout is very similar to the later-model Egg 48s. Power is 735-hp 8V92 diesels which fit nicely in the large engine room. A good-running boat, her cruising speed is an honest 26 knots, and the top speed is around 29 knots. ❏

See Page 234 for Pricing Information

PACEMAKER 30 SPORTFISHERMAN

SPECIFICATIONS

Length	30'8"	Fuel	140 gals.
Length WL	28'5"	Cockpit	80 sq. ft.
Beam	11'6"	Hull Type	Modified-V
Draft	2'6"	Deadrise Aft	NA
Weight	10,000#	Designer	Pacemaker
Clearance	9'11"	Production	1973–80
Water	20 gals.		

The Pacemaker 30 SF is a good-looking boat with a still-modern profile and comfortable accommodations below. She was offered with or without the lower helm station which came at the expense of one of the salon settees. Both floorplans have the galley and head aft in the salon where access from the cockpit is the most convenient. The Pacemaker 30 SF proved to be a popular design over the years due to her clean lines and affordable price. A competent sportfishing boat, her large cockpit should easily satisfy the requirements of most weekend anglers. In 1978, Pacemaker engineers combined the flybridge into the deck/cabin mold thus making the bridge an integral part of the superstructure. Standard 225-hp Chryslers cruise at 18–19 knots, and the top speed is around 27 knots. Note that the Pacemaker 31 Convertible (introduced by the *new* Pacemaker Yachts in 1988 and no relation to the old Pacemaker company) uses the same Pacemaker 30 tooling but includes several modern updates and design improvements. ❏

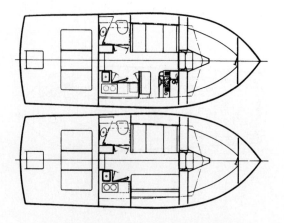

See Page 234 for Pricing Information

PACEMAKER 34 CONVERTIBLE

SPECIFICATIONS

Length	33'10"	Water	85 gals.
Beam	13'10"	Fuel	340 gals.
Draft	3'6"	Hull Type	Modified-V
Weight	15,000#	Deadrise Aft	8°
Clearance	12'0"	Designer	Pacemaker
Cockpit	75 sq. ft.	Production	1988–92

Built by the new Pacemaker company (the original firm went under in 1980), the Pacemaker 34 is built on a solid fiberglass low-deadrise hull with an exceptionally wide beam. Not surprisingly, the interior dimensions are spacious indeed, and the fact that she has a *real* salon is notable in just a 34-foot boat. There's also a separate dinette (not jammed into the salon) as well as a separate stall shower in the head compartment. Completely finished with teak cabinetry, doors, and woodwork, the full wraparound cabin windows provide plenty of outside natural lighting. The cockpit is too small for a fighting chair, although there's room for a couple of light-tackle anglers and their gear. Teak covering boards, washdowns, and a transom door are standard. Price-wise, the Pacemaker 34 was an inexpensive boat compared with other convertibles her size. Standard 454-cid gas engines cruise at 20–21 knots with a top speed of around 30 knots. Note that the Sportfish model is the same boat with a larger cockpit and reduced salon dimensions. ❏

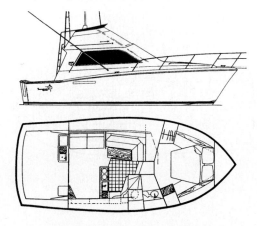

See Page 234 for Pricing Information

PACEMAKER 36 SPORTFISHERMAN

SPECIFICATIONS

Length	36'0"	Fuel	260 gals.
Beam	13'3"	Cockpit	80 sq. ft.
Draft	2'3"	Hull Type	Modified-V
Weight	17,100#	Deadrise Aft	NA
Clearance	12'2"	Designer	Pacemaker
Water	75 gals.	Production	1973–80

Introduced back in 1973 and enjoying a long and successful production run, the Pacemaker 36 SF has the traditional sportfish profile typical of many Jersey-style sportfishermen of the mid-1970s. Her large tournament flybridge and a roomy fishing cockpit made her a popular boat with a great many anglers over the years. Built on a low-deadrise, solid fiberglass hull with a wide beam, early models came with a standard two-stateroom floorplan with a salon galley and a stall shower in the head. A revised layout in 1976 moved the galley down and offered the option of replacing the guest stateroom with a dinette. This later floorplan results in a more open salon but eliminates the separate stall shower in the head. Either layout offers generally comfortable accommodations and adequate storage for brief trips. Several power options were offered. The standard 270-hp gas engines will run at 16–17 knots cruise and 25 knots top. Twin 350-hp Crusaders gas engines will cruise the Pacemaker 36 Sportfisherman around 17–18 knots and reach 26 knots wide open. ❏

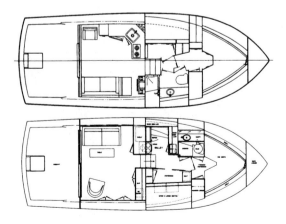

See Page 234 for Pricing Information

PACEMAKER 37 SPORTFISHERMAN

SPECIFICATIONS

Length	36'10"	Water	85 gals.
Beam	14'0"	Fuel	450 gals.
Draft	3'8"	Hull Type	Modified-V
Weight	22,000#	Deadrise Aft	8°
Clearance	16'6"	Designer	Pacemaker
Cockpit	110 sq. ft.	Production	1990–92

Introduced in 1988 by the *new* Pacemaker company (now deceased), the 37 SF is a classic Jersey-style sportfisherman with conservative lines and the traditional Pacemaker profile. She was available in two versions: the Sportfisherman (pictured above) came out in 1990 with a huge cockpit, optional front windshield, and standard hardtop; and the original Convertible model with a smaller cockpit, increased interior dimensions, and standard front cabin windshield. The oversize cockpit of the SF—one of the largest in her class—mandates a rather small interior for a boat of this size. Several floorplans were offered, and the factory was able to accommodate those seeking semi-custom layouts. The interior is finished out with teak woodwork and cabinetry, and there's a big fish box in the cockpit along with molded tackle centers and a transom door. Standard 454-cid gas engines will cruise the Pacemaker 37 SF around 19–20 knots and reach 29 knots top. Optional 450-hp Merlin diesels deliver a cruising speed of 25 knots and 29 knots wide open. ❏

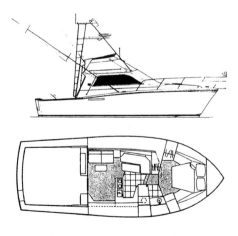

See Page 235 for Pricing Information

PACEMAKER 38 SPORTFISHERMAN

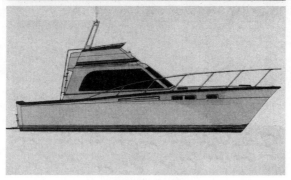

SPECIFICATIONS

LOA	41'11"	Cockpit	80 sq. ft.
Hull Length	38'5"	Water	150 gals.
Beam	14'5"	Fuel	512 gals.
Draft	3'6"	Hull Type	Modified-V
Weight	21,639#	Deadrise Aft	9°
Clearance	12'9"	Production	1979–80

A good-looking fisherman with a still-modern profile, the Pacemaker 38 was the last boat introduced by Pacemaker before the company went under in 1980. (Note that the molds were later used by Egg Harbor in the production of their 37 and 41 SF models.) Constructed on a solid fiberglass, low-deadrise hull with a comparitively wide beam, the 38 SF came with a standard two-stateroom floorplan with the galley and dinette up. This was a very open layout for a boat this size, and the large wraparound cabin windows provide excellent outside visibility. Teak woodwork is used throughout the interior, and the head compartment includes a stall shower. Outside, the cockpit features a teak sole and covering boards in addition to under-gunnel rod storage, a transom door, and room for a full-size fighting chair. The small flybridge has the controls well aft for an unobstructed view of the cockpit. Standard 350-hp gas engines will cruise the Pacemaker 38 SF at 18 knots and reach a top speed of about 28 knots. ❏

See Page 235 for Pricing Information

PACEMAKER 40 SPORTFISHERMAN

SPECIFICATIONS

Length	39'11"	Fuel, Opt	330 gals.
Beam	13'10"	Cockpit	NA
Draft	2'8"	Hull Type	Modified-V
Weight	20,098#	Deadrise Aft	8°
Clearance	12'3"	Designer	Pacemaker
Water	69 gals.	Production	1973–79
Fuel, Std	260 gals.		

With her classic sportfish styling and an aggressive profile, the Pacemaker 40 SF has the appearance of a much larger boat. She's built on a solid fiberglass hull with shallow deadrise aft and moderate beam—the same hull used for the Pacemaker 40 MY. Typical of most Jersey-style boats, the Pacemaker 40 has a flared bow and a notably attractive sheer. Two basic floorplans were offered: a two-stateroom layout (very popular), and a single-stateroom version with a dinette replacing the guest cabin. The galley is down in both arrangements, and the head has a shower stall. The engine room is small enough when equipped with the standard gas engines but becomes too small with diesels. Topside, the tournament-style flybridge offers an excellent view of the cockpit where a full-size fighting chair can easily be installed. Even with the optional 330-gallon fuel capacity, the cruising range is limited for a sportfisherman. GM 6-71s (325-hp) will cruise the Pacemaker 40 SF around 22 knots with a top speed of 24–25 knots. ❑

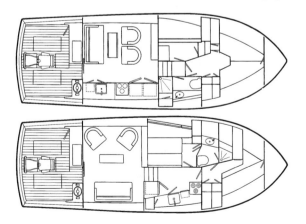

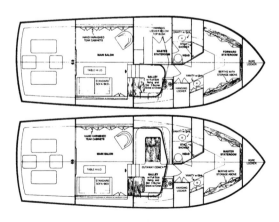

See Page 235 for Pricing Information

PACEMAKER 48 SPORTFISHERMAN

SPECIFICATIONS

Length..........................48'4"	Fuel.......610/700/880 gals.
Beam ....14'11"	Cockpit ....105 sq. ft.
Draft.............................3'10"	Hull Type.........Modified-V
Weight....................40,000#	Deadrise Aft..................NA
Clearance.......................NA	Designer ....Pacemaker
Water.....................155 gals.	Production.........1971–1980

The largest sportfishing model ever built by Pacemaker (and by far the best looking), the Pacemaker 48 SF was also one of the first boats to offer the new GM 8V92TI diesels as an option back in 1978. A pure tournament machine in all that the name implies, the 48 is a big boat designed for serious deepwater pursuits. Construction is solid fiberglass, and the long foredeck and sweeping sheer mark her as a classic East Coast fisherman. Two interior arrangements were available: a galley-down layout with two staterooms, or a galley-up version with three staterooms. Outside, the large and uncluttered fishing cockpit came with a teak sole and covering boards, a standard transom door, and molded tackle centers. The flybridge was restyled in 1976, and the fuel was increased to 880 gallons in 1978. Most Pacemaker 48s were powered with 425-hp 8V71s and cruise at 19–20 knots (23 top). Later models equipped with the 8V92TIs are capable of 24-knot cruising speeds and around 26–27 knots wide open. ❏

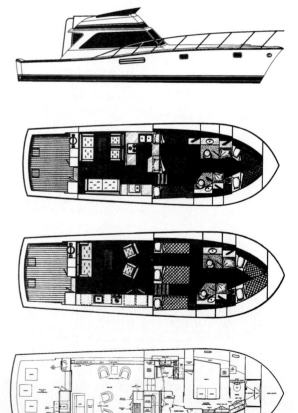

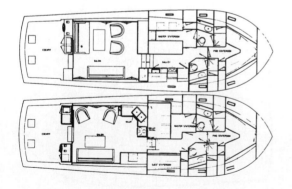

See Page 235 for Pricing Information

PACIFICA 36 SF

SPECIFICATIONS

Length..........................36'0"	Fuel........................300 gals.
Beam ....13'0"	Cockpit ....83 sq. ft.
Draft..............................3'4"	Hull Type........Modified-V
Weight.....................16,000#	Deadrise Aft...................12°
Clearance......................NA	Designer ....John Norek
Water.......................90 gals.	Production.............1974–92

A handsome boat with a distinctive profile, the Pacifica 36 is a limited-production sportfisherman designed for serious anglers. She's constructed on a modified-V hull form with a relatively deep keel for stability and generous flare at the bow. The Pacifica 36 is primarily aimed at the West Coast market and features wide side-decks and a forward helm console on the flybridge (an East Coast, tournament-style flybridge was available). The cockpit—with just over 80 sq. ft. of usable space—isn't large compared to others in her class. Inside, the Pacifica 36 can sleep six with the salon dinette and settee converted. V-berths are located in the stateroom, and the split head features a huge shower to starboard. A lower helm was standard, and the interior is finished with laminate countertops and teak trim. At 16,000 pounds, the Pacifica 36 SF is a light boat, and her performance with 375-hp Cat diesels (26 knots cruise/30 knots top) is impressive. About 25 of these boats were built during her production run. ❏

PACIFICA 44 SPORTFISHERMAN

SPECIFICATIONS

Length..........................44'0"	Fuel ....650/750 gals.
Beam ....15'0"	Cockpit ....148 sq. ft.
Draft..............................4'2"	Hull Type........Modified-V
Weight.....................33,000#	Deadrise Aft...................11°
Clearance......................NA	Designer ....John Norek
Water...................120 gals.	Production...1970–Current

The Pacifica 44 SF has been in production for two decades without undergoing any significant design changes—a remarkable testament to her popularity among West Coast sportfishermen. She's never been a high-production model (about 65 were sold), but the 44 remains Pacifica's most popular boat ever. Built on a modified-V hull with a wide beam and considerable flare at the bow, the 44 is notable for her huge fishing cockpit and rugged construction. Her interior consists of two staterooms (each with a double bed), two heads, and a handy midships lounge in the companionway that converts to over/under berths. The salon is arranged with the galley to port, and the original standard lower helm is now optional. As is the case with many West Coast sportfishermen, the wide sidedecks result in a salon of limited dimensions. A good performer, many were equipped with the 435-hp 8V71 diesels which cruise at 22–23 knots and reach 26 knots top. The larger 550-hp 6V92s will cruise around 26 knots and turn 30 wide open. ❏

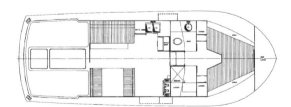

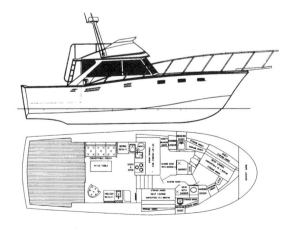

See Page 235 for Pricing Information

See Page 235 for Pricing Information

PEARSON 38 CONVERTIBLE

SPECIFICATIONS

Length	37'6"	Fuel	410 gals.
Beam	13'10"	Cockpit	NA
Draft	3'9"	Hull Type	Deep-V
Weight	24,000#	Deadrise Aft	19°
Clearance	NA	Designer	Hunt Assoc.
Water	120 gals.	Production	1987–91

Pearson Yachts developed several powerboat designs in the past, and in the early 1960s the Pearson name was no stranger to the powerboat industry. With the downturn of the sailboat market in recent years, Pearson once again decided to build powerboats. The first—the 38 Convertible pictured above—was introduced in 1987. She was designed by Hunt Associates and features their famous deep-V hull and a practical two-stateroom floorplan. This is a good-quality family cruiser/fisherman with attractive lines, a soft ride, and upscale interior accommodations. Those who have seen and inspected the Pearson 38 have been impressed, especially with the attractive oak-trimmed Formica interior decor. Hull construction, mechanical systems, and detailing are generally above average, and the engine room is quite large for a boat this size. No racehorse, standard 375-hp Caterpillar diesels will cruise the Pearson 38 at a respectable 22–23 knots and deliver a top speed in the neighborhood of 26 knots. Pearson went bankrupt in 1991, thus ending the production of this and all models. ❏

See Page 235 for Pricing Information

PERFORMER 32

SPECIFICATIONS

Length	31'6"	Fuel	210/320 gals.
Beam	10'3"	Cockpit	86 sq. ft.
Draft	2'4"	Hull Type	Deep-V
Weight	12,500#	Deadrise Aft	23°
Clearance	NA	Designer	Performer
Water	30 gals.	Production	1987–Current

The Performer 32 is recognized for her aggressive low-profile appearance and strictly-business cockpit layout. She's built on a deep-V hull using some of the most advanced construction techniques in the business. The beam is narrow and prop pockets are used to reduce the shaft angle for better speed and efficiency. The result is a rugged and seaworthy fishing platform that can haul ass. With optional J&T 300-hp 8.2s, she'll cruise at an honest 30 knots and reach 36–37 knots top *with* a tower. The compact bi-level cockpit can handle a marlin chair and comes with an in-deck fish box. The helm is superbly arranged with a full array of instruments set into a shaded dash and a comfortable bolster-type helm seat. The interior accommodations are basic, and the fiberglass surfaces, brushed aluminum trim, and snap-out carpeting make clean-up easy. A good-looking boat that lives up to her ambitious name, the Performer 32 will appeal primarily to experienced anglers who have been around the block a few times. ❏

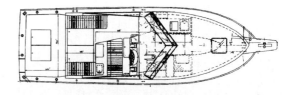

See Page 235 for Pricing Information

PHOENIX 27 WEEKENDER

SPECIFICATIONS

Length	27'3"	Fuel, Opt	250 gals.
Beam	9'10"	Cockpit	NA
Draft	1'10"	Hull Type	Deep-V
Weight	7,200#	Deadrise Aft	21°
Clearance	6'9"	Designer	Jim Wynne
Water	24 gals.	Production	1979–Current
Fuel, Std	200 gals.		

Long a popular boat, the Phoenix 27 Weekender is a straightforward offshore express without a lot of frills. Construction is solid fiberglass with a full-length inner liner bonded to the hull for added strength. As with other Jim Wynne designs, the Phoenix 27 has propeller pockets recessed into her deep-V hull. Since over half of the boat's length is devoted to the single-level cockpit, the interior is necessarily compact with V-berths, a small galley, and stand-up head with shower. The engines are located under raised engine boxes that double as bait-watching seats. In addition to the Weekender model, the 27 was offered in a "Fishbuster" version (1979–89) with the galley/tackle center located forward and to port in the cockpit (see top layout below). Standard 350-cid gas engines provide a cruising speed of about 23 knots (31+ knots top). Optional 200-hp Volvo diesels will cruise around 25 knots (29-30 top). With a pair of 250-hp Yahama outboards, the 27 Tournament will hit a top speed of 40 knots. ❏

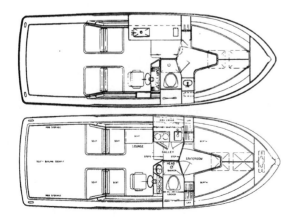

See Page 235 for Pricing Information

PHOENIX 27 TOURNAMENT

SPECIFICATIONS

Length	27'3"	Fuel, Std	220 gals.
Length WL	23'6"	Fuel, Opt	290 gals.
Beam	9'10"	Cockpit	90 sq. ft.
Draft	2'0"	Hull Type	Deep-V
Weight	8,200#	Deadrise Aft	21°
Clearance	7'6"	Designer	Jim Wynne
Water	24 gals.	Production	1990–Current

Built on the same hull as the Phoenix 27 Weekender, the 27 Tournament is a good-looking raised deck open express with a clean and uncluttered fishing layout. She's built on a rugged deep-V hull with prop pockets and a steep 21° of transom deadrise. Her bi-level cockpit eliminates the engine boxes found in the Weekender while providing much-improved helm visibility. Below, the cabin accommodations are centered around a convertible lounge/dinette forward and a small galley to port. There's standing headroom in the head, and the interior is tastefully finished with teak trim and off-white mica laminates. Additional features include a molded bow pulpit, transom door and gate, in-deck fish box, seawater washdown, lockable rod storage under the cockpit coaming, and good access to the engines. Twin 350-cid gas engines are standard (23 knots cruise/30 knots top), and Volvo 200-hp diesels are optional (25 knots cruise/29 knots wide open). A pair of 250-hp Yahama outboards will cruise at 25 knots and reach a top speed of 40 knots.❏

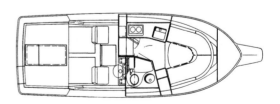

See Page 236 for Pricing Information

PHOENIX 29 CONVERTIBLE

SPECIFICATIONS

Length........................28'10"	Fuel, Opt...............260 gals.
Beam ....10'0"	Cockpit ....75 sq. ft.
Draft...........................2'4"	Hull Type ....Modified-V
Weight...................8,500#	Deadrise Aft..................21°
Clearance......................9'6"	Designer...........Jim Wynne
Water.......................50 gals.	Production.............1977–87
Fuel, Std...............160 gals.	

The Phoenix 29 Convertible had a long and successful production run before being replaced with an all-new model in 1988. Over 750 were built, and during that time she earned the respect of many anglers for her clean styling and durable construction. She has a surprisingly large interior for a boat of her size and type. There's plenty of elbow room throughout the cabin, and both the head and galley are conveniently located just inside the salon door. Berths are provided for four adults and two kids. Topside, a bench seat on the small flybridge will seat three. The cockpit is free of obstructions and clearly designed for fishing. Because of her recessed prop pockets, shaft angles are significantly reduced allowing her to run in reasonably shallow waters. On the downside, some consider the Phoenix 29 to be a bit tender. Several engine choices were offered over the years. The popular 124-hp Volvo diesels will cruise efficiently at 18 knots and turn 22 knots top. Later models with the 165-hp Volvos cruise at 20–21 knots. ❑

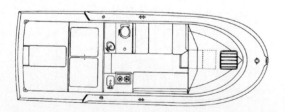

See Page 236 for Pricing Information

PHOENIX 29 SF CONVERTIBLE

SPECIFICATIONS

Length........................31'11"	Fuel, Opt...............300 gals.
Beam ....10'0"	Cockpit ....75 sq. ft.
Draft...........................2'4"	Hull Type..............Deep-V
Weight...................9,450#	Deadrise Aft..................22°
Clearance......................9'6"	Designer...........Jim Wynne
Water.......................50 gals.	Production...1988–Current
Fuel, Std...............180 gals.	

The Phoenix 29 SF is an updated and restyled version of the original Phoenix 29 (1977–87). She replaces the straightforward and businesslike profile of her predecessor with the aggressive lines of the larger Phoenix 33 Convertible. Indeed, the oversized flybridge seems almost *too* large for a 29-footer. Phoenix has introduced a number of desirable features in this model including a transom door, molded pulpit, aluminum rails, and a revamped and updated interior layout with berths for six. Stoutly built, the all-new hull features a slightly wider beam at the waterline, a redesigned entry, and extra strakes for improved lift and stability. Inside, the elimination of the forward stateroom bulkhead results in a more open interior. Borrowing again from the 33 Convertible, a unique air duct system is used to rid the cockpit of exhaust fumes while underway. Standard 350-cid gas engines will cruise about 22 knots (30 knots top). Optional 200-hp Volvo diesels cruise about 25 knots (30 knots top), and the newer Volvo 225-hp diesels cruise at 27 knots (32 top). ❑

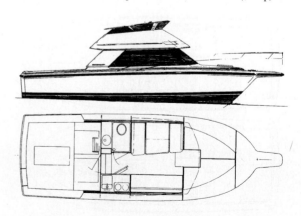

See Page 236 for Pricing Information

PHOENIX 33 CONVERTIBLE

SPECIFICATIONS

Length	33'9"	Fuel	300 gals.
Beam	13'0"	Cockpit	114 sq. ft.
Draft	2'9"	Hull Type	Deep-V
Weight, Gas	20,520#	Deadrise Aft	17°
Weight, Dsl	23,600#	Designer	Jim Wynne
Clearance	10'9"	Production	1987–Current
Water	70 gals.		

Well-built and realistically priced, the Phoenix 33 Convertible is loaded with the kind of features sure to please hard-core anglers and cruisers alike. She's a good-looking boat with a huge flybridge and a notably aggressive profile. Construction is solid fiberglass, and she rides on a beamy deep-V hull with prop pockets and a full-length inner liner. Underway, a unique vent ducting system directs fresh air into the cockpit to disperse fumes that might collect in that area. The stylish decor is impressive with berths for six and several thoughtful design features. In 1991, Phoenix introduced the SFX model for dedicated anglers with a larger salon (but no stall shower), berths for four, and a revised helm console with more room for flush-mounting electronics. Engine boxes make access to the motors easy, and the cockpit comes with a transom door, in-deck fish box, and washdowns standard. Standard 454-cid gas engines cruise the Phoenix 33 at 19 knots and reach a top speed of 30. The optional 425-hp Cats cruise around 26 knots. ❑

PHOENIX 33 TOURNAMENT

SPECIFICATIONS

Length	33'9"	Fuel, Opt	400 gals.
Beam	13'0"	Cockpit	114 sq. ft.
Draft	2'9"	Hull Type	Deep-V
Weight	20,520#	Deadrise Aft	17°
Clearance	8'4"	Designer	Jim Wynne
Water	70 gals.	Production	1990–Current
Fuel, Std	300 gals.		

The Phoenix 33 Tournament is a good-looking express with a low profile and a large, unobstructed fishing cockpit. She's built on the same hull as the 33 Convertible—a rugged deep-V with a full inner liner and recessed prop pockets. The single-level cockpit of the 33 is arranged with a dinette/lounge opposite the helm, bait and tackle centers, and lockable rod storage. The engine boxes double as convenient bait-watching seats. Additional cockpit features include an in-deck fish box, seawater washdown, excellent non-skid, and a transom door with gate. (A reinforcing plate is provided in the cockpit sole for the installation of a mounted chair.) Below, the small (but very upscale) cabin can be fitted with an island berth or V-berths. While 454-cid gas engines are standard, most anglers will likely go for one of the several diesel options available. The popular 375-hp Cats cruise at 26–27 knots (30 knots top), and the newer 412-hp Cats will cruise at a fast 28 knots and reach 32 knots wide open. ❑

See Page 236 for Pricing Information

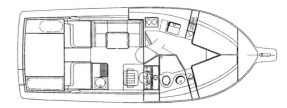

See Page 236 for Pricing Information

PHOENIX 37 SF CONVERTIBLE

SPECIFICATIONS

Length	37'10"	Fuel	440 gals.
Beam	14'0"	Cockpit	93 sq. ft.
Draft	3'7"	Hull Type	Modified-V
Weight	30,800#	Deadrise	18°
Clearance	12'7"	Designer	Jim Wynne
Water	110 gals.	Production	1989–Current

Bold styling and rugged construction characterize the 37 SF Convertible, currently the largest boat in the Phoenix fleet. She's built on basically the same hull as the earlier Phoenix 38 with a full inner liner, prop pockets, and a steep 18° of deadrise at the transom. New features include a molded pulpit, enlarged salon dimensions, a revised flybridge profile, and recessed trim tabs. Her two-stateroom, galley-up interior is arranged with an island berth forward and stacked single berths in the guest stateroom. Teak or white ash interior woodwork is offered, and a glassed-over deckhouse windshield is optional. With her large and uncluttered cockpit, the 37 is designed to meet the needs of serious fishermen. A transom door is standard along with a molded tackle center, livewell, rod storage, and two in-deck fish boxes. With the optional 375-hp Cat diesels, the Phoenix 37 will cruise at 22–23 knots and reach a top speed of 26 knots. The 485-hp 6-71s will cruise around 26–27 knots and turn 30 knots wide open. ❏

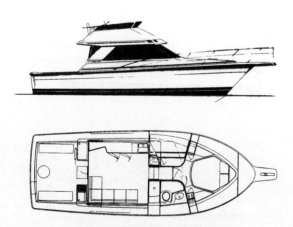

See Page 236 for Pricing Information

PHOENIX 38 CONVERTIBLE

SPECIFICATIONS

Length	38'0"	Fuel	400 gals.
Beam	14'0"	Cockpit	NA
Draft	3'7"	Hull Type	Deep-V
Weight	25,000#	Deadrise Aft	18°
Clearance	12'1"	Designer	Jim Wynne
Water	100 gals.	Production	1982–88

A good-looking fisherman with a huge cockpit to go with her aggressive profile, the Phoenix 38 is built on a solid fiberglass deep-V hull with a wide beam, a full-length inner liner, and prop pockets. Note that the salon's aft bulkhead is angled to improve the flow of fresh air in the cockpit while underway. Inside, one is immediately confronted with one of the smallest salons seen in a boat this size—a genuine drawback in an otherwise competent design. Her wide sidedecks, roomy cockpit, and excellent bridge layout make the Phoenix 38 a comfortable boat to fish. Engine room access is via a hatch in the cockpit—an innovative approach in a 38-foot boat, but the engine room is a tight fit. (Interestingly, this is the smallest production boat with a cockpit engine room door.) A solid front windshield became optional in 1988. The 375-hp Cats cruise at 20 knots and reach 24 at the top. The optional 450-hp 6-71s cruise the Phoenix 38 about 23 knots and reach 26 knots wide open. ❏

See Page 236 for Pricing Information

POST 42 SPORTFISHERMAN

SPECIFICATIONS

Length..........................42'0"	Fuel ....460/500 gals.
Beam ....15'9"	Cockpit ....115 sq. ft.
Draft..............................3'0"	Hull Type.......Modified-V
Weight....................30,000#	Deadrise Aft....................4°
Clearance....................12'6"	Designer ....Russel Post
Water....................120 gals.	Production.............1975–83

With over 230 built, the 42 SF remains the best-selling Post ever. She was introduced in 1975 as a replacement for the all-wood Post 40, and she shares her predecessor's striking Jersey-style profile. As a fishing platform, most tournament veterans rank the Post 42 among the best of the mid-range sportfishermen. Her flat aftersections and flared bow produce a relatively dry boat with good lift and speed. The glassed-over deckhouse windshield seen in later models first became available in 1979. Inside, somewhat dated mahogany woodwork was standard (a teak interior became optional in 1979), and the salon appears larger than the dimensions suggest. Her two-stateroom layout has the master stateroom located amidships and stacked single berths in the forward stateroom. Always built on a solid fiberglass hull, the Post 42 was constructed with a glass-over-wood deck and superstructure until mid-1976. Nearly all were delivered with 310-hp 6-71N diesels (18–19 knots cruise/22 knots wide open) or 410-hp 6-71s (22–23 knots cruise/26 knots top). ❏

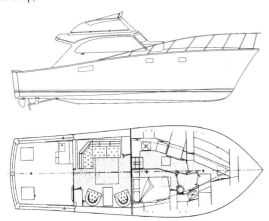

See Page 236 for Pricing Information

POST 43 SPORTFISHERMAN

SPECIFICATIONS

Length.........................43'8"	Fuel ....500/550 gals.
Beam ....15'9"	Cockpit ....125 sq. ft.
Draft..............................3'6"	Hull Type.......Modified-V
Weight....................33,000#	Deadrise Aft.....................7°
Clearance....................13'7"	Designer ......W. Nickerson
Water....................120 gals.	Production.............1984–89

The Post 43 is a revised and updated version of the classic Post 42 Sportfisherman. Introduced in 1984, the 43 underwent significant design changes for 1989 when she became the 43 II. Featuring a redesigned bottom with a deeper forefoot and increased transom deadrise (for a measurably improved ride), the Post 43 II also received a revised flybridge layout, more fuel, and a molded-in tackle center. The previously optional solid front windshield became standard, and a second sprayrail was added for improved lift and a dryer ride. Her two-stateroom interior is a blend of traditional teak woodwork and decorator fabrics. The cockpit is very large and includes a bait freezer, teak covering boards, a transom door, and two in-deck fish boxes. The bridge ladder is stepped on the tackle center and leads through a (small) opening in the flybridge overhang—a Post trademark. Twin 485-hp 6-71s will cruise the Post 43 around 25 knots with a top speed of 28 knots. The optional 550-hp 6V92s cruise at a fast 27 knots (31 knots wide open). ❏

See Page 236 for Pricing Information

155

POST 44 SPORTFISHERMAN

SPECIFICATIONS

Length..........................43'9"	Fuel........................570 gals.
Beam ....15'9"	Cockpit ....125 sq. ft.
Draft..............................3'6"	Hull Type........Modified-V
Weight....................33,000#	Deadrise Aft....................7°
Clearance....................13'7"	Designer ......W. Nickerson
Water.....................120 gals.	Production...1990–Current

The profile of the Post 44 is virtually identical to that of the 43 II model, the boat she replaced in 1990. Indeed, both are built on the same hull, and the cockpit dimensions and bridge layout are identical. But where the Post 43 II has a two-stateroom, galley-down layout, the newer 44 has a two-stateroom, two-head floorplan with a smaller salon and a mid-level galley. While the actual salon dimensions of the Post 44 are about average, the meticulous woodwork and upscale decor are characteristic of Post's elegant teak interiors. Built for the serious angler, the cockpit has a molded tackle center, two in-deck fish boxes, transom door, and teak covering boards. The helm console and flybridge layout are state of the art. Cockpit engine room access was added beginning with the 1992 models. A limited-production boat, only 10–12 Post 44s are built annually, and most have had the optional 550-hp 6V92s. She'll cruise at 27–28 knots and deliver a top speed of 31 knots. ❏

POST 46 SPORTFISHERMAN

SPECIFICATIONS

Length..........................46'9"	Fuel........................640 gals.
Beam ....15'9"	Cockpit ....NA
Draft..............................3'6"	Hull Type........Modified-V
Weight....................36,000#	Deadrise Aft....................7°
Clearance....................13'7"	Designer ......W. Nickerson
Water.....................120 gals.	Production...1978–Current

The original Post 46 was introduced in 1978 as an enlarged version of the popular Post 42. Using the 42's reworked hull, the extra length of the 46 resulted in a second head and the luxury of a dinette. The interior layout was changed in 1985 (the dinette was moved into the salon, and the master stateroom was relocated forward). In 1989, the current 46 II model came out with slightly increased transom deadrise and a deeper forefoot (for a much-improved ride), together with a rearranged flybridge, solid front windshield and a molded tackle center. Cockpit access to the engine room became standard in 1992. Below, her lush two-stateroom teak (or oak) interior remains essentially unchanged. Since the beginning, the Post 46 has been recognized as a premium tournament design with the classic Jersey-style profile long admired in the sportfishing community. With the now-standard 535-hp 6V92s, she'll cruise around 27 knots and reach 30 knots wide open. Earlier models with the 450-hp 6-71TIs will cruise around 23 knots with a top speed of 27 knots. ❏

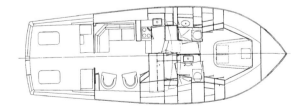

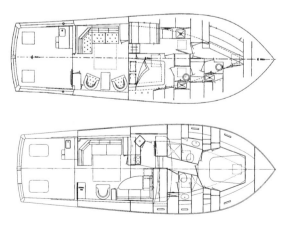

See Page 237 for Pricing Information

See Page 237 for Pricing Information

POST 50 SPORTFISHERMAN

SPECIFICATIONS

Length.........................50'7"	Fuel.......................800 gals.
Beam ....16'11"	Cockpit................147 sq. ft.
Draft...............................4'0"	Hull Type........Modified-V
Weight....................43,000#	Deadrise Aft.....................8°
Clearance...................13'10"	Designer ......W. Nickerson
Water.....................240 gals.	Production...1989–Current

There are many who find the distinctive profile of a Post to be unmatched for beauty and sex appeal. The Post 50 SF is the latest model from this New Jersey builder and their biggest tournament-class sportfisherman ever. Introduced in mid 1989 and offered on a limited production basis, the Post 50 is built on an all-new cored hull with nearly 17 feet of beam and a relatively flat 8° of transom deadrise. Her three-stateroom, mid-level galley floorplan is unique in a convertible of this size (most three-stateroom 50-foot convertibles have the galley up). The teak interior includes a dinette, and the single berths in the aft stateroom can be converted into a large double. The cockpit is set up for serious fishing with a full tackle center, cockpit controls, teak covering boards, and direct access to the engine room (where the overhead is low but outboard access is good). Performance with standard 735-hp 8V92s is excellent—an honest 29 knots at cruise and 33 knots wide open. ❏

PRECISION 2800

SPECIFICATIONS

LOA w/Pulpit............29'7"	Fuel ....204/250 gals.
Hull Length.................28'0"	Cockpit ....NA
Beam ....10'0"	Hull Type........Modified-V
Draft.............................2'9"	Deadrise Aft..................16°
Weight.....................7,900#	Designer ....J. Storie
Clearance.......................8'3"	Production...1992–Current
Water.....................22 gals.	

The Precision 2800 has that aggressive, low-slung profile that experienced anglers have come to associate with good fishing platforms. A light boat at just 7,900 pounds, her solid fiberglass hull is designed with a well-flared bow, shallow 6' keel, and a relatively steep 16° of deadrise at the transom. Note the absence of front windows in the house. The cabin sole is a step down from the cockpit level, and engine boxes flank the entryway. Inside, there are accommodations for four with V-berths forward and a convertible dinette opposite the galley. Outside, the roomy cockpit is arranged with two in-deck fish boxes along with padded coamings, washdowns, and a transom door. A helm and companion seat are fitted on the flybridge. Additional features include wide walkaround sidedecks with waist-high railings, a molded bow pulpit, and a stand-up head with shower. An efficient boat with 4-cylinder Yanmar 170-hp diesels, the Precision 2800 will cruise at 25 knots and reach a top speed of around 29–30 knots. ❏

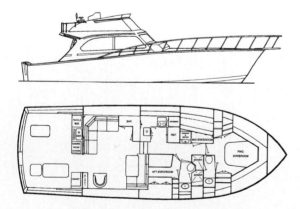

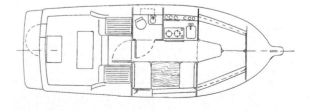

See Page 237 for Pricing Information

See Page 237 for Pricing Information

PRO-LINE 2550 MID-CABIN W/A

SPECIFICATIONS

Length w/Pulpit........27'5"	Fuel, I/O...............125 gals.
Beam ....9'10"	Cockpit ....71 sq. ft.
Hull Draft....................1'10"	Hull Type...............Deep-V
Hull Weight..............5,845#	Deadrise Aft...................19°
Clearance......................NA	Designer ....Pro-Line
Water.......................20 gals.	Production...1991–Current
Fuel, O/B..............150 gals.	

The Pro-Line 2550 is a durable and affordably priced fisherman with a walkaround cuddy cabin and a choice of outboard or stern drive power. She's built on a solid fiberglass deep-V hull with foam flotation, a relatively wide beam, and 19° of deadrise at the transom. A good-looking boat with a strictly-business profile, the uncluttered cockpit comes standard with a livewell, two in-deck fish boxes, and a pair of baitwells built into the transom. Rods racks are fitted beneath the gunwales. Belowdecks, the 2550's compact cabin is arranged with a dinette/V-berth forward, a small galley, and an enclosed head with shower. There's also a transversely mounted berth in the mid-cabin area beneath the helm. Outside, visibility from the elevated helm is excellent, and wide sidedecks make access to the bow quick and easy. Bracket-mounted 200-hp outboards will cruise the Pro-Line 2550 Walkaround at a brisk 27 knots and deliver a top speed of around 42–43 knots. The fuel capacity is limited, so don't plan any long trips. ❏

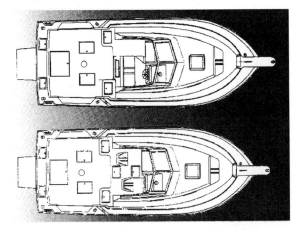

See Page 237 for Pricing Information

PRO-LINE 2700 SPORTSMAN

SPECIFICATIONS

Length w/Pulpit........27'5"	Fuel.........................200 gals.
Beam ....9'10"	Cockpit ....115 sq. ft.
Hull Draft.....................1'8"	Hull Type...............Deep-V
Hull Weight..............4,750#	Deadrise Aft...................19°
Clearance......................NA	Designer ....Pro-Line
Water.......................15 gals.	Production...1993–Current

The 2700 Sportsman is a straightforward day boat with more fishing space than most other center consoles her size. Indeed, the nearly 10' beam is very wide for a 27-footer, and the Sportsman's high freeboard is notable. She's built on a deep-V hull with 19° of deadrise at the transom, foam flotation, and a well-flared bow for a dry ride. Designed for serious anglers yet still attractively priced, the cockpit is huge and comes with a transom baitstation with livewell, sink, cutting board, and freshwater washdown. The transom door, leaning post, cockpit shower, and in-deck fish boxes are all standard. The 2700's wide helm console has space for installing some electronics, and the console itself houses tackle trays and a roomy stand-up head compartment (with shower) below. Forward of the helm is a casting platform with storage under the seats. A fast ride with 200-hp bracket-mounted outboards, the Pro-Line 2700 Sportsman will cruise efficiently at 29 knots and reach a top speed of around 43–44 knots. ❏

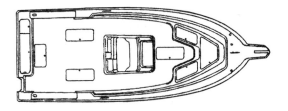

See Page 237 for Pricing Information

PRO-LINE 2950 MID-CABIN W/A

SPECIFICATIONS

Length	30'0"	Fuel	300 gals.
Beam	10'9"	Cockpit	80 sq. ft.
Hull Draft	1'10"	Hull Type	Deep-V
Hull Weight	7,500#	Deadrise Aft	19°
Clearance	6'0"	Designer	Pro-Line
Water	42 gals.	Production	1992–Current

A popular boat, the Pro-Line 2950 Mid-cabin Walkaround is one of the more affordable fishing boats in her size range. Construction is solid glass, and the wide-beam hull is packed with foam flotation. A distinguishing feature of the 2950 is her wide, deep walkaround sidedecks—the high freeboard provides unusual security, although it's a long reach over the gunwale to the water. Visibility from the raised bridgedeck is excellent, and the big 80 sq. ft. cockpit is fitted with a jump seat, in-deck fish box, rod storage, tackle drawers, and transom door. A bait-prep station is built into the transom complete with livewell and sink. Belowdecks, the cabin is arranged with V-berths, a compact galley and head, and a mid-cabin berth aft. Additional features include a stylish curved windshield, molded pulpit, a well-arranged helm console, and foredeck seating. A good-looking boat in spite of her no-frills construction, bracket-mounted 250-hp Yahamas will cruise the Pro-Line 2950 at an easy 28 knots and reach 40+ knots wide open. ❏

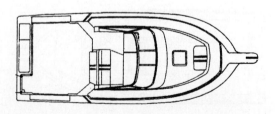

See Page 237 for Pricing Information

RADOVICH 34 SF

SPECIFICATIONS

Length	34'8"	Fuel, Std	360 gals.
Beam	13'0"	Fuel, Opt	500 gals.
Draft	2'8"	Hull Type	Modified-V
Weight	19,500#	Deadrise Aft	15°
Clearance	NA	Designer	V. Radovich
Water	100 gals.	Production	1987–Current

The Radovich 34 is a conservative West Coast fisherman with a huge cockpit, basic interior accommodations, and a distinctive low-profile appearance similar to early Luhrs, Tollycraft and Silverton designs. She's heavily built on a solid fiberglass hull, and a 15-inch keel runs about two-thirds the length of the bottom. The Radovich is a beamy boat for her length, and that—together with her raised cockpit sole—allows the motors to be mounted further outboard for improved low-speed handling. An aluminum bait tank occupies the center of the cockpit, and extra-wide sidedecks make foredeck access easy. Topside, the bridge is arranged in typical West Coast fashion with the helm forward (although variations are available). Offered with or without a lower helm, the modest no-glitz interior of the Radovich includes a dinette, stand-up head, an efficient galley, good headroom, and berths for six. Three hatches in the cockpit sole provide excellent access to the engines. Twin 320-hp Cats will cruise the Radovich at 20 knots with a top speed of around 26 knots. ❏

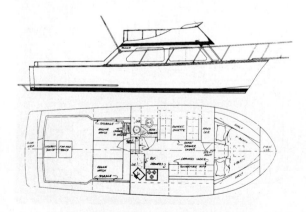

See Page 237 for Pricing Information

RAMPAGE 24 EXPRESS

SPECIFICATIONS

LOA, Inbd ....24'6"	Clearance.......................4'0"
LOA w/Platform ....26'6"	Fuel.......................130 gals.
Beam ....9'11"	Hull Type........Modified-V
Draft, Inbd.....................2'8"	Deadrise Aft...................12°
Weight, Inbd ....4,900#	Designer ....Dick Lema
Weight, O/B.............4,400#	Production.............1984–90

The Rampage 24 is a wide-beam express fisherman with a big fishing cockpit and overnight accommodations for two anglers. Like all Rampage models, she's built on a fully balsa-cored modified-V hull with moderate transom deadrise and substantial bow flare to deflect spray. A skeg protects the running gear in the inboard version. First offered as a single inboard or stern drive/jackshaft model, an outboard version with bracket became available in 1987. The cockpit is set up with twin in-deck fish boxes and rod racks under the gunwales. A centerline engine box (with a seat cushion) makes getting at the motor easy. The cuddy cabin is fitted with V-berths, a hanging locker, and portable toilet. Wide sidedecks and sturdy rails make for safe foredeck access. On balance, the overall utility and fishability of the Rampage 24 is excellent. A single 350-cid gas inboard will cruise at 22 knots and reach a top speed of about 32 knots. Twin 200-hp outboards will reach top speeds in excess of 40 knots. ❑

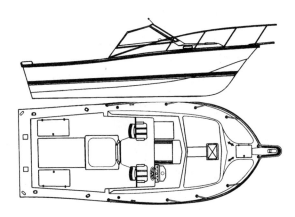

See Page 237 for Pricing Information

RAMPAGE 28 SPORTSMAN

SPECIFICATIONS

LOA ....29'6"	Fuel........................240 gals.
Hull Length................28'0"	Cockpit ....80 sq. ft.
Beam ....11'0"	Hull Type........Modified-V
Draft ....2'6"	Deadrise Aft...................10°
Weight.....................8,200#	Designer ....Dick Lema
Clearance.......................NA	Production...1986–Current
Water.......................25 gals.	

The Rampage 28 Sportsman is a good-looking day boat with a well-arranged cockpit and generous cabin accommodations. She's built on a fully cored hull with a sweeping sheer, modest transom deadrise, and a relatively sharp entry. Her relatively wide beam gives the 28 Sportsman the look and feel of a much bigger boat. About half of her length is given over to cockpit space, where there's plenty of room for a full-size fighting chair in addition to a standard livewell and transom door. Inside, the cabin is clean and attractive with enough teak woodwork and trim to keep things from looking too plain. There are berths for three (the portside backrest of the dinette/settee swings up to create the third berth), and an enclosed stand-up head compartment and compact galley complete the accommodations. Separate engine boxes below the helm and companion seats provide good access to the motors. A good performer, twin 350-cid gas inboards will cruise the Rampage 28 at a brisk 24 knots and deliver 33–34 knots top. ❑

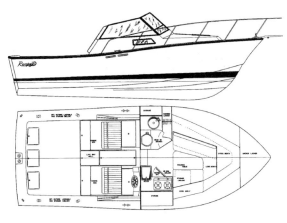

See Page 237 for Pricing Information

RAMPAGE 31 SPORTFISHERMAN

SPECIFICATIONS

LOA ....31'10"	Fuel.........................256 gals.
Hull Length...............30'10"	Cockpit ....114 sq. ft.
Beam ....11'11"	Hull Type........Modified-V
Draft..............................2'9"	Deadrise Aft..................10°
Weight....................12,000#	Designer ....Dick Lema
Clearance.......................NA	Production...1985–Current
Water.......................50 gals.	

The Rampage 31 is a good example of how a modern express fisherman combines the stringent requirements of offshore fishing with the high-tech construction techniques rapidly taking hold throughout the industry. She rides on a fully cored hull with a flared bow and moderate deadrise at the transom. Below, the cabin is snug but adequate for the needs of weekend anglers. The dinette/settee converts into a V-berth, and the backrests fold up to become bunks—a total of four berths. The bi-level cockpit is particularly well-designed with an extra-wide transom door, lockable rod storage, and a huge in-deck 85-gallon circulating livewell. There's room in the console for electronics installation, and a unique system of sliding hatches make engine access about as painless as it gets. Note the wide sidedecks and sturdy rails. Standard 454-cid gas engines will cruise the Rampage 31 around 24 knots (33 top). The popular 300-hp GM 8.2 diesels will cruise at a fast 28 knots with a top speed of 31–33 knots. ❏

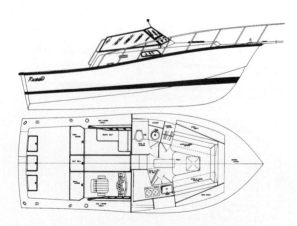

See Page 237 for Pricing Information

RAMPAGE 33 SPORTFISHERMAN

SPECIFICATIONS

LOA ....34'10"	Water.......................58 gals.
Hull Length...............32'4"	Fuel.........................300 gals.
Beam ....12'4"	Cockpit ....77 sq. ft.
Draft..............................2'7"	Hull Type...............Deep-V
Weight....................14,500#	Deadrise Aft..................18°
Clearance....................11'2"	Production...1990–Current

The Rampage 33 is designed for experienced anglers who don't mind paying for the quality that goes into a stylish and well-built offshore day boat. She's built on a fully cored deep-V hull, and her wide beam and flared bow insures a dry and stable fishing platform in a variety of weather conditions. Belowdecks, the roomy cabin will sleep four and includes a stand-up head, a big U-shaped dinette, and compact galley. The Rampage 33 is loaded with thoughtful features sure to appeal to hard-core fishermen—good engine access, an oversized transom door, big in-deck fish boxes, lockable rod storage space, a hinged helm console, underwater exhausts, windshield vents, and a completely removable aft cockpit sole. There's space in the console for most electronics, and the sidedecks are quite wide. Gas engines are standard, but most buyers will opt for diesel power. Optional Cummins 300-hp diesels will cruise economically at 24–25 knots and reach about 29 knots wide open. The bigger 320-hp Cats will run a knot faster. ❏

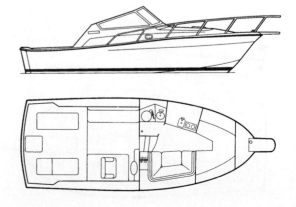

See Page 238 for Pricing Information

RAMPAGE 36 SPORTFISHERMAN

SPECIFICATIONS

LOA ....37'8"	Water.......................70 gals.
Hull Length.................35'6"	Fuel.......................435 gals.
Beam ....13'9"	Cockpit................100 sq. ft.
Draft.............................2'9"	Hull TypeModified Deep-V
Weight....................19,000#	Deadrise Aft...................17°
Clearance....................8'10"	Production...1989–Current

Built on a full-cored deep-V hull, the Rampage 36 is a beamy off-shore fisherman with the aggressive good looks and rugged construction common to all Rampage products. Chief among her attributes is a spacious bi-level fishing cockpit with insulated fish boxes, concealed rod storage, huge livewell, extra-large transom door, and molded tackle center. The helm position is elevated and features a lockable electronics panel and excellent visibility. A convenient settee is abaft the companion seat, and easy engine access is provided via a centerline hatch in the cockpit sole. Inside, the cabin layout is comfortable and well-arranged with a small galley, a full-sized convertible dinette, and an enclosed head with the toilet concealed in the shower stall. Additional features include side-dumping exhausts, chart table, and molded bow pulpit. Several diesel options have been offered. With 291-hp Cummins diesels, the Rampage 36 will cruise efficiently around 22 knots (25 knots top) and, with the big 425-hp Cats, will cruise at 25 knots and deliver 29–30 knots wide open. ❏

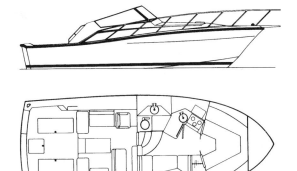

See Page 238 for Pricing Information

RAMPAGE 40 SPORTFISHERMAN

SPECIFICATIONS

Length..........................41'9"	Fuel.......................575 gals.
Beam ....15'2"	Cockpit................102 sq. ft.
Draft.............................3'6"	Hull Type........Modified-V
Weight....................25,000#	Deadrise Aft.................NA
Clearance....................13'3"	Designer.............Rampage
Water.....................100 gals.	Production.............1988–90

Not a notably popular boat, the styling of the Rampage 40 is unusual in that she features a rather unattractive trunk cabin foredeck rather than the conventional flush foredeck seen in most convertibles this size. Like all Rampage products, the 40 is constructed on a fully cored hull with a wide beam and moderate deadrise at the transom. A unique underwater exhaust system is located midships, just below the salon. The roomy two-stateroom interior is arranged with the galley aft in the salon (unusual in a fishing boat). A cavernous rod locker is built into the salon overhead, and the cherry woodwork is impressive. Topside, the wraparound helm console has two large electronics lockers properly angled for easy viewing. A transom door, circulating livewell, bait prep station, and two fish boxes were all standard. A well-built boat, 485-hp 6-71s will cruise the Rampage 40 around 23–24 knots. The bigger 550-hp 6V92 diesels will cruise at 27 knots and reach 30 knots top. Note that she was called the Rampage 42 Sportfisherman in 1990. ❏

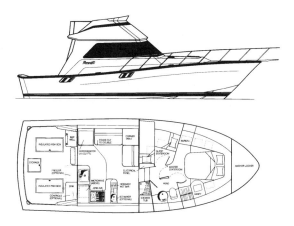

See Page 238 for Pricing Information

RONIN 38 CONVERTIBLE

SPECIFICATIONS

Length	38'3"	Fuel	370 gals.
Beam	13'11"	Cockpit	108 sq. ft.
Draft	3'6"	Hull Type	Modified-V
Weight	26,000#	Deadrise Aft	15°
Clearance	12'8"	Designer	Unknown
Water	100 gals.	Production	1986–92

Built in Taiwan, the Ronin 38 is constructed on a conventional modified-V hull with a wide beam and balsa coring in the hull-sides. Three separate molds were required—hull, superstructure, and flybridge—so there are no seams in the cockpit or screws on the bridge. A good-looking boat with a handsome profile, the Ronin 38 was available with a galley-down, single-stateroom layout or with the galley in the salon and two staterooms forward. The interior is finished in solid teak or light oak woodwork and good craftsmanship is evident throughout. A hatch in the salon sole reveals a well-organized engine room with good access to motors and generator. Outside, the large cockpit is set up for serious fishing and includes a transom door and gate, livewell, freezer, and freshwater washdown. Standard Cat 375-hp diesels cruise the Ronin 38 at 22–23 knots and reach a top speed of 27. The optional 485-hp 6-71s provide a cruising speed of 25–26 knots and a top speed of about 29 knots. ❏

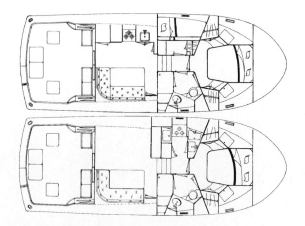

See Page 238 for Pricing Information

RONIN 48 CONVERTIBLE

SPECIFICATIONS

Length	48'8"	Fuel	850 gals.
Beam	15'10"	Cockpit	NA
Draft	4'0"	Hull Type	Modified-V
Weight	46,000#	Deadrise Aft	15°
Clearance	14'3"	Designer	Unknown
Water	200 gals.	Production	1987–92

To date, Ronin is one of the *very* few Taiwan sportfishermen to have at least cracked the long-standing resistance to Asian imports among hard-core anglers. Like the smaller Ronin 38, the 48 Convertible is built on a conventional modified-V hull with generous flare at the bow and 15° of deadrise at the transom. The hull-sides are cored with balsa, and the boat is assembled with only three separate molds, which adds strength and rigidity while reducing seals and leaks. In appearance, the Ronin 48 Convertible has a strong resemblance to Brand H (as in Hatteras). The styling is contemporary and completely in line with popular sportfish trends. Inside, the 48 offered a choice of two or three staterooms with the galley up or down. The teak (or light oak) interior woodwork is very attractive, and the large engine room is arranged with good access to the motors. With optional 735-hp 8V92s, the Ronin 48 will cruise around 27 knots and reach 30+ knots wide open. Twin 840-hp MAN diesels became optional in 1990. ❏

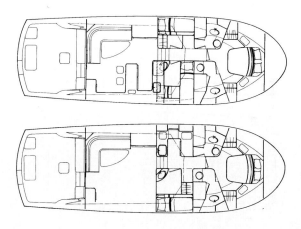

See Page 238 for Pricing Information

RYBO RUNNER 30 CENTER CONSOLE

SEA RAY 270 AMBERJACK

SPECIFICATIONS

Length	30'0"	Fuel	200 gals.
Beam	10'8"	Cockpit	NA
Draft	3'0"	Hull Type	Deep-V
Weight	6,500#	Deadrise Aft	24°
Clearance	NA	Designer	Rybovich
Water	None	Production	1983–89

SPECIFICATIONS

LOA	29'3"	Water	28 gals.
Hull Length	27'7"	Fuel	200 gals.
Beam	10'0"	Cockpit	NA
Draft, drive down	2'8"	Hull Type	Deep-V
Drave, drive up	1'3"	Deadrise Aft	22°
Weight	7,000#	Production	1986–90

The Rybo Runner is a high-speed fisherman from Rybovich with a unique double-step hull designed to reduce wetted area when planing by creating air pockets behind the steps. Hull construction is solid fiberglass, and a full-length inner liner adds a good deal of rigidity to the hull. The center console has space for flush-mounting some electronics, and there's room inside the console for a stand-up head and shower. Abaft the console, the leaning post is a molded fiberglass unit with rod holders, tackle storage, and an optional baitwell. In the cockpit sole are two long lift-out fish boxes, and there are four rod holders in the gunwales. The cockpit can easily accommodate a fighting chair. Rybo Runners were semi-custom boats, and most were equipped with an optional Rybovich tower and outriggers. Power options included twin outboards, 205-hp OMC SeaDrives, twin 270-hp gas inboards, or a single 8.2 diesel. The Sea Drives will cruise at 24 knots (42–43 knots top), and the gas inboards also cruise around 24 knots (31 top).   ❏

A good-selling boat for Sea Ray, the 270 Amberjack is a roomy express cruiser with an unusually large cockpit to go with her basic cabin accommodations. Construction is solid fiberglass, and her 10-foot beam is wide for a 27-footer. (Note that the maximum beam is carried well aft resulting in plenty of cockpit space but a relatively narrow cabin.) The single-level cockpit is arranged with a fore-and-aft companion seat opposite the helm and fold-away bench seating at the transom. There's a storage bin between the two seats, and additional storage is located under the gunwales. Inside, the cabin is fitted with V-berths, an enclosed stand-up head compartment with shower, and a compact galley area. A single hatch at the transom provides good access to the engines. Additional features include a small transom door, swim platform with ladder, teak bow pulpit, and teak covering boards. Popular 260-hp stern drives will cruise the 270 Amberjack at an easy 23 knots and reach a top speed of 32–33 knots.   ❏

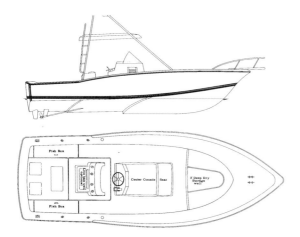

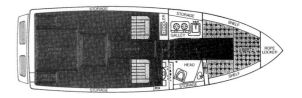

See Page 238 for Pricing Information

See Page 238 for Pricing Information

SEA RAY LAGUNA 29 WALKAROUND

SPECIFICATIONS

LOA	31'6"	Water	30 gals.
Hull Length	29'2"	Fuel	200 gals.
Beam	10'6"	Cockpit	66 sq. ft.
Draft, drive down	2'8"	Hull Type	Deep-V
Drave, drive up	1'11"	Deadrise Aft	21°
Weight	9,200#	Production	1993 Only
Clearance	6'8"		

I t's not often that Sea Ray misfires with a new model, but that appears to have been the case with the Laguna 29 Walkaround, an attractive and well-designed day boat aimed at the market for family fishermen. Originally built for the Japanese market, production lasted only a year. Constructed on a solid fiberglass deep-V hull, the Laguna 29 lacks the curved windshield and integrated swim platform seen in most modern express boats. Neither does she carry enough fuel—200 gallons just doesn't get it in a boat this size. On the plus side, the mid-cabin interior (with its compact galley and stand-up head) will sleep four, and the deep walkaround decks are perfect for fighting fish or maintaining the security of little ones. The transom is fitted with a lift-out fish box and livewell, and the extra-wide swim platform is removable. Powered with V-drive 350-cid gas inboards, the Laguna 29 will cruise at 20 knots and reach a top speed of 27–28 knots. Stern drives were optional. ❏

SEA RAY 310 AMBERJACK

SPECIFICATIONS

Length	31'2"	Water	40 gals.
Beam	11'5"	Fuel	296 gals.
Draft	3'1"	Hull Type	Deep-V
Weight	10,500#	Deadrise Aft	18°
Cockpit	57 sq. ft.	Designer	Sea Ray
Clearance	NA	Production	1991–Current

A nglers will find much to like in the 310 Amberjack, a good-looking dayboat with the aggressive low-profile silhouette of a small Bertram or Blackfin. She's built on a deep-V hull with cored hullsides, a wide beam, prop pockets, and 18° of transom deadrise. Like any well-planned fisherman, the Amberjack's original emphasis was in the large and well-organized cockpit. In 1994, however, Sea Ray replaced the convenient dinette opposite the helm with an elevated lounge area. The cockpit can be fitted with in-deck fish boxes, rod holders, and a transom livewell. While cabin space is at a premium, the 310 AJ manages to include overnight berths for two plus a stand-up head with shower, small galley, and convertible dinette. The sidedecks are a foot wide, and the motors are accessed via engine boxes. A good performer with twin 454-cid MerCruiser gas engines, she'll cruise at an easy 24 knots and reach 31–32 knots top. Note that she was called the Sea Ray Laguna 31 in 1993. ❏

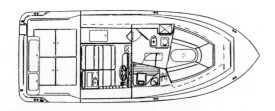

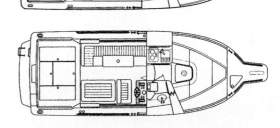

See Page 238 for Pricing Information

See Page 238 for Pricing Information

SEA RAY 310 SPORT BRIDGE

SPECIFICATIONS

LOA	33'8"	Water	40 gals.
Hull Length	31'2"	Fuel	296 gals.
Beam	11'5"	Hull Type	Deep-V
Draft	3'1"	Deadrise Aft	18°
Weight	11,500#	Designer	Sea Ray
Clearance	9'6"	Production	1992–93
Cockpit	57 sq. ft.		

A great-looking boat with aggressive styling and a low-profile appearance, the 310 Sport Bridge is basically a 310 Amberjack with a flybridge and semi-enclosed lower helm. She's built on a deep-V hull with a wide beam, side-dumping exhausts, and prop pockets. Like any well-planned sedan fisherman, she comes with a spacious cockpit—a wide-open affair consuming well over half of the boat's LOA. There's plenty of guest seating including a sunpad and dinette, and the cockpit can be fitted with in-deck fish boxes, rod holders, and a transom livewell. While cabin space is at a premium, the 310 manages to include overnight berths for two plus a stand-up head with shower, small galley, and convertible dinette. The bridge is small with seating for two. Hinged motor boxes provide good access to the engines, and the sidedecks are a foot wide. Twin 454-cid gas engines will cruise at 23 knots (30–31 knots top), and optional 291-hp Cummins diesels will cruise around 27 knots (31 knots top). ❑

SEA RAY 390 SEDAN SF

SPECIFICATIONS

Length	39'0"	Fuel	400 gals.
Beam	13'11"	Cockpit	116 sq. ft.
Draft	2'5"	Hull Type	Deep-V
Weight	18,400#	Deadrise Aft	19°
Clearance	NA	Designer	Sea Ray
Water	100 gals.	Production	1983–86

The 390 Sedan SF is a stretched version of the popular Sea Ray 360 Sedan built from 1980 to 1983. The extra length went into the cockpit, which is easily the boat's most impressive feature. She was built on the same one-piece fiberglass hull as the 360 and 390 Express Cruisers—a deep-V design with a relatively wide beam, 19° of transom deadrise, and propeller pockets. The original floorplan was updated in 1985 to include a centerline queen berth in the forward stateroom and a more open salon area. Single berths are located in the guest cabin, and a serving counter separates the galley from the salon. The comfortable interior arrangements of the 390 Sedan make her an excellent all-purpose family cruiser, and, with plenty of fuel and a big cockpit, she's capable of fishing activities. Standard 350-hp gas engines will cruise around 17 knots and reach a top speed of 25 knots. Optional 320-hp Cat diesels cruise the 390 Sedan SF at an economical 21 knots and reach 24 knots top. ❑

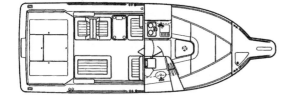

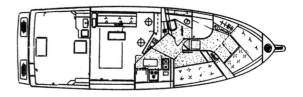

See Page 238 for Pricing Information

See Page 238 for Pricing Information

SEA RAY 440 CONVERTIBLE

SPECIFICATIONS

LOA ....49'1"	Fuel.......................500 gals.
Hull Length................43'6"	Cockpit ....NA
Beam ....13'11"	Hull Type..............Deep-V
Draft..............................2'8"	Deadrise Aft..................17°
Weight...................23,000#	Designer................Sea Ray
Clearance....................10'9"	Production.............1988–91
Water....................132 gals.	

Aimed at the market for offshore fishermen, the 440 Convertible was styled after the larger Sea Ray 460 Convertible (1987–88) with a low foredeck, stepped sheer, and modern deckhouse profile. Introduced in 1988 as the 430 Convertible, the 440 designation came in 1989. Built on a rugged deep-V hull with plenty of beam, she's more family cruiser than fishing boat. Below, the high-style European interior theme of the 440 (no teak anywhere) was updated in 1990 with a modest amount of teak trim and compares well with many of today's contemporary family convertibles. The floorplan—with its mid-level galley and athwartships guest stateroom—is innovative and well-arranged. Also unusual (in a 43' boat) is the cockpit engine room access where a hatch opens into a somewhat tight engine compartment. Standard features include a transom door, removable fish box, salon and flybridge wet bars, cockpit shower, and a swim platform. With the optional 375-hp Cat diesels, the 440 Convertible will cruise around 21 knots and reach 25 knots wide open. ❏

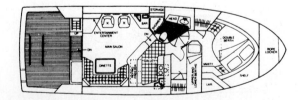

See Page 238 for Pricing Information

SEA RAY 460 CONVERTIBLE

SPECIFICATIONS

Length.........................45'6"	Fuel.......................700 gals.
Beam ....14'11"	Cockpit ....105 sq. ft.
Draft..............................3'2"	Hull Type..............Deep-V
Weight....................34,000#	Deadrise Aft..................17°
Clearance....................13'1"	Designer................Sea Ray
Water....................150 gals.	Production.............1987–88

The 460 Convertible was Sea Ray's first venture into the serious sportfishing market and represented a bold departure from the company's past devotion to family-oriented cruisers and sportboats. She was built on a relatively lightweight deep-V hull with prop pockets, and her aggressive, Eurostyle appearance remains stylish today. Still, the 460 Convertible wasn't a big seller, and production lasted only two years until she was replaced in 1988 with the less-expensive 440 model. A comfortable boat, her two-stateroom interior was plush in the extreme (too plush for some anglers) with a combination of ultrasuedes and vinyls matched with grey Formica galley counters and cabinetry—a Eurostyle decor with luxury touches seldom found in an offshore fisherman. Outside, the cockpit is large enough for a full-size fighting chair, and the flybridge ladder is mounted sideways to save space. Caterpillar diesels were standard, but the best performance is achieved with the 550-hp 6V92s. With those engines, the Sea Ray 460 Convertible will cruise around 24 knots and reach 27 knots at full throttle. ❏

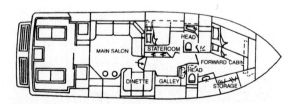

See Page 238 for Pricing Information

SHAMROCK 31 GRAND SLAM

SPECIFICATIONS

Length	31'0"	Fuel, Opt	340 gals.
Beam	11'4"	Cockpit	142 sq. ft.
Draft	3'4"	Hull Type	Deep-V
Weight	9,250#	Deadrise Aft	19°
Clearance	18'0"	Designer	Shamrock
Water	40 gals.	Production	1987–94
Fuel, Std	290 gals.		

Shamrock Marine is a well-regarded South Florida builder of small fishing and utility boats featuring unique "keel drive" hull designs. Unlike the rest of the Shamrock series, however, the 31 Grand Slam is built on a conventional deep-V hull. At first glance, she appears to be a fairly standard open sportfisherman with attractive lines and a large fishing cockpit. A closer look reveals several interesting features. The helm seat, for example, can be converted into a leaning post. Engine access is good—a unique central service bay houses all the mechanical and electrical systems. The cockpit features modular tackle centers, rod holders, and storage bins. For accommodations, there are four single berths below (the dinette seatbacks convert to single bunks) and a stand-up head with shower. Standard gas engines have not proved popular with buyers. Early models with optional 250-hp Cummins diesels cruise at 28 knots (2 mpg!) and reach 33 wide open. Cummins 300-hp diesels (available since 1990) cruise at 31 knots and deliver 34–35 knots top. Over 160 were built. ❏

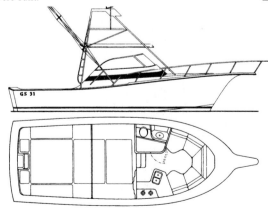

See Page 238 for Pricing Information

SILVERTON 31 CONVERTIBLE (EARLY)

1977–81

1982–87

SPECIFICATIONS

Length	31'0"	Fuel	220 gals.
Beam	11'11"	Cockpit	82 sq. ft.
Draft	2'11"	Hull Type	Modified-V
Weight	11,400#	Deadrise Aft	NA
Clearance	10'8"	Designer	Silverton
Water	40 gals.	Production	1977–87

The appeal of the Silverton 31 Convertible (production ran for a full decade) had much to do with her roomy accommodations, attractive design, and an affordable price tag. Compared with other convertibles and family sedans of her size, the Silverton 31 gets high marks for a spacious salon area—a rare luxury in a boat this small—with enough room to seat four or five comfortably without being cramped. Her large cockpit provides a good platform for swimming and casual fishing activities. On the downside, the flybridge is notably small with seating for just three persons. The Silverton 31 Convertible received a major styling update in 1982, when the deckhouse was redesigned with a much-improved profile. Light oak interior woodwork was added in the 1985 model. Throughout her long production run the Silverton 31 Convertible retained the same basic interior floorplan with the galley and head forward and down from the salon. Twin 220-hp gas engines with V-drives will provide a cruising speed of around 17–18 knots and a cruising speed of about 27 knots. ❏

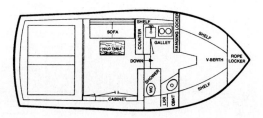

See Page 238 for Pricing Information

SILVERTON 37 CONVERTIBLE

SPECIFICATIONS

Length	37'4"	Fuel	375 gals.
Beam	13'11"	Cockpit	80 sq. ft.
Draft	3'9"	Hull Type	Modified-V
Weight	21,000#	Deadrise Aft	17°
Clearance	14'0"	Designer	M. Peters
Water	100 gals.	Production	1990–Current

With her contemporary profile and upscale interior, the newest Silverton 37 (the original 37 Convertible ran from 1980 to 1989) is one of the most affordable family cruisers available in this size range. Like most Silverton models, she's a lot of boat for the money. Her solid fiberglass hull has a shallow keel and a fairly steep 17° of deadrise at the transom. Belowdecks, the spacious single-stateroom interior is arranged with the galley and dinette down and but still open to the salon. The light oak interior woodwork, white galley laminates, and wraparound cabin windows create a bright and pleasant interior. The cockpit is too small for a fighting chair, but coaming pads, an in-deck fish box, and a transom door and swim platform are standard. The flybridge seats six with bench seating forward of the helm, and the well-planned console has space for flush-mounting some electronics. No racehorse, the performance of the Silverton 37 with standard 454-cid gas engines is a modest 15–16 knots, at cruise and the top speed is about 25 knots. ❏

SILVERTON 41 CONVERTIBLE

SPECIFICATIONS

Length	41'3"	Water	200 gals.
Beam	14'10"	Fuel	516 gals.
Draft	3'9"	Hull Type	Modified-V
Weight	27,000#	Deadrise Aft	NA
Clearance	15'5"	Designer	Silverton
Cockpit	98 sq. ft.	Production	1991–Current

The Silverton 41 Convertible is a moderately priced sedan cruiser with a clean-cut profile and a practical two-stateroom interior layout. With her long foredeck, step-down sheer, and raked bridge, the 41 has the look of a sportfisherman (although Silvertons have never been noted for building tournament-level boats). The cockpit is large enough for a fighting chair, and there's a good-size fish box below the sole. Inside, wraparound cabin windows provide excellent natural lighting. The light oak interior is arranged with the galley and (big) dinette down from the salon level, a double-entry head with a stall shower, over/under single berths in the guest cabin, and an island berth in the master stateroom. Additional features include a reasonably spacious flybridge with plenty of seating, side exhausts, transom door, and swim platform. Standard 502-cid gas engines will cruise the Silverton 41 Convertible at 19–20 knots (about 28 knots top), and the optional 425-hp Caterpillar diesels will cruise at 24–25 knots and reach 28 knots wide open. ❏

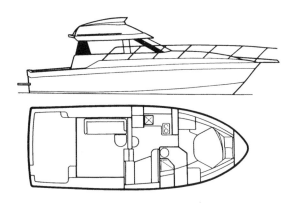

See Page 239 for Pricing Information

See Page 239 for Pricing Information

SOUTHERN CROSS 44 SF

SPECIFICATIONS

Length.........................44'2"	Fuel......................550 gals.
Beam ....14'6"	Cockpit................110 sq. ft.
Draft..............................3'0"	Hull Type........Modified-V
Weight...................28,000#	Deadrise Aft..................NA
Clearance....................12'6"	Designer............Tom Fexas
Water.....................100 gals.	Production.............1987–90

A great-looking design from Tom Fexas, the Southern Cross 44 is an Australian import with a number of innovative and practical design features. Beginning with a fully cored hull, her unique chamfered transom allows the 44 to back down hard with less tendency to flood the cockpit. The air intakes are hidden in the after edge of the house, and underwater exhausts run through the stringers. At 28,000 lbs., the Southern Cross 44 is a relatively light boat for her size, and those who have run her agree that her seakeeping characteristics are good. The cockpit is equipped with controls, a bait prep station, transom door, and livewell. Access to the spacious engine room is provided via a cockpit door. *Four* steps up from the cockpit, the salon features silver ash woodwork and stylish fabrics to create an especially attractive interior. A good-running boat with a comfortable ride, twin 540-hp 6V92 diesels will cruise the Southern Cross 44 Convertible around 27 knots, and the top speed is 30 knots. ❏

SOUTHERN CROSS 52 SF

SPECIFICATIONS

Length.........................52'0"	Fuel....................1,000 gals.
Beam ....15'6"	Cockpit ....144 sq. ft.
Draft..............................3'6"	Hull Type........Modified-V
Weight...................38,000#	Deadrise Aft..................NA
Clearance......................NA	Designer............Tom Fexas
Water.....................150 gals.	Production 1986-1990

Southern Cross was the Australian builder who ran those full-page ads some years ago promising to blow Bertram and Hatteras out of the "bloody water." They were talking about the Southern Cross 52, a sleek Fexas design with plenty of high-tech construction and not a lot of weight. She never really caught on with serious anglers (her eagerly awaited introduction at the '85 Lauderdale boat show was a bust), and only seven were sold before Southern Cross closed down in 1991. In some ways, she was ahead of her time—lightweight, fully cored construction, and ash interiors have since become popular in the sportfishing community. Several floorplans were offered (early models had the galley aft in the salon) with the three-stateroom, galley-up layout preferred. Narrow in the beam and with a very low cockpit, the 52 SF never attained the promised 37-knot performance. Instead, she turned a still-fast 34 knots wide open with just 740-hp 8V92s (which isn't bad—a late model Hatteras 52 barely manages 27 knots top with the same motors). ❏

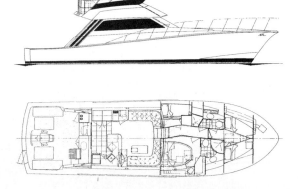

See Page 239 for Pricing Information

See Page 239 for Pricing Information

STAMAS 288 LIBERTY

SPECIFICATIONS

LOA w/Pulpit...........30'2"	Fuel........................196 gals.
Hull Length................28'4"	Cockpit ....NA
Beam..............................11'2'	Hull Type........Modified-V
Draft..............................1'6"	Deadrise Aft...................18°
Weight......................9,500#	Designer..............P. Stamas
Clearance.....................7'6"	Production...1987–Current
Water......................20 gals.	

The 288 Liberty is an affordably priced fishing boat with the styling, appointments, and performance that anglers expect in a strictly-business day boat. A popular model (she's now called the Stamas 288 Family Fisherman), the hull is constructed of solid fiberglass with a wide beam and a gently flared bow. Key to the success of the boat is her practical deck plan and spacious mid-cabin interior layout. The single-level cockpit is arranged with two forward fish wells, two live baitwells, and an icebox. The helm is elevated, and a motor box occupies the aft end of the cockpit in the stern drive version. Inside, there are berths for four in the roomy cabin with a stand-up head and a small galley—accommodations suitable for a small family. Additional features include wide sidedecks, a molded pulpit, and excellent storage. Those with 230-hp I/Os will cruise around 23 knots (36 knots top). Bracket-mounted 200-hp outboards will cruise around 21 knots and reach 30+ knots wide open. ❏

STAMAS 290 EXPRESS

SPECIFICATIONS

LOA w/Pulpit...........31'7"	Fuel........................200 gals.
Hull Length................29'0"	Cockpit ....95 sq. ft.
Beam..............................10'4"	Hull Type........Modified-V
Draft..............................1'6"	Deadrise Aft...................18°
Weight......................7,010#	Designer..............P. Stamas
Clearance.....................7'2"	Production...1992–Current
Water......................27 gals.	

The 290 Express is a scaled-down version of the Stamas 310 Express with a similar profile and the exact same mid-cabin interior layout. A good-looking boat with a molded pulpit and a fully integrated bracket platform, the 290 Express is a versatile boat with the ability to serve as a competent offshore fisherman or capable family cruiser. The single-level cockpit is arranged with a transom baitwell, washdowns, and a starboard-side transom door. The helm seat is elevated (to make room for the mid-cabin below), and visibility is excellent. Belowdecks, the compact cabin has a V-berth/dinette forward, stand-up head with shower, compact galley, and an athwartships double berth in the small mid-cabin. The accommodations are basic but well-finished and comfortable. Additional features include wide sidedecks, a stylish curved windshield, four opening ports, and an attractive price. Twin Yahama 200-hp O/Bs will cruise the Stamas 290 Express at a respectable 24 knots and deliver top speeds of just under 40 knots. ❏

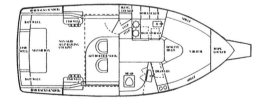

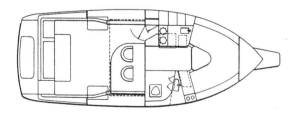

See Page 239 for Pricing Information

See Page 239 for Pricing Information

STAMAS 310 EXPRESS

SPECIFICATIONS

LOA w/Pulpit	32'6"	Fuel	204 gals.
Hull Length	30'9"	Cockpit	106 sq. ft.
Beam	11'2"	Hull Type	Modified-V
Draft	1'7"	Deadrise Aft	18°
Weight	8,800#	Designer	P. Stamas
Clearance	7'2"	Production	1993–Current
Water	40 gals.		

The Stamas 310 Express is an enlarged version of the smaller 290 Express with a similar profile and the same mid-cabin interior layout. She's a roomy boat thanks to her wide beam, and the solid fiberglass hull is designed with 18° of deadrise at the transom. While the 310 is likely to be viewed by many as a fishing boat (thanks to the Stamas nameplate), the roomy mid-cabin accommodations are well-suited to family cruising. There are berths for four with a convertible dinette/V-berth forward and a double berth in the mid cabin. Outside, the cockpit is big enough for three or four anglers, and the flush-deck layout results in an excellent fishing platform. A transom door is standard, and a deep fish box is built into the transom. Two hatches in the cockpit sole provide excellent access to the motors, and visibility from the elevated helm is outstanding. A good performer with standard 350-cid gas engines, she'll cruise efficiently at 20 knots and reach 28–29 knots wide open. ❑

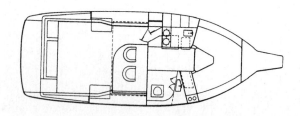

STAMAS 32 FLYBRIDGE SF

SPECIFICATIONS

Length	32'3"	Fuel	250 gals.
Length WL	28'0"	Cockpit	90 sq. ft.
Beam	12'0"	Hull Type	Modified-V
Draft:	2'9"	Deadrise Aft	NA
Weight	12,800#	Designer	Stamas
Clearance	11'6"	Production	1977–87
Water	55 gals.		

The Stamas 32 has earned a reputation as a durable sportfisherman as well as a competent no-frills family cruiser. Introduced in 1977, she's built on a solid fiberglass hull with a wide beam and moderate transom deadrise. Stamas offered the 32 in a Sport Sedan (with a salon bulkhead) and Flybridge Sportfisherman versions (with no aft bulkhead and a semi-enclosed deckhouse). She features a big fishing cockpit, comfortable interior accommodations, and a proven record as a competent fishing platform. Her good all-around handling qualities are well known by now, and the ride is dry and stable in most conditions. Attention to practical details is evident in the extra-wide sidedecks and cockpit coaming. Visibility from the lower helm is excellent, and the cockpit is open and completely unobstructed. Inside, the layout is arranged with Vee berths forward, an efficient galley area, and a roomy head compartment with a shower. No lightweight, the Stamas 32 will cruise at 20–21 knots and top out around 30 knots with optional 454-cid gas engines. ❑

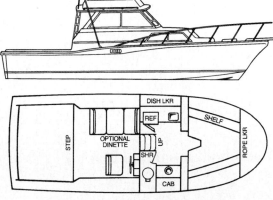

See Page 239 for Pricing Information

See Page 239 for Pricing Information

174

RUN OFFSHORE WITH CONFIDENCE

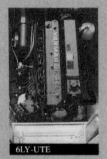

6LY-UTE

DESIGNED FROM THE GROUND UP for the rigors of marine use, this 315hp engine represents state-of-the-art in marine diesel technology.

Diesel economy has never before been available in such a quiet, compact, lightweight and powerful package.

Every aspect of the engine's design is eminently practical including the decision to keep all maintenance points on top. Everything from filter changes to turbocharger cleaning and lube refills is easily done from above.

For full details and specifications, contact your nearest Stamas Dealer.

STAMAS 290 EXPRESS

ABOARD A STAMAS POWERED BY YANMAR.

Every so often a boat and motor combination comes along that catches the imagination of even the most hardened offshore angler. Such is the case with Stamas' 290 Express. Built to withstand the rigors of offshore fishing, the 290's innovative hull design provides excellent handling characteristics in all sea conditions. Inshore, its unique shoal draft further expands fishing and cruising opportunities.

Introduce the dependability, cruising range and fuel economy of a state-of-the-art diesel engine, and the 290 nears perfection. Cruising range with a single 315hp Yanmar is 350 nautical miles at 27 knots. Throttle back to 21 knots, and your range jumps to 450 nm.

Featuring the industry's best horsepower to weight ratio, Yanmar's compact 315 fits nicely into the 290's engine bay, assuring ample room for easy maintenance.

If you haven't seen the 290 yet, now may be the time to examine one up close. You'll see and feel the difference immediately. It lies in the attention to detail and level of performance that only an uncompromising builder can deliver. It lies in the confidence that only Stamas delivers.

STAMAS
BOATS FOR PEOPLE WHO KNOW BOATS

The heavy duty construction and the attention to detail of a Stamas require close inspection. See one up close at your nearest dealer. Eight models from 24´-36´. Call (800) 782-6271 or write for more information.
STAMAS YACHT INC. 300 Pampas Avenue, Tarpon Springs, FL 34689
USA FAX - (813) 934-1339 • Int'l Ph. - (305) 731-7888 • Int'l FAX - (305) 731-7985

POWERED BY:
YANMAR
DIESEL ENGINES

STAMAS 360 EXPRESS

SPECIFICATIONS

Length w/Pulpit ....36'6"	Fuel.......................372 gals.
Beam ....13'2"	Cockpit ....155 sq. ft.
Draft.............................2'4"	Hull Type........Modified-V
Weight....................16,975#	Deadrise Aft.................18°
Clearance......................8'3"	Designer...........Jim Wynne
Water.......................90 gals.	Production...1992–Current

At first glance, the Stamas 360 appears to be just another attractive mid-cabin family express with contemporary styling and a big cockpit. But Stamas has built their reputation on fishing boats, and the 360 Express is more than a good-looking express. Like the Tiara 36, she's designed to serve as a stable fishing platform as well as a comfortable day cruiser. Hull construction is solid fiberglass with a wide beam, prop pockets, and a steep 18° of transom deadrise. Note that she has a long keel of sufficient depth to protect the running gear. In a departure from most of today's mid-cabin designs, the Stamas 360 has a single-level cockpit instead of a raised bridgedeck. Her mid-cabin accommodations are attractive and well-arranged, however the forward stateroom lacks a privacy door—a disappointing omission in a boat this size. Cockpit features include flush-mounted rod holders, an insulated fish box, baitwell, and transom storage. A competent performer with 454-cid gas engines, she'll cruise around 18–19 knots and reach 27 knots wide open. ❏

STRIKE 29 SPORTFISHERMAN

SPECIFICATIONS

Length..........................29'0"	Fuel.......................215 gals.
Beam ....10'11"	Cockpit ....NA
Draft.............................2'6"	Hull Type..............Deep-V
Weight......................7,500#	Deadrise Aft.................20°
Clearance ....7'6"	Designer ....J. Fourtney
Water.......................20 gals.	Production.............1985–89

The Strike 29 displays the quality workmanship and simplicity of layout that experienced anglers always admire. Built on a deep-V hull with propeller pockets, she has the look and feel of a custom boat. The deck plan is ideal for fishermen who want the overnight capability of a small cuddy while still retaining the walkaround fish-fighting attributes of a center console. The accommodations are basic—V-berths with a head under—but well-finished and sufficient for an occasional offshore weekend. The forward section of the huge center console lifts up for easy access to the diesels. The cockpit itself (with padded coaming) is large enough for the installation of a full-size chair. The Strike 29 can easily handle the addition of a tower thanks to her wide beam and low center of gravity. A total of 35 were built, and the original teak cockpit sole was replaced with a fiberglass liner beginning with hull #5. Twin 240-hp Perkins diesels (optional) deliver a 25-knot cruising speed (29 knots top) and a range of 350–400 miles. ❏

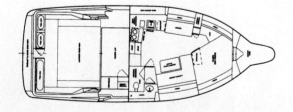

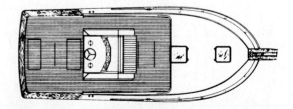

See Page 239 for Pricing Information

See Page 239 for Pricing Information

STRIKER 34 CANYON RUNNER

SPECIFICATIONS

Length	34'0"	Cockpit	100 sq. ft.
Beam	13'7"	Hull Type	Modified-V
Draft	2'3"	Deadrise Aft	NA
Weight	16,500#	Construction	Aluminum
Clearance	NA	Designer	T. DeGroot
Water	100 gals.	Production	1973–75
Fuel	400 gals.		

The 34 Canyon Runner was introduced in 1973 as a scaled-down version of the popular Striker 44 SF. She was built of welded aluminum in Norway and utilized the same exclusive hull design of the bigger Strikers. With her serious profile and ship-like construction, the 34 set the tone for future models in the Canyon Runner series. She was specifically designed for the type of offshore running typical of the Jersey and Maryland coasts. Her wide beam provides a stable fishing platform, and she has the range to go long distances without refueling. Inside, the cabin is arranged to meet the basic overnight needs of a couple of anglers with V-berths, a convertible dinette area, and a small galley and head. The interior is trimmed with teak woodwork and Formica counters—not a particularly stylish decor, but maintenance is easy. A rugged little vessel still occasionally found on the used market, the Striker 34 Canyon Runner with the 240-hp V555M Cummins diesels will cruise at 15 knots and reach a top speed of 18–19 knots. ❏

STRIKER 37 CANYON RUNNER

SPECIFICATIONS

Length	37'4"	Cockpit	100 sq. ft.
Beam	14'7"	Hull Type	Modified-V
Draft	2'8"	Deadrise Aft	NA
Weight	24,000#	Construction	Aluminum
Clearance	13'1"	Designer	T. DeGroot
Water	150 gals.	Production	1988–90
Fuel	750 gals.		

The 37 Canyon Runner is an enlarged version of the original 34 Canyon Runner. She started out as a 36-foot prototype in 1987 but was lengthened the following year to gain additional cockpit space. The 37 can be characterized as a serious gamefishing machine with battleship construction. Like all Strikers, the 37's hull and superstructure are heavy-gauge welded marine aluminum. The beam is unusually wide, and the deepest part of the keel provides protection for the props. (Notably, she's the only US-built Striker ever.) Inside, the compact layout has a single stateroom forward, a small head (without a shower stall), convertible dinette, and a very small galley. What appears to be a window in the aft bulkhead is actually a complete fold-up bait prep center. A good-looking boat with a lean and mean appearance, standard 485-hp 6-71 diesels will cruise at 27–28 knots. Note the large 750-gallon fuel capacity. For the record, the Striker 37 Canyon Runner was at the top of the scale when it came to price. ❏

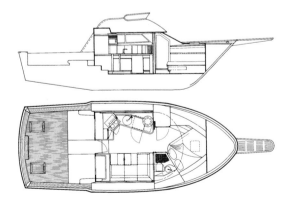

See Page 239 for Pricing Information

See Page 239 for Pricing Information

STRIKER 41 SPORTFISHERMAN

SPECIFICATIONS

Length..........................41'0"	Cockpit ....NA
Draft..............................2'4"	Hull Type........Modified-V
Beam ....14'9"	Deadrise Aft..................NA
Weight.....................16,250#	Construction....Aluminum
Clearance.....................13'6"	Designer..........T. DeGroot
Water.....................100 gals.	Production.............1981–83
Fuel, Std...............650 gals.	

A good-looking boat, the Striker 41 SF is a stable offshore fisherman built for serious tournament-level pursuits. She was constructed of aluminum on a wide-beam hull with a shallow draft, and at only 16,250 lbs. she's an incredibly light boat for her size. Her two-stateroom layout is very spacious and open (in spite of the dark teak woodwork) and includes *two* heads as well as a big galley on the lower level. Thanks to her wide beam, the generous interior accommodations of the Striker 41 don't intrude into the cockpit, where there's space for a complete set of tackle centers and a mounted chair. The flybridge is large for a 41-footer, and the sidedecks are very wide. Additional features include a teak cockpit sole and covering boards, foredeck seating, sturdy tubular deck rails, and a big engine room with good outboard service access. All six Striker 41s were fitted with 410-hp 6-71s and cruise around 23 knots and reach a top speed of 26–27 knots. ❏

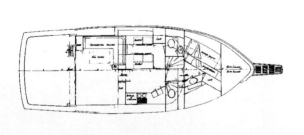

See Page 239 for Pricing Information

STRIKER 44 SPORTFISHERMAN

SPECIFICATIONS

Length..........................44'0"	Fuel, Opt...............705 gals.
Beam ....15'9"	Cockpit ....NA
Draft..............................2'9"	Hull Type........Modified-V
Weight.....................20,000#	Deadrise Aft..................NA
Clearance.....................14'6"	Construction....Aluminum
Water.....................235 gals.	Designer ......Tom DeGroot
Fuel, Std...............470 gals.	Production.............1968–75

The 44 Sportfisherman was the best-selling Striker ever. A total of 99 were built in Norway, and used models still seem to be in demand around serious sportfishing markets. Her popularity stems from the rugged welded aluminum construction and the massive brawn common to all Striker yachts. The 44 quickly gained a reputation as a capable offshore sportfisherman with a distinctive profile and superb offshore handling characteristics. As a fishing boat, she has very good range, a first-class working cockpit, and unusually wide and secure sidedecks with beefy deck hardware and rails. The more popular two-stateroom, galley-down layout is well suited to the needs of extended cruising. Among many notable features are a sea chest to eliminate unnecessary through-hull fittings, a serviceable engine room, an expansive flybridge, teak cockpit sole, and teak covering boards. Most Striker 44s were powered with 310-hp 6-71s and cruise at around 17 knots with a top speed of 20 knots. The 370-hp Cummins cruise at 20 knots and top out at 23. ❏

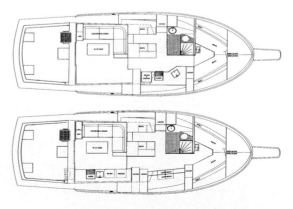

See Page 239 for Pricing Information

STRIKER 50 SPORTFISHERMAN

SPECIFICATIONS

Length......................49'11"	Cockpit................100 sq. ft.
Beam..........................16'8"	Hull Type........Modified-V
Draft...........................3'9"	Deadrise Aft..................NA
Weight..................41,000#	Construction....Aluminum
Clearance...................12'6"	Designer..........T. DeGroot
Water....................250 gals.	Production.............1979–82
Fuel..................1,100 gals.	1987–89

The first Striker 50s were built in Korea beginning in 1979. Five were constructed through 1982, and each was a semi-custom yacht built to suit the needs of her owner. Production was resumed in 1987, when a yard in Chile was selected to build the boats. These newer Striker 50s incorporated major design changes in the deckhouse, cockpit, engine room, and flybridge. Her two-stateroom interior was available with the galley up or down, the difference being the size of the owner's stateroom and the salon arrangement. Featuring a luxurious decor (for her day), the spacious accommodations available in the Striker 50's living areas are impressive. Outside, the cockpit is set up for serious fishing with cockpit controls and a teak sole standard, together with direct access to the roomy engine room. Additional features include wide sidedecks with sturdy rails, an upright rod locker in the cockpit, a huge flybridge, and an unusually long welded pulpit. A good-running boat, she'll cruise at a fast 25 knots and reach a top speed of 28 with 735-hp 8V92 diesels. ❏

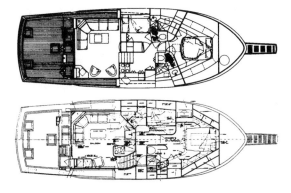

See Page 239 for Pricing Information

STRIKER 54 SPORTFISHERMAN

SPECIFICATIONS

Length..........................54'0"	Fuel, Opt............1,275 gals.
Beam ....17'0"	Cockpit.................170 sq. ft.
Draft.............................3'6"	Hull Type........Modified-V
Weight..................34,000#	Deadrise Aft..................NA
Clearance...................14'9"	Construction....Aluminum
Water....................350 gals.	Designer..........T. DeGroot
Fuel, Std ....925 gals.	Production.............1970–75

The Striker 54 evolved from the successful Striker 36 and 44 models and all were designed for long-range, tournament-level events. A total of 18 were built in Norway. Her distinctive profile, welded aluminum construction, super-wide beam, and unique modified-V hull design set her apart from the competition. The first impression of a Striker 54 is of size—she's a big 54-footer. Inside, her three-stateroom interior is finished in solid teak and features an expansive 20-foot-long salon wide open to the galley. Each stateroom is fitted with twin berths, and each has a private head. Like all Strikers, the 54 features a sea chest to eliminate through-hull fittings, self-cooling integral fuel tanks, protection for the underwater running gear, very wide sidedecks, and massive aluminum rails for on-deck security. Still in demand as a used boat, she'll cruise at 17 knots and run 20 knots wide open with 12V71N diesels. With the larger 12V71TI versions, she'll cruise at 21 knots and reach a top speed of 24 knots. ❏

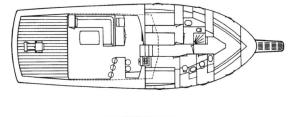

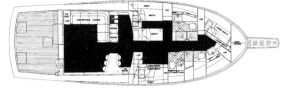

See Page 239 for Pricing Information

STRIKER 58/60 SPORTFISHERMEN

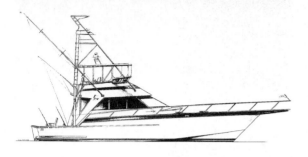

STRIKER 62 SPORTFISHERMAN

SPECIFICATIONS

Length..........................58'6"	Cockpit ....149 sq. ft.
Beam ....19'6"	Hull Type........Modified-V
Draft.............................3'11"	Deadrise Aft..................NA
Weight ....51,480#	Construction....Aluminum
Clearance....................15'6"	Designer...........T. DeGroot
Water.....................315 gals.	Production.............1988–90
Fuel....................1,550 gals.	

SPECIFICATIONS

Length..........................62'0"	Cockpit ....146 sq. ft.
Beam ....21'0"	Hull Type........Modified-V
Draft.............................3'10"	Deadrise Aft..................NA
Weight ....68,000#	Construction....Aluminum
Clearance.....................NA	Designer...........T. DeGroot
Water.....................315 gals.	Production.............1986–90
Fuel....................2,280 gals.	

Built in Chile, the Striker 58 SF is actually a revised and updated version of the earlier Striker 60 SF built in Korea from 1979–82. She has the same hull but changes were made to the deckhouse, cockpit, engine room, and flybridge. Like all Striker yachts, she was constructed of welded aluminum on a wide-beamed hull with the shallow keel providing protection to the props and running gear. At heart, the Striker 58/60 is a world-class tournament fisherman with the strength and endurance to match any boat in the fleet. The spacious cockpit is set up for serious fishing and—as with the Striker 62 and 70 models—the 58 also has a unique on-deck day head. While all were delivered with semi-custom layouts, the interior of the 58 was redesigned early in her production run (see lower floorplan) and featured an all-new decor package. A good-running boat, 1,080-hp 12V92s will cruise the Striker 58/60 at 26 knots and reach a top speed of around 28 knots. ❏

Only a few production yachts received the media attention of the Striker 62 SF when she was introduced in 1986. Aside from the fact that she was at the time the largest all-aluminum sportfisherman ever built, what set her apart from earlier Strikers was her lush interior decor and incredible 21-foot beam. Built in Holland (a total of nine were delivered), the Striker 62s were priced at the top of the chart compared to other yachts in her size range. The lavish three-stateroom accommodations must be seen to be appreciated—indeed, with a 21-foot beam, the floorplan dimensions are huge and the equal of many motor yachts. Among several innovative design features, the steps in the cockpit can be raised hydraulically for engine room access, and the electronics can be hidden within the flybridge helm console until needed. Standard 1,080-hp 12V92s cruise about 23 knots (at around 100 gph) and reach a top speed of 26–27 knots. Optional 1,300-hp 12-cylinder MTUs offer a 27-knot cruising speed and about 30 knots wide open. ❏

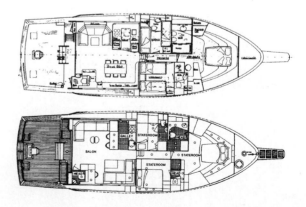

See Page 239 for Pricing Information

See Page 239 for Pricing Information

STRIKER 70 SPORTFISHERMAN

SPECIFICATIONS

Length	70'6"	Fuel	4,000 gals.
Beam	23'6"	Cockpit	221 sq. ft.
Draft	3'4"	Hull Type	Modified-V
Weight	75,000#	Deadrise Aft	NA
Clearance	17'4"	Designer	T. DeGroot
Water	450 gals.	Production	1983–89

The 70 Sportfisherman was the largest model ever offered by Striker Yachts. A total of seven of these custom yachts were built—two in Korea and five in Holland. With her welded aluminum construction, beefy systems, and enormous interiors, the Striker 70 is actually a small ship with the range to reach the most remote fishing grounds. The huge 221-sq. ft. cockpit is awesome in size and comes equipped with a vast array of features including the popular day head seen in some smaller Striker models. The salon steps lift up at the touch of a button to provide direct cockpit access to the engine room, and (like all Strikers) the gin pole serves as an air duct to ventilate the engine room. The interior layout and decor of the 70s were generally customized to meet the tastes of the owner. Those powered with the 1,300-hp MTUs will cruise at 17–18 knots. The 1,900-hp MTUs will cruise the Striker 70 at 22 knots and reach a top speed of 25 knots. ❏

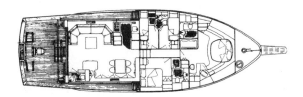

See Page 239 for Pricing Information

THE KEY TO ANY ACQUISITION IS TO STRIKE QUICKLY AND OUTMANEUVER YOUR OPPONENT.

New 3100 Open

Tiara Yachts offer everything the really serious fisherman needs to outwit a worthy adversary. The power. The renowned smooth, stable, dry ride. The spacious, well-designed cockpits with sure-footed nonskid surfaces. The enormous storage compartments. See why Tiara Yachts are the premier fishing machines. So formidable, you could be accused of not giving an opponent a sporting chance. For literature and dealer information, call us at 1-800-843-3172.

Tiara®

YACHTS

Pride in Motion

PURSUIT 2600 CUDDY CABIN

PURSUIT 2655 EXPRESS FISHERMAN

SPECIFICATIONS

LOA w/pulpit............27'0"	Water.......................20 gals.
Hull Length.................25'6"	Fuel, O/B..............155 gals.
Beam ....8'9"	Fuel, I/O...............107 gals.
Draft.............................2'6"	Cockpit.................80 sq. ft.
Weight, O/B.............3,800#	Hull Type........Modified-V
Weight, I/O..............4,600#	Designer ....Tiara
Clearance.......................6'7"	Production.............1986–88

SPECIFICATIONS

Length w/Pulpit......28'10"	Water.......................19 gals.
Hull Length.................26'5"	Fuel.........................234 gals.
Beam ....9'7"	Hull Type..............Deep-V
Hull Draft....................1'5"	Designer ....20°
Weight.......................4,800#	Production...1989–Current
Clearance.......................NA	

A good-looking fisherman, the Pursuit 2600 will appeal to family-oriented anglers who need the overnight capabilities a small cuddy cabin (with only a V-berth) can't provide. The hull is solid fiberglass with a shallow skeg below, and the moderate 8'9" beam makes her legally trailerable in several states. Like all Tiaras, the 2600 is a well-built boat with better than average detailing. The cockpit is arranged with two in-deck fish boxes, and (in the I/O version) two insulated wells are built into the transom. Inside, the cabin has a dinette/V-berths forward, a compact galley, and a stand-up head with shower—a basic but well-finished interior that's easy to clean. Additional features include wide sidedecks, under-gunnel rod storage, space at the helm for flush-mounting some electronics, teak covering boards, and a superb windshield with opening panels. The 2600 Cuddy was available with stern drive or outboard power. With a single 350-cid I/O, she'll cruise efficiently at 22 knots (about 9 gph) and reach about 33 knots top. ❑

Perhaps better known to many as the Pursuit 2650 Cuddy Cabin, Tiara changed the model designation in 1993 to the current 2655 Express Fisherman. This is a stylish fishboat (observe the curved windshield) with an expanded cuddy cabin that many anglers are sure to like. She's built on a balsa-cored deep-V hull with a sharp entry, a wide beam, and reverse chines. The cockpit has room for a mounted chair and features a first-class rigging station at the transom with a circulating livewell, sink, and bait storage compartment. A fish box is built into the sole, and a raw water washdown is standard. Wide sidedecks and secure railings make foredeck access easy. Inside, the cuddy is set up with V-berths forward, a decent galley area with plenty of counter space, and a stand-up head with shower. A good-handling boat, twin 200-hp Yahamas will cruise at 28 knots and reach a top speed of 40+ knots. Note that the opening ports were relocated from the hullsides to the cabinsides in 1993. ❑

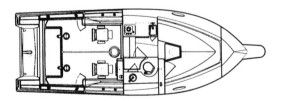

See Page 239 for Pricing Information

See Page 240 for Pricing Information

SPECIFICATIONS

Length w/Pulpit	28'10"	Water	20 gals.
Hull Length	26'5"	Fuel	234 gals.
Beam	9'7"	Hull Type	Deep-V
Hull Draft	1'5"	Deadrise Aft	20°
Weight	4,600#	Designer	Pursuit
Clearance	NA	Production	1992–Current

SPECIFICATIONS

LOA	29'5"	Water	20 gals.
Hull Length	27'0"	Fuel	240 gals.
Beam	10'0"	Hull Type	Deep-V
Draft	2'0"	Deadrise Aft	22°
Weight	7,500#	Designer	L. Slikkers
Clearance	7'0"	Production	1982–93

A good-looking small fisherman, the Pursuit 2655 Center Console (originally called the Pursuit 2650) is built on a lightweight deep-V hull with a wide beam, sharp entry, and reverse outer chines to keep the spray down. The deck layout—big enough for a party of five or six anglers—includes a first-class rigging station at the transom with a circulating livewell, sink, and bait storage compartment. The helm console is big enough for flush-mounting electronics, and the leaning post doubles as a tackle center. A stand-up head compartment is located inside the helm console. The absence of a cuddy cabin forward allows the entire length of the hull to be used for fishing—a fact not lost on serious anglers. Additional features include a molded pulpit, good range, raw water washdown, and a built-in cooler forward. Available in an outboard bracket model only, twin 200-hp Yahama outboards will cruise the Pursuit 2655 at a fast 28 knots and a top speed in the neighborhood of 40+ knots. ❏

B etter known to anglers as the Pursuit 2700, the Tiara 2700 Open is a scaled-down version of the company's successful 3100 Open fisherman. (Note that Pursuit—sister company of Tiara—marketed this boat for many years in fishing trim as the 2700 Pursuit and later, the 2700 Express Fisherman.) She's built on a deep-V hull with moderate beam, balsa-cored hullsides, and a steep 22° of deadrise at the transom—a good offshore design with proven handling characteristics. The popularity of this boat has much to do with her built-in versatility. As a fisherman, her spacious single-level cockpit is completely uncluttered and large enough for a mounted chair. As a family cruiser, the 2700 Open offers the advantages of inboard power (most of her competitors have outboards) and a proven offshore hull to go with her upscale interior. Features include engine boxes, wide sidedecks, excellent detailing, and good resale values. Standard 350-cid gas engines will cruise the Tiara 2700 around 23 knots with a top speed of 30–31 knots. ❏

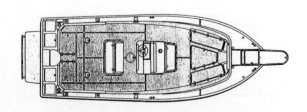

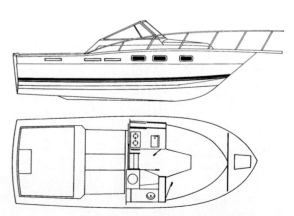

See Page 240 for Pricing Information

See Page 240 for Pricing Information

PURSUIT 2800 OPEN

SPECIFICATIONS

LOA w/Pulpit............30'4"	Fuel.......................290 gals.
Hull Length.................28'2"	Cockpit ....NA
Beam ....10'0"	Hull Type..............Deep-V
Hull Draft.....................1'9"	Deadrise Aft..................20°
Weight.......................5,500#	Designer.................Pursuit
Clearance.....................6'9"	Production 1989-92
Water......................22 gals.	

A stylish design with plenty of eye appeal, this outboard-powered day fisherman manages to combine excellent offshore performance with a practical cockpit layout and surprisingly spacious cabin accommodations. (While she's better known among anglers as the 2800 Open—her original name—she was also called the 2800 Express Fisherman during 1991–92.) Her deep-V hull is balsa-cored from the chines up, and the wide ten-foot beam results in a stable fishing platform easily able to handle a small tower. Her cockpit is arranged with a 5' in-deck fish box plus rod holders and storage under the cabin wings. An insulated cooler is built into the companion seat, and a tackle center is behind the helm seat. Note the attractive curved windshield and molded pulpit. Inside, the well-finished cabin includes berths for two in addition to a roomy galley and stand-up head compartment. The level of finish and detailing is excellent. Twin 225-hp outboards will cruise the Pursuit 2800 easily at 26 knots and deliver top speeds in the neighborhood of 38–39 knots. ❏

PURSUIT 2855 EXPRESS FISHERMAN

SPECIFICATIONS

LOA w/Pulpit............32'4"	Fuel.......................300 gals.
Hull Length.................28'0"	Cockpit ....57 sq. ft.
Beam ....10'3"	Hull Type..............Deep-V
Hull Draft.....................1'9"	Deadrise Aft..................20°
Weight.......................6,500#	Designer.................Pursuit
Clearance.....................8'6"	Production...1993–Current
Water......................30 gals.	

Like Grady-White's Marlin 28, the Pursuit 2855 Express Fisherman is an upscale fisherman for people with a taste for quality. She's a good-looking boat with her crisp styling and molded engine bracket, and the layout and detailing are well above average—a first-class boat from a top-quality builder. The cockpit features a full-height transom with a built-in bait and tackle rigging station, livewell, and transom door. A pair of fish boxes are located abaft the helm and companion seats, and the helm console is wide enough for flush-mounting most necessary electronics. Belowdecks, the 2855 will sleep four (the dinette converts to a double berth, and the seat backs swing up to form two more bunks) and includes a small galley area and a stand-up head. Additional features include fairly wide sidedecks, a molded bow pulpit, balsa coring in the hullsides, and a windshield center vent. Twin 250-hp outboards will cruise the Pursuit 2855 Express at 25 knots and reach a top speed of around 38 knots. ❏

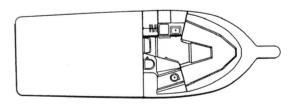

See Page 240 for Pricing Information   **See Page 240 for Pricing Information**

TIARA 2900 OPEN

SPECIFICATIONS

LOA w/Pulpit	30'9"	Fuel	200 gals.
Hull Length	28'9"	Cockpit	60 sq. ft.
Beam	11'4"	Hull Type	Deep-V
Hull Draft	2'2"	Deadrise Aft	19°
Weight	8,200#	Designer	Tiara
Clearance	7'8"	Production	1993–Current
Water	30 gals.		

With her conservative styling and quality construction, the Tiara 2900 Open will appeal to those looking for an upscale express cruiser with genuine offshore capabilities. She's built on a proven deep-V hull design with cored hullsides, a wide beam, and a relatively steep 19° of deadrise at the transom. Note the lack of an integrated swim platform—the 2900 retains a traditional full-height transom configuration with a bolt-on platform. Unlike most other contemporary family sportboats, the 2900 does not have a mid-cabin interior layout (but neither does she require the V-drives found in mid-cabin designs to deliver the power). The cabin appointments are lush indeed, and the level of finish is excellent. Additional features include hide-away bench seating at the transom, a hinged helm console, molded pulpit, and a transom door. The bridge deck can be raised hydraulically for engine access. Standard 260-hp gas inboards will cruise the 2900 Open at 18 knots (about 30 knots top), and optional 170-hp Yanmar diesels will cruise efficiently at 25 knots (29–30 top). ❏

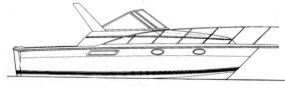

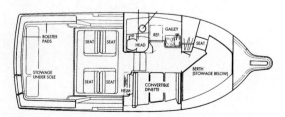

See Page 240 for Pricing Information

TIARA 3100 OPEN (EARLY)

SPECIFICATIONS

Length	31'3"	Fuel, Std	196 gals.
Beam	12'0"	Cockpit	144 sq. ft.
Draft	2'9"	Hull Type	Modified-V
Weight	10,500#	Deadrise Aft	16°
Clearance	7'6"	Designer	L. Slikkers
Water	36 gals.	Production	1979–92

Originally called the 3100 Pursuit, the Tiara 3100 Open has long been considered a serious tournament-level contender in coastal sportfishing circles. After more than a decade in production, she remained basically unchanged until she was replaced with a new 3100 model in 1992. Her popularity derives from her large cockpit and good offshore handling, but behind her reputation as a fishing boat is the realization that she's well-engineered and built to high standards. The addition of the optional radar arch, swim platform, and bench seating in the cockpit transforms the 3100 into a conservative but good-looking family sportboat with genuine eye appeal. Although more than half of her LOA is committed to the cockpit, the interior accommodations are plush if somewhat compact. Built on a rugged modified-V hull, standard 454 gas engines will cruise at 22–23 knots and reach a top speed of around 32 knots. GM 8.2 diesels (300-hp) were a popular option (22–23 knots cruise). Note that the Tiara 3100 FB Convertible model is the same boat with a flybridge. ❏

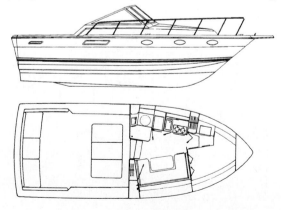

See Page 240 for Pricing Information

TIARA 3100 OPEN

SPECIFICATIONS

LOA w/Pulpit..........33'10"	Water......................38 gals.
Hull Length ....31'3"	Fuel.......................246 gals.
Beam ....12'0"	Hull Type...............Deep-V
Draft............................2'9"	Deadrise Aft..................18°
Weight ....11,500#	Designer ....Tiara
Clearance.....................7'9"	Production...1992–Current
Cockpit ....NA	

The new Tiara 3100 Open is a complete update of the original 3100 Open model. Her reworked hull features a sharper entry, additional transom deadrise (18° vs. 16°), greater bow flare for a dryer ride, and prop pockets for shallow draft. The 3100 also has a new bi-level cockpit layout which allows for the installation of optional Volvo, Cat, or Cummins diesels in an enlarged engine compartment. Tiara has always been a conservative builder, and it's no surprise that the new 3100 looks a lot like the original—basically a no-glitz express with good-quality construction, systems, and hardware. The slightly enlarged interior of the 3100 has more headroom than before, and there's also a bigger U-shaped dinette. Additional updates include increased fuel, a tilt-away helm console, recessed trim tabs, and an in-deck fish box and livewell in the cockpit. A transom door became standard in 1994. Standard 454-cid gas engines will cruise at 21-22 knots (30 knots top), and 291-hp 3116 Cat diesels will cruise at 25 knots (30 knots wide open). ❏

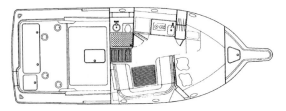

See Page 240 for Pricing Information

TIARA 3100 CONVERTIBLE

SPECIFICATIONS

Length..........................31'3"	Fuel, Opt...............286 gals.
Beam ....12'0"	Cockpit ....NA
Draft............................2'11"	Hull Type........Modified-V
Weight....................13,200#	Deadrise Aft..................16°
Clearance....................12'2"	Designer ....L. Slikkers
Water......................36 gals.	Production.............1982–92
Fuel, Std................206 gals.	

The Tiara 3100 Convertible is an upscale family cruiser with attractive lines and good overall performance. She was originally introduced in 1982 as the 3100 Continental, a designation that lasted through 1986. Built on the same hull used for the original 3100 Open, the Convertible offers the added comforts of a salon and an enclosed lower helm, along with the ability to sleep six persons overnight. The stylish interior of the 3100 Convertible is a blend of quality fabrics and teak trim with off-white mica cabinets featured in the galley. This is, in fact, one of the more appealing layouts to be found in any 31' convertible, and most will find it well suited to the demands of family cruising. Additional features include a good-size cockpit, wide sidedecks, a molded bow pulpit, and decent engine access. The relatively small flybridge has bench seating forward of the helm console for three guests. Standard 454-cid gas engines will cruise the Tiara 3100 Convertible at 20 knots with a top speed of about 29 knots. ❏

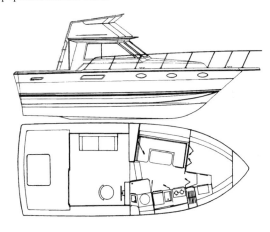

See Page 240 for Pricing Information

PURSUIT 3250

SPECIFICATIONS

Length...........................33'0"	Fuel.......................,305 gals.
Beam ....12'6"	Cockpit...............115 sq. ft.
Draft..............................2'8"	Hull Type........Modified-V
Weight...................13,500#	Deadrise Aft..................18°
Clearance......................8'4"	Designer ....L. Slikkers
Water......................50 gals.	Production.............1990–93

Largest of the Pursuit series of offshore fishermen, the 3250 (called the 3250 Express in 1992 and the 3300 Express in 1993) is an upscale canyon runner designed to appeal to well-heeled anglers with a taste for quality. She's built on a reworked version of the popular 3300 hull—a deep-V design with a wide beam and balsa coring in the hullsides. An inner liner is used to create a rugged one-piece hull of extraordinary strength. Below, the cabin layout is arranged with V-berths forward, a compact galley, dinette, and stand-up head. The 3250's bi-level fishing cockpit features an over-size transom door, an in-deck fish box, livewell, molded steps, and fresh- and salt-water washdowns. Push a button and hydraulic hatches rise to expose both engines. Gas engines were standard (just 15 knots cruise/24 top), but most 3250s were delivered with one of several diesel installations. The 300-hp Cummins, 296-hp Volvos, and 300-hp Cats will all cruise around 26-28 knots and deliver top speeds of 30+ knots. ❑

TIARA 3300 FLYBRIDGE

SPECIFICATIONS

Length.......................32'10"	Fuel......................295 gals.
Beam ....12'6"	Cockpit.................75 sq. ft.
Draft..............................2'8"	Hull Type........Modified-V
Weight...................13,000#	Deadrise Aft..................14°
Clearance....................11'6"	Designer ....L. Slikkers
Water......................46 gals.	Production.............1986–92

A good-looking boat with a low profile and big cockpit, the Tiara 3300 Flybridge is thirty-three feet of solid construction and good performance. Her rakish profile and glassed-in windshield combine with a practical deck layout to create an extremely capable fishing platform. Note the offset companionway hatch which allows space in the cockpit for the full-size tackle center. The moderate-deadrise hull is balsa-cored above the waterline, and side exhausts exit just forward of the transom. The ride is dry and comfortable with good lateral stability at trolling speeds. Inside, the upscale cabin is modest in size but well-suited to the needs of four anglers. Unlike other Tiaras with their abundant teak woodwork, the interior in the 3300 uses only a modest amount of teak trim and plenty of easily cleaned laminates. A hydraulically operated hatch in the bridge deck provides excellent access to the motors. Standard 454-cid Crusaders will cruise at 20–21 knots, and optional 300-hp GM 8.2 diesels (or 320-hp Cats) cruise around 24–25 knots. ❑

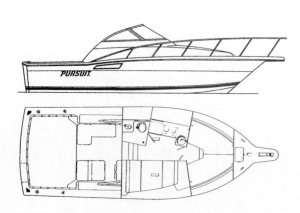

See Page 240 for Pricing Information

See Page 240 for Pricing Information

TIARA 3300 OPEN

SPECIFICATIONS

LOA w/Pulpit ....35'8"	Water......................46 gals.
Hull Length ....32'10"	Fuel........................295 gals.
Beam ....12'6"	Cockpit ....117 sq. ft.
Draft ....2'3"	Hull Type........Modified-V
Weight....................11,500#	Deadrise Aft..................14°
Clearance......................8'8"	Production.............1988–94

Tiara's 3300 Open is a stylish family cruiser whose conservative design and top quality construction have made her an attractive alternative to the built-in glitz of competitive models in this size range. She's built on a rugged modified-V hull with a shallow skeg and balsa coring in the hullsides. Unlike the Tiara 3100 Open, the 3300 was not designed as a dedicated fisherman. Instead, she's more at home in the family cruiser role where her plush interior and sport-boat profile are most appreciated. Her well-designed interior features overnight berths for six in a cabin of unusual elegance and luxury. The interior is finished with grain-matched teak joinerwork, and the galley features white Formica cabinetry. In spite of her generous interior dimensions, the 3300 still manages to provide an excellent fishing cockpit with a transom door, inwale padding, and cockpit washdown as standard equipment. Standard 454-cid gas engines will cruise the Tiara 3300 Open at 22 knots (32 knots top), and optional 300-hp GM 8.2 diesels will cruise at about 24 knots. ❑

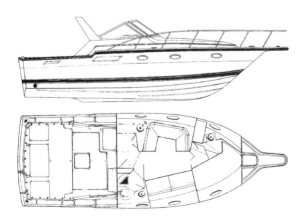

See Page 240 for Pricing Information

TIARA 3600 OPEN

SPECIFICATIONS

LOA w/Pulpit ....36'8"	Water......................85 gals.
Hull Length...............36'8"	Fuel........................396 gals.
Beam ....13'9"	Cockpit ....NA
Draft ....2'11"	Hull Type ....Modified-V
Weight....................16,500#	Deadrise Aft..................14°
Clearance......................9'7"	Production...1985–Current

A hugely popular boat, the 3600 Open is a wide-beamed express with conservative lines, top-shelf construction, and very upscale interior accommodations. What sets the 3600 apart from much of the competition is her excellent all-round fishability, although it's no secret that the ride can be wet in a chop. The spacious bi-level cockpit is fitted with an in-deck big fish box on the centerline along with two circulating livewells, rod storage, and a transom door. The interior accommodations are finished with traditional teak cabinetry and designer fabrics throughout. An island berth is forward in the original "A" Plan, and the alternate "B" layout (new in 1989) has a settee opposite the dinette and overnight berths for six, but no stall shower. The bridgedeck has a hydraulic lift for easy access to the engines. Standard 454-cid gas engines provide a 20–knot cruising speed and a top speed of about 29 knots. Optional 375-hp Cats offer cruising speeds at a respectable 26 knots and reach 32+ knots wide open. ❑

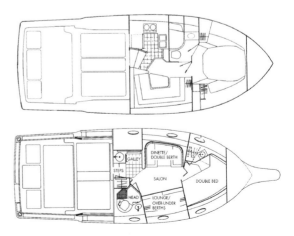

See Page 240 for Pricing Information

189

TIARA 3600 CONVERTIBLE

SPECIFICATIONS

LOA w/Pulpit	39'8"	Water	85 gals.
Hull Length	36'8"	Fuel	396 gals.
Beam	13'9"	Cockpit	NA
Draft	3'0"	Hull Type	Modified-V
Weight	18,300#	Deadrise Aft	14°
Clearance	12'6"	Production	1987–Current

The Tiara 3600 Convertible is a good-looking flybridge sedan with a very practical interior layout to go with her attractive lines. She's built on the same hull used for the 3600 Open—a proven offshore design with cored hullsides and a relatively wide beam. Inside, a lower helm is optional, and the light-grain interior wood work and decorator fabrics make for an impressive interior. Two floorplans are available: a two-stateroom arrangement or a single-stateroom floorplan with a dinette. Both have a mid-level galley and include a stall shower in the head. The cockpit is equipped with a transom door and gate, and wide walkaround decks provide safe access to the bow. Unfortunately, the cockpit isn't notably roomy and makes no allowance for the addition of tackle centers—a definite drawback for anglers. Standard 454-cid gas engines cruise the Tiara 3600 at a steady 19-20 knots and reach 28 knots wide open. Optional Cat 375-hp diesels cruise at 25 knots and deliver a top speed of 29–30 knots. ❑

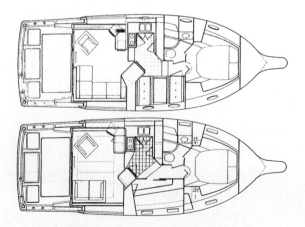

See Page 241 for Pricing Information

TIARA 4300 CONVERTIBLE

SPECIFICATIONS

LOA w/Pulpit	46'7"	Fuel	640 gals.
Hull Length	43'2"	Cockpit	121 sq. ft.
Beam	15'2"	Hull Type	Modified-V
Draft	4'0"	Deadrise Aft	16°
Weight	31,000#	Designer	J. Garland
Clearance	13'5"	Production	1990–Current
Water	160 gals.		

A good-running boat with plenty of eye appeal, the Tiara 4300 Convertible is an upscale sportfisherman with an exceptionally roomy and well-arranged interior. She's built on a beamy modified-V hull with a stepped sheer and balsa-cored hullsides. Two floorplans are offered: The original two-stateroom, two-head layout has the mid-level galley separated from the salon by a breakfast bar. An alternate floorplan introduced in 1992 trades out the guest cabin for a large U-shaped dinette and an enlarged master stateroom. The cockpit is huge and comes with a transom door, in-deck storage boxes, cockpit steps, and (beginning in 1994) direct access to the engine room. Topside, there's plenty of space in the helm console for flush-mounting an array of electronics. Additional features include overhead rod storage in the salon, molded tackle center and pulpit, wide sidedecks, and a choice of teak or oak interior wood-work. No hot rod, the Tiara 4300 will cruise at a respectable 24–25 knots with standard 550-hp 6V92s and reach 28 knots top. ❑

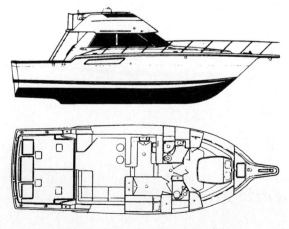

See Page 241 for Pricing Information

190

TIARA 4300 OPEN

SPECIFICATIONS

LOA w/Pulpit............46'7"	Water....................150 gals.
Hull Length ....43'2"	Fuel......................525 gals.
Beam ....15'2"	Hull Type.......Modified-V
Draft.............................4'0"	Deadrise Aft..................16°
Weight ....28,000#	Designer............J. Garland
Clearance...................10'4"	Production...1991–Current
Cockpit...............167 sq. ft.	

Conservatively styled (note the absence of an integrated swim platform) and elegantly appointed, the Tiara 4300 Open is one of the larger—and more expensive—production sportboats available in today's market. Built on the same wide-beam hull used in the 4300 Convertible, she's aimed at the market for upscale express cruisers, although she can easily be converted into a serious fishing platform. The belowdeck accommodations are plush with light ash woodwork, leather upholstery, a teak and holly cabin sole, hydraulically operated dinette, and a huge master stateroom with a walkaround island berth and built-in TV. Outside, the huge bi-level cockpit—reinforced for a mounted chair—provides seating for ten with in-deck storage compartments, cockpit steps, and a transom door with gate. Additional features include a superb helm console with room for flush-mounting an array of electronics, wide sidedecks, excellent engine room access, and hide-away bench seating at the transom. A surprisingly fast boat with 535-hp 6V92s, she'll cruise around 27 knots and reach 30 knots wide open. ❏

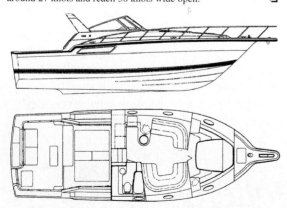

See Page 241 for Pricing Information

TOLLYCRAFT 40 SPORT SEDAN

SPECIFICATIONS

Length ....40'2"	Fuel........................500 gals.
Beam ....14'8"	Cockpit ....101 sq. ft.
Draft.............................3'0"	Hull Type.......Modified-V
Weight.....................26,000#	Deadrise Aft...................10°
Clearance ....12'4"	Designer ....Ed Monk, Jr.
Water....................140 gals.	Production.............1987–93

A good sea boat, the 40 Sport Sedan is the only serious sportfishing design ever offered by Tollycraft. Introduced in 1987 as the Convertible Sportfisherman, she's built using the modified-V hull originally designed for the Tollycraft 40 Sundeck MY. In 1989, Tollycraft gave the boat a new profile and a revised interior layout while toning down the emphasis on fishing, renaming her the 40 Sport Sedan. Her slightly reduced cockpit (101 vs. 112 sq. ft.) is still large enough to accommodate a mounted chair and tackle center, and molded steps provide easy access to the wide sidedecks. The original two-stateroom, galley-up floorplan was revised in 1989 with the galley moved forward to a mid-level position. (A dinette could be ordered in place of the guest cabin.) The helm console can be located aft on the flybridge or forward in the West Coast style. A good seaboat, Caterpillar 375-hp diesels will cruise at 23 knots (27 top), and the 485-hp 6-71s will cruise around 27 knots and deliver 30 knots wide open. ❏

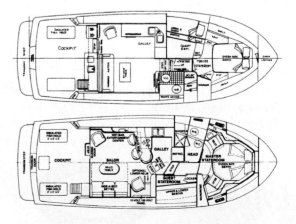

See Page 241 for Pricing Information

TOLLYCRAFT 48 CONVERTIBLE

SPECIFICATIONS

Length	48'2"	Fuel	600 gals.
Beam	15'2"	Cockpit	120 sq. ft.
Draft	3'8"	Hull Type	Semi-Disp.
Weight	40,000#	Deadrise Aft	10°
Clearance	14'3"	Designer	Ed Monk
Water	200 gals.	Production	1982–85

Sharing the same semi-displacement hull as the 48 Cockpit MY, the Tollycraft 48 Convertible is a truly handsome yacht with traditional styling and go-anywhere construction. With her fine entry, moderate deadrise, and long keel, the Tolly 48 earned a reputation as a good all-round sea boat. Not developed as an out-and-out sportfisherman, she's designed instead for part-time anglers who enjoy a comfortable family cruising yacht with genuine offshore fishing capabilities. Among her features are two staterooms and heads, a lower helm station, cored hull construction, a *giant* (and deep) cockpit with transom door, and an enormous flybridge. The owner's stateroom is huge and rivals those found in many motor yachts for size and comfort. Her easy-running hull will cruise efficiently at 16 knots with any of several diesel options, and the big 8V92TIs will reach a top speed of nearly 30 knots. With 600 gallons of fuel and a cruising economy approaching one mile-per-gallon at 15 knots, the 48 Convertible is indeed a long-range yacht.❏

TOPAZ 29 SPORTFISHERMAN

SPECIFICATIONS

Length	29'0"	Fuel	225 gals.
Beam	10'3"	Cockpit	65 sq. ft.
Draft	2'6"	Hull Type	Modified-V
Weight	8,100#	Deadrise Aft	NA
Clearance	NA	Designer	Topaz
Water	30 gals.	Production	1983–88

The Topaz 29 proved to be a popular boat over the years due to her rugged construction and single-minded approach to sportfishing. Like all Topaz models, the bi-cockpit dominates the layout and measures about half of the LOA. The engines are located beneath the raised bridgedeck, and there's room for a full-size marlin chair on the lower level where a large insulated fish box is built into the cockpit sole. A companion seat/tackle center (optional) is to port, and engine access is via a removable centerline hatch. Below, the cabin accommodations are simple and straightforward with upper and lower berths forward that will sleep three plus a mini galley and stand-up head with shower. Recognized as a competent and good-handling offshore fisherman, most Topaz 29s were sold with the factory tower and Volvo diesels. The popular 200-hp TAMD41s cruise at a brisk 26 knots and reach a top speed of around 30 knots. Topaz sold the molds in 1988, and today the boat is in production as the Bimini 29. ❏

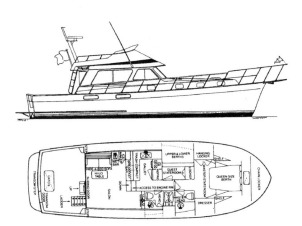

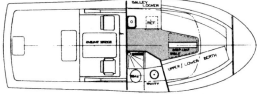

See Page 241 for Pricing Information

See Page 241 for Pricing Information

TOPAZ 32 SPORTFISHERMAN

SPECIFICATIONS

Length..........................32'8"	Fuel........................300 gals.
Beam ....12'2"	Cockpit ....NA
Draft..............................2'1"	Hull Type..............Deep-V
Weight....................16,500#	Deadrise Aft...................18°
Clearance.......................NA	Designer ....Pat Patterson
Water......................40 gals.	Production.............1986–91

The Topaz 32 is an attractive open sportfisherman with a large cockpit, stable handling characteristics, and good-quality construction. She was built on a good-running deep-V hull with a relatively wide beam and considerable flare at the bow. The hull is solid fiberglass, and beefy aluminum frames support the engine mounts. Inside, the cabin accommodations are comfortable and extremely well-finished with durable fabrics and superb teak joinerwork throughout. The 32's bi-level cockpit is quite spacious and reinforced to handle a mounted fighting chair. An in-deck removable fish box is just forward of the transom, and two roomy storage bins are also built into the cockpit sole. The raised bridgedeck provides excellent visibility from the helm, and a hatch between the seats offers good access to the diesel engines. (The entire bridgedeck can be raised for major engine work.) The Topaz 32 was available with 306-hp Volvo or 320-hp Cat diesels. She'll cruise around 25 knots with the Cats and reach a top speed of 29 knots. ❏

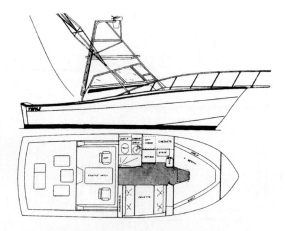

See Page 241 for Pricing Information

TOPAZ 32 ROYALE

SPECIFICATIONS

Length..........................32'8"	Fuel........................350 gals.
Beam ....12'2"	Cockpit ....NA
Draft..............................2'1"	Hull Type..............Deep-V
Weight....................16,500#	Deadrise Aft...................18°
Clearance.......................NA	Designer ....Pat Patterson
Water......................40 gals.	Production 1990-91

The Topaz 32 Royale incorporates the same dramatic styling and sleek European profile seen in the popular 39 Royale model. Indeed, with her sweeping sheer and curved windshield, the Royale is easily one of the more stylish boats in her class. Designed to meet the needs of sportboat enthusiasts as well as the demands of offshore fishermen, the Royale is built on the proven deep-V hull used for the Topaz 32 SF. She features a bi-level cockpit layout with the engines located below the bridgedeck. Visibility from the raised portside helm position is excellent, and a lounge/dinette opposite provides seating for guests and anglers. The cockpit is large enough for a fighting chair and includes an in-deck fish box and removable floor. Below, the stylish cabin is arranged with a convertible dinette, stand-up head, and a compact galley. No lightweight, 320-hp Cat diesels will cruise the 32 Royale at 21–22 knots. The larger 375-hp Cats cruise at 23 knots and reach a top speed of around 27 knots. ❏

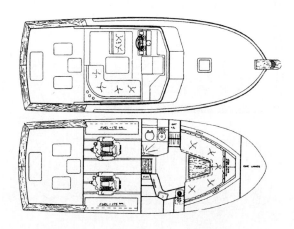

See Page 241 for Pricing Information

TOPAZ 36 SPORTFISHERMAN

SPECIFICATIONS

Length	36'2"	Fuel	300 gals.
Beam	13'0"	Cockpit	NA
Draft	2'5"	Hull Type	Modified-V
Weight	17,800#	Deadrise Aft	NA
Clearance	NA	Designer	Pat Patterson
Water	50 gals.	Production	1980-85

Forerunner of the popular Topaz 37 and a good-selling boat in her own right, the Topaz 36 established the company's name with offshore fishermen in the early 1980s. She was constructed on a solid glass hull with a fairly wide beam and modest transom deadrise. With her low center of gravity, the 36 is a stable boat with a tower, but her relatively flat aftersections can mean a hard ride in a chop. She was designed as a dedicated sportfisherman, and her spacious bi-level cockpit is arranged to meet the requirements of tournament-level anglers. There's room for a full-size tuna chair in the cockpit, and a large in-deck fish box and teak covering boards were standard. The belowdecks accommodations are comfortable and adequate for overnight expeditions with V-berths, convertible dinette, small galley, and a stand-up head compartment with stall shower. The Topaz 36 was available with a variety of diesel engine options from Volvo, GM, and Caterpillar. The popular 355-hp Cats will cruise economically at 23 knots and reach 26–27 knots wide open.   ❏

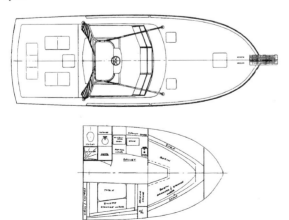

See Page 241 for Pricing Information

TOPAZ 37 SPORTFISHERMAN

SPECIFICATIONS

Length	37'6"	Fuel	350 gals.
Beam	13'0"	Cockpit	81 sq. ft.
Draft	3'4"	Hull Type	Modified-V
Weight	19,800#	Deadrise Aft	NA
Clearance	NA	Designer	Pat Patterson
Water	60 gals.	Production	1986–91

Still a good-selling boat in resale markets, the Topaz 37 SF is a reworked version of the popular Topaz 36 with additional fuel, increased bow flare (for a dryer ride), a larger interior, and improved performance. She was built of solid fiberglass on a modified-V bottom with a relatively wide beam. Offshore, she has a reputation for a solid ride and good handling characteristics. A low center of gravity makes her a stable boat at trolling speeds. The cockpit is a bi-level arrangement with the engines located beneath the raised bridgedeck. (Access to the engines is much improved from the Topaz 36.) The open helm provides good visibility, and there's room on the console for flush-mounting any electronics not fitted in an overhead cabinet. The cabin is set up to sleep four and includes a U-shaped dinette, complete galley, and a separate stall shower in the head. The only engines installed in the Topaz 37 were 375-hp Cat diesels. She'll cruise at 25 knots and reach a top speed of around 28–29 knots.   ❏

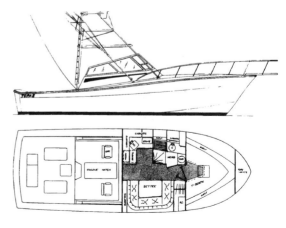

See Page 241 for Pricing Information

195

TOPAZ 38 FLYBRIDGE SF

SPECIFICATIONS

Length	38'2"	Fuel	430 gals.
Beam	13'0"	Cockpit	125 sq. ft.
Draft	2'7"	Hull Type	Modified Deep-V
Weight	22,700#	Deadrise Aft	17°
Clearance	11'3"	Designer	Pat Patterson
Water	160 gals.	Production	1985–87

With the distinctive profile of a pure-bred South Florida custom boat, the Topaz 38 Flybridge is a stylish East Coast canyon runner with a practical interior layout and excellent speed to go with her great looks. Aside from her outright sex appeal, serious anglers are attracted to the large and uncluttered fishing cockpit with port and starboard tackle centers, in-deck fish box, transom door, and space for a full-size fighting chair. Unlike most convertibles in this size range, the Topaz 38 was offered with only a single-stateroom floorplan—a fact that limits her aftermarket appeal among those who use their boat for family cruising. In an effort to keep the profile low, the salon settee and dinette are elevated from the salon sole. This—combined with the outboard saddle tanks—makes for a very tight engine room. Additional features include teak covering boards, an offset bridge ladder, and a teak bow pulpit. A fast boat (with a stiff ride), 450-hp 6-71s will cruise the Topaz 38 at 26 knots and deliver about 30 knots top. ❏

See Page 241 for Pricing Information

TOPAZ 39 ROYALE

SPECIFICATIONS

Length	39'1"	Fuel	400 gals.
Beam	13'0"	Cockpit	NA
Draft	3'1"	Hull Type	Modified Deep-V
Weight	21,900#	Deadrise Aft	17°
Clearance	NA	Designer	Pat Patterson
Water	60 gals.	Production	1988–91

Before Topaz ceased operations in 1991 the 39 Royale was one of their best-selling boats. Designed to appeal to the upscale end of the family cruiser market as well as the style-conscious sportfisherman, the 39 Royale is an extremely handsome design with an aggressive low-profile appearance and good rough-water performance. She was built on a modified-V hull form with moderate beam and generous flare at the bow—the same hull used in the production of the earlier Topaz 38. Her graceful lines are enhanced by the wraparound windshield and oval portlights in the hullsides. Below, the accommodations are compact but still comfortable with berths for four or five depending on the floorplan. The head is fitted with a stall shower, and the interior is finished with mica counters and teak woodwork. A popular sportboat, the 39 Royale is equally at home as a fisherman and comes equipped with a molded tackle center and a large in-deck fish box. She'll cruise at a fast 30 knots with 485-hp 6-71s and reach 33–34 knots top. ❏

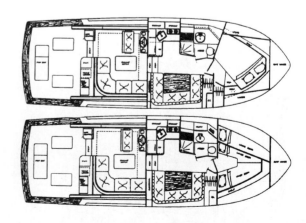

See Page 241 for Pricing Information

TOPAZ 44 FB SPORTFISHERMAN

SPECIFICATIONS

Length	44'3"	Fuel	640 gals.
Beam	15'4"	Cockpit	152 sq. ft.
Draft	3'11"	Hull Type	Modified-V
Weight	37,500#	Deadrise Aft	NA
Clearance	12'8"	Designer	Topaz
Water	125 gals.	Production	1987–89

An attention-getter on any dock, the Topaz 44 never became a big seller (only four were built) in spite of her near-custom South Florida profile. Topaz introduced this model in 1987 in a further departure from the company's past reliance on the open skiff-type day boats. The cockpit is somewhat larger than most boats her size (note that the beam is carried well aft) and features a huge in-deck fish box, a molded tackle center with freezer, cockpit controls, and distinctive teak covering boards. A bridge overhang provides protection from the weather, and the bridge ladder is mounted flush against the salon bulkhead. The flybridge is large for a 44-footer and features bench seating forward and to starboard of the helm console. The 44's fashionable two-stateroom interior is somewhat marred by the lack of a second head compartment. Easily serviced in a spacious engine room, the standard 565-hp 6V92 diesels will cruise the Topaz 44 at 26 knots and reach a top speed of around 29 knots. ❏

See Page 241 for Pricing Information

TROJAN 12 METER CONVERTIBLE

SPECIFICATIONS

Length	39'9"	Fuel	400 gals.
Beam	14'3"	Cockpit	110 sq. ft.
Draft	3'6"	Hull Type	Modified-V
Weight	19,000#	Deadrise Aft	12°
Clearance	12'6"	Designer	H. Schoell
Water	100 gals.	Production	1986–92

The 12 Meter Convertible was a serious attempt by Trojan to field a legitimate sportfishing boat. She is, in fact, a fairly good-looking boat although most anglers will probably frown at the dramatic Eurostyle hull graphics. With over 14' of beam, the 12 Meter is a roomy boat both inside and out. Since the accent is on fishability, the cockpit is set up with built-in fish boxes, seawater washdown, transom door, and tackle center. Her low-profile flybridge provides a good view of the cockpit action below, and the upscale interior came standard with a built-in entertainment center, wet bar, and icemaker. Until 1989, the dinette in the single-stateroom version could be replaced with a guest cabin for a two-stateroom floorplan. A revised two-stateroom layout with a deckhouse settee was introduced for 1990. Crusader 454-cid gas engines were standard. Optional 375-hp Cats deliver a cruising speed of 22 knots. The larger 485-hp 6-71s will cruise the 12 Meter at a fast 26 knots and reach around 30 knots wide open. ❏

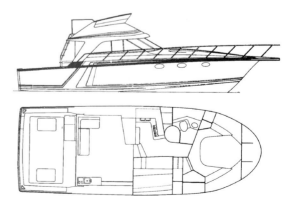

See Page 241 for Pricing Information

TROJAN 44 CONVERTIBLE

SPECIFICATIONS

Length	43'3"	Fuel, Opt	700 gals.
Beam	14'11"	Cockpit	150 sq. ft.
Draft	3'9"	Hull Type	Modified-V
Weight	33,750#	Deadrise Aft	8°
Clearance	12'6"	Designer	Trojan
Water	200 gals.	Production	1974–78
Fuel, Std	400 gals.		

The Trojan 44 Convertible was built on the same hull as the Trojan 44 MY—a modified-V affair with a modest 8° of deadrise aft, plenty of bow flare, and a long skeg ending just forward of the shafts. With her sweeping sheer, the profile of the 44 Convertible is quite handsome. Notably, this was Trojan's first (and only) attempt at a serious sportfisherman prior to the 1980s. There were two interior arrangements: Plan "A" was a Mediterranean version with crew quarters forward with one head for the huge master stateroom and guest cabin; Plan "B" (which became standard) is a more conventional layout with a deckhouse galley, two staterooms, and two heads. Outside, the 44's cockpit is huge, with room for a mounted chair and optional tackle center and controls. Several diesel options were available during her production run. The Cummins VT-903-Ms (400-hp) provide a top speed of 23 knots and an average cruising speed of about 19 knots. Market-wise, the Trojan 44 Convertible was not considered a notably successful sportfishing design. ❏

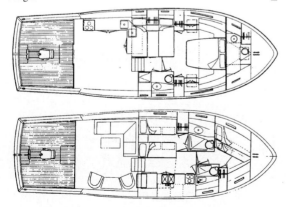

See Page 242 for Pricing Information

TROJAN 14 METER CONVERTIBLE

SPECIFICATIONS

Length	46'3"	Fuel	710 gals.
Beam	16'3"	Cockpit	130 sq. ft.
Draft	3'6"	Hull Type	Modified-V
Weight	34,000#	Deadrise Aft	12°
Clearance	13'7"	Designer	H. Schoell
Water	175 gals.	Production	1988–92

The Trojan 14 Meter Convertible was built on a stretched 13 Meter hull with moderate transom deadrise, fairly low freeboard, and a super-wide beam. She has essentially the same interior floorplan as the previous 13 Meter Sedan (1986–87) with the extra three feet of length used to create a much larger cockpit area. A stylish boat (in spite of the hull graphics), everything about the 14 Meter is on a grand scale. The extra beam creates huge volumes of space in both the cockpit and the interior. Although aimed at the sportfishing market, her luxurious two-stateroom floorplan features an extravagant main salon, a spacious galley, and two staterooms—each with a double berth and private head with stall shower. Outside, the uncluttered fishing cockpit is arranged for tournament-level activities with a transom door and tackle center to port. The huge flybridge has its own wet bar and seating for as many as ten. Optional 750-hp 8V92s will cruise the 14 Meter Convertible at 26 knots and reach a top speed of 29 knots. ❏

See Page 242 for Pricing Information

UNIFLITE 28 SALTY DOG

SPECIFICATIONS

Length	28'2"	Water	30 gals.
Length WL	24'5"	Fuel	150/210 gals.
Beam	10'10"	Cockpit	90 sq. ft.
Draft	2'10"	Hull Type	Modified-V
Weight	9,000#	Designer	Uniflite
Clearance	8'0"	Production	1971–1984

The 28 Salty Dog has long been recognized as a sturdy and well-crafted day fisherman. With nearly 100 sq. ft. of usable cockpit space, she's one of the best fishing platforms in her size range. A molded-in fish well was standard, and the engine access is very good. Although the Salty Dog is rather a plain-Jane boat in her stock form, the addition of a tower and outriggers adds much to her appearance. The cabin accommodations are basic but still comfortable for an occasional offshore weekend. The elevated portside helm is close to the action, and visibility is excellent. The Salty Dog came with several power options including single and twin gas or diesel engines. The standard single Crusader 270-hp gas engine will cruise at 17 knots (25 knots top), and the twin 220s cruise at around 22 knots and reach 30+ wide open. Note that the fuel capacity was increased in 1982. Following Uniflite's demise in 1984, the Salty Dog enjoyed brief resurgence as Chris Craft 282 SF in 1985–86.❏

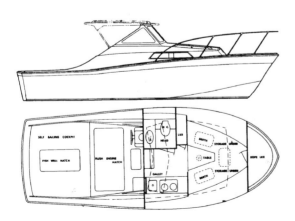

See Page 242 for Pricing Information

UNIFLITE 34 SPORT SEDAN

SPECIFICATIONS

Length	34'2"	Fuel	200 gals.
Beam	11'11"	Cockpit	75 sq. ft.
Draft	2'9"	Hull	Modified-V
Weight	17,000#	Deadrise Aft	15°
Clearance	11'11"	Designer	Uniflite
Water	100 gals.	Production	1974–84

The Uniflite 34 was introduced in 1974 in two configurations: the Tournament Fisherman with helm aft on the bridge and extra fuel capacity (300 gallons); and the Sport Sedan model (pictured above) with the helm console forward on the bridge in the West Coast fashion. Her lines are more attractive than those of the Uniflite 32 (whose hull was stretched in the design of the 34). She was built on a solid fiberglass modified-V hull with generous flare at the bow, a relatively wide beam, and moderate transom deadrise. The result was a rugged family cruiser/offshore fisherman with conservative lines and good seakeeping characteristics. The basic galley-down interior layout features a stall shower in the head, a roomy galley area, well-crafted teak interior woodwork, berths for six, and big wraparound salon windows. In a notable update, the original sliding glass salon doors were replaced in 1977 with a single hinged door. With the 454-cid Crusader gas engines, the Uniflite 34 Sedan will cruise around 20 knots and reach 29–30 knots at full throttle.❏

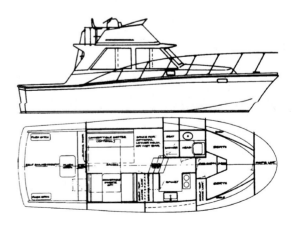

See Page 242 for Pricing Information

UNIFLITE 36 SPORT SEDAN

SPECIFICATIONS

Length..........................36'0"	Fuel, Opt...............300 gals.
Beam ....12'4"	Cockpit................. 80 sq. ft.
Draft..............................3'4"	Hull Type........Modified-V
Weight...................20,000#	Deadrise Aft...................11°
Clearance.....................NA	Designer.......A. Nordtvedt
Water.....................100 gals.	Production.............1970–84
Fuel, Std................216 gals.	

The Uniflite 36 Sport Sedan is a traditional sedan-style design with a smart profile and a rugged personality. Built on the same solid fiberglass hull as the 36 Double Cabin (a modified-V with single chines and 11° of deadrise at the transom), she was offered with two basic interior layouts during her production years. The two-stateroom version has an in-line galley to port in the salon, while, in the single-stateroom arrangement, the galley replaces the guest stateroom on the lower level, and the salon is considerably enlarged. Outside, the cockpit is large enough for serious fishing, and the wide sidedecks are notable. The flybridge is exceptionally large for a 36' boat with the helm console set all the way forward in the West Coast fashion. Standard Crusader 454-cid gas engines will cruise the Uniflite 36 Sport Sedan around 19 knots and reach a top speed of 28–29 knots. The optional 210-hp Caterpillar diesels cruise at 16 knots and reach a top speed of about 18–19 knots. ❑

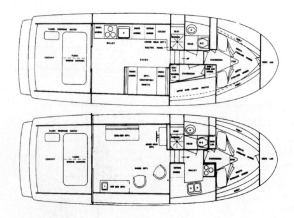

See Page 242 for Pricing Information

UNIFLITE 38 CONVERTIBLE

SPECIFICATIONS

Length..........................38'0"	Fuel.......................400 gals.
Beam ....13'11"	Cockpit.................92 sq. ft.
Draft..............................3'8"	Hull Type........Modified-V
Weight...................24,000#	Deadrise Aft.................NA
Clearance....................12'8"	Designer ....Uniflite
Water.....................100 gals.	Production.............1977–84

The 38 Convertible is a comfortable family cruising yacht and a competent offshore sportfisherman. Heavily built, she was available with two basic floorplans: a single-stateroom, galley-down arrangement and the standard two-stateroom, galley-up plan—the latter being somewhat notable for the small galley wedged into the forward corner of the salon. Both layouts had the convenience of a double-entry head, stall shower, and large staterooms. The 38's salon is spacious for a boat of this size. The portside lower helm station was an option, and most were so equipped. As a sportfisherman, the 38 has a large and uncluttered cockpit with a molded-in fish box and wide sidedecks. While the 400-gallon fuel capacity is adequate in the diesel-powered models, those with gas engines carry only 300 gallons—definitely on the light side. Optional 310-hp J&T 6-71Ns will cruise the Uniflite 38 at a steady 19 knots and reach 22 knots at full throttle. Note that in 1985 Chris Craft reintroduced this boat as the 382 Commander. ❑

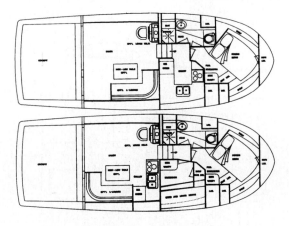

See Page 242 for Pricing Information

UNIFLITE 42 CONVERTIBLE

SPECIFICATIONS

Length	42'0"	Fuel	450/500 gals.
Beam	14'9"	Cockpit	102 sq. ft.
Draft	3'9"	Hull Type	Modified-V
Weight	35,000#	Designer	A. Nordtvedt
Clearance	12'10"	Production	1972–84
Water	160 gals.		

The Uniflite 42 is a sturdy West Coast fisherman with a conservative profile masking her rugged construction. She's built on a solid glass hull with a wide beam and moderate transom deadrise. There were two interior layouts offered: The original plan has the galley and dinette at the lower level with a single stateroom forward, and later models have a two-stateroom interior with the galley down (no dinette) and a choice of one or two heads. A lower station is generally found in the salon. Standard 350-hp gas engines cruise at just 17 knots (about 24 knots wide open). Optional 310-hp 6-71s cruise around 18–19 knots, and the more powerful 410-hp 6-71 diesels will cruise the Uniflite 42 Convertible at a solid 24 knots. Note that the standard fuel capacity increased to 500 gallons in 1977. A tournament-style flybridge (with the helm aft rather than forward) was offered for East Coast markets. With the optional 600-gallon fuel capacity, the Uniflite 42 has the ability to range far offshore. ❏

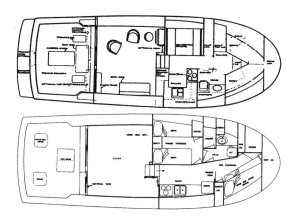

See Page 242 for Pricing Information

UNIFLITE 48 CONVERTIBLE

SPECIFICATIONS

Length	48'10"	Fuel	780 gals.
Beam	15'9"	Cockpit	133 sq. ft.
Draft	4'9"	Hull Type	Modified-V
Weight	48,000#	Deadrise Aft	14°
Clearance	13'9"	Designer	A. Nordtvedt
Water	200 gals.	Production	1980–84

The Uniflite 48 Convertible is a handsome and good-running offshore sportfisherman built to compete in tournament-level events. She's constructed on a solid fiberglass modified-V hull design with balsa coring in the hullsides from the waterline up. This was Uniflite's largest (and last) foray into the big-boat sportfishing market. Once considered a relatively fast boat, the Uniflite 48 was one of the early production applications of the then-new 8V92 diesels. Several three-stateroom interior layouts were available, and buyers could choose between having the master stateroom amidships or forward at the bow. Outside, the 48's huge cockpit came with in-deck storage and direct access to the engine room. The flybridge is arranged with the helm console aft on the centerline with bench seating forward. The sidedecks are notably wide. Known for her agile handling, 550-hp 8V92 diesels will cruise the Uniflite 48 Convertible at 24–25 knots and reach 28 knots wide open. Note that these hull molds were later used by Chris Craft in the construction of their 482 Commander. ❏

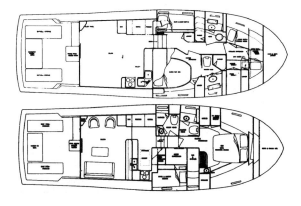

See Page 242 for Pricing Information

VIKING 35 CONVERTIBLE

1975-84

1985-92

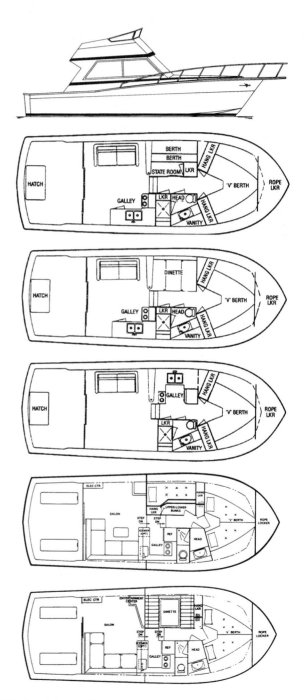

SPECIFICATIONS

Length	35'0"	Fuel	275/300 gals.
Beam	13'1"	Cockpit	80 sq. ft.
Draft	2'5"	Hull Type	Modified-V
Weight	20,000#	Deadrise Aft	15.5°
Clearance	12'4"	Designer	Viking
Water	75 gals.	Production	1975–92

A popular and durable family convertible, the Viking 35 has been recognized as a successful design since her introduction in 1975. She combines the essential elements of modern convertible styling with an attractive interior layout, superior construction, and proven offshore capabilities. Built on a beefed-up modified-V hull with 15.5° of deadrise aft, the hullsides are balsa-cored for weight reduction and strength. She was extensively redesigned and updated in 1985 with a solid front windshield, a completely restyled fly-bridge, and a luxurious teak interior with a choice of one or two staterooms. (The original wood-grain mica interior was replaced with teak in 1980.) Also in 1985, the generator was relocated from beneath the cockpit to the engine room. With her uncluttered cock-pit and comfortable interior, the Viking 35 can easily double as a weekend family cruiser. A stiff ride in a chop, 454-cid gas engines will cruise at 18–19 knots with a top speed of nearly 30 knots. Cat 375-hp diesels provide a cruising speed of 24–25 knots and 28 knots top. ❏

See Page 242 for Pricing Information

203

VIKING 35 SPORTFISHERMAN

SPECIFICATIONS

Length	35'0"	Fuel	300 gals.
Beam	13'1"	Cockpit	NA
Draft	2'5"	Hull Type	Modified-V
Weight	19,000#	Deadrise Aft	15.5°
Clearance	8'6"	Designer	Viking
Water	70 gals.	Production	1984–86

The 35 Sportfisherman was Viking's first entry into the market for open express fishing boats. Designed with a roomy and completely uncluttered cockpit and featuring modest interior comforts, the 35 SF was built on the same proven hull as the Viking 35 Convertible. Her large bi-level cockpit is equipped with two in-deck fish boxes, a built-in tackle cabinet, and full-length lounge seating port and starboard. Engine access, however, is not one of her selling points—working space is at a premium and access is tight. Below, the stylish teak interior provides overnight accommodations for four with a V-berths forward and a convertible dinette. Note that the toilet is fitted in the shower stall compartment to save space (just as in the 35 Convertible). Standard gas engines will cruise the Viking 45 SF around 19 knots with a top speed of 28. The 355-hp Cats cruise at a fast 27 knots and reach over 30 knots wide open. Some thirty-two of these boats were built until production was discontinued in 1986. ❏

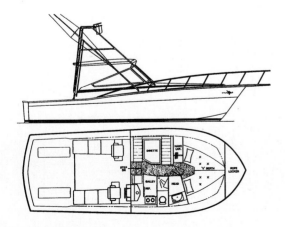

See Page 243 for Pricing Information

VIKING 38 CONVERTIBLE

SPECIFICATIONS

Length	39'4"	Fuel	430 gals.
Beam	14'2"	Cockpit	108 sq. ft.
Draft	4'1"	Hull Type	Modified-V
Weight	32,890#	Deadrise Aft	15.5°
Clearance	11'10"	Designer	B. Wilson
Water	110 gals.	Production	1990–Current

A handsome boat with tremendous eye appeal, the Viking 38 (she's actually over 39') is at the top of the class in today's mid-size convertible market. She's built on a modified-V hull with cored hullsides and better than 14 feet of beam—wide indeed for a 38-footer. Inside, the truly expansive interior of the Viking 38, with its rich teak paneling and upscale fabrics, is the largest to be found in a boat of this size. Two floorplans are offered, and both retain the convenient mid-level galley arrangement and double-entry head. The salon in the dinette layout seems huge—more like a 45-footer. The cockpit has over 100 sq. ft. of uncluttered space and comes with an in-deck fish box, transom door, and molded tackle centers. Topside, the spacious flybridge will seat eight. Crusader gas engines were standard until 1992, when they were replaced with 485-hp 6-71 diesels. A great-running boat, the Viking 38 Convertible will cruise around 26 knots and reach 29+ knots wide open. ❏

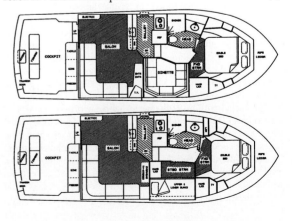

See Page 243 for Pricing Information

VIKING 40 SEDAN

SPECIFICATIONS

Length..........................40'4"
Beam ....14'6"
Draft..............................3'6"
Weight....................30,000#
Clearance....................11'9"
Water......................90 gals.

Fuel ....300/350 gals.
Cockpit.................100 sq. ft.
Hull TypeModified Deep-V
Deadrise Aft...................18°
Designer..............B. Wilson
Production.............1973–83

A major sales success with over 400 sold, the 40 Sedan contributed mightily to Viking's reputation as a quality East Coast builder. Boasting an aggressive profile and rugged hull construction, the Viking 40's cockpit and spacious interior are big for a 40-footer. Notable, too, are the balsa-cored hullsides—the Viking 40 was one of the early production boats to pioneer this technology. Steel engine mounts were also employed, which have now become a Viking trademark. Three interior layouts were offered with the differences affecting only the lower living area. Early models featured a simulated-wood laminate interior, but in 1982 Viking switched to a more luxurious teak interior. Another update (this one in 1980) moved the generator from under the cockpit to the engine room. Gas power was standard, but most Viking 40 Sedans were equipped with one of several diesel options. The popular 310-hp J&T 6-71Ns and 300-hp Cats will cruise around 20 knots (23–24 knots top), and the larger 410-hp 6-71TIs cruise at 23 knots (26 knots top).   ❏

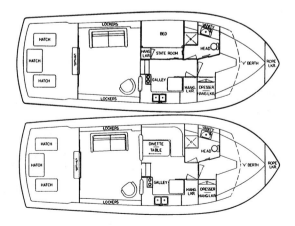

See Page 243 for Pricing Information

VIKING 41 CONVERTIBLE

SPECIFICATIONS

Length	41'2"	Fuel	380/430 gals.
Beam	14'10"	Cockpit	108 sq. ft.
Draft	4'3"	Hull Type	Modified-V
Weight	32,000#	Deadrise Aft	15.5°
Clearance	12'0"	Designer	Viking
Water	125 gals.	Production	1983–89

A popular boat with plenty of eye appeal, the Viking 41 is an upscale tournament-level sportfisherman with classic convertible styling and top-quality construction. She's built on a beamy modified-V hull with a sharp entry, plenty of bow flare, and balsa coring in the hullsides. Several floorplans were offered over the years: The two-stateroom layout sold best, although the single-stateroom arrangement with a full dinette was also quite popular. Indeed, with its wide open dinette and galley, this floorplan gives the interior of the Viking 41 the appearance of a *much* larger boat. The matched teak woodwork, top-quality hardware, and decorator fabrics are impressive. Outside, the large and unobstructed cockpit is fitted with in-deck fish boxes and a tackle center as standard equipment. The sidedecks are quite wide, and the flybridge will seat six easily. Fast and agile and possessing good seakeeping characteristics, the Viking 41 Convertible will turn an honest 30 knots wide open and cruise at 26 knots with the 485-hp 6-71 diesels. ❑

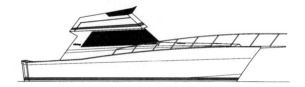

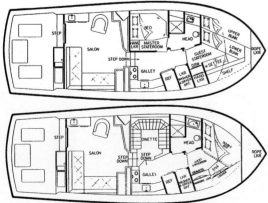

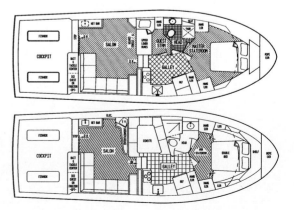

See Page 243 for Pricing Information

206

VIKING 43 CONVERTIBLE

SPECIFICATIONS

Length..........................43'0"	Fuel.......................525 gals.
Beam ....15'3"	Cockpit................116 sq. ft.
Draft..............................4'3"	Hull Type.......Modified-V
Weight....................38,595#	Deadrise Aft...............15.5°
Clearance.....................12'3"	Designer.............B. Wilson
Water....................115 gals.	Production...1990–Current

Replacing the popular 41 Convertible in 1990, the Viking 43 shares the same aggressive flybridge and deckhouse styling seen in the newest generation of Viking Convertibles. She has more beam and fuel capacity than the 41, and like her predecessor she offers a choice of a dinette in lieu of a second stateroom. Either way, the mid-level galley is wide open to the salon, and the head compartment and master stateroom are both very spacious. The interior is comprised of rich teak woodwork and cabinetry throughout with quality appliances, excellent detailing, and the latest in designer fabrics—upscale accommodations indeed for a tournament-capable fishing boat. Topside, the flybridge is among the largest in her class and features a particularly well-arranged helm console. The cockpit includes a transom door, molded tackle center, and a big in-deck fish box. A good-running sea boat with the original 485-hp 6-71s (24 knots cruise/28 top), now-standard 535-hp 6V-92s will cruise the Viking 43 at a fast 26 knots and reach 30 knots top. ❏

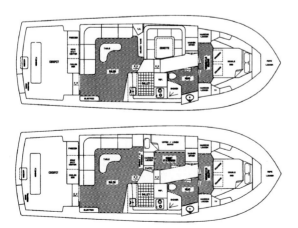

See Page 243 for Pricing Information

VIKING 43 SPORTFISH

SPECIFICATIONS

Length..........................43'0"	Fuel.......................525 gals.
Beam ....15'3"	Cockpit................116 sq. ft.
Draft..............................4'3"	Hull Type.......Modified-V
Weight....................34,500#	Deadrise Aft...............15.5°
Clearance.......................8'6"	Designer.............B. Wilson
Water....................115 gals.	Production...1994–Current

Built on the existing 43 Convertible hull, the Viking 43 Sportfish is one of the largest full-production express fishermen available in today's market. She's a good-looking boat with her wraparound windshield and aggressive profile, and the absence of a bow pulpit adds to her appearance. The deck plan is somewhat unusual: the helm is *centered* on the raised bridgedeck (note the wraparound lounge seating), and the steps leading down to the cockpit are offset to starboard. This permits a full set of in-line tackle centers and a centerline access door to the nearly stand-up engine room. A fish box is built into the cockpit sole, and a transom door and livewell are standard. Inside, the plush single-stateroom floorplan features a spacious salon/galley area along with a big stateroom forward and plenty of storage—close to what many consider to be the perfect day boat layout. Standard 535-hp 6V92s will cruise at 28 knots and reach 32 knots wide open. An Express version is available with an optional two-stateroom layout and an integrated swim platform. ❏

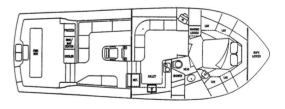

See Page 243 for Pricing Information

VIKING 45 CONVERTIBLE

SPECIFICATIONS

Length	45'5"	Fuel	600 gals.
Beam	15'0"	Cockpit	120 sq. ft.
Draft	4'0"	Hull Type	Modified-V
Weight	44,400#	Deadrise Aft	15.5°
Clearance	12'5"	Designer	B. Wilson
Water	160 gals.	Production	1987–93

The Viking 45 Convertible is one of those rare cases where the product is so well-matched to the market that her success was assured. (Indeed, 250 were built in six years.) A superb blend of good looks and impressive performance, she's constructed on Viking's standard modified-V hull form with moderate transom deadrise, a wide beam, and balsa coring in the hullsides. Originally offered with two staterooms and two heads, in late 1988 a spacious two-stateroom dinette layout became available at the expense of one of the head compartments. Both floorplans feature a mid-level galley, and the beautiful teak interior woodwork and stylish decor package are most impressive. The cockpit is set up for serious fishing (molded tackle center, transom door, etc.), and the big flybridge will seat eight comfortably. A good performer with standard 485-hp 6-71s, the Viking 45 Convertible will cruise at 24 knots and turn 27 knots on the wall. The 550-hp 6V92s (since 1990) will cruise at a fast 27 knots and reach a top speed of 30 knots. ❑

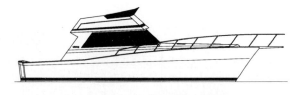

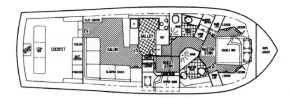

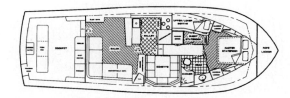

See Page 243 for Pricing Information

VIKING 46 CONVERTIBLE

SPECIFICATIONS

Length..........................46'6"	Fuel ....620/750 gals.
Beam ....16'0"	Cockpit................120 sq. ft.
Draft..............................4'0"	Hull Type........Modified-V
Weight....................44,000#	Deadrise Aft...............15.5°
Clearance......................NA	Designer..............B. Wilson
Water....................200 gals.	Production.............1981–85

The first to display the graceful profile of today's modern Viking yachts, the 46 Convertible is a good-looking canyon runner with plenty of muscle and speed. Built on the standard Viking hull with moderate transom deadrise and reversed chines, the hull bottom is grid-reinforced, and the engines rest on rigid steel beds. The Viking 46 has a reputation for being quite agile, although the ride can be hard in a chop. Her lush two-stateroom, galley-down interior includes an incredibly spacious master stateroom. A triple-stateroom layout—unusual in an under 50' convertible—became available in 1982. The interior is finished with traditional teak woodwork and top-quality furnishings, appliances, and hardware. The cockpit can easily handle a full-size chair, and the flybridge will seat six comfortably. The engine room is tight (air intakes are located under the gunnels). Originally offered with 500-hp 6V92s (24 knots cruise/28 top), 675-hp 8V92s became available in 1983 raising the cruising speed to a fast 27–28 knots and the top speed to 31 knots. ❏

VIKING 47 CONVERTIBLE

SPECIFICATIONS

Length..........................47'2"	Fuel........................700 gals.
Beam ....15'6"	Cockpit...............110 sq. ft.
Draft..............................4'5"	Hull Type........Modified-V
Weight....................46,300#	Deadrise Aft...............15.5°
Clearance....................12'9"	Designer..................Viking
Water....................160 gals.	Production...1994–Current

Replacing the popular 45 Convertible in the Viking line-up in 1994, the new Viking 47 is a great-looking boat with tremendous eye appeal and good overall performance. She rides on a new hull design with a deepened forefoot for improved headsea handling and additional flare at the bow for deflecting spray. The hull is solid fiberglass below the waterline and balsa-cored above. Inside, the two-stateroom layout is unusual in that the salon, galley and dinette are on a single level—completely unique in a modern convertible under 50'. The master stateroom is huge, and both head compartments have stall showers. Viking interiors are an elegant blend of grain-matched teak cabinetry and designer fabrics, and the 47's accommodations are plush indeed. Note the starboard-side (rather than centerline) salon door. Outside, the cockpit comes with an in-deck fish box in addition to a molded tackle center and direct access to the spacious engine room. Standard 680-hp MAN diesels will cruise the Viking 47 at a fast 28 knots and reach 31 knots top. ❏

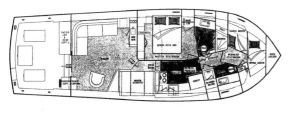

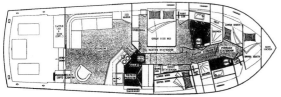

See Page 243 for Pricing Information

See Page 243 for Pricing Information

SPECIFICATIONS

Length	48'7"	Fuel	680 gals.
Beam	16'0"	Cockpit	144 sq. ft.
Draft	4'7"	Hull Type	Modified-V
Weight	45,500#	Deadrise Aft	15.5°
Clearance	12'5"	Designer	B. Wilson
Water	200 gals.	Production	1985–90

Built on a lengthened and reworked Viking 46 hull, the popular 48 Convertible used the additional hull length to create a huge 144 sq. ft. fishing cockpit. Unlike the 46 Convertible, the 48 has a solid front windshield and a much-improved engine room. In the original floorplan the galley and dinette are at mid-level. An alternate three-stateroom layout replaced the dinette with a small private cabin, and in 1989 the Plan "C" arrangement offered an L-shaped dinette on the deckhouse level and two very spacious staterooms. The 48's massive cockpit is fitted with two in-deck fish boxes, a tackle center, and a transom door—all standard. The flybridge has seating for eight. Additional features include reasonably wide sidedecks, a molded pulpit, and an optional hardtop. A stiff ride in a chop, the Viking 48 will cruise at 23–24 knots with 550-hp 6V92s (about 26 knots top). With the 735-hp 8V92s (standard in later models), the cruising speed is a blistering 27–28 knots, and the top speed is about 31 knots. ❑

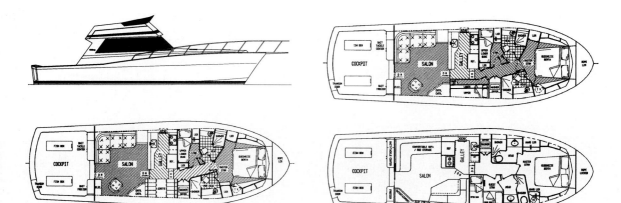

See Page 243 for Pricing Information

VIKING 50 CONVERTIBLE

SPECIFICATIONS

Length	50'7"	Fuel	850 gals.
Beam	16'4"	Hull Type	Modified-V
Draft	4'9"	Deadrise Aft	15.5°
Weight	58,814#	Designer	B. Wilson
Clearance	13'10"	Production	1991–Current
Water	208 gals.		

In many respects, the Viking 50 is best described as a scaled-down version of the popular Viking 53 Convertible introduced a few years ago. She's built on a modified-V hull with a wide beam, moderate transom deadrise, and balsa coring in the hullsides. Inside, her three-stateroom layout is virtually identical to the 53 with only slightly reduced interior dimensions. Note that the salon, galley, and dinette are on the same level. Two or three staterooms are available forward; either way, the master stateroom is amidships where the ride is the most comfortable. Additional features include a stand-up engine room, a *huge* in-deck fish box, relatively wide sidedecks, direct cockpit engine room access, and a superb bridge layout. At 60,000 lbs., the Viking 50 is no lightweight. Standard power in 1991 was 730-hp 8V92s (27 knots cruise/30 top), however they were replaced in 1992 with 820-hp MANs. A great-running boat, she'll cruise at a fast 30 knots and deliver a top speed of 33 knots. ❏

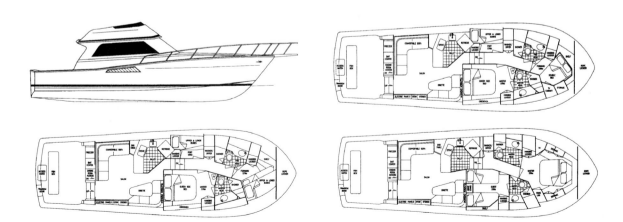

See Page 243 for Pricing Information

211

VIKING 53 CONVERTIBLE

SPECIFICATIONS

Length	53'7"	Fuel	900/1,100 gals.
Beam	16'7"	Cockpit	148 sq. ft.
Draft	4'10"	Hull Type	Modified-V
Weight	68,600#	Deadrise Aft	15°
Clearance	13'4"	Designer	B. Wilson
Water	200 gals.	Production	1990–Current

A popular boat, the Viking 53 is a sleek and well-proportioned sportfisherman with the angular good looks common to all modern Viking designs. She's built on a modified-V hull with cored hullsides, wide chines, and a shallow keel. The galley-up floorplan of the Viking 53 includes three staterooms and two heads on the lower level with the master stateroom to starboard. (Note that in 1991 the galley was rearranged, and in 1992 a queen bed forward became standard.) The salon, galley, and dinette are on the same level. With its elegant decor, lush teak woodwork, and clever use of mirrors, the high-style interior is slightly overwhelming for a tournament-level fisherman. The cockpit features a full tackle center, transom door, in-deck fish box, and access to an award-winning engine room. The flybridge is equally large and features a superb helm console. Standard 845-hp MANs will cruise at a fast 27–28 knots (33 knots top), and 1,000-hp MANs (optional beginning in 1992) cruise at 31 knots and deliver 35 knots top. ❑

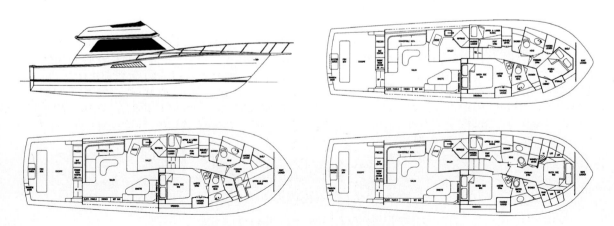

See Page 243 for Pricing Information

VIKING 57 CONVERTIBLE

SPECIFICATIONS

Length	57'2"	Fuel	1,500 gals.
Beam	18'0"	Cockpit	176 sq. ft.
Draft	5'3"	Hull Type	Modified-V
Weight	69,000#	Deadrise Aft	15.5°
Clearance	14'6"	Designer	B. Wilson
Water	250 gals.	Production	1989–91

A good-looking boat with a superb layout to go with her modern styling, the Viking 57 Convertible was built on the standard Viking hull form with a flat keel section, reversed outer chines, and 15.5° of deadrise at the transom. Inside, the three-stateroom interior is arranged with the salon, galley, and dinette all on the same level. Needless to say, the decor is upscale in the extreme—especially the elegant teak woodwork—and each stateroom has a private head. Note that the master stateroom is forward in this layout. The tournament-size fishing cockpit is fitted with molded tackle centers, transom door, teak covering boards, and direct access to the spacious (and well-arranged) stand-up engine room. The only engines ever used in the Viking 57 Convertible were the 1,080-hp 12V92s. A good performer, she'll cruise at 28 knots and reach a top speed of 32 knots. Fast and agile but wet in a headsea, the Viking 57 was replaced in 1992 with the new 58 Convertible. A total of 29 were built. ❏

VIKING 58 CONVERTIBLE

SPECIFICATIONS

Length	58'11"	Fuel	1,500 gals.
Beam	18'0"	Cockpit	165 sq. ft.
Draft	5'3"	Hull Type	Modified-V
Weight	81,500#	Deadrise Aft	15.5°
Clearance	14'6"	Designer	B. Wilson
Water	260 gals.	Production	1991–Current

The Viking 58 is basically an updated version of the earlier 57 Convertible with a sharper entry, additional bow flare, and a redesigned transom. She's a dryer boat than her predecessor with slightly better headsea and backing-down characteristics. Her modified-V hull retains the same 15.5° of transom deadrise, and the hullsides are cored with balsa. The superstructure—from pulpit to cockpit—is a single-piece mold. Inside, the lush interior of the Viking 58 is quite similar to the 57, although the galley has been slightly enlarged by moving the companionway to starboard. Note that the master stateroom is now amidships rather than forward. All three heads have separate stall showers. The cockpit and flybridge are designed to tournament-level standards, and the meticulously arranged engine room is among the best to be found in a boat this size. A great-running boat with tremendous eye appeal, standard 1,100-hp MAN diesels will cruise the Viking 58 Convertible at a fast 29–30 knots and deliver a top speed of about 33 knots. ❏

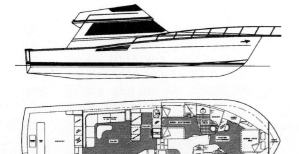

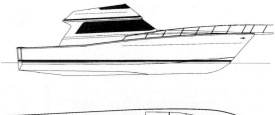

See Page 243 for Pricing Information

See Page 243 for Pricing Information

VISTA 48/50 SPORTFISHERMAN

SPECIFICATIONS

Length ....48'0"	Fuel........................700 gals.
Beam ....16'0"	Cockpit ....NA
Draft...............................3'1"	Hull Type........Modified-V
Weight.....................36,000#	Deadrise Aft..................NA
Clearance...................13'10"	Designer............Tom Fexas
Water.....................180 gals.	Production.............1986–92

The Vista 48 and 50 SF are basically the same boat with the 50 having a slightly larger salon. Built on a beamy, fully cored hull, the Vista weighs in at a relatively light 36,000 pounds. Note the raked flybridge and distinctive foredeck "arms" extending from both sides of the deckhouse. The accommodations of the Vista 48 are spacious and very open. The standard two-stateroom layout includes two heads with stall showers, and the alternate three-stateroom floorplan moves the galley up into the salon. Teak paneling and trim are used throughout the interior, and light oak woodwork was available. A sliding door opens into the huge and unobstructed fishing cockpit which is down two steps from the salon level. A molded tackle center is standard along with cockpit controls, transom door, fish box, etc., and there's cockpit access to the enormous engine room. Engine options include 375-hp Cats, 550-hp 6V92s, and 735-hp 8V92s. The popular 6V92s will cruise at an honest 24 knots and deliver a top speed of around 28 knots. ❏

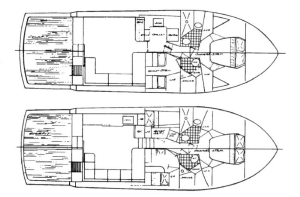

See Page 243 for Pricing Information

WELLCRAFT 2600 COASTAL

SPECIFICATIONS

LOA w/Pulpit ....28'0"	Water.......................20 gals.
Hull Length.................26'1"	Fuel ....150/200 gals.
Beam ....9'8"	Cockpit ....NA
Draft, Down ....3'0"	Hull Type...............Deep-V
Hull Weight O/B ....5,500#	Deadrise Aft...................18°
Weight, I/Os ....7,100#	Designer ....B. Collier
Clearance......................7'3"	Production...1990–Current

The Wellcraft 2600 is an open-transom express fisherman with conservative lines and good open-water performance. She's built on a solid fiberglass deep-V hull with a well-flared bow and a relatively wide 9'8" beam. Available in outboard and stern drive versions, the 2600 is a sturdy boat with a big cockpit and good belowdecks accommodations. The cabin will sleep four and includes a convertible dinette, compact galley, and stand-up head with shower. (Note that the head was slightly enlarged in 1994 at the expense of galley space.) The bi-level cockpit is arranged with elevated helm and companion seats forward with under-gunwale rod storage, tackle drawers, and a circulating livewell beneath the companion seat. An in-deck fish box is standard in outboard models, and a full-height wave gate became available in 1993. The sidedecks are quite wide on this boat, and foredeck access is very good. With twin 200-hp outboards, the 2600 Coastal will cruise at 26 knots and reach a top speed in the neighborhood of 42–43 knots. ❏

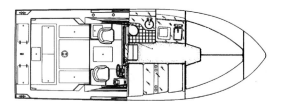

See Page 243 for Pricing Information

215

WELLCRAFT 2800 COASTAL

SPECIFICATIONS

LOA w/Pulpit............29'8"	Water.......................20 gals.
Hull Length................27'7"	Fuel........................182 gals.
Beam ....9'11"	Cockpit ....55 sq. ft.
Draft..............................2'4"	Hull Type........Modified-V
Weight......................8,200#	Deadrise Aft...................16°
Clearance.....................7'6"	Production...1986–Current

The 2800 Coastal is a versatile express boat with a conservative profile and several notable design features. Built on a modified-V hull with moderate beam, she's a capable fisherman able to meet the needs of most weekend anglers. While the Coastal has wide side-decks and a large cockpit, she still manages to provide a surprisingly spacious interior layout below with good headroom, a small galley area, compact head with shower, and berths for four. For most, how-ever, the chief attraction of the 2800 Coastal is her practical and well-arranged deck plan. The large bi-level cockpit has a fiberglass liner for easy clean up and comes standard with removable in-deck fish boxes and a transom door. The helm seat is mounted on an above-deck livewell, and the companion seat pod contains a tackle center with sink. Updates in 1990 included new deckhouse window styling and upgraded tackle centers, and in 1993 a dinette floorplan became standard. With 350-cid gas engines, the 2800 Coastal will cruise around 20 knots and reach 29–30 knots top. ❏

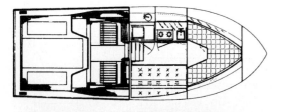

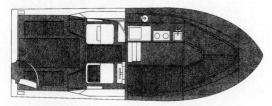

See Page 244 for Pricing Information

WELLCRAFT 2900 SPORT BRIDGE

SPECIFICATIONS

Length..........................28'8"	Fuel........................200 gals.
Beam ....10'8"	Cockpit Area.................NA
Draft..............................2'6"	Hull Type........Modified-V
Weight......................9,200#	Deadrise Aft...................16°
Clearance.......................NA	Designer ....B. Collier
Fresh Water............45 gals.	Production.............1983–86

The 2900 Sport Bridge is a good-looking flybridge fisherman with a big fishing cockpit and an attractive low-profile appearance. She was built on a conventional modified-V hull form with 16° of deadrise at the transom and generous flare at the bow. The compact cabin layout of the Sport Bridge is straightforward and efficient with the head conveniently located just inside the cabin door. The small galley is to port across from the convertible dinette, and V-berths are fitted in the forward stateroom. This is a practical layout for a small convertible and one that will suit the needs of family cruisers as well as a couple of overnight anglers. Engines are accessed via hatches in the raised engine deck, and the flybridge will accommodate three with a bench seat. Additional features include rod holders, swim platform, and a well-arranged and unobstructed fishing cockpit. A popular model, the 2900 Sport Bridge will cruise economically around 20 knots and reach 28 knots top with the optional Crusader 270-hp (or Volvo 260-hp) gas engines. ❏

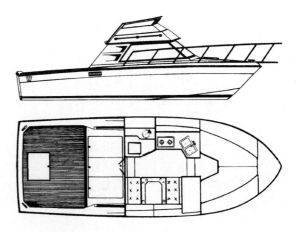

See Page 244 for Pricing Information

WELLCRAFT 3200 COASTAL

SPECIFICATIONS

Length	32'0"	Fuel	290 gals.
Beam	11'6"	Cockpit	71 sq. ft.
Draft	3'0"	Hull Type	Modified-V
Weight	13,200#	Deadrise Aft	14°
Clearance	8'3"	Designer	B. Collier
Water	80 gals.	Production	1984–86

One of the early fishboat designs from Wellcraft, the 3200 Coastal is a good-looking express fisherman with a well-arranged deck plan and a comfortable interior layout. She was built on a solid fiberglass, modified-V hull form and features wide walkaround sidedecks and a molded bow pulpit. No longer in production, 3200 Coastals are popular today because of a solid and dry ride, good all-around handling qualities, and a large, unobstructed fishing cockpit. Below, the roomy teak-paneled cabin will sleep four and includes a full galley and a stand-up head with shower. The Coastal's bi-level cockpit includes a 19" transom door (that unfortunately opens into the cockpit rather than out), and rod storage beneath the gunwales. An optional 60 gallons of fuel (or a generator instead) provide a cruising range of close to 300 miles. Twin 350-hp Crusaders will cruise the 3200 Coastal around 22 knots with a top speed of 30 knots. The Wellcraft 3200 Sport Bridge (1985–86) is essentially the same boat with a flybridge and salon. ❏

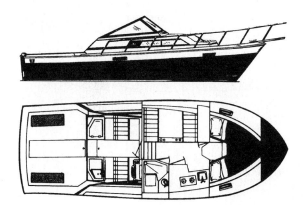

See Page 244 for Pricing Information

WELLCRAFT 3300 COASTAL

SPECIFICATIONS

LOA w/Pulpit	36'6"	Water	52 gals.
HullLength	33'4"	Fuel	288 gals.
Beam	12'8"	Hull Type	Modified-V
Draft	2'8"	Deadrise Aft	16°
Weight	13,800#	Designer	Wellcraft
Clearance	8'4"	Production	1989–Current

Together with the 3300 Sport Bridge, the 3300 Coastal is the largest model in Wellcraft's fleet of fishing boats. Introduced in 1989, she's constructed on a modified-V hull form with 16° of deadrise aft and prop pockets below (side exhausts were added in 1992). Designed as a dedicated sportfisherman, the 3300 Coastal comes standard with synchronized throttle controls, insulated in-deck fish boxes, bow pulpit, and the same inward-opening transom door found on the earlier 3200 Coastal. A factory marlin or tuna tower is optional. The bi-level cockpit is fitted with under-gunwale storage and padded coaming. Both helm and companion seats are mounted on raised boxes (with built-in livewell and bait prep station) that swing back for engine access. Although she's primarily a fishing boat, the accommodations aboard the 3300 Coastal are suitable for weekend cruising. A popular boat, standard 454-cid gas engines will cruise the 3300 Coastal at 20–21 knots with a top speed of about 30 knots. Optional 375-hp Cat diesels will cruise around 25 knots. ❏

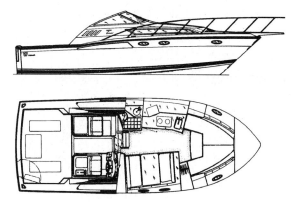

See Page 244 for Pricing Information

WELLCRAFT 3300 SPORT BRIDGE

SPECIFICATIONS

Length ....33'4"	Fuel........................274 gals.
Beam ....12'8"	Cockpit...............104 sq. ft.
Draft............................2'10"	Hull Type........Modified-V
Weight ....15,300#	Designer ....Wellcraft
Clearance.....................9'9"	Production.............1991–92
Water.......................50 gals.	

A good-looking boat, the 3300 Sport Bridge is built on the same wide-beam hull used in the production of the 3300 Coastal. Although she's most at home as a fisherman, her upscale interior and wide-open deck layout makes her an equally competent family cruiser. The floorplan is arranged with an island berth forward, compact galley, and a stand-up head. The salon is quite roomy, and rod storage is located below the sole. Outside, there's seating for five on the small bridge, and the cockpit includes in-deck fish boxes, tackle center, and an inward-opening transom door (a dubious feature that Wellcraft seems to favor in their fishing boats). Prop pockets in the hull allow the engines to be located aft of the salon bulkhead where they're accessible via flush hatches in the forward part of the cockpit. This design allows for a lower overall deckhouse profile without the use of engine boxes. Standard 454-cid gas engines will cruise the 3300 Sport Bridge at 19 knots and deliver a top speed of around 27 knots. ❏

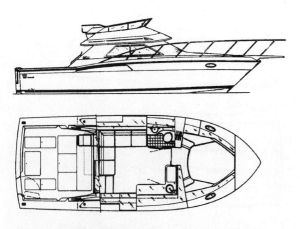

See Page 244 for Pricing Information

WELLCRAFT 3700 COZUMEL

SPECIFICATIONS

Length........................36'11"	Fuel........................400 gals.
Beam ....13'6"	Cockpit.................90 sq. ft.
Draft..............................3'3"	Hull Type........Modified-V
Weight....................21,000#	Deadrise Aft...............16.5°
Clearance....................12'3"	Designer ....B. Collier
Water.......................90 gals.	Production.............1988–89

The 3700 Cozumel had a rather short production run lasting just two years before she was retired from the Wellcraft line-up. Aimed at the market for affordably priced convertibles, her upscale two-stateroom layout with mid-level galley is a contemporary blend of white mica surfaces and attractive fabrics—a stylish decor for a fishing boat with some of the glitz and personality of the luxurious Portifino and San Remo interiors. The Cozumel's hull was designed with a relatively steep 16.5° of deadrise at the transom, and prop pockets are built into the hull. Her large and uncluttered cockpit came equipped with lockable rod storage compartments, a transom door, inwale padding, and a fish box. A recessed lounge cushion is provided on the foredeck for sunbathing. Topside, the tournament-style flybridge provides good cockpit visibility and includes bench seating forward of the helm console. Twin 454-cid gas engines were standard (about 20 knots cruise/29 top). Optional 375-hp Cat diesels will cruise the 3700 Cozumel around 24 knots with a top speed of 28 knots. ❏

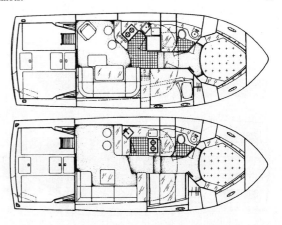

See Page 244 for Pricing Information

New & Used Boat Prices

A single asterisk (*) indicates that the price is for the hull only and does not include the outboard motor.

Four asterisks (****) indicate boats whose production runs were prior to 1975.

Six asterisks (******) indicate insufficient data to render a value for a particular year.

S designates single engine models; T, twins.

Year	Power	Retail Low	Retail High	Year	Power	Retail Low	Retail High	Year	Power	Retail Low	Retail High
Albemarle 27 Express				1986	T/Diesel	43,610	49,000	1991	T/Diesel	105,100	118,090
1994	T/IO	68,032	76,440	1985	T/IO	30,527	34,300	1990	T/Gas	82,859	93,100
1994	T/Gas	77,190	86,730	1984	T/IO	28,783	32,340	**Albin 28 Tournament Express**			
1994	T/Diesel	85,040	95,550	1983	T/IO	27,038	30,380				
1993	T/IO	59,746	67,130	**Albemarle 32 FB**				1994	S/T/Diesel	68,904	77,420
1993	T/Gas	68,032	76,440	1994	T/Gas	126,033	141,610	1993	S/T/Diesel	64,543	72,520
1993	T/Diesel	76,754	86,240	1994	T/Diesel	145,657	163,660	**Albin 32 Sportfisher**			
1992	T/IO	53,204	59,780	1993	T/Gas	111,206	124,950	1994	S/T/Diesel	119,491	134,260
1992	T/Gas	60,618	68,110	1993	T/Diesel	132,574	148,960	1994	T/Diesel	145,657	163,660
1992	T/Diesel	69,776	78,400	1992	T/Gas	98,559	110,740	1993	S/T/Diesel	105,100	118,090
1991	T/IO	47,971	53,900	1992	T/Diesel	120,800	135,730	1993	T/Diesel	134,319	150,920
1991	T/Gas	54,512	61,250	1991	T/Gas	92,453	103,880	1992	S/T/Diesel	99,867	112,210
1991	T/Diesel	63,671	71,540	1991	T/Diesel	112,514	126,420	1992	T/Diesel	125,161	140,630
1990	T/IO	44,046	49,490	1990	T/Gas	87,220	98,000	1991	S/T/Diesel	90,273	101,430
1990	T/Gas	49,715	55,860	1990	T/Diesel	105,100	118,090	1991	T/Diesel	114,694	128,870
1990	T/Diesel	58,001	65,170	1989	T/Gas	79,806	89,670	1990	S/T/Diesel	73,701	82,810
1989	T/IO	40,993	46,060	1989	T/Diesel	95,070	106,820	1990	T/Diesel	105,536	118,580
1989	T/Gas	45,790	51,450	1988	T/Gas	75,445	84,770	1989	S/T/Diesel	64,979	73,010
1989	T/Diesel	53,640	60,270	**Albemarle 32 Express**				1989	T/Diesel	96,814	108,780
1988	T/IO	38,377	43,120	1994	T/Gas	109,897	123,480	**Aquasport 290 Tournament**			
1988	T/Gas	41,430	46,550	1994	T/Diesel	141,732	159,250	1990	T/Gas	60,182	67,620
1988	T/Diesel	49,715	55,860	1993	T/Gas	101,175	113,680	1989	T/Gas	56,693	63,700
1987	T/IO	34,888	39,200	1993	T/Diesel	128,650	144,550	1988	T/Gas	53,640	60,270
1987	T/Gas	38,377	43,120	1992	T/Gas	93,762	105,350	1987	T/Gas	46,227	51,940
1987	T/Diesel	46,227	51,940	1992	T/Diesel	116,439	130,830	1986	T/Gas	42,738	48,020
1986	T/IO	32,271	36,260	1991	T/Gas	87,656	98,490	1985	T/Gas	34,888	39,200
1986	T/Gas	35,760	40,180								

Year	Power	Retail Low	Retail High
1984	T/Gas	28,783	32,340

Atlantic 34 Sportsman

Year	Power	Retail Low	Retail High
1992	T/Gas	88,092	98,980
1992	T/Diesel	113,386	127,400
1991	T/Gas	77,626	87,220
1991	T/Diesel	103,792	116,620
1990	T/Gas	68,468	76,930
1990	T/Diesel	95,942	107,800
1989	T/Gas	61,926	69,580
1989	T/Diesel	89,400	100,450
1988	T/Gas	57,565	64,680
1988	T/Diesel	83,731	94,080

Bayliner 2502 Trophy

Year	Power	Retail Low	Retail High
1994	O/B*	23,113	25,970
1993	O/B*	19,188	21,560
1992	O/B*	17,008	19,110

Bayliner 2860 Trophy

Year	Power	Retail Low	Retail High
1987	S/IO	16,572	18,620
1987	T/Gas	25,294	28,420
1986	S/IO	15,700	17,640
1986	T/Gas	22,677	25,480
1985	S/IO	14,827	16,660
1985	T/Gas	20,061	22,540
1984	S/IO	13,955	15,680
1984	T/Gas	18,316	20,580

Bertram 28 FBC

Year	Power	Retail Low	Retail High
1994	T/Gas	109,025	122,500
1994	T/Diesel	127,341	143,080
1993	T/Gas	100,303	112,700
1993	T/Diesel	116,439	130,830
1992	T/Gas	90,709	101,920
1992	T/Diesel	104,228	117,110
1991	T/Gas	81,115	91,140
1991	T/Diesel	92,889	104,370
1990	T/Gas	72,829	81,830
1989	T/Gas	67,159	75,460
1988	T/Gas	61,490	69,090
1987	T/Gas	57,129	64,190
1986	T/Gas	52,768	59,290
1985	T/Gas	47,535	53,410
1984	T/Gas	45,790	51,450
1983	T/Gas	42,738	48,020
1982	T/Gas	37,941	42,630
1981	T/Gas	33,144	37,240
1980	T/Gas	26,166	29,400
1979	T/Gas	23,986	26,950
1978	T/Gas	22,241	24,990
1977	T/Gas	20,933	23,520
1976	T/Gas	20,061	22,540
1975	T/Gas	19,188	21,560

Bertram 28 SF

Year	Power	Retail Low	Retail High
1983	T/Gas	37,941	42,630
1982	T/Gas	34,452	38,710
1981	T/Gas	31,399	35,280
1980	T/Gas	24,422	27,440
1979	T/Gas	23,113	25,970
1978	T/Gas	21,369	24,010
1977	T/Gas	20,061	22,540
1976	T/Gas	19,188	21,560
1975	T/Gas	18,316	20,580

Bertram 28 Bahia Mar

Year	Power	Retail Low	Retail High
1992	T/Gas	82,859	93,100
1992	T/Diesel	98,995	111,230
1991	T/Gas	76,754	86,240
1991	T/Diesel	90,273	101,430
1990	T/Gas	70,212	78,890
1989	T/Gas	64,107	72,030
1988	T/Gas	57,129	64,190
1987	T/Gas	52,768	59,290
1986	T/Gas	51,024	57,330
1985	T/Gas	45,354	50,960
1984	T/Gas	43,174	48,510

Bertram 28 Moppie

Year	Power	Retail Low	Retail High
1994	T/Gas	100,303	112,700
1993	T/Gas	96,814	108,780
1992	T/Gas	84,603	95,060
1991	T/Gas	75,009	84,280
1990	T/Gas	67,596	75,950
1989	T/Gas	61,926	69,580
1988	T/Gas	53,204	59,780
1987	T/Gas	41,866	47,040

Bertram 30 FBC

Year	Power	Retail Low	Retail High
1985	T/Gas	60,182	67,620
1985	T/Diesel	76,318	85,750
1984	T/Gas	58,437	65,660
1984	T/Diesel	73,265	82,320

Bertram 30 Moppie

Year	Power	Retail Low	Retail High
1994	T/Gas	109,897	123,480
1994	T/Diesel	143,041	160,720

Bertram 31 FBC

Year	Power	Retail Low	Retail High
1986	T/Gas	75,009	84,280
1983	T/Gas	52,768	59,290
1983	T/Diesel	68,032	76,440
1982	T/Gas	47,971	53,900
1982	T/Diesel	63,234	71,050
1981	T/Gas	44,046	49,490
1981	T/Diesel	55,385	62,230
1980	T/Gas	40,121	45,080
1980	T/Diesel	46,663	52,430
1979	T/Gas	34,888	39,200
1979	T/Diesel	41,866	47,040
1978	T/Gas	31,835	35,770
1978	T/Diesel	37,941	42,630
1977	T/Gas	29,655	33,320
1977	T/Diesel	34,888	39,200
1976	T/Gas	27,910	31,360
1976	T/Diesel	31,399	35,280
1975	T/Gas	26,166	29,400
1975	T/Diesel	28,783	32,340

Bertram 31 SF

Year	Power	Retail Low	Retail High
1982	T/Gas	46,663	52,430
1982	T/Diesel	60,182	67,620
1981	T/Gas	49,279	55,370
1981	T/Diesel	52,332	58,800
1980	T/Gas	37,068	41,650
1980	T/Diesel	42,738	48,020
1979	T/Gas	34,888	39,200
1979	T/Diesel	39,249	44,100
1978	T/Gas	31,399	35,280
1978	T/Diesel	34,888	39,200
1977	T/Gas	27,038	30,380
1977	T/Diesel	32,271	36,260
1976	T/Gas	24,422	27,440
1976	T/Diesel	28,783	32,340
1975	T/Gas	21,805	24,500
1975	T/Diesel	25,294	28,420

Bertram 31 Bahia Mar

Year	Power	Retail Low	Retail High
1981	T/Gas	37,068	41,650
1981	T/Diesel	45,354	50,960
1980	T/Gas	34,888	39,200

Year	Power	Retail Low	Retail High
1980	T/Diesel	40,121	45,080
1979	T/Gas	32,271	36,260
1979	T/Diesel	36,632	41,160
1978	T/Gas	29,655	33,320
1978	T/Diesel	31,399	35,280
1977	T/Gas	26,602	29,890
1977	T/Diesel	28,783	32,340
1976	T/Gas	23,549	26,460
1976	T/Diesel	26,166	29,400
1975	T/Gas	20,933	23,520
1975	T/Diesel	22,677	25,480

Bertram 33 FBC

Year	Power	Retail Low	Retail High
1992	T/Gas	151,763	170,520
1992	T/Diesel	191,884	215,600
1991	T/Gas	133,447	149,940
1991	T/Diesel	170,079	191,100
1990	T/Gas	125,597	141,120
1990	T/Diesel	154,379	173,460
1989	T/Gas	119,491	134,260
1989	T/Diesel	139,552	156,800
1988	T/Gas	107,717	121,030
1988	T/Diesel	130,830	147,000
1987	T/Gas	98,559	110,740
1987	T/Diesel	122,108	137,200
1986	T/Gas	92,017	103,390
1986	T/Diesel	113,386	127,400
1985	T/Gas	84,167	94,570
1985	T/Diesel	104,664	117,600
1984	T/Gas	78,062	87,710
1984	T/Diesel	96,814	108,780
1983	T/Gas	71,956	80,850
1983	T/Diesel	88,964	99,960
1982	T/Gas	66,287	74,480
1982	T/Diesel	81,115	91,140
1981	T/Gas	61,490	69,090
1981	T/Diesel	74,137	83,300
1980	T/Gas	54,949	61,740
1980	T/Diesel	75,009	84,280
1979	T/Gas	47,971	53,900
1979	T/Diesel	65,415	73,500
1978	T/Gas	43,610	49,000
1978	T/Diesel	61,926	69,580
1977	T/Gas	40,121	45,080
1977	T/Diesel	57,565	64,680
1976	T/Gas	35,760	40,180
1976	T/Diesel	52,332	58,800

Year	Power	Retail Low	Retail High
1975	T/Gas	33,144	37,240
1975	T/Diesel	47,099	52,920

Bertram 33 SF

Year	Power	Retail Low	Retail High
1992	T/Gas	143,477	161,210
1992	T/Diesel	187,523	210,700
1991	T/Gas	132,574	148,960
1991	T/Diesel	176,184	197,960
1990	T/Gas	119,491	134,260
1990	T/Diesel	159,613	179,340
1989	T/Gas	110,333	123,970
1989	T/Diesel	143,477	161,210
1988	T/Gas	101,611	114,170
1988	T/Diesel	129,522	145,530
1987	T/Gas	98,995	111,230
1987	T/Diesel	125,161	140,630
1986	T/Gas	86,784	97,510
1986	T/Diesel	109,025	122,500
1985	T/Gas	83,295	93,590
1985	T/Diesel	108,589	122,010
1984	T/Gas	76,754	86,240
1984	T/Diesel	98,122	110,250
1983	T/Gas	71,084	79,870
1983	T/Diesel	92,889	104,370
1982	T/Gas	63,234	71,050
1982	T/Diesel	85,476	96,040
1981	T/Gas	58,001	65,170
1981	T/Diesel	77,626	87,220
1980	T/Gas	56,693	63,700
1980	T/Diesel	73,701	82,810
1979	T/Gas	53,204	59,780
1979	T/Diesel	68,904	77,420

Bertram 35 Convertible

Year	Power	Retail Low	Retail High
1986	T/Gas	98,122	110,250
1986	T/Diesel	127,341	143,080
1985	T/Gas	89,837	100,940
1985	T/Diesel	118,619	133,280
1984	T/Gas	86,348	97,020
1984	T/Diesel	112,950	126,910
1983	T/Gas	82,423	92,610
1983	T/Diesel	109,461	122,990
1982	T/Gas	72,829	81,830
1982	T/Diesel	97,686	109,760
1981	T/Gas	66,723	74,970
1981	T/Diesel	83,731	94,080
1980	T/Gas	63,234	71,050

Year	Power	Retail Low	Retail High
1980	T/Diesel	74,573	83,790
1979	T/Gas	59,746	67,130
1979	T/Diesel	69,776	78,400
1978	T/Gas	54,076	60,760
1978	T/Diesel	65,415	73,500
1977	T/Gas	47,099	52,920
1977	T/Diesel	61,054	68,600
1976	T/Gas	40,993	46,060
1976	T/Diesel	56,693	63,700
1975	T/Gas	37,505	42,140
1975	T/Diesel	52,332	58,800

Bertram 37 Convertible

Year	Power	Retail Low	Retail High
1994	450D	345,391	388,080
1994	550D	366,324	411,600
1993	375D	266,021	298,900
1993	450D	309,631	347,900
1993	550D	334,925	376,320
1992	375D	245,960	276,360
1992	450D	284,337	319,480
1992	550D	307,014	344,960
1991	375D	217,178	244,020
1991	450D	261,660	294,000
1990	375D	200,606	225,400
1990	450D	231,133	259,700
1989	375D	187,523	210,700
1989	450D	209,328	235,200
1988	375D	174,440	196,000
1988	450D	191,884	215,600
1987	375D	165,718	186,200
1987	435D	176,184	197,960
1987	450D	174,440	196,000
1986	375D	158,740	178,360
1986	435D	170,079	191,100

Bertram 38 Convertible

Year	Power	Retail Low	Retail High
1976	T/Diesel	69,340	77,910
1975	T/Diesel	62,798	70,560

Bertram 38 III Convertible

Year	Power	Retail Low	Retail High
1986	T/Diesel	163,974	184,240
1985	T/Diesel	148,710	167,090
1984	T/Diesel	140,860	158,270
1983	T/Diesel	133,883	150,430
1982	T/Diesel	123,852	139,160
1981	T/Diesel	103,792	116,620
1980	T/Diesel	96,814	108,780

Year	Power	Retail Low	Retail High
1979	T/Diesel	91,581	102,900
1978	T/Diesel	80,242	90,160

Bertram 38 Special

Year	Power	Retail Low	Retail High
1987	375D	156,996	176,400
1987	435D	175,312	196,980
1986	375D	149,146	167,580
1986	435D	122,980	138,180

Bertram 42 Convertible

Year	Power	Retail Low	Retail High
1987	T/Diesel	236,366	265,580
1986	T/Diesel	223,719	251,370
1985	T/Diesel	208,456	234,220
1984	T/Diesel	195,373	219,520
1983	T/Diesel	180,545	202,860
1982	T/Diesel	170,079	191,100
1981	T/Diesel	158,740	178,360
1980	T/Diesel	147,402	165,620
1979	T/Diesel	139,552	156,800
1978	T/Diesel	132,574	148,960
1977	T/Diesel	123,852	139,160
1976	T/Diesel	109,025	122,500

Bertram 43 Convertible

Year	Power	Retail Low	Retail High
1994	T/Diesel	462,266	519,400
1993	T/Diesel	422,145	474,320
1992	T/Diesel	409,934	460,600
1991	T/Diesel	348,880	392,000
1990	T/Diesel	322,714	362,600
1989	T/Diesel	304,398	342,020
1988	T/Diesel	289,570	325,360

Bertram 46 Convertible

Year	Power	Retail Low	Retail High
1987	T/Diesel	305,706	343,490
1986	T/Diesel	292,623	328,790
1985	T/Diesel	259,916	292,040
1984	T/Diesel	253,374	284,690
1983	T/Diesel	232,877	261,660
1982	T/Diesel	209,764	235,690
1981	T/Diesel	191,448	215,110
1980	T/Diesel	174,876	196,490
1979	T/Diesel	163,974	184,240
1978	T/Diesel	152,199	171,010
1977	T/Diesel	139,552	156,800
1976	T/Diesel	130,830	147,000
1975	T/Diesel	126,469	142,100

Bertram 46 Moppie

Year	Power	Retail Low	Retail High
1994	T/Diesel	523,320	588,000
1993	T/Diesel	505,876	568,400

Bertram 50 Convertible

Year	Power	Retail Low	Retail High
1994	735D	675,955	759,500
1994	900D	757,942	851,620
1993	735D	614,901	690,900
1992	735D		
	Galley up	584,374	656,600
	Galley down	566,930	637,000
1991	735D		
	Galley up	553,847	622,300
	Galley down	536,403	602,700
1991	840D		
	Galley up	588,735	661,500
	Galley down	571,291	641,900
1990	735D		
	Galley up	507,620	570,360
	Galley down	494,537	555,660
1990	840D		
	Galley up	540,764	607,600
	Galley down	527,681	592,900
1989	735D		
	Galley up	470,988	529,200
	Galley down	457,905	514,500
1989	840D		
	Galley up	505,876	568,400
	Galley down	492,793	553,700
1988	735D		
	Galley up	449,183	504,700
	Galley down	436,100	490,000
1987	735D	427,378	480,200

Bertram 54 Convertible

Year	Power	Retail Low	Retail High
1993	T/Diesel	885,283	994,700
1992	T/Diesel	891,824	1,002,050
1991	T/Diesel	815,943	916,790
1990	T/Diesel	732,648	823,200
1989	T/Diesel	654,150	735,000
1988	T/Diesel	566,930	637,000
1987	T/Diesel	523,320	588,000
1986	T/Diesel	462,266	519,400
1985	T/Diesel	425,634	478,240
1984	T/Diesel	401,212	450,800
1983	T/Diesel	388,129	436,100
1982	T/Diesel	364,144	409,150

Year	Power	Retail Low	Retail High
1981	T/Diesel	348,444	391,510

Bertram 58 Convertible

Year	Power	Retail Low	Retail High
1983	T/Diesel	466,627	524,300
1982	T/Diesel	439,589	493,920
1981	T/Diesel	409,498	460,110
1980	T/Diesel	357,602	401,800
1979	T/Diesel	333,616	374,850
1978	T/Diesel	309,631	347,900
1977	T/Diesel	296,548	333,200

Bertram 60 Convertible

Year	Power	Retail Low	Retail High
1994	T/Diesel	1,308,300	1,470,000
1993	T/Diesel	1,221,080	1,372,000
1992	T/Diesel	1,142,582	1,283,800
1991	T/Diesel	1,061,904	1,193,150
1990	T/Diesel	886,591	996,170

Bertram 72 Convertible

Year	Power	Retail Low	Retail High
1994	T/Diesel	*****	******
1993	T/Diesel	*****	******
1992	T/Diesel	*****	******
1991	T/Diesel	*****	******
1990	T/Diesel	*****	******

Bimini 245 Tournament

Year	Power	Retail Low	Retail High
1994	T/Gas	48,843	54,880
1993	T/Gas	45,790	51,450
1992	T/Gas	42,302	47,530
1991	T/Gas	31,399	35,280

Bimini 29

Year	Power	Retail Low	Retail High
1994	T/Gas	76,754	86,240
1994	T/Diesel	91,581	102,900
1993	T/Gas	73,265	82,320
1993	T/Diesel	85,040	95,550
1992	T/Gas	66,723	74,970
1992	T/Diesel	77,190	86,730
1991	T/Gas	61,054	68,600
1991	T/Diesel	68,032	76,440
1990	T/Gas	57,129	64,190
1990	T/Diesel	63,671	71,540
1989	T/Gas	53,640	60,270
1989	T/Diesel	59,746	67,130

Black Watch 26 SF

Year	Power	Retail Low	Retail High
1994	O/B*	47,099	52,920
1994	T/Gas	75,009	84,280
1993	O/B*	45,354	50,960

Year	Power	Retail Low	Retail High
1993	T/Gas	71,520	80,360
1992	O/B*	40,993	46,060
1992	T/Gas	68,904	77,420
1991	O/B*	37,068	41,650
1991	T/Gas	63,234	71,050
1990	O/B*	34,016	38,220
1990	T/Gas	57,129	64,190
1989	O/B*	30,091	33,810
1989	T/Gas	49,715	55,860
1988	O/B*	26,166	29,400
1988	T/Gas	42,738	48,020

Black Watch 30 SF

Year	Power	Retail Low	Retail High
1994	T/Gas	102,920	115,640
1994	T/Diesel	124,288	139,650
1993	T/Gas	91,581	102,900
1993	T/Diesel	113,386	127,400
1992	T/Gas	81,115	91,140
1992	T/Diesel	102,047	114,660
1991	T/Gas	70,648	79,380
1991	T/Diesel	94,634	106,330
1990	T/Gas	66,287	74,480
1990	T/Diesel	85,476	96,040
1989	T/Gas	57,565	64,680
1989	T/Diesel	71,520	80,360
1988	T/Gas	48,843	54,880
1988	T/Diesel	64,543	72,520
1987	T/Gas	42,738	48,020
1987	T/Diesel	60,182	67,620
1986	T/Gas	39,249	44,100
1986	T/Diesel	50,588	56,840

Black Watch 30 FB

Year	Power	Retail Low	Retail High
1994	T/Gas	129,086	145,040
1994	T/Diesel	154,379	173,460
1993	T/Gas	115,130	129,360
1993	T/Diesel	142,605	160,230
1992	T/Gas	100,303	112,700
1992	T/Diesel	112,950	126,910
1991	T/Gas	87,656	98,490
1991	T/Diesel	106,844	120,050
1990	T/Gas	80,242	90,160
1990	T/Diesel	98,559	110,740
1989	T/Gas	70,648	79,380
1989	T/Diesel	83,295	93,590

Black Watch 36 FB

Year	Power	Retail Low	Retail High
1994	T/Gas	146,530	164,640
1994	T/Diesel	183,162	205,800
1993	T/Gas	139,116	156,310
1993	T/Diesel	170,515	191,590
1992	T/Gas	127,341	143,080
1992	T/Diesel	152,635	171,500
1991	T/Gas	117,747	132,300
1991	T/Diesel	146,094	164,150

Blackfin 27 Combi

Year	Power	Retail Low	Retail High
1992	O/B*	47,099	52,920
1992	T/Gas	67,596	75,950
1991	O/B*	43,610	49,000
1991	T/Gas	60,618	68,110
1990	O/B*	37,941	42,630
1990	T/Gas	54,949	61,740
1989	O/B*	34,452	38,710
1989	T/Gas	48,407	54,390
1988	O/B*	30,963	34,790
1988	T/Gas	44,046	49,490
1987	O/B*	28,783	32,340
1987	T/Gas	42,738	48,020
1986	O/B*	25,730	28,910
1986	T/Gas	38,377	43,120
1985	O/B*	23,986	26,950
1985	T/Gas	35,760	40,180

Blackfin 27 Fisherman

Year	Power	Retail Low	Retail High
1991	O/B*	41,866	47,040
1991	T/Gas	59,310	66,640
1990	O/B*	37,505	42,140
1990	T/Gas	54,076	60,760
1989	O/B*	33,580	37,730
1989	T/Gas	47,971	53,900
1988	O/B*	30,091	33,810
1988	T/Gas	44,046	49,490
1987	O/B*	27,910	31,360
1987	T/Gas	41,430	46,550
1986	O/B*	24,858	27,930
1986	T/Gas	37,505	42,140
1985	O/B*	23,113	25,970
1985	T/Gas	34,016	38,220

Blackfin 29 Combi

Year	Power	Retail Low	Retail High
1994	T/Gas	104,664	117,600
1994	T/Diesel	127,777	143,570

Year	Power	Retail Low	Retail High
1993	T/Gas	93,849	105,448
1993	T/Diesel	114,694	128,870
1992	T/Gas	84,167	94,570
1992	T/Diesel	103,356	116,130
1991	T/Gas	75,445	84,770
1991	T/Diesel	92,889	104,370
1990	T/Gas	70,212	78,890
1990	T/Diesel	81,987	92,120
1989	T/Gas	59,310	66,640
1989	T/Diesel	74,137	83,300
1988	T/Gas	52,768	59,290
1988	T/Diesel	65,851	73,990
1987	T/Gas	49,279	55,370
1987	T/Diesel	61,054	68,600
1986	T/Gas	45,354	50,960
1986	T/Diesel	56,257	63,210
1985	T/Gas	41,430	46,550
1985	T/Diesel	52,768	59,290
1984	T/Gas	37,505	42,140
1984	T/Diesel	49,279	55,370
1983	T/Gas	35,324	39,690
1983	T/Diesel	46,227	51,940

Blackfin 29 FB SF

Year	Power	Retail Low	Retail High
1994	T/Gas	116,875	131,320
1994	T/Diesel	150,891	169,540
1993	T/Gas	105,972	119,070
1993	T/Diesel	140,860	158,270
1992	T/Gas	94,634	106,330
1992	T/Diesel	125,161	140,630
1991	T/Gas	85,040	95,550
1991	T/Diesel	113,386	127,400
1990	T/Gas	76,318	85,750
1990	T/Diesel	95,506	107,310
1989	T/Gas	67,596	75,950
1989	T/Diesel	84,603	95,060
1988	T/Gas	61,490	69,090
1988	T/Diesel	76,754	86,240
1987	T/Gas	57,129	64,190
1987	T/Diesel	71,956	80,850
1986	T/Gas	48,407	54,390
1986	T/Diesel	64,543	72,520

Blackfin 31 Combi

Year	Power	Retail Low	Retail High
1994	T/Gas	135,191	151,900
1994	T/Diesel	181,854	204,330
1993	T/Gas	131,266	147,490

Year	Power	Retail Low	Retail High
1993	T/Diesel	163,974	184,240

Blackfin 32 SF

Year	Power	Retail Low	Retail High
1991	T/Gas	105,536	118,580
1991	300D	136,935	153,860
1991	375D	156,124	175,420
1990	T/Gas	95,942	107,800
1990	300D	122,980	138,180
1990	375D	142,169	159,740
1989	T/Gas	88,092	98,980
1989	300D	110,769	124,460
1989	375D	131,702	147,980
1988	T/Gas	80,242	90,160
1988	300D	106,844	120,050
1988	375D	120,364	135,240
1987	T/Gas	74,573	83,790
1987	300D	100,303	112,700
1987	375D	112,514	126,420
1986	T/Gas	67,596	75,950
1986	300D	93,325	104,860
1986	375D	102,920	115,640
1985	T/Gas	64,107	72,030
1985	300D	87,220	98,000
1985	355D	96,814	108,780
1984	T/Gas	54,949	61,740
1984	300D	72,829	81,830
1984	355D	86,348	97,020
1983	T/Gas	51,024	57,330
1983	300D	70,648	79,380
1983	355D	77,625	87,220
1982	T/Gas	44,482	49,980
1982	300D	62,362	70,070
1981	T/Gas	41,866	47,040
1981	300D	60,182	67,620
1980	T/Gas	37,068	41,650
1980	T/Diesel	49,715	55,860

Blackfin 32 Combi

Year	Power	Retail Low	Retail High
1992	T/Gas	112,514	126,420
1992	T/Diesel	146,094	164,150
1991	T/Gas	101,175	113,680
1991	T/Diesel	131,702	147,980
1990	T/Gas	88,092	98,980
1990	T/Diesel	118,619	133,280
1989	T/Gas	80,678	90,650
1989	T/Diesel	107,717	121,030
1988	T/Gas	77,626	87,220

Year	Power	Retail Low	Retail High
1988	T/Diesel	103,792	116,620

Blackfin 33 SF

Year	Power	Retail Low	Retail High
1984	O/B*	28,346	31,850
1984	T/Gas	44,046	49,490
1984	T/Diesel	55,385	62,230
1983	O/B*	26,166	29,400
1983	T/Gas	40,557	45,570
1983	T/Diesel	50,588	56,840
1982	O/B*	23,113	25,970
1982	T/Gas	38,377	43,120
1982	T/Diesel	47,099	52,920
1981	O/B*	20,933	23,520
1981	T/Gas	35,324	39,690
1981	T/Diesel	44,046	49,490
1980	O/B*	20,061	22,540
1980	T/Gas	33,144	37,240
1980	T/Diesel	42,302	47,530
1979	O/B*	17,880	20,090
1979	T/Gas	30,527	34,300
1979	T/Diesel	37,941	42,630
1978	O/B*	16,572	18,620
1978	T/Gas	29,219	32,830
1978	T/Diesel	36,196	40,670

Blackfin 33 Combi

Year	Power	Retail Low	Retail High
1994	T/Gas	166,590	187,180
1994	T/Diesel	222,411	249,900

Blackfin 33 FB

Year	Power	Retail Low	Retail High
1994	T/Gas	156,124	175,420
1994	320D	214,561	241,080
1994	425D	237,238	266,560
1993	T/Gas	137,372	154,350
1993	320D	186,651	209,720
1993	425D	213,689	240,100
1992	T/Gas	126,469	142,100
1992	320D	172,260	193,550
1992	425D	192,320	216,090
1991	T/Gas	110,769	124,460
1991	320D	154,816	173,950
1991	425D	171,823	193,060
1990	T/Gas	92,453	103,880
1990	T/Diesel	137,372	154,350

Blackfin 38 Combi

Year	Power	Retail Low	Retail High
1994	485D	340,158	382,200
1994	550D	364,144	409,150

Year	Power	Retail Low	Retail High
1993	485D	310,503	348,880
1993	550D	320,970	360,640
1992	485D	279,540	314,090
1992	550D	290,443	326,340
1991	485D	251,194	282,240
1991	550D	264,277	296,940
1990	485D	212,381	238,630
1990	550D	225,028	252,840
1989	485D	195,373	219,520
1989	550D	205,839	231,280

Blackfin 38 Convertible

Year	Power	Retail Low	Retail High
1994	485D	346,263	389,060
1994	550D	366,324	411,600
1993	485D	324,458	364,560
1993	550D	335,797	377,300
1992	485D	293,931	330,260
1992	550D	305,270	343,000
1991	485D	266,893	299,880
1991	550D	276,051	310,170
1990	485D	227,644	255,780
1990	550D	240,291	269,990
1989	485D	197,553	221,970
1989	550D	203,223	228,340

Boston Whaler 31L

Year	Power	Retail Low	Retail High
1992	T/Gas	120,364	135,240
1992	T/Diesel	139,552	156,800
1991	T/Gas	145,221	163,170
1991	T/Diesel	125,161	140,630
1990	T/Gas	88,964	99,960
1990	T/Diesel	106,408	119,560
1989	T/Gas	73,265	82,320
1989	T/Diesel	93,325	104,860
1988	T/Gas	64,979	73,010
1988	T/Diesel	83,731	94,080

Cabo 35 FB SF

Year	Power	Retail Low	Retail High
1994	T/Diesel	244,216	274,400
1993	T/Diesel	225,028	252,840
1992	T/Diesel	232,877	261,660

Cabo 35 Express SF

Year	Power	Retail Low	Retail High
1994	T/Diesel	240,727	270,480
1993	T/Diesel	222,411	249,900

Californian 48 Convertible

Year	Power	Retail Low	Retail High
1989	T/Diesel	261,660	294,000

Year	Power	Retail Low	Retail High
1988	T/Diesel	244,216	274,400
1987	T/Diesel	220,667	247,940
1986	T/Diesel	197,117	221,480

Chase 38 SF

Year	Power	Retail Low	Retail High
1992	T/Diesel	221,975	249,410
1991	T/Diesel	207,584	233,240
1990	T/Diesel	194,064	218,050
1989	T/Diesel	180,109	202,370
1988	T/Diesel	170,515	191,590

Cheoy Lee 48 Sport Yacht

Year	Power	Retail Low	Retail High
1986	T/Diesel	230,261	258,720
1985	T/Diesel	218,922	245,980
1984	T/Diesel	210,200	236,180
1983	T/Diesel	201,042	225,890
1982	T/Diesel	186,215	209,230
1981	T/Diesel	177,929	199,920
1980	T/Diesel	169,643	190,610

Cheoy Lee 50 Sport Yacht

Year	Power	Retail Low	Retail High
1994	T/Diesel	540,764	607,600
1993	T/Diesel	505,440	567,910
1992	T/Diesel	458,777	515,480
1991	T/Diesel	420,400	472,360
1990	T/Diesel	395,979	444,920
1989	T/Diesel	369,813	415,520
1988	T/Diesel	346,700	389,550
1987	T/Diesel	331,436	372,400

Cheoy Lee 58 Sport Yacht

Year	Power	Retail Low	Retail High
1994	T/Diesel	743,987	835,940
1993	T/Diesel	697,760	784,000
1992	T/Diesel	648,045	728,140
1991	T/Diesel	609,232	684,530
1990	T/Diesel	560,825	630,140
1989	T/Diesel	494,537	555,660
1988	T/Diesel	462,702	519,890
1987	T/Diesel	444,386	499,310
1986	T/Diesel	423,889	476,280

Cheoy Lee 66 Sport Yacht

Year	Power	Retail Low	Retail High
1987	T/Diesel	687,294	772,240
1986	T/Diesel	640,195	719,320
1985	T/Diesel	604,871	679,630
1984	T/Diesel	559,080	628,180

Chris 30 Tournament SF

Year	Power	Retail Low	Retail High
1977	T/Gas	14,827	16,660
1976	T/Gas	13,519	15,190
1975	T/Gas	12,211	13,720

Chris 315 Sport Sedan

Year	Power	Retail Low	Retail High
1990	T/Gas	56,257	63,210
1990	T/Diesel	68,904	77,420
1989	T/Gas	50,588	56,840
1989	T/Diesel	64,543	72,520
1988	T/Gas	47,099	52,920
1988	T/Diesel	60,618	68,110
1987	T/Gas	46,227	51,940
1987	T/Diesel	58,437	65,660
1986	T/Gas	43,610	49,000
1986	T/Diesel	57,565	64,680
1985	T/Gas	41,430	46,550
1985	T/Diesel	52,768	59,290
1984	T/Gas	38,377	43,120
1984	T/Diesel	49,279	55,370
1983	T/Gas	35,324	39,690
1983	T/Diesel	45,354	50,960

Chris 360 Sport Sedan

Year	Power	Retail Low	Retail High
1986	T/Gas	77,626	87,220
1986	T/Diesel	101,175	113,680
1985	T/Gas	71,520	80,360
1985	T/Diesel	93,325	104,860
1984	T/Gas	68,032	76,440
1984	T/Diesel	89,400	100,450
1983	T/Gas	63,671	71,540
1983	T/Diesel	83,731	94,080
1982	T/Gas	58,001	65,170
1982	T/Diesel	80,242	90,160
1981	T/Gas	56,257	63,210
1981	T/Diesel	71,956	80,850
1980	T/Gas	51,460	57,820
1980	T/Diesel	65,851	73,990
1979	T/Gas	47,971	53,900
1979	T/Diesel	61,490	69,090
1978	T/Gas	42,738	48,020
1978	T/Diesel	54,076	60,760
1977	T/Gas	39,249	44,100
1977	T/Diesel	50,588	56,840
1976	T/Gas	35,324	39,690
1976	T/Diesel	44,046	49,490
1975	T/Gas	31,835	35,770
1975	T/Diesel	39,249	44,100

Chris 382/392 Commander

Year	Power	Retail Low	Retail High
1990	T/Gas	119,055	133,770
1990	T/Diesel	149,582	168,070
1989	T/Gas	107,281	120,540
1989	T/Diesel	136,935	153,860
1988	T/Gas	98,559	110,740
1988	T/Diesel	125,597	141,120
1987	T/Gas	93,325	104,860
1987	T/Diesel	114,258	128,380
1986	T/Gas	89,837	100,940
1986	T/Diesel	108,589	122,010
1985	T/Gas	82,423	92,610
1985	T/Diesel	102,920	115,640

Chris 422 Sport Sedan

Year	Power	Retail Low	Retail High
1990	T/Diesel	210,200	236,180
1989	T/Diesel	189,752	213,204
1988	T/Diesel	168,335	189,140
1987	T/Diesel	156,560	175,910
1986	T/Diesel	149,146	167,580
1985	T/Diesel	143,477	161,210
1984	T/Diesel	138,680	155,820
1983	T/Diesel	134,319	150,920
1982	T/Diesel	125,161	140,630
1981	T/Diesel	115,130	129,360
1980	T/Diesel	107,281	120,540
1979	T/Diesel	95,506	107,310
1978	T/Diesel	84,603	95,060
1977	T/Diesel	80,242	90,160
1976	T/Diesel	75,881	85,260
1975	T/Diesel	69,776	78,400

Chris 45 Commander SF

Year	Power	Retail Low	Retail High
1981	T/Diesel	143,041	160,720
1980	T/Diesel	128,213	144,060
1979	T/Diesel	114,694	128,870
1978	T/Diesel	107,281	120,540
1977	T/Diesel	99,867	112,210
1976	T/Diesel	93,325	104,860
1975	T/Diesel	86,784	97,510

Chris 482 Convertible

Year	Power	Retail Low	Retail High
1988	T/Diesel	259,916	292,040
1987	T/Diesel	246,833	277,340
1986	T/Diesel	234,186	263,130
1985	T/Diesel	217,614	244,510

Year	Power	Retail Low	Retail High
Contender 35			
1994	O/B*	65,415	73,500
1994	T/Diesel	113,386	127,400
1993	O/B*	61,054	68,600
1993	T/Diesel	104,664	117,600
1992	O/B*	56,693	63,700
1992	T/Diesel	95,942	107,800
1991	O/B*	53,204	59,780
1991	T/Diesel	87,220	98,000
1990	O/B*	49,715	55,860
1990	T/Diesel	81,115	91,140
1989	O/B*	47,099	52,920
1989	T/Diesel	74,137	83,300
Cruisers 3210 Sea Devil			
1990	T/Gas	51,896	58,310
1989	T/Gas	45,790	51,450
1988	T/Gas	38,377	43,120
Davis 44 SF			
1993	T/Diesel	327,075	367,500
1992	T/Diesel	300,909	338,100
1991	T/Diesel	270,382	303,800
Davis 44 Express SF			
1993	T/Diesel	318,353	357,700
1992	T/Diesel	292,187	328,300
Davis 47 Flybridge SF			
1993	T/Diesel	427,378	480,200
1992	T/Diesel	409,934	460,600
1991	T/Diesel	398,595	447,860
1990	T/Diesel	372,429	418,460
1989	T/Diesel	341,902	384,160
1988	T/Diesel	324,022	364,070
1987	T/Diesel	300,473	337,610
1986	T/Diesel	277,360	311,640
Davis 61 Flybridge SF			
1993	T/Diesel	907,088	1,019,200
1992	T/Diesel	872,200	980,000
1991	T/Diesel	819,868	921,200
1990	T/Diesel	767,536	862,400
1989	T/Diesel	723,926	813,400
1988	T/Diesel	684,677	769,300
1987	T/Diesel	645,428	725,200
Dawson 38 SF			
1994	T/Diesel	302,653	340,060
1993	T/Diesel	261,660	294,000
1992	T/Diesel	231,133	259,700
1991	T/Diesel	200,606	225,400
1990	T/Diesel	185,779	208,740
1989	T/Diesel	170,079	191,100
1988	T/Diesel	155,252	174,440
1987	T/Diesel	141,296	158,760
Delta 36 SFX			
1994	T/Diesel	199,734	224,420
1993	T/Diesel	188,395	211,680
1992	T/Diesel	165,718	186,200
1991	T/Diesel	151,763	170,520
1990	T/Diesel	134,319	150,920
1989	T/Diesel	120,364	135,240
1988	T/Diesel	108,153	121,520
1987	T/Diesel	99,431	111,720
Delta 38 SF			
1994	T/Diesel	161,793	181,790
1993	T/Diesel	153,507	172,480
1992	T/Diesel	144,349	162,190
1991	T/Diesel	133,883	150,430
1990	T/Diesel	122,108	137,200
1989	T/Diesel	113,822	127,890
1988	T/Diesel	105,536	118,580
1987	T/Diesel	95,942	107,800
1986	T/Diesel	86,348	97,020
1985	T/Diesel	77,626	87,220
1984	T/Diesel	71,956	80,850
Donzi 65 SF			
1994	T/Diesel	1,500,184	1,685,600
1993	T/Diesel	1,404,242	1,577,800
1992	T/Diesel	1,308,300	1,470,000
1991	T/Diesel	1,229,802	1,381,800
1990	T/Diesel	1,142,582	1,283,800
1989	T/Diesel	1,055,362	1,185,800
1988	T/Diesel	955,059	1,073,100
1987	T/Diesel	863,478	970,200
Dorado 30			
1994	O/B*	47,971	53,900
1994	T/IO Dsl. (S)	68,032	76,440
1994	S/T/Diesel	68,904	77,420
1993	O/B*	43,610	49,000
1993	T/IO Dsl. (S)	57,565	64,680
1993	S/T/Diesel	61,926	69,580
1992	O/B*	41,866	47,040
1992	T/IO Dsl. (S)	55,821	62,720
1992	S/T/Diesel	57,565	64,680
1991	O/B*	40,121	45,080
1991	T/IO Dsl. (S)	54,076	60,760
1991	S/T/Diesel	54,076	60,760
1990	O/B*	37,505	42,140
1990	T/IO Dsl. (S)	50,588	56,840
1990	S/T/Diesel	50,588	56,840
1989	O/B*	34,016	38,220
1989	T/IO Dsl. (S)	47,099	52,920
1989	S/T/Diesel	47,099	52,920
1988	O/B*	30,527	34,300
1988	T/IO Dsl. (S)	44,482	49,980
1988	S/T/Diesel	44,482	49,980
Dyer 29			
1994	S/T/Gas	78,498	88,200
1993	S/T/Gas	67,159	75,460
1992	S/T/Gas	60,182	67,620
1991	S/T/Gas	53,204	59,780
1990	S/T/Gas	48,843	54,880
1989	S/T/Gas	42,738	48,020
1988	S/T/Gas	38,377	43,120
1987	S/T/Gas	35,760	40,180
1986	S/T/Gas	32,271	36,260
1985	S/T/Gas	28,783	32,340
1984	S/T/Gas	25,294	28,420
1983	S/T/Gas	21,805	24,500
1982	S/T/Gas	20,933	23,520
1981	S/T/Gas	20,061	22,540
1980	S/T/Gas	19,188	21,560
1979	S/T/Gas	18,316	20,580
1978	S/T/Gas	17,444	19,600
1977	S/T/Gas	16,572	18,620
1976	S/T/Gas	15,700	17,640
1975	S/T/Gas	14,827	16,660
Egg Harbor 33 Sedan			
1981	T/Gas	46,663	52,430
1981	T/Diesel	61,490	69,090
1980	T/Gas	44,482	49,980
1980	T/Diesel	51,896	58,310
1979	T/Gas	41,430	46,550
1979	T/Diesel	48,407	54,390
1978	T/Gas	37,505	42,140
1978	T/Diesel	48,843	54,880

Year	Power	Retail Low	Retail High
1977	T/Gas	35,324	39,690
1977	T/Diesel	44,918	50,470
1976	T/Gas	31,835	35,770
1976	T/Diesel	40,993	46,060
1975	T/Gas	28,783	32,340
1975	T/Diesel	38,377	43,120

Egg Harbor 33 Convertible

Year	Power	Retail Low	Retail High
1989	T/Gas	93,325	104,860
1989	T/Diesel	118,619	133,280
1988	T/Gas	86,784	97,510
1988	T/Diesel	110,769	124,460
1987	T/Gas	80,242	90,160
1987	T/Diesel	98,995	111,230
1986	T/Gas	75,445	84,770
1986	T/Diesel	92,017	103,390
1985	T/Gas	70,648	79,380
1985	T/Diesel	86,784	97,510
1984	T/Gas	65,415	73,500
1984	T/Diesel	81,551	91,630
1983	T/Gas	59,746	67,130
1983	T/Diesel	76,754	86,240
1982	T/Gas	55,385	62,230
1982	T/Diesel	71,520	80,360

Egg Harbor 34 Golden Egg

Year	Power	Retail Low	Retail High
1994	T/Gas	161,357	181,300
1994	T/Diesel	213,689	240,100
1993	T/Gas	143,913	161,700
1993	T/Diesel	188,831	212,170
1992	T/Gas	119,928	134,750
1992	T/Diesel	157,868	177,380
1991	T/Gas	114,258	128,380
1991	T/Diesel	148,274	166,600
1990	T/Gas	109,025	122,500
1990	T/Diesel	139,552	156,800

Egg Harbor 36 Sedan

Year	Power	Retail Low	Retail High
1985	T/Gas	93,325	104,860
1985	T/Diesel	113,822	127,890
1984	T/Gas	78,062	87,710
1984	T/Diesel	100,303	112,700
1983	T/Gas	73,265	82,320
1983	T/Diesel	92,889	104,370
1982	T/Gas	66,287	74,480
1982	T/Diesel	85,040	95,550
1981	T/Gas	61,054	68,600

Year	Power	Retail Low	Retail High
1981	T/Diesel	76,754	86,240
1980	T/Gas	57,129	64,190
1980	T/Diesel	69,340	77,910
1979	T/Gas	54,076	60,760
1979	T/Diesel	65,415	73,500
1978	T/Gas	47,971	53,900
1978	T/Diesel	61,490	69,090
1977	T/Gas	40,993	46,060
1977	T/Diesel	51,024	57,330
1976	T/Gas	37,505	42,140
1976	T/Diesel	48,407	54,390

Egg Harbor 37 Convertible

Year	Power	Retail Low	Retail High
1989	T/Gas	126,469	142,100
1989	T/Diesel	171,823	193,060
1988	T/Gas	135,191	151,900
1988	T/Diesel	157,432	176,890
1987	T/Gas	113,386	127,400
1987	T/Diesel	141,732	159,250
1986	T/Gas	106,408	119,560
1986	T/Diesel	132,138	148,470
1985	T/Gas	100,303	112,700
1985	T/Diesel	125,161	140,630

Egg Harbor 38 Golden Egg

Year	Power	Retail Low	Retail High
1994	T/Gas	226,772	254,800
1994	T/Diesel	292,187	328,300
1993	T/Gas	205,839	231,280
1993	T/Diesel	249,449	280,280
1992	T/Gas	184,906	207,760
1992	T/Diesel	221,103	248,430
1991	T/Gas	180,545	202,860
1991	T/Diesel	210,636	236,670
1990	T/Gas	156,124	175,420
1990	T/Diesel	189,267	212,660

Egg Harbor 40 Sedan

Year	Power	Retail Low	Retail High
1986	T/Gas	128,650	144,550
1986	T/Diesel	162,229	182,280
1985	T/Gas	120,800	135,730
1985	T/Diesel	151,763	170,520
1984	T/Gas	105,536	118,580
1984	T/Diesel	137,808	154,840
1983	T/Gas	98,122	110,250
1983	T/Diesel	128,650	144,550
1982	T/Gas	85,040	95,550
1982	T/Diesel	114,694	128,870

Year	Power	Retail Low	Retail High
1981	T/Gas	78,062	87,710
1981	T/Diesel	104,664	117,600
1980	T/Gas	73,701	82,810
1980	T/Diesel	98,122	110,250
1979	T/Gas	68,468	76,930
1979	T/Diesel	87,220	98,000
1978	T/Gas	61,054	68,600
1978	T/Diesel	77,626	87,220
1977	T/Gas	52,768	59,290
1977	T/Diesel	66,723	74,970
1976	T/Gas	50,588	56,840
1976	T/Diesel	62,798	70,560
1975	T/Gas	48,407	54,390
1975	T/Diesel	59,310	66,640

Egg Harbor 41 SF

Year	Power	Retail Low	Retail High
1989	375D	191,884	215,600
1989	485D	208,456	234,220
1988	375D	183,162	205,800
1988	485D	197,117	221,480
1987	375D	168,335	189,140
1987	485D	179,673	201,880
1986	355D	155,688	174,930
1986	450D	169,207	190,120
1985	355D	147,402	165,620
1985	450D	160,921	180,810
1984	355D	128,213	144,060
1984	450D	136,499	153,370

Egg Harbor 42 Golden Egg

Year	Power	Retail Low	Retail High
1994	435D	331,436	372,400
1994	485D	348,880	392,000
1993	425D	304,834	342,510
1993	485D	327,075	367,500
1992	425D	288,698	324,380
1992	485D	301,345	338,590
1991	425D	273,871	307,720
1991	485D	286,082	321,440
1990	375D	244,216	274,400
1990	485D	258,171	290,080

Egg Harbor 43 SF

Year	Power	Retail Low	Retail High
1989	375D	219,358	246,470
1989	485D	236,366	265,580
1988	375D	205,403	230,790
1988	485D	218,922	245,980
1987	355D	188,395	211,680

Year	Power	Retail Low	Retail High
1987	485D	201,914	226,870
1986	355D	182,290	204,820
1986	485D	191,448	215,110

Egg Harbor 46 Sedan

Year	Power	Retail Low	Retail High
1983	T/Diesel	183,598	206,290
1982	T/Diesel	164,846	185,220
1981	T/Diesel	160,049	179,830
1980	T/Diesel	152,635	171,500
1979	T/Diesel	142,169	159,740
1978	T/Diesel	127,341	143,080
1977	T/Diesel	109,025	122,500
1976	T/Diesel	98,995	111,230
1975	T/Diesel	89,400	100,450

Egg Harbor 48 SF

Year	Power	Retail Low	Retail High
1986	540D	244,216	274,400
1986	675D	263,404	295,960
1985	500D	216,742	243,530
1985	675D	236,802	266,070
1984	500D	194,937	219,030
1984	675D	221,975	249,410
1983	T/Diesel	185,779	208,740
1982	T/Diesel	174,440	196,000
1981	T/Diesel	163,974	184,240
1980	T/Diesel	154,379	173,460
1979	T/Diesel	145,221	163,170
1978	T/Diesel	130,830	147,000

Egg Harbor 54 Convertible

Year	Power	Retail Low	Retail High
1994	735D	697,760	784,000
1994	900D	784,980	882,000
1993	735D	697,324	783,510
1993	900D	754,453	847,700
1992	735D	623,187	700,210
1992	900D	675,955	759,500
1991	735D	588,735	661,500
1991	900D	660,255	741,860
1990	735D	543,817	611,030
1990	900D	590,479	663,460
1989	735D	456,161	512,540

Egg Harbor 58 Golden Egg

Year	Power	Retail Low	Retail High
1994	900D	846,034	950,600
1994	1080D	889,644	999,600
1993	900D	811,146	911,400
1993	1080D	850,395	955,500
1992	900D	758,814	852,600

Year	Power	Retail Low	Retail High
1992	1080D	817,251	918,260
1991	900D	732,212	822,710
1991	1080D	772,333	867,790
1990	900D	673,774	757,050
1990	1080D	706,482	793,800

Egg Harbor 60 Convertible

Year	Power	Retail Low	Retail High
1990	900D	655,022	735,980
1989	1080D	693,835	779,590
1988	900D	623,623	700,700
1988	1080D	651,970	732,550
1987	870D	587,863	660,520
1987	1000D	626,240	703,640
1986	870D	539,456	606,130
1986	1000D	566,930	637,000

Gamefisherman 40

Year	Power	Retail Low	Retail High
1994	T/Diesel	353,241	396,900
1993	T/Diesel	331,436	372,400
1992	T/Diesel	313,992	352,800
1991	T/Diesel	300,909	338,100
1990	T/Diesel	287,826	323,400
1989	T/Diesel	274,743	308,700
1988	T/Diesel	261,660	294,000
1987	T/Diesel	248,577	279,300
1986	T/Diesel	235,494	264,600

Garlington 44

Year	Power	Retail Low	Retail High
1994	T/Diesel	488,432	548,800
1993	T/Diesel	457,905	514,500
1992	T/Diesel	436,100	490,000
1991	T/Diesel	392,490	441,000
1990	T/Diesel	370,685	416,500

Grady-White Sailfish 25

Year	Power	Retail Low	Retail High
1994	O/B*	40,121	45,080
1994	T/IO	50,588	56,840
1993	O/B*	36,196	40,670
1993	T/IO	44,482	49,980
1992	O/B*	31,399	35,280
1992	T/IO	40,121	45,080
1991	O/B*	27,474	30,870
1991	T/IO	35,760	40,180
1990	O/B*	23,549	26,460
1990	T/IO	32,271	36,260
1989	O/B*	21,369	24,010
1989	T/IO	28,346	31,850
1988	O/B*	19,624	22,050

Year	Power	Retail Low	Retail High
1988	T/IO	24,858	27,930
1987	O/B*	17,880	20,090
1987	T/IO	23,549	26,460
1986	O/B*	17,008	19,110
1986	T/IO	21,805	24,500
1985	O/B*	15,700	17,640
1985	T/IO	20,497	23,030
1984	O/B*	14,827	16,660
1984	T/IO	18,752	21,070
1983	O/B*	13,955	15,680
1983	T/IO	17,444	19,600
1982	O/B*	12,211	13,720
1982	T/IO	16,572	18,620
1981	O/B*	11,339	12,740
1981	T/IO	15,264	17,150
1980	O/B*	10,902	12,250
1980	T/IO	13,083	14,700

Grady-White Marlin 28

Year	Power	Retail Low	Retail High
1994	O/B*	64,543	72,520
1993	O/B*	55,821	62,720
1992	O/B*	48,843	54,880
1991	O/B*	44,046	49,490
1990	O/B*	39,685	44,590
1989	O/B*	36,196	40,670

Grand Banks 42 Sport Cruiser

Year	Power	Retail Low	Retail High
1992	135D	187,523	210,700
1992	375D	260,788	293,020
1991	135D	178,801	200,900
1991	375D	248,577	279,300
1990	135D	165,718	186,200
1990	375D	222,411	249,900
1989	135D	152,635	171,500
1989	375D	209,328	235,200
1988	375D	200,606	225,400
1987	375D	191,884	215,600
1986	375D	183,162	205,800
1985	355D	174,440	196,000
1984	210D	148,274	166,600
1984	355D	165,718	186,200
1983	210D	143,913	161,700
1982	210D	135,191	151,900
1981	210D	126,469	142,100

Hatteras 32 FB SF

Year	Power	Retail Low	Retail High
1986	T/Gas	76,318	85,750

Year	Power	Retail Low	Retail High
1986	T/Diesel	110,769	124,460
1985	T/Gas	72,393	81,340
1985	T/Diesel	108,153	121,520
1984	T/Gas	69,340	77,910
1984	T/Diesel	97,686	109,760
1983	T/Gas	66,287	74,480
1983	T/Diesel	92,889	104,370
1982	T/Gas	61,054	68,600
1982	T/Diesel	88,964	99,960

Hatteras 36 Convertible (Early)

Year	Power	Retail Low	Retail High
1977	T/Gas	50,152	56,350
1977	T/Diesel	61,490	69,090
1976	T/Gas	44,918	50,470
1976	T/Diesel	56,257	63,210
1975	T/Gas	41,866	47,040
1975	T/Diesel	51,896	58,310

Hatteras 36 Convertible

Year	Power	Retail Low	Retail High
1987	T/Gas	114,258	128,380
1987	T/Diesel	152,635	171,500
1986	T/Gas	102,484	115,150
1986	T/Diesel	137,372	154,350
1985	T/Gas	99,431	111,720
1985	T/Diesel	127,341	143,080
1984	T/Gas	94,198	105,840
1984	T/Diesel	118,619	133,280
1983	T/Gas	89,837	100,940
1983	T/Diesel	113,386	127,400

Hatteras 36 SF

Year	Power	Retail Low	Retail High
1986	T/Gas	100,739	113,190
1986	T/Diesel	129,086	145,040
1985	T/Gas	92,889	104,370
1985	T/Diesel	122,108	137,200
1984	T/Gas	87,220	98,000
1984	T/Diesel	113,822	127,890
1983	T/Gas	83,295	93,590
1983	T/Diesel	104,664	117,600

Hatteras 37 Convertible

Year	Power	Retail Low	Retail High
1983	T/Diesel	132,574	148,960
1982	T/Diesel	122,544	137,690
1981	T/Diesel	109,897	123,480
1980	T/Diesel	100,303	112,700
1979	T/Diesel	93,325	104,860
1978	T/Diesel	88,964	99,960

Year	Power	Retail Low	Retail High
1977	T/Diesel	85,040	95,550

Hatteras 38 Convertible (Early)
****

Hatteras 38 Convertible

Year	Power	Retail Low	Retail High
1993	T/Diesel	312,248	350,840
1992	T/Diesel	288,262	323,890
1991	T/Diesel	260,788	293,020
1990	T/Diesel	237,238	266,560
1989	T/Diesel	218,486	245,490
1988	T/Diesel	206,711	232,260

Hatteras 39 Convertible

Year	Power	Retail Low	Retail High
1994	465D	173,655	195,118

Hatteras 41 Convertible (Early)
****

Hatteras 41 Convertible

Year	Power	Retail Low	Retail High
1991	535D	318,353	357,700
1990	465D	278,232	312,620
1990	535D	288,698	324,380
1989	465D	246,396	276,850
1989	535D	256,427	288,120
1988	465D	220,667	247,940
1988	535D	272,999	306,740
1987	465D	205,403	230,790
1986	450D	188,395	211,680

Hatteras 42 Convertible

Year	Power	Retail Low	Retail High
1978	T/Diesel	111,642	125,440
1977	T/Diesel	101,611	114,170
1976	T/Diesel	89,837	100,940
1975	T/Diesel	79,370	89,180

Hatteras 43 Convertible (Early)

Year	Power	Retail Low	Retail High
1984	T/Diesel	193,628	217,560
1983	T/Diesel	181,854	204,330
1982	T/Diesel	167,898	188,650
1981	T/Diesel	155,252	174,440
1980	T/Diesel	143,041	160,720
1979	T/Diesel	134,755	151,410

Hatteras 43 Convertible

Year	Power	Retail Low	Retail High
1994	T/Diesel	411,678	462,560
1993	T/Diesel	371,557	417,480

Year	Power	Retail Low	Retail High
1992	T/Diesel	337,541	379,260
1991	T/Diesel	313,120	351,820

Hatteras 45 Convertible (Early)
****

Hatteras 45 Convertible

Year	Power	Retail Low	Retail High
1991	T/Diesel	374,174	420,420
1990	T/Diesel	337,541	379,260
1989	T/Diesel	296,112	332,710
1988	T/Diesel	266,021	298,900
1987	T/Diesel	246,396	276,850
1986	T/Diesel	230,261	258,720
1985	T/Diesel	215,433	242,060
1984	T/Diesel	202,786	227,850

Hatteras 46 Convertible (Early)

Year	Power	Retail Low	Retail High
1985	650D	240,727	270,480
1984	650D	234,622	263,620
1983	650D	223,283	250,880
1982	650D	204,095	229,320
1981	435D	174,440	196,000
1980	435D	165,718	186,200
1979	435D	157,868	177,380
1978	435D	148,274	166,600
1977	435D	142,169	159,740
1976	435D	136,063	152,880
1975	435D	130,830	147,000
1974	435D	126,469	142,100

Hatteras 46 Convertible

Year	Power	Retail Low	Retail High
1994	T/Diesel	619,262	695,800
1993	T/Diesel	550,358	618,380
1992	T/Diesel	492,793	553,700

Hatteras 48 Convertible

Year	Power	Retail Low	Retail High
1991	T/Diesel	444,822	499,800
1990	T/Diesel	436,972	490,980
1989	T/Diesel	406,009	456,190
1988	T/Diesel	373,302	419,440
1987	T/Diesel	348,880	392,000

Hatteras 50 Convertible (Early)
****

Year	Power	Retail Low	Retail High
Hatteras 50 Convertible			
1983	T/Diesel	272,562	306,250
1982	T/Diesel	258,607	290,570
1981	T/Diesel	231,133	259,700
1980	T/Diesel	214,997	241,570
Hatteras 50 Convertible (Current)			
1994	720D	671,594	754,600
1994	780D	710,843	798,700
1994	870D	771,897	867,300
1993	720D	641,067	720,300
1993	780D	669,850	752,640
1993	870D	715,204	803,600
1992	720D	587,863	660,520
1992	780D	610,540	686,000
1992	870D	643,684	723,240
1991	720D	549,486	617,400
1991	780D	570,419	640,920
1991	870D	600,946	675,220
Hatteras 52 Convertible			
1991	T/Diesel	523,320	588,000
1990	T/Diesel	489,304	549,780
1989	T/Diesel	462,266	519,400
1988	T/Diesel	427,378	480,200
1987	T/Diesel	375,482	421,890
1986	T/Diesel	348,880	392,000
1985	T/Diesel	322,714	362,600
1984	T/Diesel	305,270	343,000
Hatteras 53 Convertible			
1980	T/Diesel	233,314	262,150
1979	T/Diesel	220,230	247,450
1978	T/Diesel	208,020	233,730
1977	T/Diesel	189,267	212,660
1976	T/Diesel	168,335	189,140
1975	T/Diesel	141,732	159,250
Hatteras 54 Convertible			
1994	870D	889,644	999,600
1994	1040D	941,976	1,058,400
1993	870D	846,034	950,600
1993	1040D	889,644	999,600
1992	870D	769,280	864,360
1992	1040D	826,846	929,040
1991	870D	741,370	833,000
1991	1040D	784,980	882,000
Hatteras 55 Convertible			
1989	T/Diesel	631,473	709,520
1988	T/Diesel	566,930	637,000
1987	T/Diesel	530,734	596,330
1986	T/Diesel	457,469	514,010
1985	T/Diesel	433,047	486,570
1984	T/Diesel	405,573	455,700
1983	T/Diesel	382,896	430,220
1982	T/Diesel	359,782	404,250
1981	T/Diesel	299,165	336,140
1980	T/Diesel	272,999	306,740
Hatteras 58 Convertible			
1994	1040D	1,177,470	1,323,000
1994	1350D	1,330,105	1,494,500
1993	1040D	1,068,445	1,200,500
1993	1350D	1,221,080	1,372,000
1992	1040D	959,420	1,078,000
1992	1350D	1,090,250	1,225,000
1991	1040D	841,673	945,700
1991	1350D	959,420	1,078,000
1990	1040D	737,009	828,100
1990	1350D	850,395	955,500
Hatteras 60 Convertible			
1986	840D	566,058	636,020
1985	650D	497,154	558,600
1985	840D	532,914	598,780
1984	650D	460,958	517,930
1984	840D	498,898	560,560
1983	650D	443,078	497,840
1983	840D	477,093	536,060
1982	650D	418,220	469,910
1982	840D	440,025	494,410
1981	650D	363,271	408,170
1980	650D	342,775	385,140
1979	650D	327,075	367,500
1978	650D	313,992	352,800
1977	650D	300,909	338,100
Hatteras 65 Convertible			
1994	1035D	1,308,300	1,470,000
1994	1350D	1,517,628	1,705,200
1993	1035D	1,327,924	1,492,050
1993	1350D	1,417,325	1,592,500
1992	1035D	1,212,794	1,362,690
1992	1350D	1,324,000	1,487,640
1991	1035D	1,130,371	1,270,080
1991	1235D	1,225,005	1,376,410
1990	1035D	972,503	1,092,700
1990	1235D	1,063,212	1,194,620
1989	1035D	886,155	995,680
1989	1235D	978,172	1,099,070
1988	1035D	808,093	907,970
1988	1235D	904,035	1,015,770
1987	1035D	751,836	844,760
1987	1235D	833,387	936,390
Hatteras 82 Convertible			
1994	D	******	******
1993	D	******	******
1992	D	******	******
Henriques 35 Maine Coaster			
1994	T/Diesel	143,913	161,700
1993	T/Diesel	129,086	145,040
1992	T/Diesel	117,747	132,300
1991	T/Diesel	113,386	127,400
1990	T/Diesel	105,536	118,580
1989	T/Diesel	100,303	112,700
1988	T/Diesel	91,581	102,900
1987	T/Diesel	81,987	92,120
1986	T/Diesel	73,265	82,320
1985	T/Diesel	65,415	73,500
1984	T/Diesel	58,437	65,660
1983	T/Diesel	56,693	63,700
1982	T/Diesel	54,949	61,740
1981	T/Diesel	52,332	58,800
1980	T/Diesel	50,588	56,840
1979	T/Diesel	47,971	53,900
1978	T/Diesel	44,482	49,980
1977	T/Diesel	42,738	48,020
Henriques 38 SF			
1994	T/Diesel	222,411	249,900
1993	T/Diesel	200,606	225,400
1992	T/Diesel	187,523	210,700
1991	T/Diesel	178,801	200,900
1990	T/Diesel	165,718	186,200
1989	T/Diesel	156,996	176,400
1988	T/Diesel	148,274	166,600
Henriques 38 El Bravo			
1994	T/Diesel	222,411	249,900
1993	T/Diesel	204,967	230,300

Year	Power	Retail Low	Retail High
1992	T/Diesel	191,884	215,600
1991	T/Diesel	183,162	205,800

Henriques 44 SF

Year	Power	Retail Low	Retail High
1994	T/Diesel	309,631	347,900
1993	T/Diesel	283,465	318,500
1992	T/Diesel	266,021	298,900
1991	T/Diesel	235,494	264,600
1990	T/Diesel	219,794	246,960
1989	T/Diesel	209,328	235,200
1988	T/Diesel	187,523	210,700
1987	T/Diesel	161,357	181,300
1986	T/Diesel	143,913	161,700
1985	T/Diesel	130,830	147,000
1984	T/Diesel	122,108	137,200
1983	T/Diesel	113,386	127,400

Hydra-Sports 2550 WA

Year	Power	Retail Low	Retail High
1994	O/B*	42,738	48,020
1993	O/B*	39,249	44,100
1992	O/B*	37,505	42,140
1991	O/B*	32,271	36,260

Hydra-Sports 2800 SF

Year	Power	Retail Low	Retail High
1994	O/B*	74,137	83,300
1993	O/B*	66,287	74,480
1992	O/B*	59,310	66,640
1991	O/B*	51,460	57,820

Hydra-Sports 3300 SF

Year	Power	Retail Low	Retail High
1992	O/B*	66,287	74,480
1991	O/B*	58,437	65,660
1990	O/B*	51,896	58,310
1989	O/B*	46,663	52,430

Hylas 47 Convertible

Year	Power	Retail Low	Retail High
1993	T/Diesel	259,043	291,060
1992	T/Diesel	239,855	269,500
1991	T/Diesel	204,967	230,300
1990	T/Diesel	182,290	204,820

Innovator 31

Year	Power	Retail Low	Retail High
1991	T/Gas	******	******
1991	T/Diesel	******	******
1990	T/Gas	******	******
1990	T/Diesel	******	******
1989	T/Gas	******	******
1989	T/Diesel	******	******
1988	T/Gas	******	******

Year	Power	Retail Low	Retail High
1988	T/Diesel	******	******

Intrepid 30

Year	Power	Retail Low	Retail High
1994	O/B*	35,760	40,180
1993	O/B*	31,399	35,280
1992	O/B*	27,910	31,360
1991	O/B*	25,294	28,420

Intrepid 33

Year	Power	Retail Low	Retail High
1994	O/B*	78,498	88,200
1993	O/B*	71,520	80,360

Intrepid 38

Year	Power	Retail Low	Retail High
1993	T/Diesel	161,357	181,300
1992	T/Diesel	145,657	163,660
1991	T/Diesel	127,341	143,080

Island Gypsy 32 SF

Year	Power	Retail Low	Retail High
1994	S/T/Diesel	122,108	137,200
1994	T/Diesel	140,424	157,780
1993	S/T/Diesel	110,769	124,460
1993	T/Diesel	128,650	144,550
1992	S/T/Diesel	100,739	113,190
1992	T/Diesel	121,672	136,710
1991	S/T/Diesel	92,889	104,370
1991	T/Diesel	114,258	128,380
1990	S/T/Diesel	84,603	95,060
1990	T/Diesel	102,484	115,150
1989	S/T/Diesel	75,445	84,770
1989	T/Diesel	93,762	105,350
1988	S/T/Diesel	63,234	71,050
1988	T/Diesel	77,190	86,730
1987	S/T/Diesel	54,512	61,250
1987	T/Diesel	63,234	71,050

Jersey 36 Convertible SF

Year	Power	Retail Low	Retail High
1993	T/Gas	156,996	176,400
1993	T/Diesel	184,906	207,760
1992	T/Gas	143,913	161,700
1992	T/Diesel	170,079	191,100
1991	T/Gas	130,830	147,000
1991	T/Diesel	156,996	176,400
1990	T/Gas	117,747	132,300
1990	T/Diesel	143,913	161,700
1989	T/Gas	109,025	122,500
1989	T/Diesel	130,830	147,000
1988	T/Gas	100,303	112,700
1988	T/Diesel	122,108	137,200

Year	Power	Retail Low	Retail High
1987	T/Gas	91,581	102,900
1987	T/Diesel	113,386	127,400
1986	T/Gas	82,859	93,100
1986	T/Diesel	104,664	117,600

Jersey 40 Dawn Convertible

Year	Power	Retail Low	Retail High
1988	T/Diesel	163,101	183,260
1987	T/Diesel	143,913	161,700
1986	T/Diesel	134,319	150,920
1985	T/Diesel	119,491	134,260
1984	T/Diesel	109,025	122,500
1983	T/Diesel	100,739	113,190
1982	T/Diesel	91,581	102,900
1981	T/Diesel	84,603	95,060
1980	T/Diesel	77,626	87,220
1979	T/Diesel	71,520	80,360
1978	T/Diesel	66,287	74,480
1977	T/Diesel	61,054	68,600
1976	T/Diesel	57,129	64,190
1975	T/Diesel	53,640	60,270

Jersey Devil 44 SF

Year	Power	Retail Low	Retail High
1985	T/Diesel	146,530	164,640
1984	T/Diesel	138,244	155,330
1983	T/Diesel	125,161	140,630
1982	T/Diesel	117,747	132,300
1981	T/Diesel	105,100	118,090
1980	T/Diesel	94,634	106,330

Jersey 44 Convertible SF

Year	Power	Retail Low	Retail High
1993	T/Diesel	322,714	362,600
1992	T/Diesel	300,909	338,100
1991	T/Diesel	274,743	308,700
1990	T/Diesel	244,216	274,400
1989	T/Diesel	218,050	245,000

Jersey 47 Convertible

Year	Power	Retail Low	Retail High
1993	T/Diesel	331,436	372,400
1992	T/Diesel	308,759	346,920
1991	T/Diesel	292,187	328,300
1990	T/Diesel	279,104	313,600
1898	T/Diesel	266,021	298,900
1988	T/Diesel	251,194	282,240
1987	T/Diesel	226,772	254,800

Luhrs 250 Open

Year	Power	Retail Low	Retail High
1994	S/T/Gas	50,588	56,840
1994	T/Gas	58,437	65,660

Year	Power	Retail Low	Retail High
1994	S/T/Diesel	61,926	69,580
1994	T/Diesel	65,415	73,500
1993	S/T/Gas	47,971	53,900
1993	T/Gas	55,821	62,720
1993	S/T/Diesel	58,437	65,660
1993	T/Diesel	61,926	69,580

Luhrs 290 (Early)

Year	Power	Retail Low	Retail High
1988	T/Gas	35,760	40,180
1987	T/Gas	34,452	38,710
1986	T/Gas	30,527	34,300

Luhrs 290

Year	Power	Retail Low	Retail High
1991	T/Gas	41,866	47,040
1990	T/Gas	38,813	43,610
1989	T/Gas	35,760	40,180

Luhrs 290 Open

Year	Power	Retail Low	Retail High
1994	T/Gas	78,498	88,200
1994	T/Diesel	95,942	107,800
1993	T/Gas	69,776	78,400
1993	T/Diesel	87,220	98,000
1992	T/Gas	61,054	68,600
1992	T/Diesel	78,498	88,200

Luhrs Alura 30

Year	Power	Retail Low	Retail High
1990	S/T/Gas	32,271	36,260
1989	S/T/Gas	28,346	31,850
1988	S/T/Gas	25,730	28,910
1987	S/T/Gas	21,805	24,500

Luhrs 300 SF

Year	Power	Retail Low	Retail High
1994	T/Gas	75,881	85,260
1994	T/Diesel	95,942	107,800
1993	T/Gas	71,084	79,870
1993	T/Diesel	89,837	100,940
1992	T/Gas	64,979	73,010
1992	T/Diesel	81,987	92,120
1991	T/Gas	48,843	54,880
1991	T/Diesel	60,618	68,110

Luhrs 320

Year	Power	Retail Low	Retail High
1994	T/Gas	95,070	106,820
1994	T/Diesel	132,574	148,960
1993	T/Gas	83,731	94,080
1993	T/Diesel	116,439	130,830
1992	T/Gas	75,445	84,770
1992	T/Diesel	101,175	113,680
1991	T/Gas	68,032	76,440
1991	T/Diesel	87,220	98,000
1990	T/Gas	52,332	58,800
1990	T/Diesel	72,393	81,340
1989	T/Gas	47,971	53,900
1989	T/Diesel	62,798	70,560
1988	T/Gas	42,302	47,530
1988	T/Diesel	55,385	62,230

Luhrs 320 Open

Year	Power	Retail Low	Retail High
1994	T/Gas	97,686	109,760
1994	T/Diesel	142,169	159,740

Luhrs 340 SF

Year	Power	Retail Low	Retail High
1987	T/Gas	52,768	59,290
1987	T/Diesel	62,798	70,560
1986	T/Gas	47,535	53,410
1986	T/Diesel	56,693	63,700
1985	T/Gas	44,918	50,470
1985	T/Diesel	52,332	58,800
1984	T/Gas	42,302	47,530
1984	T/Diesel	48,843	54,880
1983	T/Gas	36,632	41,160
1983	T/Diesel	45,354	50,960

Luhrs 342

Year	Power	Retail Low	Retail High
1989	T/Gas	60,182	67,620
1989	T/Diesel	72,829	81,830
1988	T/Gas	57,129	64,190
1988	T/Diesel	68,032	76,440
1987	T/Gas	52,332	58,800
1987	T/Diesel	63,671	71,540
1986	T/Gas	47,535	53,410
1986	T/Diesel	54,949	61,740

Luhrs Alura 35

Year	Power	Retail Low	Retail High
1989	T/Gas	55,821	62,720
1989	T/Diesel	69,776	78,400
1988	T/Gas	52,332	58,800
1988	T/Diesel	63,671	71,540

Luhrs 350

Year	Power	Retail Low	Retail High
1994	T/Gas	125,597	141,120
1994	T/Diesel	163,101	183,260
1993	T/Gas	110,769	124,460
1993	T/Diesel	151,327	170,030
1992	T/Gas	101,175	113,680
1992	T/Diesel	135,191	151,900
1991	T/Gas	92,889	104,370
1991	T/Diesel	123,416	138,670
1990	T/Gas	82,859	93,100
1990	T/Diesel	112,514	126,420

Luhrs 380

Year	Power	Retail Low	Retail High
1994	T/Diesel	257,299	289,100
1993	T/Diesel	234,622	263,620
1992	T/Diesel	208,456	234,220
1991	T/Diesel	188,831	212,170
1990	T/Diesel	171,387	192,570
1989	T/Diesel	156,996	176,400

Luhrs 380 Open

Year	Power	Retail Low	Retail High
1994	T/Diesel	257,299	289,100
1993	T/Diesel	234,622	263,620
1992	T/Diesel	209,328	235,200
1991	T/Diesel	186,651	209,720

Luhrs 400

Year	Power	Retail Low	Retail High
1990	T/Gas	127,341	143,080
1990	T/Diesel	152,635	171,500
1989	T/Gas	111,206	124,950
1989	T/Diesel	140,424	157,780
1988	T/Gas	102,047	114,660
1988	T/Diesel	130,830	147,000
1987	T/Gas	95,506	107,310
1987	T/Diesel	122,544	137,690

Mako 263 Walkaround

Year	Power	Retail Low	Retail High
1994	O/B*	34,016	38,220
1993	O/B*	26,166	29,400

Mako 286 Inboard

Year	Power	Retail Low	Retail High
1994	T/Gas	80,242	90,160
1993	T/Gas	74,137	83,300
1992	T/Gas	64,543	72,520
1991	T/Gas	55,821	62,720
1990	T/Gas	47,099	52,920
1989	T/Gas	43,174	48,510
1988	T/Gas	39,685	44,590
1987	T/Gas	35,760	40,180
1986	T/Gas	31,835	35,770
1985	T/Gas	29,219	32,830

Mako 295 Dual Console

Year	Power	Retail Low	Retail High
1994	O/B*	48,843	54,880
1993	O/B*	43,610	49,000

Marlin 35 Sportfish

Year	Power	Retail Low	Retail High
1994	O/B* (w/engines)	69,776	78,400

Year	Power	Retail Low	Retail High
1993	O/B* (w/engines)	61,054	68,600
Matthews 46 SF			
1975	T/Diesel	82,859	93,100
Matthews 56 SF			
1975	T/Diesel	131,702	147,980
Mediterranean 38 Convertible			
1994	T/Diesel	191,884	215,600
1993	T/Diesel	170,079	191,100
1992	T/Diesel	159,613	179,340
1991	T/Diesel	147,838	166,110
1990	T/Diesel	135,191	151,900
1989	T/Diesel	125,161	140,630
1988	T/Diesel	119,055	133,770
1987	T/Diesel	112,078	125,930
1986	T/Diesel	106,408	119,560
1985	T/Diesel	102,920	115,640
Mikelson 50 Sedan SF			
1994	T/Diesel	468,371	526,260
1993	T/Diesel	446,130	501,270
1992	T/Diesel	414,295	465,500
1991	T/Diesel	363,707	408,660
1990	T/Diesel	337,105	378,770
Mikelson 60 Sportfisher			
1994	T/Diesel	651,970	732,550
1993	T/Diesel	610,540	686,000
1992	T/Diesel	536,403	602,700
North Coast 31 SF			
1990	T/Gas	61,054	68,600
1990	T/Diesel	101,611	114,170
1989	T/Gas	56,693	63,700
1989	T/Diesel	94,198	105,840
1988	T/Gas	52,332	58,800
1988	T/Diesel	82,859	93,100
Ocean 29 SS			
1992	T/Gas	97,250	109,270
1992	T/Diesel	112,078	125,930
1991	T/Gas	85,476	96,040
1991	T/Diesel	100,739	113,190
1990	T/Gas	78,498	88,200
1990	T/Diesel	88,092	98,980
Ocean 32 SS			
1992	T/Gas	113,386	127,400
1992	T/Diesel	135,627	152,390
1991	T/Gas	102,920	115,640
1991	T/Diesel	122,544	137,690
1990	T/Gas	95,070	106,820
1990	T/Diesel	111,206	124,950
1989	T/Gas	86,348	97,020
1989	T/Diesel	99,431	111,720
Ocean 35 SS			
1994	T/Diesel	196,245	220,500
1993	T/Diesel	174,440	196,000
1992	T/Gas	136,063	152,880
1992	T/Diesel	160,049	179,830
1991	T/Gas	122,980	138,180
1991	T/Diesel	146,966	165,130
1990	T/Gas	112,514	126,420
1990	T/Diesel	132,138	148,470
1989	T/Gas	104,664	117,600
1989	T/Diesel	122,544	137,690
1988	T/Gas	98,122	110,250
1988	T/Diesel	116,439	130,830
Ocean 35 Sport Cruiser SF			
1993	T/Diesel	155,252	174,440
1992	T/Gas	124,725	140,140
1992	T/Diesel	143,041	160,720
1991	T/Gas	105,972	119,070
1991	T/Diesel	128,213	144,060
1990	T/Gas	100,303	112,700
1990	T/Diesel	122,108	137,200
Ocean 38 SS (Early)			
1991	T/Diesel	170,079	191,100
1990	T/Gas	125,597	141,120
1990	T/Diesel	161,357	181,300
1989	T/Gas	118,183	132,790
1989	T/Diesel	150,018	168,560
1988	T/Gas	109,897	123,480
1988	T/Diesel	141,296	158,760
1987	T/Gas	102,920	115,640
1987	T/Diesel	134,319	150,920
1986	T/Gas	95,506	107,310
1986	T/Diesel	121,236	136,220
1985	T/Gas	87,220	98,000
1985	T/Diesel	116,003	130,340
1984	T/Gas	78,498	88,200
1984	T/Diesel	106,408	119,560
Ocean 38 SS			
1994	T/Diesel	270,382	303,800
1993	T/Diesel	247,705	278,320
1992	T/Diesel	226,772	254,800
Ocean 40 SS			
1980	T/Diesel	91,581	102,900
1979	T/Diesel	82,859	93,100
1978	T/Diesel	77,190	86,730
1977	T/Diesel	69,776	78,400
Ocean 42 SS (Early)			
1983	T/Diesel	125,597	141,120
1982	T/Diesel	117,311	131,810
1981	T/Diesel	107,281	120,540
1980	T/Diesel	100,303	112,700
Ocean 42 SS			
1994	435D	305,270	343,000
1994	485D	322,714	362,600
1993	425D	287,826	323,400
1993	485D	301,781	339,080
1992	425D	266,021	298,900
1992	485D	277,360	311,640
1991	425D	241,163	270,970
1991	485D	252,938	284,200
Ocean 44 SS			
1991	T/Diesel	257,299	289,100
1990	T/Diesel	246,833	277,340
1989	T/Diesel	227,644	255,780
1988	T/Diesel	211,945	238,140
1987	T/Diesel	199,734	224,420
1986	T/Diesel	186,215	209,230
1985	T/Diesel	171,823	193,060
Ocean 46 SS			
1985	T/Diesel	176,184	197,960
1984	T/Diesel	166,590	187,180
1983	T/Diesel	157,868	177,380
Ocean 48 SS (Early)			
1990	T/Diesel	287,826	323,400
1989	T/Diesel	266,021	298,900
1988	T/Diesel	247,705	278,320
1987	T/Diesel	226,772	254,800

Year	Power	Retail Low	Retail High
1986	T/Diesel	204,967	230,300

Ocean 48 SS

Year	Power	Retail Low	Retail High
1994	550D	418,656	470,400
1994	735D	444,822	499,800
1993	T/Diesel	375,046	421,400
1992	T/Diesel	336,669	378,280
1991	T/Diesel	306,142	343,980

Ocean 50 SS

Year	Power	Retail Low	Retail High
1985	T/Diesel	229,389	257,740
1984	T/Diesel	209,328	235,200
1983	T/Diesel	191,884	215,600
1982	T/Diesel	174,440	196,000

Ocean 53 SS

Year	Power	Retail Low	Retail High
1994	760D	584,374	656,600
1994	820D	601,818	676,200
1993	760D	536,403	602,700
1993	820D	553,847	622,300
1992	735D	493,229	554,190
1992	820D	508,056	570,850
1991	735D	449,183	504,700
1991	820D	462,266	519,400

Ocean 55 SS

Year	Power	Retail Low	Retail High
1990	T/Diesel	436,100	490,000
1989	T/Diesel	388,129	436,100
1988	T/Diesel	340,158	382,200
1987	T/Diesel	313,992	352,800
1986	T/Diesel	296,548	333,200
1985	T/Diesel	279,104	313,600
1984	T/Diesel	266,021	298,900
1983	T/Diesel	252,938	284,200
1982	T/Diesel	241,599	271,460
1981	T/Diesel	226,772	254,800

Ocean 58 SS

Year	Power	Retail Low	Retail High
1994	1080 DD	819,868	921,200
1994	1100 MAN	872,200	980,000
1993	1080 DD	737,009	828,100
1993	1100 MAN	784,980	882,000
1992	1050 MAN	706,482	793,800
1992	1080 DD	662,872	744,800
1991	1050 MAN	662,872	744,800
1991	1080 DD	623,623	700,700
1990	1050 MAN	610,540	686,000
1990	1080 DD	593,096	666,400

Ocean 63 SS

Year	Power	Retail Low	Retail High
1991	1050DD	789,341	886,900
1991	1050MAN	815,507	916,300
1990	1050DD	741,370	833,000
1990	1050MAN	767,536	862,400
1989	1050DD	693,399	779,100
1989	1050MAN	719,565	808,500
1988	1050DD	636,706	715,400
1987	1050DD	571,291	641,900
1986	1050DD	523,320	588,000

Ocean 66 SS

Year	Power	Retail Low	Retail High
1994	1080DD	1,072,806	1,205,400
1994	1100MAN	1,125,138	1,264,200
1993	1040DD	994,308	1,117,200
1993	1100MAN	1,046,640	1,176,000

Ocean Master 31 CC

Year	Power	Retail Low	Retail High
1994	O/B*	42,738	48,020
1993	O/B*	39,249	44,100
1992	O/B*	35,760	40,180
1991	O/B*	33,144	37,240
1990	O/B*	31,399	35,280
1989	O/B*	29,655	33,320
1988	O/B*	27,910	31,360
1987	O/B*	27,038	30,380
1986	O/B*	26,166	29,400
1985	O/B*	25,294	28,420
1984	O/B*	24,422	27,440
1983	O/B*	23,549	26,460
1982	O/B*	22,677	25,480
1981	O/B*	21,805	24,500
1980	O/B*	20,933	23,520
1979	O/B*	20,061	22,540
1978	O/B*	19,188	21,560
1977	O/B*	18,316	20,580
1976	O/B*	17,444	19,600
1975	O/B*	16,572	18,620

Orca 36

Year	Power	Retail Low	Retail High
1994	T/Diesel	******	******
1993	T/Diesel	******	******
1992	T/Diesel	******	******
1991	T/Diesel	******	******
1990	T/Diesel	******	******

Pace 36 SF

Year	Power	Retail Low	Retail High
1992	T/Gas	113,386	127,400

Year	Power	Retail Low	Retail High
1992	T/Diesel	130,830	147,000
1991	T/Gas	104,664	117,600
1991	T/Diesel	122,108	137,200
1990	T/Gas	96,814	108,780
1990	T/Diesel	115,130	129,360
1989	T/Gas	87,220	98,000
1989	T/Diesel	106,408	119,560
1988	T/Gas	78,498	88,200
1988	T/Diesel	98,559	110,740

Pace 40 SF

Year	Power	Retail Low	Retail High
1992	T/Diesel	167,462	188,160
1991	T/Diesel	156,996	176,400
1990	T/Diesel	147,402	165,620
1989	T/Diesel	139,552	156,800
1988	T/Diesel	130,830	147,000

Pace 48 SF

Year	Power	Retail Low	Retail High
1992	T/Diesel	272,126	305,760
1991	T/Diesel	252,938	284,200
1990	T/Diesel	229,389	257,740
1989	T/Diesel	209,328	235,200
1988	T/Diesel	192,756	216,580
1987	T/Diesel	171,823	193,060

Pacemaker 30 SF

Year	Power	Retail Low	Retail High
1980	T/Gas	25,730	28,910
1979	T/Gas	21,805	24,500
1978	T/Gas	19,624	22,050
1977	T/Gas	18,316	20,580
1976	T/Gas	17,008	19,110
1975	T/Gas	15,700	17,640

Pacemaker 34 Convertible

Year	Power	Retail Low	Retail High
1992	T/Gas	113,386	127,400
1992	T/Diesel	136,063	152,880
1991	T/Gas	99,431	111,720
1991	T/Diesel	119,491	134,260
1990	T/Gas	91,581	102,900
1990	T/Diesel	104,664	117,600
1989	T/Gas	82,859	93,100
1989	T/Diesel	98,995	111,230
1988	T/Gas	73,265	82,320
1988	T/Diesel	91,581	102,900

Pacemaker 36 SF

Year	Power	Retail Low	Retail High
1980	T/Gas	52,332	58,800
1980	T/Diesel	59,310	66,640

Year	Power	Retail Low	Retail High
1979	T/Gas	47,099	52,920
1979	T/Diesel	54,949	61,740
1978	T/Gas	41,866	47,040
1977	T/Gas	35,760	40,180
1976	T/Gas	30,527	34,300
1975	T/Gas	27,038	30,380

Pacemaker 37 SF

Year	Power	Retail Low	Retail High
1992	T/Gas	139,552	156,800
1992	T/Diesel	185,342	208,250
1991	T/Gas	125,161	140,630
1991	T/Diesel	154,379	173,460
1990	T/Gas	113,386	127,400
1990	T/Diesel	140,424	157,780

Pacemaker 38 SF

Year	Power	Retail Low	Retail High
1980	T/Gas	64,107	72,030
1980	T/Diesel	81,115	91,140
1979	T/Gas	57,565	64,680
1979	T/Diesel	74,137	83,300

Pacemaker 40 SF

Year	Power	Retail Low	Retail High
1979	T/Gas	63,671	71,540
1979	T/Diesel	77,626	87,220
1978	T/Gas	54,076	60,760
1978	T/Diesel	66,287	74,480
1977	T/Gas	45,354	50,960
1977	T/Diesel	54,949	61,740
1976	T/Gas	34,888	39,200
1976	T/Diesel	46,227	51,940
1975	T/Gas	31,399	35,280
1975	T/Diesel	38,377	43,120

Pacemaker 48 SF

Year	Power	Retail Low	Retail High
1980	T/Diesel	137,808	154,840
1979	T/Diesel	129,086	145,040
1978	T/Diesel	119,491	134,260
1977	T/Diesel	109,025	122,500
1976	T/Diesel	92,453	103,880
1975	T/Diesel	76,754	86,240

Pacifica 36 SF

Year	Power	Retail Low	Retail High
1992	300D	188,395	211,680
1992	375D	198,862	223,440
1991	300D	175,748	197,470
1991	375D	190,140	213,640
1990	300D	159,176	178,850
1990	375D	172,260	193,550

Year	Power	Retail Low	Retail High
1989	300D	147,838	166,110
1989	375D	162,229	182,280
1988	300D	91,145	102,410
1988	375D	145,221	163,170
1987	300D	124,725	140,140
1987	375D	134,755	151,410
1986	300D	114,258	128,380
1986	355D	123,416	138,670
1985	300D	105,972	119,070
1985	355D	115,566	129,850
1984	T/Diesel	102,047	114,660
1983	T/Diesel	92,453	103,880
1982	T/Diesel	86,348	97,020
1981	T/Diesel	80,678	90,650
1980	T/Diesel	70,212	78,890
1979	T/Diesel	64,979	73,010
1978	T/Diesel	59,746	67,130
1977	T/Diesel	56,693	63,700
1976	T/Diesel	53,640	60,270
1975	T/Diesel	51,024	57,330

Pacifica 44 SF

Year	Power	Retail Low	Retail High
1994	485D	423,017	475,300
1994	550D	453,544	509,600
1993	485D	389,001	437,080
1993	550D	404,701	454,720
1992	485D	361,963	406,700
1992	550D	370,685	416,500
1991	485D	332,308	373,380
1991	550D	339,286	381,220
1990	485D	300,909	338,100
1990	550D	309,631	347,900
1989	485D	280,848	315,560
1989	550D	293,931	330,260
1988	485D	263,404	295,960
1988	550D	278,232	312,620
1987	485D	248,141	278,810
1987	550D	263,404	295,960
1986	450D	232,005	260,680
1986	535D	245,960	276,360
1985	450D	217,614	244,510
1985	535D	228,516	256,760
1984	450D	203,223	228,340
1984	535D	213,689	240,100
1983	450D	188,395	211,680
1983	535D	196,245	220,500
1982	T/Diesel	180,109	202,370

Year	Power	Retail Low	Retail High
1981	T/Diesel	168,335	189,140
1980	T/Diesel	146,530	164,640
1979	T/Diesel	137,372	154,350
1978	T/Diesel	130,830	147,000
1977	T/Diesel	122,980	138,180
1976	T/Diesel	116,003	130,340
1975	T/Diesel	111,642	125,440

Pearson 38 Convertible

Year	Power	Retail Low	Retail High
1991	T/Diesel	165,718	186,200
1990	T/Diesel	148,274	166,600
1989	T/Diesel	130,830	147,000
1988	T/Diesel	122,108	137,200
1987	T/Diesel	113,386	127,400

Performer 32

Year	Power	Retail Low	Retail High
1994	T/Diesel	130,830	147,000
1993	T/Diesel	122,108	137,200
1992	T/Diesel	112,514	126,420
1991	T/Diesel	100,303	112,700
1990	T/Diesel	89,837	100,940
1989	T/Diesel	78,498	88,200
1988	T/Diesel	68,904	77,420
1987	T/Diesel	60,182	67,620

Phoenix 27 Weekender

Year	Power	Retail Low	Retail High
1994	O/B*	47,971	53,900
1994	T/Gas	76,754	86,240
1994	T/Diesel	94,198	105,840
1993	O/B*	44,482	49,980
1993	T/Gas	69,340	77,910
1993	T/Diesel	84,603	95,060
1992	O/B*	40,993	46,060
1992	T/Gas	62,798	70,560
1992	T/Diesel	76,754	86,240
1991	O/B*	34,016	38,220
1991	T/Gas	57,565	64,680
1991	T/Diesel	67,159	75,460
1990	O/B*	29,655	33,320
1990	T/Gas	50,588	56,840
1990	T/Diesel	62,362	70,070
1989	O/B*	26,166	29,400
1989	T/Gas	45,354	50,960
1989	T/Diesel	56,693	63,700
1988	O/B*	24,422	27,440
1988	T/Gas	40,557	45,570
1988	T/Diesel	52,332	58,800

Year	Power	Retail Low	Retail High
1987	O/B*	23,113	25,970
1987	T/Gas	37,505	42,140
1987	T/Diesel	49,715	55,860
1986	O/B*	21,805	24,500
1986	T/Gas	34,888	39,200
1986	T/Diesel	46,663	52,430
1985	O/B*	20,061	22,540
1985	T/Gas	33,144	37,240
1985	T/Diesel	43,610	49,000
1984	O/B*	18,316	20,580
1984	T/Gas	30,527	34,300
1984	T/Diesel	40,993	46,060
1983	O/B*	16,572	18,620
1983	T/Gas	27,910	31,360
1983	T/Diesel	37,505	42,140
1982	O/B*	14,827	16,660
1982	T/Gas	26,166	29,400
1982	T/Diesel	34,016	38,220
1981	O/B*	13,083	14,700
1981	T/Gas	23,986	26,950
1981	T/Diesel	28,783	32,340
1980	O/B*	12,211	13,720
1980	T/Gas	21,805	24,500
1980	T/Diesel	27,474	30,870
1979	O/B*	11,339	12,740
1979	T/Gas	20,933	23,520
1979	T/Diesel	25,730	28,910

Phoenix 27 Tournament

Year	Power	Retail Low	Retail High
1994	T/Gas	84,603	95,060
1994	T/Diesel	109,897	123,480
1993	T/Gas	75,445	84,770
1993	T/Diesel	95,942	107,800
1992	T/Gas	71,520	80,360
1992	T/Diesel	88,092	98,980
1991	T/Gas	61,926	69,580
1991	T/Diesel	77,190	86,730
1990	T/Gas	51,896	58,310
1990	T/Diesel	67,159	75,460

Phoenix 29 Convertible

Year	Power	Retail Low	Retail High
1987	T/Gas	44,918	50,470
1987	T/Diesel	57,565	64,680
1986	T/Gas	42,738	48,020
1986	T/Diesel	52,332	58,800
1985	T/Gas	40,121	45,080
1985	T/Diesel	48,407	54,390

Year	Power	Retail Low	Retail High
1984	T/Gas	37,505	42,140
1984	T/Diesel	45,790	51,450
1983	T/Gas	34,016	38,220
1983	T/Diesel	40,993	46,060
1982	T/Gas	30,527	34,300
1982	T/Diesel	37,941	42,630
1981	T/Gas	28,346	31,850
1981	T/Diesel	34,888	39,200
1980	T/Gas	26,166	29,400
1980	T/Diesel	32,271	36,260
1979	T/Gas	23,549	26,460
1979	T/Diesel	29,655	33,320
1978	T/Gas	21,805	24,500
1978	T/Diesel	28,346	31,850
1977	T/Gas	20,061	22,540
1977	T/Diesel	26,166	29,400

Phoenix 29 SF Convertible

Year	Power	Retail Low	Retail High
1994	T/Gas	107,281	120,540
1994	T/Diesel	119,491	134,260
1993	T/Gas	92,017	103,390
1993	T/Diesel	106,844	120,050
1992	T/Gas	81,551	91,630
1992	T/Diesel	95,942	107,800
1991	T/Gas	69,340	77,910
1991	T/Diesel	86,348	97,020
1990	T/Gas	60,618	68,110
1990	T/Diesel	78,498	88,200
1989	T/Gas	55,821	62,720
1989	T/Diesel	70,648	79,380
1988	T/Gas	47,971	53,900
1988	T/Diesel	58,437	65,660

Phoenix 33 Convertible

Year	Power	Retail Low	Retail High
1994	T/Gas	171,823	193,060
1994	T/Diesel	218,922	245,980
1993	T/Gas	160,485	180,320
1993	T/Diesel	206,275	231,770
1992	T/Gas	136,063	152,880
1992	T/Diesel	184,906	207,760
1991	T/Gas	122,108	137,200
1991	T/Diesel	166,590	187,180
1990	T/Gas	112,950	126,910
1990	T/Diesel	158,740	178,360
1989	T/Gas	94,198	105,840
1989	T/Diesel	132,574	148,960
1988	T/Gas	83,295	93,590

Year	Power	Retail Low	Retail High
1988	T/Diesel	119,491	134,260
1987	T/Gas	76,754	86,240
1987	T/Diesel	109,025	122,500

Phoenix 33 Tournament

Year	Power	Retail Low	Retail High
1994	T/Gas	177,057	198,940
1994	T/Diesel	215,433	242,060
1993	T/Gas	161,357	181,300
1993	T/Diesel	204,095	229,320
1992	T/Gas	145,221	163,170
1992	T/Diesel	187,523	210,700
1991	T/Gas	115,130	129,360
1991	T/Diesel	165,718	186,200
1990	T/Gas	105,536	118,580
1990	T/Diesel	154,379	173,460

Phoenix 37 SF Convertible

Year	Power	Retail Low	Retail High
1994	375D	299,165	336,140
1994	485D	318,353	357,700
1993	375D	274,743	308,700
1993	485D	293,931	330,260
1992	375D	246,833	277,340
1992	485D	265,149	297,920
1991	375D	219,794	246,960
1991	485D	226,772	254,800
1990	375D	196,681	220,990
1990	485D	217,614	244,510
1989	375D	167,898	188,650
1989	485D	179,673	201,880

Phoenix 38 Convertible

Year	Power	Retail Low	Retail High
1988	375D	147,838	166,110
1988	485D	160,485	180,320
1987	375D	139,552	156,800
1987	450D	150,018	168,560
1986	375D	133,447	149,940
1986	450D	137,372	154,350
1985	355D	125,161	140,630
1985	410D	129,086	145,040
1984	355D	113,386	127,400
1984	410D	122,108	137,200
1983	300D	108,153	121,520
1983	410D	116,003	130,340
1982	300D	97,686	109,760
1982	410D	110,769	124,460

Post 42 SF

Year	Power	Retail Low	Retail High
1983	310D	129,086	145,040

Year	Power	Retail Low	Retail High
1983	450D	150,891	169,540
1982	310D	126,469	142,100
1982	450D	144,785	162,680
1981	310D	126,469	142,100
1981	410D	136,935	153,860
1980	310D	116,003	130,340
1980	410D	128,213	144,060
1979	T/Diesel	111,642	125,440
1978	T/Diesel	104,664	117,600
1977	T/Diesel	96,814	108,780
1976	T/Diesel	88,092	98,980
1975	T/Diesel	83,731	94,080

Post 43 SF

Year	Power	Retail Low	Retail High
1989	T/Diesel	241,599	271,460
1988	T/Diesel	218,050	245,000
1987	T/Diesel	206,711	232,260
1986	T/Diesel	187,523	210,700
1985	T/Diesel	170,079	191,100
1984	T/Diesel	161,357	181,300

Post 44 SF

Year	Power	Retail Low	Retail High
1994	T/Diesel	389,873	438,060
1993	T/Diesel	335,797	377,300
1992	T/Diesel	305,270	343,000
1991	T/Diesel	279,104	313,600
1990	T/Diesel	257,299	289,100

Post 46 SF

Year	Power	Retail Low	Retail High
1994	T/Diesel	457,905	514,500
1993	T/Diesel	383,768	431,200
1992	T/Diesel	340,158	382,200
1991	T/Diesel	318,353	357,700
1990	T/Diesel	295,676	332,220
1989	T/Diesel	272,126	305,760
1988	T/Diesel	252,066	283,220
1987	T/Diesel	222,411	249,900
1986	T/Diesel	197,117	221,480
1985	T/Diesel	190,140	213,640
1984	T/Diesel	183,162	205,800
1983	T/Diesel	176,184	197,960
1982	T/Diesel	168,335	189,140
1981	T/Diesel	159,613	179,340
1980	T/Diesel	150,891	169,540
1979	T/Diesel	140,424	157,780
1978	T/Diesel	130,830	147,000
1977	T/Diesel	126,469	142,100

Year	Power	Retail Low	Retail High
1976	T/Diesel	122,108	137,200
1975	T/Diesel	117,747	132,300

Post 50 SF

Year	Power	Retail Low	Retail High
1994	T/Diesel	575,652	646,800
1993	T/Diesel	523,320	588,000
1992	T/Diesel	479,710	539,000
1991	T/Diesel	440,461	494,900
1990	T/Diesel	401,212	450,800
1989	T/Diesel	361,963	406,700

Precision 2800

Year	Power	Retail Low	Retail High
1994	T/Diesel	87,220	98,000
1993	T/Diesel	79,370	89,180
1992	T/Diesel	70,648	79,380

Pro-Line 2550 Mid-Cabin

Year	Power	Retail Low	Retail High
1994	O/B*	40,121	45,080
1994	T/IO T/Gas	44,482	49,980
1993	O/B*	34,888	39,200
1993	T/IO T/Gas	40,993	46,060
1992	O/B*	29,655	33,320
1992	T/IO T/Gas	36,632	41,160
1991	O/B*	25,294	28,420
1991	T/IO T/Gas	31,399	35,280

Pro-Line 2700 Sportsman

Year	Power	Retail Low	Retail High
1994	O/B*	40,993	46,060
1993	O/B*	32,271	36,260

Pro-Line 2950 Mid-Cabin

Year	Power	Retail Low	Retail High
1994	O/B*	57,565	64,680
1994	T/IO T/Gas	65,415	73,500
1993	O/B*	47,971	53,900
1993	T/IO T/Gas	55,821	62,720
1992	O/B*	38,377	43,120
1992	T/IO T/Gas	46,227	51,940

Radovich 34 SF

Year	Power	Retail Low	Retail High
1994	T/Gas	******	******
1994	T/Diesel	******	******
1993	T/Gas	******	******
1993	T/Diesel	******	******
1992	T/Gas	******	******
1992	T/Diesel	******	******
1991	T/Gas	******	******
1991	T/Diesel	******	******
1990	T/Gas	******	******
1990	T/Diesel	******	******

Year	Power	Retail Low	Retail High
1989	T/Gas	******	******
1989	T/Diesel	******	******
1988	T/Gas	******	******
1988	T/Diesel	******	******

Rampage 24 Express

Year	Power	Retail Low	Retail High
1990	O/B*	19,624	22,050
1990	T/Gas	28,346	31,850
1989	O/B*	18,316	20,580
1989	T/Gas	26,166	29,400
1988	T/Gas	24,422	27,440
1987	T/Gas	22,241	24,990
1986	T/Gas	20,497	23,030
1985	T/Gas	19,624	22,050
1984	T/Gas	18,316	20,580

Rampage 28 Sportsman

Year	Power	Retail Low	Retail High
1994	T/Gas	78,498	88,200
1994	T/Diesel	98,559	110,740
1993	T/Gas	72,393	81,340
1993	T/Diesel	89,837	100,940
1992	T/Gas	64,107	72,030
1992	T/Diesel	80,242	90,160
1991	T/Gas	59,310	66,640
1991	T/Diesel	73,265	82,320
1990	T/Gas	50,588	56,840
1990	T/Diesel	62,362	70,070
1989	T/Gas	47,971	53,900
1988	T/Gas	42,302	47,530
1987	T/Gas	40,121	45,080
1986	T/Gas	36,632	41,160

Rampage 31 SF

Year	Power	Retail Low	Retail High
1994	T/Gas	104,664	117,600
1994	T/Diesel	129,958	146,020
1993	T/Gas	96,814	108,780
1993	T/Diesel	123,416	138,670
1992	T/Gas	88,092	98,980
1992	T/Diesel	108,589	122,010
1991	T/Gas	82,859	93,100
1991	T/Diesel	99,431	111,720
1990	T/Gas	70,648	79,380
1990	T/Diesel	91,581	102,900
1989	T/Gas	61,054	68,600
1989	T/Diesel	85,476	96,040
1988	T/Gas	49,715	55,860
1988	T/Diesel	80,678	90,650

Year	Power	Retail Low	Retail High
1987	T/Gas	46,227	51,940
1987	T/Diesel	66,723	74,970
1986	T/Gas	44,046	49,490
1986	T/Diesel	60,618	68,110
1985	T/Gas	42,302	47,530
1985	T/Diesel	53,204	59,780

Rampage 33 SF

Year	Power	Retail Low	Retail High
1994	T/Gas	126,469	142,100
1994	T/Diesel	157,868	177,380
1993	T/Gas	121,236	136,220
1993	T/Diesel	148,274	166,600
1992	T/Gas	112,950	126,910
1992	T/Diesel	135,191	151,900
1991	T/Gas	106,844	120,050
1991	T/Diesel	126,905	142,590
1990	T/Gas	101,611	114,170
1990	T/Diesel	120,800	135,730

Rampage 36 SF

Year	Power	Retail Low	Retail High
1994	T/Diesel	218,050	245,000
1993	T/Diesel	206,711	232,260
1992	T/Diesel	189,267	212,660
1991	T/Diesel	172,696	194,040
1990	T/Diesel	160,485	180,320
1989	T/Diesel	148,274	166,600

Rampage 40 SF

Year	Power	Retail Low	Retail High
1990	T/Diesel	208,456	234,220
1989	T/Diesel	184,034	206,780
1988	T/Diesel	156,996	176,400

Ronin 38 Convertible

Year	Power	Retail Low	Retail High
1992	T/Diesel	191,884	215,600
1991	T/Diesel	183,162	205,800
1990	T/Diesel	171,823	193,060
1989	T/Diesel	163,974	184,240
1988	T/Diesel	148,274	166,600
1987	T/Diesel	139,552	156,800
1986	T/Diesel	129,958	146,020

Ronin 48 Convertible

Year	Power	Retail Low	Retail High
1992	T/Diesel	326,203	366,520
1991	T/Diesel	311,375	349,860
1990	T/Diesel	294,804	331,240
1989	T/Diesel	279,104	313,600
1988	T/Diesel	258,171	290,080
1987	T/Diesel	231,133	259,700

Rybo Runner 30 CC

Year	Power	Retail Low	Retail High
1989	Seadrive	43,610	49,000
1989	T/Gas	61,054	68,600
1988	Seadrive	41,866	47,040
1988	T/Gas	56,693	63,700
1987	Seadrive	40,121	45,080
1987	T/Gas	53,204	59,780
1986	Seadrive	37,068	41,650
1986	T/Gas	46,663	52,430
1985	Seadrive	34,016	38,220
1985	T/Gas	42,738	48,020
1984	Seadrive	30,527	34,300
1984	T/Gas	39,249	44,100
1983	Seadrive	27,038	30,380
1983	T/Gas	36,632	41,160

Sea Ray 270 Amberjack

Year	Power	Retail Low	Retail High
1990	175 T/IO	32,271	36,260
1990	260 T/IO	37,068	41,650
1989	175 T/IO	30,527	34,300
1989	260 T/IO	34,016	38,220
1988	175 T/IO	27,474	30,870
1988	260 T/IO	30,963	34,790
1987	175 T/IO	24,422	27,440
1987	260 T/IO	26,602	29,890
1986	175 T/IO	22,241	24,990
1986	260 T/IO	24,858	27,930

Sea Ray Laguna 29 WA

Year	Power	Retail Low	Retail High
1993	T/Gas	67,159	75,460

Sea Ray 310 Amberjack

Year	Power	Retail Low	Retail High
1994	T/Gas	82,859	93,100
1994	T/Diesel	125,597	141,120
1993	T/Gas	77,626	87,220
1993	T/Diesel	116,003	130,340
1992	T/Gas	69,340	77,910
1992	T/Diesel	102,047	114,660
1991	T/Gas	61,926	69,580
1991	T/Diesel	90,709	101,920

Sea Ray 310 Sport Bridge

Year	Power	Retail Low	Retail High
1993	T/Gas	87,220	98,000
1993	T/Diesel	113,386	127,400
1992	T/Gas	78,498	88,200
1992	T/Diesel	104,664	117,600

Sea Ray 390 Sedan SF

Year	Power	Retail Low	Retail High
1986	T/Gas	81,115	91,140

Year	Power	Retail Low	Retail High
1986	T/Diesel	104,664	117,600
1985	T/Gas	77,626	87,220
1985	T/Diesel	100,303	112,700
1984	T/Gas	73,265	82,320
1984	T/Diesel	87,220	98,000
1983	T/Gas	68,032	76,440
1983	T/Diesel	87,656	98,490

Sea Ray 440 Convertible

Year	Power	Retail Low	Retail High
1991	T/Diesel	200,606	225,400
1990	T/Diesel	182,290	204,820
1989	T/Diesel	160,485	180,320
1988	T/Diesel	148,274	166,600

Sea Ray 460 Convertible

Year	Power	Retail Low	Retail High
1988	375D	194,501	218,540
1988	550D	218,050	245,000
1987	375D	175,312	196,980
1987	550D	195,373	219,520

Shamrock 31 Grand Slam

Year	Power	Retail Low	Retail High
1994	T/Gas	90,709	101,920
1994	T/Diesel	117,747	132,300
1993	T/Gas	85,476	96,040
1993	T/Diesel	109,025	122,500
1992	T/Gas	82,859	93,100
1992	T/Diesel	95,942	107,800
1991	T/Gas	75,009	84,280
1991	T/Diesel	88,092	98,980
1990	T/Gas	69,776	78,400
1990	T/Diesel	81,987	92,120
1989	T/Gas	66,723	74,970
1989	T/Diesel	78,062	87,710
1988	T/Gas	62,798	70,560
1988	T/Diesel	73,701	82,810
1987	T/Gas	58,437	65,660
1987	T/Diesel	67,159	75,460

Silverton 31 Convertible (Early)

Year	Power	Retail Low	Retail High
1987	T/Gas	40,557	45,570
1986	T/Gas	37,941	42,630
1985	T/Gas	35,324	39,690
1984	T/Gas	33,580	37,730
1983	T/Gas	31,835	35,770
1982	T/Gas	29,219	32,830
1981	T/Gas	27,474	30,870
1980	T/Gas	24,858	27,930

Year	Power	Retail Low	Retail High
1979	T/Gas	23,113	25,970
1978	T/Gas	21,805	24,500
1977	T/Gas	20,933	23,520

Silverton 37 Convertible

Year	Power	Retail Low	Retail High
1994	T/Gas	130,830	147,000
1994	T/Diesel	165,718	186,200
1993	T/Gas	125,597	141,120
1993	T/Diesel	156,996	176,400
1992	T/Gas	115,130	129,360
1992	T/Diesel	146,530	164,640
1991	T/Gas	98,559	110,740
1991	T/Diesel	133,010	149,450
1990	T/Gas	88,964	99,960
1990	T/Diesel	115,130	129,360

Silverton 41 Convertible

Year	Power	Retail Low	Retail High
1994	T/Gas	174,440	196,000
1994	T/Diesel	216,306	243,040
1993	T/Gas	161,357	181,300
1993	T/Diesel	200,606	225,400
1992	T/Gas	147,402	165,620
1992	T/Diesel	184,906	207,760
1991	T/Gas	135,191	151,900
1991	T/Diesel	165,718	186,200

Southern Cross 44 SF

Year	Power	Retail Low	Retail High
1990	T/Diesel	244,216	274,400
1989	T/Diesel	235,494	264,600
1988	T/Diesel	226,772	254,800
1987	T/Diesel	209,328	235,200

Southern Cross 52 SF

Year	Power	Retail Low	Retail High
1990	T/Diesel	361,963	406,700
1989	T/Diesel	340,158	382,200
1988	T/Diesel	318,353	357,700
1987	T/Diesel	300,909	338,100
1986	T/Diesel	283,465	318,500

Stamas 288 Liberty

Year	Power	Retail Low	Retail High
1994	T/IO T/Gas	64,543	72,520
1993	O/B*	46,227	51,940
1993	T/IO T/Gas	56,693	63,700
1992	O/B*	40,121	45,080
1992	T/IO T/Gas	50,152	56,350
1991	O/B*	36,632	41,160
1991	T/IO T/Gas	46,663	52,430
1990	O/B*	33,144	37,240

Year	Power	Retail Low	Retail High
1990	T/IO T/Gas	43,174	48,510
1989	O/B*	32,271	36,260
1989	T/IO T/Gas	40,557	45,570
1988	O/B*	29,655	33,320
1988	T/IO T/Gas	37,941	42,630
1987	O/B*	26,166	29,400
1987	T/IO T/Gas	36,196	40,670

Stamas 290 Express

Year	Power	Retail Low	Retail High
1994	O/B*	56,693	63,700
1993	O/B*	48,843	54,880
1992	O/B*	40,993	46,060

Stamas 310 Express

Year	Power	Retail Low	Retail High
1994	O/B*	73,265	82,320
1994	T/Gas	78,498	88,200
1993	O/B*	66,287	74,480
1993	T/Gas	70,648	79,380

Stamas 32 FB SF

Year	Power	Retail Low	Retail High
1987	T/Gas	58,437	65,660
1986	T/Gas	54,949	61,740
1985	T/Gas	49,279	55,370
1984	T/Gas	47,971	53,900
1983	T/Gas	44,046	49,490
1982	T/Gas	40,993	46,060
1981	T/Gas	37,505	42,140
1980	T/Gas	32,271	36,260
1979	T/Gas	28,346	31,850
1978	T/Gas	26,602	29,890
1977	T/Gas	22,677	25,480

Stamas 360 Express

Year	Power	Retail Low	Retail High
1994	T/Gas	143,913	161,700
1994	T/Diesel	171,823	193,060
1993	T/Gas	125,597	141,120
1993	T/Diesel	152,635	171,500
1992	T/Gas	107,281	120,540
1992	T/Diesel	137,808	154,840

Strike 29 SF

Year	Power	Retail Low	Retail High
1989	T/Gas	56,693	63,700
1989	T/Diesel	65,415	73,500
1988	T/Gas	52,332	58,800
1988	T/Diesel	59,310	66,640
1987	T/Gas	49,715	55,860
1987	T/Diesel	55,821	62,720
1986	T/Gas	43,610	49,000

Year	Power	Retail Low	Retail High
1986	T/Diesel	50,588	56,840
1985	T/Gas	36,632	41,160
1985	T/Diesel	44,482	49,980

Striker 34 Canyon Runner

Year	Power	Retail Low	Retail High
1975	T/Diesel	40,121	45,080

Striker 37 Canyon Runner

Year	Power	Retail Low	Retail High
1990	T/Diesel	209,328	235,200
1989	T/Diesel	196,245	220,500
1988	T/Diesel	178,801	200,900

Striker 41 SF

Year	Power	Retail Low	Retail High
1983	T/Diesel	165,718	186,200
1982	T/Diesel	156,996	176,400
1981	T/Diesel	148,274	166,600

Striker 44 SF

Year	Power	Retail Low	Retail High
1975	T/Diesel	113,386	127,400

Striker 50 SF

Year	Power	Retail Low	Retail High
1989	T/Diesel	479,710	539,000
1988	T/Diesel	443,078	497,840
1987	T/Diesel	414,295	465,500

Striker 54 SF

Year	Power	Retail Low	Retail High
1975	T/Diesel	209,328	235,200

Striker 58/60 SF

Year	Power	Retail Low	Retail High
1990	T/Diesel	784,980	882,000
1989	T/Diesel	719,565	808,500
1988	T/Diesel	662,872	744,800

Striker 62 SF

Year	Power	Retail Low	Retail High
1990	T/Diesel	1,046,640	1,176,000
1989	T/Diesel	981,225	1,102,500
1988	T/Diesel	911,449	1,024,100
1987	T/Diesel	841,673	945,700
1986	T/Diesel	767,536	862,400

Striker 70 SF

Year	Power	Retail Low	Retail High
1989	T/Diesel	1,443,491	1,621,900
1988	T/Diesel	1,360,632	1,528,800
1987	T/Diesel	1,278,645	1,436,680
1986	T/Diesel	1,207,997	1,357,300
1985	T/Diesel	1,125,138	1,264,200
1984	T/Diesel	1,046,640	1,176,000
1983	T/Diesel	976,864	1,097,600

Pursuit 2600 Cuddy Cabin

Year	Power	Retail Low	Retail High
1988	O/B*	16,572	18,620

Year	Power	Retail Low	Retail High
1988	1/O (S)	24,422	27,440
1987	O/B*	14,827	16,660
1987	1/O (S)	22,677	25,480
1986	O/B*	13,083	14,700
1986	1/O (S)	20,933	23,520

Pursuit 2655 Express

Year	Power	Retail Low	Retail High
1994	O/B*	39,249	44,100
1994	1/O (S)	50,588	56,840
1993	O/B*	34,888	39,200
1993	1/O (S)	46,227	51,940
1992	O/B*	29,219	32,830
1992	1/O (S)	40,993	46,060
1991	O/B*	26,166	29,400
1991	1/O (S)	37,505	42,140
1990	O/B*	23,549	26,460
1990	1/O (S)	32,271	36,260
1989	O/B*	21,369	24,010
1989	1/O (S)	29,219	32,830

Pursuit 2655 CC

Year	Power	Retail Low	Retail High
1994	O/B*	36,632	41,160
1993	O/B*	33,144	37,240
1992	O/B*	29,655	33,320

Tiara 2700 Open

Year	Power	Retail Low	Retail High
1993	T/Gas	67,159	75,460
1992	T/Gas	58,437	65,660
1991	T/Gas	51,896	58,310
1990	T/Gas	48,843	54,880
1989	T/Gas	44,918	50,470
1988	T/Gas	42,302	47,530
1987	T/Gas	39,249	44,100
1986	T/Gas	37,068	41,650
1985	T/Gas	34,888	39,200
1984	T/Gas	32,708	36,750
1983	T/Gas	29,655	33,320
1982	T/Gas	27,038	30,380

Pursuit 2800 Open

Year	Power	Retail Low	Retail High
1992	O/B*	35,760	40,180
1991	O/B*	31,399	35,280
1990	O/B*	27,910	31,360
1989	O/B*	24,422	27,440

Pursuit 2855 Express

Year	Power	Retail Low	Retail High
1994	O/B*	55,821	62,720
1993	O/B*	48,843	54,880

Tiara 2900 Open

Year	Power	Retail Low	Retail High
1994	T/Gas	82,859	93,100
1993	T/Gas	75,881	85,260

Tiara 3100 Convertible

Year	Power	Retail Low	Retail High
1992	T/Gas	96,814	108,780
1991	T/Gas	88,528	99,470
1990	T/Gas	82,859	93,100
1989	T/Gas	75,009	84,280
1988	T/Gas	71,520	80,360
1987	T/Gas	68,904	77,420
1986	T/Gas	62,362	70,070
1985	T/Gas	59,746	67,130
1984	T/Gas	55,821	62,720
1983	T/Gas	51,896	58,310
1982	T/Gas	47,535	53,410

Tiara 3100 Open (Early)

Year	Power	Retail Low	Retail High
1992	T/Gas	90,273	101,430
1992	T/Diesel	107,717	121,030
1991	T/Gas	78,498	88,200
1991	T/Diesel	101,175	113,680
1990	T/Gas	72,829	81,830
1990	T/Diesel	94,198	105,840
1989	T/Gas	67,159	75,460
1989	T/Diesel	85,476	96,040
1988	T/Gas	61,490	69,090
1988	T/Diesel	76,318	85,750
1987	T/Gas	60,182	67,620
1987	T/Diesel	70,648	79,380
1986	T/Gas	54,512	61,250
1986	T/Diesel	65,415	73,500
1985	T/Gas	50,588	56,840
1985	T/Diesel	60,618	68,110
1984	T/Gas	48,843	54,880
1984	T/Diesel	52,332	58,800
1983	T/Gas	38,377	43,120
1983	T/Diesel	43,610	49,000
1982	T/Gas	35,760	40,180
1981	T/Gas	31,835	35,770
1980	T/Gas	27,910	31,360
1979	T/Gas	26,166	29,400

Tiara 3100 Open

Year	Power	Retail Low	Retail High
1994	T/Gas	107,281	120,540
1994	T/Diesel	137,808	154,840
1993	T/Gas	95,942	107,800
1993	T/Diesel	126,469	142,100
1992	T/Gas	86,348	97,020
1992	T/Diesel	104,664	117,600

Pursuit 3250

Year	Power	Retail Low	Retail High
1993	T/Gas	112,514	126,420
1993	T/Diesel	142,169	159,740
1992	T/Gas	105,536	118,580
1992	T/Diesel	125,597	141,120
1991	T/Gas	93,325	104,860
1991	T/Diesel	113,386	127,400
1990	T/Gas	83,731	94,080
1990	T/Diesel	104,664	117,600

Tiara 3300 FB

Year	Power	Retail Low	Retail High
1992	T/Gas	113,386	127,400
1992	T/Diesel	130,830	147,000
1991	T/Gas	102,484	115,150
1991	T/Diesel	122,108	137,200
1990	T/Gas	88,092	98,980
1990	T/Diesel	112,950	126,910
1989	T/Gas	81,987	92,120
1989	T/Diesel	106,408	119,560
1988	T/Gas	75,009	84,280
1988	T/Diesel	98,995	111,230
1987	T/Gas	71,956	80,850
1987	T/Diesel	95,070	106,820
1986	T/Gas	68,468	76,930
1986	T/Diesel	90,709	101,920

Tiara 3300 Open

Year	Power	Retail Low	Retail High
1994	T/Gas	117,747	132,300
1994	T/Diesel	153,507	172,480
1993	T/Gas	109,461	122,990
1993	T/Diesel	142,169	159,740
1992	T/Gas	102,047	114,660
1992	T/Diesel	128,213	144,060
1991	T/Gas	92,889	104,370
1991	T/Diesel	116,875	131,320
1990	T/Gas	85,912	96,530
1990	T/Diesel	109,025	122,500
1989	T/Gas	79,806	89,670
1989	T/Diesel	101,611	114,170
1988	T/Gas	72,829	81,830
1988	T/Diesel	89,837	100,940

Tiara 3600 Open

Year	Power	Retail Low	Retail High
1994	T/Gas	158,740	178,360

Year	Power	Retail Low	Retail High
1994	T/Diesel	213,689	240,100
1993	T/Gas	158,304	177,870
1993	T/Diesel	200,606	225,400
1992	T/Gas	136,063	152,880
1992	T/Diesel	180,109	202,370
1991	T/Gas	124,725	140,140
1991	T/Diesel	164,846	185,220
1990	T/Gas	114,694	128,870
1990	T/Diesel	154,379	173,460
1989	T/Gas	105,536	118,580
1989	T/Diesel	142,169	159,740
1988	T/Gas	97,686	109,760
1988	T/Diesel	129,958	146,020
1987	T/Gas	91,581	102,900
1987	T/Diesel	114,258	128,380
1986	T/Gas	85,912	96,530
1986	T/Diesel	114,258	128,380
1985	T/Gas	80,678	90,650
1985	T/Diesel	104,664	117,600

Tiara 3600 Convertible

Year	Power	Retail Low	Retail High
1994	T/Gas	179,673	201,880
1994	T/Diesel	232,877	261,660
1993	T/Gas	173,568	195,020
1993	T/Diesel	220,230	247,450
1992	T/Gas	148,710	167,090
1992	T/Diesel	193,628	217,560
1991	T/Gas	135,191	151,900
1991	T/Diesel	177,057	198,940
1990	T/Gas	124,725	140,140
1990	T/Diesel	164,410	184,730
1989	T/Gas	115,130	129,360
1989	T/Diesel	153,507	172,480
1988	T/Gas	105,972	119,070
1988	T/Diesel	140,424	157,780
1987	T/Gas	100,303	112,700
1987	T/Diesel	133,447	149,940

Tiara 4300 Convertible

Year	Power	Retail Low	Retail High
1994	T/Diesel	423,017	475,300
1993	T/Diesel	377,663	424,340
1992	T/Diesel	335,797	377,300
1991	T/Diesel	303,526	341,040
1990	T/Diesel	283,465	318,500

Tiara 4300 Open

Year	Power	Retail Low	Retail High
1994	T/Diesel	348,880	392,000

Year	Power	Retail Low	Retail High
1993	T/Diesel	333,180	374,360
1992	T/Diesel	320,097	359,660
1991	T/Diesel	297,420	334,180

Tollycraft 40 Sport Sedan

Year	Power	Retail Low	Retail High
1993	T/Gas	226,772	254,800
1993	T/Diesel	267,765	300,860
1992	T/Gas	211,508	237,650
1992	T/Diesel	245,088	275,380
1991	T/Gas	178,801	200,900
1991	T/Diesel	217,614	244,510
1990	T/Gas	167,462	188,160
1990	T/Diesel	206,275	231,770
1989	T/Gas	154,379	173,460
1989	T/Diesel	190,140	213,640
1988	T/Gas	131,702	147,980
1988	T/Diesel	168,335	189,140
1987	T/Gas	125,161	140,630
1987	T/Diesel	156,996	176,400

Tollycraft 48 Convertible

Year	Power	Retail Low	Retail High
1985	300D	205,839	231,280
1985	550D	233,750	262,640
1984	300D	192,756	216,580
1984	550D	226,336	254,310
1983	300D	184,470	207,270
1983	550D	213,689	240,100
1982	300D	169,207	190,120
1982	550D	202,350	227,360

Topaz 29 SF

Year	Power	Retail Low	Retail High
1988	T/Gas	43,610	49,000
1988	T/Diesel	53,204	59,780
1987	T/Gas	40,993	46,060
1987	T/Diesel	48,407	54,390
1986	T/Gas	39,249	44,100
1986	T/Diesel	45,790	51,450
1985	T/Gas	35,324	39,690
1985	T/Diesel	41,866	47,040
1984	T/Gas	32,271	36,260
1984	T/Diesel	39,685	44,590
1983	T/Gas	30,527	34,300
1983	T/Diesel	37,941	42,630

Topaz 32 SF

Year	Power	Retail Low	Retail High
1991	T/Diesel	127,341	143,080
1990	T/Diesel	115,566	129,850
1989	T/Diesel	109,025	122,500

Year	Power	Retail Low	Retail High
1988	T/Diesel	100,303	112,700
1987	T/Diesel	92,889	104,370
1986	T/Diesel	88,092	98,980

Topaz 32 Royale

Year	Power	Retail Low	Retail High
1991	T/Diesel	131,702	147,980
1990	T/Diesel	116,003	130,340

Topaz 36 SF

Year	Power	Retail Low	Retail High
1985	T/Diesel	92,453	103,880
1984	T/Diesel	88,092	98,980
1983	T/Diesel	82,859	93,100
1982	T/Diesel	75,881	85,260
1981	T/Diesel	67,159	75,460
1980	T/Diesel	60,182	67,620

Topaz 37 SF

Year	Power	Retail Low	Retail High
1991	T/Diesel	171,823	193,060
1990	T/Diesel	163,101	183,260
1989	T/Diesel	153,507	172,480
1988	T/Diesel	144,785	162,680
1987	T/Diesel	135,191	151,900
1986	T/Diesel	126,469	142,100

Topaz 38 FB SF

Year	Power	Retail Low	Retail High
1987	T/Diesel	143,913	161,700
1986	T/Diesel	136,935	153,860
1985	T/Diesel	126,469	142,100

Topaz 39 Royale

Year	Power	Retail Low	Retail High
1991	T/Diesel	208,456	234,220
1990	T/Diesel	185,779	208,740
1989	T/Diesel	176,184	197,960
1988	T/Diesel	165,718	186,200

Topaz 44 FB SF

Year	Power	Retail Low	Retail High
1989	T/Diesel	239,855	269,500
1988	T/Diesel	209,328	235,200
1987	T/Diesel	187,523	210,700

Trojan 12 Meter Convertible

Year	Power	Retail Low	Retail High
1992	T/Gas	178,801	200,900
1992	T/Diesel	218,050	245,000
1991	T/Gas	161,357	181,300
1991	T/Diesel	205,839	231,280
1990	T/Gas	154,379	173,460
1990	T/Diesel	191,884	215,600
1989	T/Gas	139,552	156,800
1989	T/Diesel	171,387	192,570

Year	Power	Retail Low	Retail High
1988	T/Gas	132,574	148,960
1988	T/Diesel	159,613	179,340
1987	T/Gas	120,800	135,730
1987	T/Diesel	146,966	165,130
1986	T/Gas	111,206	124,950
1986	T/Diesel	134,319	150,920

Trojan 44 Convertible
Year	Power	Retail Low	Retail High
1978	T/Diesel	103,792	116,620
1977	T/Diesel	95,942	107,800
1976	T/Diesel	87,220	98,000
1975	T/Diesel	82,859	93,100

Trojan 14 Meter Convertible
Year	Power	Retail Low	Retail High
1992	485D	366,324	411,600
1992	735D	418,656	470,400
1991	485D	338,414	380,240
1991	735D	392,490	441,000
1990	485D	313,992	352,800
1990	735D	357,602	401,800
1989	485D	279,104	313,600
1989	735D	318,353	357,700
1988	450D	252,938	284,200
1988	735D	296,548	333,200

Uniflite 28 Salty Dog
Year	Power	Retail Low	Retail High
1984	T/Gas	31,399	35,280
1983	T/Gas	29,655	33,320
1982	T/Gas	26,166	29,400
1981	S/T/Gas	20,061	22,540
1981	T/Gas	24,858	27,930
1980	S/T/Gas	17,880	20,090
1980	T/Gas	21,369	24,010
1979	S/T/Gas	15,700	17,640
1979	T/Gas	18,752	21,070
1978	S/T/Gas	13,955	15,680
1978	T/Gas	17,444	19,600
1977	S/T/Gas	13,083	14,700
1977	T/Gas	16,136	18,130
1976	S/T/Gas	12,211	13,720
1976	T/Gas	14,827	16,660
1975	S/T/Gas	11,339	12,740
1975	T/Gas	13,519	15,190

Uniflite 34 Sport Sedan
Year	Power	Retail Low	Retail High
1984	T/Gas	61,926	69,580
1984	T/Diesel	73,265	82,320
1983	T/Gas	57,129	64,190
1983	T/Diesel	71,520	80,360
1982	T/Gas	54,949	61,740
1982	T/Diesel	67,596	75,950
1981	T/Gas	51,024	57,330
1981	T/Diesel	61,490	69,090
1980	T/Gas	47,099	52,920
1980	T/Diesel	55,821	62,720
1979	T/Gas	40,121	45,080
1979	T/Diesel	51,460	57,820
1978	T/Gas	35,760	40,180
1978	T/Diesel	47,099	52,920
1977	T/Gas	32,271	36,260
1977	T/Diesel	41,866	47,040
1976	T/Gas	30,527	34,300
1976	T/Diesel	38,377	43,120
1975	T/Gas	27,474	30,870
1975	T/Diesel	35,760	40,180

Uniflite 36 Sport Sedan
Year	Power	Retail Low	Retail High
1984	T/Gas	72,393	81,340
1984	T/Diesel	85,476	96,040
1983	T/Gas	68,468	76,930
1983	T/Diesel	81,987	92,120
1982	T/Gas	65,415	73,500
1982	T/Diesel	76,754	86,240
1981	T/Gas	59,746	67,130
1981	T/Diesel	72,829	81,830
1980	T/Gas	54,512	61,250
1980	T/Diesel	63,671	71,540
1979	T/Gas	47,099	52,920
1979	T/Diesel	56,693	63,700
1978	T/Gas	44,482	49,980
1978	T/Diesel	51,896	58,310
1977	T/Gas	40,557	45,570
1977	T/Diesel	47,099	52,920
1976	T/Gas	35,760	40,180
1976	T/Diesel	42,738	48,020
1975	T/Gas	36,196	40,670
1975	T/Diesel	39,249	44,100

Uniflite 38 Convertible
Year	Power	Retail Low	Retail High
1984	T/Diesel	120,364	135,240
1983	T/Diesel	111,206	124,950
1982	T/Diesel	103,792	116,620
1981	T/Diesel	98,122	110,250
1980	T/Diesel	90,709	101,920
1979	T/Diesel	82,423	92,610
1978	T/Diesel	78,498	88,200
1977	T/Diesel	72,393	81,340

Uniflite 42 Convertible
Year	Power	Retail Low	Retail High
1984	T/Diesel	148,274	166,600
1983	T/Diesel	139,116	156,310
1982	T/Diesel	132,138	148,470
1981	T/Diesel	121,236	136,220
1980	T/Diesel	107,717	121,030
1979	T/Diesel	98,995	111,230
1978	T/Diesel	90,709	101,920
1977	T/Diesel	85,476	96,040
1976	T/Diesel	80,242	90,160
1975	T/Diesel	75,009	84,280

Uniflite 48 Convertible
Year	Power	Retail Low	Retail High
1984	T/Diesel	213,689	240,100
1983	T/Diesel	204,967	230,300
1982	T/Diesel	191,884	215,600
1981	T/Diesel	180,545	202,860
1980	T/Diesel	171,823	193,060

Viking 35 Convertible
Year	Power	Retail Low	Retail High
1992	T/Gas	143,041	160,720
1992	T/Diesel	171,823	193,060
1991	T/Gas	123,852	139,160
1991	T/Diesel	158,740	178,360
1990	T/Gas	113,386	127,400
1990	T/Diesel	146,530	164,640
1989	T/Gas	104,228	117,110
1989	T/Diesel	133,883	150,430
1988	T/Gas	98,559	110,740
1988	T/Diesel	125,161	140,630
1987	T/Gas	94,198	105,840
1987	T/Diesel	120,364	135,240
1986	T/Gas	93,325	104,860
1986	T/Diesel	114,258	128,380
1985	T/Gas	89,837	100,940
1985	T/Diesel	109,897	123,480
1984	T/Gas	80,242	90,160
1984	T/Diesel	95,942	107,800
1983	T/Gas	76,754	86,240
1983	T/Diesel	87,220	98,000
1982	T/Gas	70,648	79,380
1982	T/Diesel	81,115	91,140
1981	T/Gas	64,979	73,010
1981	T/Diesel	77,626	87,220

Year	Power	Retail Low	Retail High
1980	T/Gas	61,490	69,090
1980	T/Diesel	73,265	82,320
1979	T/Gas	58,874	66,150
1979	T/Diesel	68,904	77,420
1978	T/Gas	55,821	62,720
1978	T/Diesel	64,543	72,520
1977	T/Gas	54,076	60,760
1977	T/Diesel	61,054	68,600
1976	T/Gas	51,024	57,330
1976	T/Diesel	57,565	64,680
1975	T/Gas	49,279	55,370
1975	T/Diesel	54,949	61,740

Viking 35 SF

Year	Power	Retail Low	Retail High
1986	T/Gas	80,678	90,650
1986	T/Diesel	103,792	116,620
1985	T/Gas	74,137	83,300
1985	T/Diesel	94,634	106,330
1984	T/Gas	67,159	75,460
1984	T/Diesel	85,476	96,040

Viking 38 Convertible

Year	Power	Retail Low	Retail High
1994	T/Diesel	333,180	374,360
1993	T/Diesel	307,887	345,940
1992	T/Diesel	277,796	312,130
1991	T/Diesel	246,833	277,340
1990	T/Diesel	225,900	253,820

Viking 40 Sedan

Year	Power	Retail Low	Retail High
1983	T/Gas	121,236	136,220
1983	T/Diesel	135,191	151,900
1982	T/Gas	105,536	118,580
1982	T/Diesel	126,469	142,100
1981	T/Gas	99,431	111,720
1981	T/Diesel	119,491	134,260
1980	T/Gas	93,325	104,860
1980	T/Diesel	108,153	121,520
1979	T/Gas	87,220	98,000
1979	T/Diesel	97,686	109,760
1978	T/Gas	80,242	90,160
1978	T/Diesel	88,092	98,980
1977	T/Gas	71,956	80,850
1977	T/Diesel	83,295	93,590
1976	T/Gas	65,415	73,500
1976	T/Diesel	77,626	87,220
1975	T/Gas	56,693	63,700
1975	T/Diesel	73,265	82,320

Viking 41 Convertible

Year	Power	Retail Low	Retail High
1989	T/Gas	174,440	196,000
1989	T/Diesel	229,389	257,740
1988	T/Gas	163,974	184,240
1988	T/Diesel	210,200	236,180
1987	T/Gas	155,252	174,440
1987	T/Diesel	174,440	196,000
1986	T/Gas	141,296	158,760
1986	T/Diesel	174,876	196,490
1985	T/Gas	132,138	148,470
1985	T/Diesel	163,974	184,240
1984	T/Gas	124,725	140,140
1984	T/Diesel	154,379	173,460
1983	T/Gas	117,311	131,810
1983	T/Diesel	146,530	164,640

Viking 43 Convertible

Year	Power	Retail Low	Retail High
1994	T/Diesel	392,490	441,000
1993	T/Diesel	361,963	406,700
1992	T/Diesel	327,075	367,500
1991	T/Diesel	296,548	333,200
1990	T/Diesel	279,104	313,600

Viking 43 SF

Year	Power	Retail Low	Retail High
1994	T/Diesel	375,046	421,400

Viking 45 Convertible

Year	Power	Retail Low	Retail High
1993	T/Diesel	383,768	431,200
1992	T/Diesel	353,241	396,900
1991	T/Diesel	322,714	362,600
1990	T/Diesel	296,548	333,200
1989	T/Diesel	270,382	303,800
1988	T/Diesel	250,321	281,260
1987	T/Diesel	235,494	264,600

Viking 46 Convertible

Year	Power	Retail Low	Retail High
1985	T/Diesel	234,186	263,130
1984	T/Diesel	215,870	242,550
1983	T/Diesel	205,839	231,280
1982	T/Diesel	194,937	219,030
1981	T/Diesel	184,906	207,760

Viking 47 Convertible

Year	Power	Retail Low	Retail High
1994	T/Diesel	549,486	617,400

Viking 48 Convertible

Year	Power	Retail Low	Retail High
1990	T/Diesel	367,196	412,580
1989	T/Diesel	347,136	390,040

Year	Power	Retail Low	Retail High
1988	T/Diesel	322,714	362,600
1987	T/Diesel	293,059	329,280
1986	T/Diesel	271,690	305,270
1985	T/Diesel	257,299	289,100

Viking 50 Convertible

Year	Power	Retail Low	Retail High
1994	820D	671,594	754,600
1993	735D	588,735	661,500
1993	820D	632,345	710,500
1992	735D	545,125	612,500
1992	820D	588,735	661,500
1991	735D	505,876	568,400

Viking 53 Convertible

Year	Power	Retail Low	Retail High
1994	T/Diesel	784,980	882,000
1993	T/Diesel	715,204	803,600
1992	T/Diesel	662,872	744,800
1991	T/Diesel	593,096	666,400
1990	T/Diesel	531,170	596,820

Viking 57 Convertible

Year	Power	Retail Low	Retail High
1991	T/Diesel	723,926	813,400
1990	T/Diesel	672,466	755,580
1989	T/Diesel	627,984	705,600

Viking 58 Convertible

Year	Power	Retail Low	Retail High
1994	T/Diesel	959,420	1,078,000
1993	T/Diesel	889,644	999,600
1992	T/Diesel	872,200	980,000
1991	T/Diesel	828,590	931,000

Vista 48/50 SF

Year	Power	Retail Low	Retail High
1992	425D	298,292	335,160
1992	735D	322,714	362,600
1991	425D	270,382	303,800
1991	735D	296,548	333,200
1990	425D	248,577	279,300
1990	735D	274,743	308,700
1989	425D	224,155	251,860
1989	735D	248,577	279,300
1988	375D	200,606	225,400
1988	650D	229,389	257,740
1987	375D	191,884	215,600
1987	650D	218,050	245,000
1986	375D	178,801	200,900
1986	650D	204,967	230,300

Wellcraft 2600 Coastal

Year	Power	Retail Low	Retail High
1994	O/B*	34,888	39,200

Year	Power	Retail Low	Retail High
1994	T/IO	44,482	49,980
1993	O/B*	27,474	30,870
1993	T/IO	40,993	46,060
1992	O/B*	23,549	26,460
1992	T/IO	36,196	40,670
1991	O/B*	20,933	23,520
1991	T/IO	31,835	35,770
1990	O/B*	18,316	20,580
1990	T/IO	29,219	32,830

Wellcraft 2800 Coastal

Year	Power	Retail Low	Retail High
1994	T/Gas	61,926	69,580
1993	T/Gas	52,332	58,800
1992	T/Gas	48,407	54,390
1991	T/Gas	44,482	49,980
1990	T/Gas	39,249	44,100
1989	T/Gas	36,196	40,670

Year	Power	Retail Low	Retail High
1988	T/Gas	33,580	37,730
1987	T/Gas	31,399	35,280
1986	T/Gas	29,655	33,320

Wellcraft 2900 Sport Bridge

Year	Power	Retail Low	Retail High
1986	T/Gas	34,888	39,200
1985	T/Gas	33,144	37,240
1984	T/Gas	30,527	34,300
1983	T/Gas	27,910	31,360

Wellcraft 3200 Coastal

Year	Power	Retail Low	Retail High
1986	T/Gas	46,227	51,940
1985	T/Gas	43,174	48,510
1984	T/Gas	40,121	45,080

Wellcraft 3300 Coastal

Year	Power	Retail Low	Retail High
1994	T/Gas	94,634	106,330
1993	T/Gas	86,348	97,020

Year	Power	Retail Low	Retail High
1992	T/Gas	78,934	88,690
1991	T/Gas	74,137	83,300
1990	T/Gas	65,415	73,500
1989	T/Gas	58,437	65,660

Wellcraft 3300 Sport Bridge

Year	Power	Retail Low	Retail High
1992	T/Gas	87,656	98,490
1991	T/Gas	78,062	87,710

Wellcraft 3700 Cozumel

Year	Power	Retail Low	Retail High
1989	T/Gas	95,070	106,820
1988	T/Gas	88,528	99,470

Cross Reference Guide

Can't Find:	Go To:
Bertram 30 Express Cruiser	Bertram 30 FB Cruiser
Blackfin 36 Combi	Blackfin 38 Combi
Blackfin 36 Convertible	Blackfin 38 Convertible
Chris Craft 502 Convertible	Chris Craft 482 Convertible
Egg Harbor 35 SF	Egg Harbor 33 Convertible
Grady-White Dolphin 25	Grady-White Sailfish 25
Hatteras 32 Sport Fisherman	Hatteras 32 FB
Hatteras 36 Sedan Cruiser	Hatteras 36 Convertible
Mikelson 48 SF	Mikelson 50 Sedan
North Coast 24	Bimini 245 Tournament
Ocean 38 Super Sportfisherman	Ocean 38 SS (Early)
Pacemaker 31 Convertible	Pacemaker 30 Sportfisherman
Pursuit 2650 Cuddy Cabin	Pursuit 2655 Express Fisherman
Rampage 42 Sportfisherman	Rampage 40 Sportfisherman
Sea Ray 360 Sedan	Sea Ray 390 Sedan SF
Sea Ray Laguna 31	Sea Ray 310 Amberjack
Stamas 288 Family Fisherman	Stamas 288 Liberty
Tiara 3100 FB Convertible	Tiara 3100 Open (Early)
Wellcraft 3200 Sport Bridge	Wellcraft 3200 Coastal

Advertiser's Index